Louisiana Women

THEIR LIVES AND TIMES

EDITED BY

Janet Allured and Judith F. Gentry

❀   ❀   ❀

The University of Georgia Press   *Athens and London*

© 2009 by the University of Georgia Press
Athens, Georgia 30602
www.ugapress.org
All rights reserved
Set in Minion by Graphic Composition, Inc.
Printed and bound by Thomson-Shore

The paper in this book meets the guidelines for
permanence and durability of the Committee on
Production Guidelines for Book Longevity of the
Council on Library Resources.

Printed in the United States of America

09 10 11 12 13   P   5 4 3 2

Library of Congress Cataloging-in-Publication Data

Louisiana women : their lives and times / edited by Janet Allured and Judith F. Gentry.
p.   cm.
Includes bibliographical references and index.
ISBN-13: 978-0-8203-2946-8 (cloth : alk. paper)
ISBN-10: 0-8203-2946-0 (cloth : alk. paper)
ISBN-13: 978-0-8203-2947-5 (pbk. : alk. paper)
ISBN-10: 0-8203-2947-9 (pbk. : alk. paper)
1. Women—Louisiana—Biography. 2. Louisiana—Biography.
I. Allured, Janet. II. Gentry, Judith F., 1942–
CT3262.L6 L68   2009
920.7209763—dc22   2008049614

British Library Cataloging-in-Publication Data available

Louisiana Women

*To the scholars in the Louisiana Historical Association,
a learned community that never fails to provide
warm scholarly assistance and a good beer.*

Contents

Acknowledgments

The editors and authors wish to thank the following people for their critiques of individual essays: Eva Baham, Carol Crown, Barbara Ewell, Adam Fairclough, Cynthia Fleming, Meghan Fleming, Dolores Janiewski, Elizabeth Shown Mills, Theda Purdue, Giselle Roberts, John Troutman, and Dan Usner. Ray Miles, dean of the College of Liberal Arts at McNeese and an American Indian specialist, took time from his administrative duties to comment on two of the essays. Emily Clark cast a learned eye on no fewer than three; her keen but friendly criticism was invaluable. We are grateful, also, to Emily Toth, who was truly a professional "Ms. Mentor" from the beginning; to Elizabeth Payne, for putting Janet in touch with Nancy Grayson at the University of Georgia Press as well as for her continued friendship and advice; to our editors at the press, Nancy Grayson and Courtney Denney, who have been patient and encouraging as well as a pleasure to work with; to McNeese State University for providing Janet Allured with a sabbatical leave; and to the anonymous readers of this manuscript in its early stages for pointing us in new directions on several of the essays. We appreciate MJ Devaney, copyeditor, for improving our writing immeasurably. We wish to thank the contributors for their patience with our repeated requests for changes, edits, and further information as we hammered out essays that are both scholarly and accessible to multiple audiences.

Lastly, we wish to acknowledge the historians of Louisiana women, whose work has laid the foundation for this book. We donate the proceeds to a prize honoring the memory of one of them, Kimberly S. Hanger (1962–1999), whose premature death cut short a promising career and constituted a sad loss for the history profession in our state. Her respected publications on free people of color of the Spanish colonial era include "Landlords, Shopkeepers, Farmers, and Slave-Owners: Free Black Female Property-Holders in Colonial New Orleans" (in *Beyond Bondage: Free Women of Color in the Americas*, ed. David Barry Gaspar and Darlene Clark Hine). The Kimberly S. Hanger Prize is awarded annually to the best undergraduate-level paper presented at a Phi Alpha Theta session of the annual Louisiana Historical Association conference.

East Carroll Parish

Shreveport

Catahoula Parish

Mississippi River

Natchitoches

Red River

Cloutierville

Archafalaya River

Elton

Baton Rouge

Mississippi River

Lake Charles

Crowley

Lake Pontchartrain

St. Bernard Parish

New Orleans

Grand Isle

Louisiana Women

Introduction

JANET ALLURED

❀ ❀ ❀

Few young people entering college today are familiar with Louisiana women's history. Since the late 1990s, Emily Toth has taught a course at Louisiana State University on Louisiana women, and she always begins by asking her students to name famous Louisiana women. The students almost always come up with the same three, all of whom are still alive: Anne Rice, Britney Spears, and either Kathleen Blanco or Mary Landrieu. None can name any famous Louisiana women from the past. This book is an attempt to change that. From the first European settlement within the modern boundaries of Louisiana to the aftermath of Hurricane Katrina, this book documents and interprets the lives of a select group of women. It showcases a few of the many eccentric, courageous, passionate, and inventive women who have helped create Louisiana over the centuries.

We chose the subjects for this collection because they represent a cross-section, a sampling, as it were, of different time periods and ethnicities. Profiled are women of African American, Euro-American, and Native American ancestry, and one who was a mixture of all three; Creole women whose native language was French as well as "Anglos" (as the Creoles called the newly arriving Americans in 1803) whose native tongue was English; women who lived lavish lives and those who got most of their sustenance from the land and water around them; women who commanded slaves and women who were slaves or descended from slaves. Each essay therefore serves as a microhistory of its time, each woman as an exemplar of the era in which she lived.

We have several goals that we wish to achieve with this book. The first is to reconceptualize the history of Louisiana by including women in the story, not as an addendum to the male version of events but as an integral part of the state's sometimes checkered and certainly colorful past. The second goal is to provide a resource for teachers of Louisiana history, geography, literature, and women's studies courses. To that end, this book is organized chronologically by date of the subject's birth. Although the records for the earlier centuries are much harder to come by, eight essays discuss women born before the advent of the Civil War and nine consider women born afterward. We could not cover everybody, and there are many worthy subjects whose stories still need to be told. The third goal, then, is to inspire other researchers, master's and doctoral students as well as established academic historians, to continue to fill in the many remaining gaps in the history of women in Louisiana.

The essays in this volume illustrate for the general reader what historians began to recognize in the 1960s—that historical actors need not be powerful, famous, rich, white, or male to make a positive contribution to the world they inhabit and to be worthy of historical study. Before the women's movement of the 1970s, when nearly all historians were men, the subjects that interested them were (largely) the exercise of political, economic, and military power. The traditional focus on "top-down" and male history left women—as well as a lot of other people—out of the picture. Thanks to the influence of the New Left and the modern feminist movement, social historians began to write about women, first about great and extraordinary ones (along the model of "Great Men") and eventually about ordinary women. The first studies focused on women in New England and along the mid-Atlantic coast. About fifteen years later, histories of women in southern states began to appear.

Yet there was almost nothing known or written about Louisiana women. Tour guides in New Orleans in the 1980s, for example, talked about only three: Marie Laveau, whom they portrayed as a witch; Madame Lalaurie, who was notorious for torturing her slaves; and Baroness Pontalba, whose famous buildings flank Jackson Square. Only fairly recently have historians of Louisiana begun recapturing the history of marginalized and relatively powerless groups, including women. Doing so requires perseverance and a willingness to spend many bleary-eyed hours reading microfilm, combing through dusty stacks of poorly organized government records, and tracking down relatives all over the country. But even when researchers are successful in locating sources, the passage of time and the decay inherent to a torrid, semitropical climate means they often find that few traces of their elusive subject have survived. Most people simply did not generate much of a paper trail, and what papers they may have left behind have long since rotted in the heat and dampness. Thus, historians have turned to federal census records; church, state, and local government records; newspapers; and court documents—both civil and criminal.[1] Such records yield raw data, but they too seldom give us what we most long to hear—the tenor of a human voice. Or the soprano.

Nonetheless, thanks to many researchers' doggedness, the number of works about women in Louisiana has grown dramatically in recent years. Mary Gehman, New Orleans feminist and writer, was shocked to find out in the early 1970s that not one of her feminist friends had ever heard of Sara Mayo, the doctor for whom the women's hospital in New Orleans was named. Gehman researched and wrote a popular history of women in New Orleans, the first of its kind.[2] The earliest scholarly work on Louisiana women tended to focus on those women who were activists and reformers, especially those who had sought a larger public role for women. One of the first such studies was Carmen Lindig's *The Path from the Parlor*, which looked at women involved in the club movement, Progressive reform, and suffrage. Sarah Towles Reed, radical teacher and labor organizer, is the subject of an excellent biography by Leslie Gale Parr. Historians of the Progressive era have studied Kate and Jean Gordon of New Orleans, leading suffragists (or antisuffragists, depending on your point of view) and reformers. Politically active white reformers of the 1930s through the 1960s are the focus of Pamela Tyler's *Silk Stockings and Ballot Boxes: Women and Politics in New Orleans, 1920–1963*. Kim Lacy Rogers, Lee Sartain, and Shannon Frystak make the work of white and black women in the civil rights movement the subjects of their research.[3]

Because the courts are a rich source of records when little else exists, we know a good bit about "disorderly women." Prostitutes in Storyville, the legal red light district in New Orleans just behind the French Quarter, are an example.[4] Likewise, the notorious Myra Clark Gaines, daughter of Daniel Clark, one of the richest men in America, has been the topic of several works because Gaines sued repeatedly seeking to establish her right to a portion of her father's vast estate. The infamous Marie Laveau is the focus of three recent books, including one by Carolyn Long, author of the essay in this collection on the Voudou Queen. Long's work is indicative of more recent trends, in which historians attempt to evoke the history of women who were not reform-minded public activists but who were just ordinary people navigating their daily lives as best they could, women who had no hopes of changing the world or ever becoming famous. Ironically, though, Marie Laveau's tomb is now one of the top tourist attractions in New Orleans. The work by Carolyn Ware on Cajun women and Mardi Gras and those on free women of color by Kimberly Hanger, Ginger Gould, and Emily Clark are examples of some of the first-rate pieces of social history produced only in the last couple of decades. Although Judith Kelleher Schafer specializes in legal history, her research is a valuable resource for studying slave women and the women who owned them in the antebellum period.[5] These works add nuances to the field of "women's history," showing that women's experiences vary depending on location as well as class and ethnicity.

As always, women of the upper class are most likely to have their histories written, for they left the largest documentary trail. They corresponded with relatives, preserved letters, maintained estates, and often kept diaries.[6] The record for some of them, such as the baroness Pontalba, is fairly large, as the baroness's father owned most of what is today the Jackson Square area in New Orleans. But the less well-placed—including Native Americans, slaves, and yeoman farmers of all races—who constituted a majority of Louisiana's population in the years before the Civil War, left us nothing in their own hand. To write these women's biographies, authors have had to tease out their lives from civil and court records, from what others wrote about them, and from the recollections of their descendants.

Researching the history of African American women is a particular challenge. The law in antebellum Louisiana prohibited teaching slaves to read. Free girls of color had greater educational choices, but even after the war, when the state established meager, poorly funded, dual public school systems for black and white, the educational opportunities available to them were still severely limited. As a group they were always less affluent than Euro-Americans. Nonetheless, the state had a small but growing black middle class, and when they organized groups such as the Louisiana Colored Teachers Association in 1901 and the American Federation of Teachers in 1937, they left records that historians can plumb. Additionally, black women were active in community and civil rights organizations.[7]

The women of African descent in this anthology were exceptional in many ways. Clementine Hunter took up "marking pictures" in her advanced age, and before she died at 101 became renowned as a self-taught artist. Marie Laveau, a legend even in her own day for her reputed powers to alter fate, has become almost a cult figure for New Age and feminist spiritualists. Oretha Castle Haley was a civil rights activist who became leader of the New Orleans chapter of the Congress of Racial Equality. But most African American women worked and lived outside the spotlight; historians still need to locate them and tell their stories.[8]

Women who lived in New Orleans figure prominently in this volume partly because New Orleans has numerous archives and large repositories of documents. Even though no more than a quarter of the state's total population ever lived in the city, its influence was colossal (and, often, deeply resented by the rest of the state). The seat of government throughout the colonial period and for the first decades after the Louisiana Purchase, New Orleans in 1860 was the second largest city in the South, behind Baltimore, with a population of 168,675. Baton Rouge, the capital after 1846, was the state's third-largest city (behind Algiers, a New Orleans suburb), with a population of only 5,428. Outside New Orleans, in other words, Louisiana was overwhelmingly a rural state sprinkled with very small towns, and recapturing the history of the women living there is a particularly difficult task.[9]

Yet our knowledge of women in New Orleans is limited, too, simply because most women lived private, inconspicuous lives. Prevailing notions of femininity constrained women, which is why, as Laurel Thatcher Ulrich famously said, "well-behaved women seldom make history." Ordinary men, because they were heads of household, show up in property records, on voting rolls, in jury pools, in unions, as businessmen, and of course in military records. Most women, though, if living as society dictated, married and thereafter stayed home and out of sight—or at least out of the sight of historians.

Given that marrying had a tendency to erase women from the historical record for as long as the marriage lasted, it's not surprising that quite a few of the white women profiled here either never married or were widowed. Naturalist and environmentalist Caroline Dormon, writer Grace King, and physician Rowena Spencer remained single. Kate Chopin began writing after her husband's death, as writing was respectable and could be done from home. Eliza Jane Nicholson broke into the male field of newspaper publishing when she inherited the nearly bankrupt *New Orleans Picayune* upon her husband's death. Much to everyone's surprise (and against well-meaning advice), she decided not only to try to save it from bankruptcy but to manage it herself. In her case, marriage gave her the property, but it was widowhood that gave her the freedom—and the power—to make decisions affecting her life. (Before her second marriage, she insisted on a prenuptial contract in which she maintained her separate financial property.)

Furthermore, nearly all the white women in these essays who wed did not follow the traditional path. Mary Land married multiple times, despite the shame that divorce brought to women. Cleoma Breaux Falcon divorced once and married twice. As if her divorce was not disgraceful enough, Cleoma sang in dance-halls as well as honky-tonks during her marriages, unheard of for Cajun women in the 1930s. Others were trapped in disastrous unions: the baroness Pontalba's father-in-law tried to kill her, and her husband eventually lost his mind; Dorothy Dix's husband also suffered from mental illness and was confined to a sanitarium in his later life.

Unlike the Euro-Americans, the women of color in this volume—Marie Thérèse Coincoin, Marie Laveau, the Coushatta women, Clementine Hunter, and Oretha Castle Haley—not only married but, in most cases, raised large families. In that sense, their lives more closely paralleled those of ordinary Louisiana women. Despite the 1950s image of the nuclear family that most people carry in their minds, working-class and even middle-income women of all races frequently worked outside the home.

Many of our subjects were not only unconventional in their tendency toward single status but also in their "assertive" or "prickly" personalities. They did not live up to, or refused to remain confined by, the standards of decorous behavior defined for women of their day. In short, they were not "ladylike." They were described by their contemporaries as like "vinegar," as "fussy," gruff, indecorous, intimidating (for a woman). For those for whom there are no extant personal descriptions, their behavior indicates that they were willing to challenge accepted notions of propriety. Marie Laveau, for example, led Voudou ceremonies, an activity not characteristic of "ladies" regardless of their race. Although some of our subjects were properly submissive, devout, well-behaved gentlewomen (for example, Kate Stone, Grace King), others acted without regard to what others might think about them and let correctness be damned. Marie Thérèse Coincoin, who lived in a slave-master relationship, was prosecuted as a "public concubine" by the priest in Natchitoches ("nack-i-tosh"). Kate Chopin set tongues wagging in her tiny village of Cloutierville over a reputed affair with a married neighbor. Gender roles for women were so constricting that it took a strong personality to step out of the bounds of propriety.

Even the women who conformed to and defended the status quo were different from the average Louisiana woman in certain ways. Kate Stone was from an elite family of great wealth (which is what made her politically conservative). Dorothy Dix, Grace King, and the baroness Pontalba were well traveled and cosmopolitan. Pontalba spent more time away from the United States than in it, and King felt as comfortable in Europe, particularly France and Paris, as she did in New Orleans. Dix traveled widely on assignments and spent many years living in New York.

A few women in this book come to our attention not because they lived unusual private lives but because they got involved in public reform efforts. Some, but not all, of these women were politically liberal, as the term was understood in their day. Some—the St. Mark's Methodist women, for example—were even radical. The women who mobilized to improve the process of cleaning up and rebuilding New Orleans after Hurricane Katrina also pushed for change. Among other things, they helped get legislation passed that improved efficiency in the city's governance. Activist women such as these, whether knowingly or not, expanded the boundary of acceptable behavior for southern women and broadened attitudes toward progressive reform while they were at it. Though few of them questioned the appropriateness of male dominance in public life, by their very actions they eroded it.

What made the subjects of these essays so unusual? The authors explore that question, looking at the influences that helped to make each woman what she became, including education, the culture of the surrounding community, intellectual and organizational networks, the natural environment, and other women. Many of our subjects had strong female role models in their own family. For others, networks of women friends were the predominant factor in their life's work. Eliza Jane Nicholson, owner-editor of the *New Orleans Picayune*, was committed to employing women journalists such as Elizabeth Meriwether Gilmer ("Dorothy Dix") and to promoting their careers. Caroline Dormon lived her entire adult life with her married-but-separated sister Virginia and was close friends with Cammie Henry, the "mistress of Melrose" Plantation. A few, such as Mary Land, were encouraged by their fathers to defy confining notions of proper womanhood. Dorothy Dix's adoring father, like Mary Land's, also supported her tomboy ways, and Eliza Jane Nicholson's adoptive parents gave their little charge the freedom to wander the countryside and riverbanks near their home. As author Patricia Brady writes, they encouraged her "love of nature and the outdoors, of animals, of poetry and literature." And Oretha Castle Haley was supported in her activism by her family as well as by her husband, Richard Haley, also a civil rights organizer.

Despite their different influences, one characteristic the women seem to share is an unusual grit that allowed them to turn trying circumstances (or even catastrophic ones) into opportunity. In some cases, their efforts earned them scorn; in others, a grudging respect. Occasionally, they even won admiration and accolades. It is hard not to admire their ingenuity and fortitude as they made a better place in the world for themselves, for their children, and very often for other women as well. Given the relative lack of power and opportunity for women, their actions were nothing short of astonishing. Faced with adversity or opportunity, they reinvented themselves, shedding convention and creating new roles for themselves and, sometimes coincidentally, for other women. In so doing, they stretched the definition of what it meant to be a Louisiana woman and also, by extension, the very concept of "southern womanhood."

NOTES

1. Information about the New Orleans tours comes from the author's interview with Mary Gehman, April 11, 2008. Works of social history in Louisiana include Ann Patton Malone, *Sweet Chariot: Slave Family and Household Structure in Nineteenth-Century Louisiana* (Chapel Hill: University of North Carolina Press, 1992); Judith Kelleher Schafer, *Slavery, the Civil Law, and the Su-*

preme Court of Louisiana (Baton Rouge: Louisiana State University Press, 1994); Judith Kelleher Schafer, *Becoming Free, Remaining Free: Manumission and Enslavement in New Orleans, 1846–1862* (Baton Rouge: Louisiana State University Press, 2003); Caryn Cossé Bell, *Revolution, Romanticism, and the Afro-Creole Protest Tradition in Louisiana, 1718–1868* (Baton Rouge: Louisiana State University Press, 1997); Carl Brasseaux, *The Founding of New Acadia: The Beginnings of Acadian Life in Louisiana, 1765–1803* (Baton Rouge: Louisiana State University Press, 1987); Carl Brasseaux, *Acadian to Cajun: Transformation of a People, 1803–1877* (Jackson: University Press of Mississippi, 1992). With Keith P. Fontenot and Claude F. Oubre, Brasseaux has also written *Creoles of Color in the Bayou Country* (Jackson: University Press of Mississippi, 1994). Shane K. Bernard, *The Cajuns: Americanization of a People* (Jackson: University Press of Mississippi, 2003).

2. Author's interview with Mary Gehman, April 11, 2008; Gehman, *Women and New Orleans* (New Orleans: Margaret Media, 1985). Sara Mayo was the great-aunt of Rowena Spencer, who is the subject of one of the chapters in this volume.

3. Carmen Lindig, *The Path from the Parlor: Louisiana Women, 1879–1920* (Lafayette: Center for Louisiana Studies, University of Louisiana at Lafayette, 1986); Kathryn W. Kemp, "Jean and Kate Gordon: New Orleans Social Reformers, 1898–1933," *Louisiana History* 24 (Fall 1983): 389–401; B. H. Gilley, "Kate Gordon and Louisiana Woman Suffrage," *Louisiana History* 24 (Summer 1983): 289–306; Elna C. Green, "The Rest of the Story: Kate Gordon and the Opposition to the Nineteenth Amendment in the South," *Louisiana History* 33 (Spring 1992): 171–89; Kenneth R. Johnson, "Kate Gordon and the Woman-Suffrage Movement in the South," *Journal of Southern History* 38 (August 1972): 365–92; Leslie Gale Parr, *A Will of Her Own: Sarah Towles Reed and the Pursuit of Democracy in Southern Public Education* (Athens: University of Georgia Press, 1998); Kim Lacy Rogers, *Righteous Lives: Narratives of the New Orleans Civil Rights Movement* (New York: New York University Press, 1993); Pamela Tyler, *Silk Stockings and Ballot Boxes: Women and Politics in New Orleans, 1920–1963* (Athens: University of Georgia Press, 1996); Shannon Frystak, "African-American Women Civil Rights Activists in Louisiana," in *Southern Black Women in the Civil Rights Era (1954–1974): A State by State Study*, ed. Bruce A. Glasrud and Merline Pitre (College Station: Texas A & M University Press, forthcoming); Shannon Frystak, "A Dissenting Tradition: Women and the Black Struggle for Equality, 1924–1968," in *Louisiana, Race, and Civil Rights*, ed. Michael S. Martin (Baton Rouge: Louisiana State University Press, forthcoming); Shannon Frystak, "The Integration of the League of Women Voters of New Orleans, 1953–1963," in *Searching for Their Places: Women in the South Across Four Centuries*, ed. Tom Appleton and Angela Boswell (Columbia: University of Missouri Press, 2003), 261–84.

4. Alecia P. Long, *The Great Southern Babylon: Sex, Race, and Respectability in New Orleans, 1865–1920* (Baton Rouge: Louisiana State University Press, 2004).

5. Elizabeth Urban Alexander, *Notorious Woman: The Celebrated Case of Myra Clark Gaines* (Baton Rouge: Louisiana State University Press, 2001); Kimberly S. Hanger, "The Fortunes of Women in America: Spanish New Orleans' Free Women of African Descent and Their Relations with Slave Women," in *Discovering the Women in Slavery: Emancipating Perspectives on the American Past*, ed. Patricia Morton (Athens: University of Georgia Press, 1996), 153–78; Virginia Meacham Gould, "In Full Enjoyment of Their Liberty: The Free Women of Color of the Gulf Ports of New Orleans, Mobile, and Pensacola, 1769–1860" (PhD diss., Emory University, 1991); Violet Harrington Bryan, "Race and Gender in the Early Works of Alice Dunbar-Nelson," in *Louisiana Literature and Literary Figures*, ed. Mathé Allain, vol. 17 of *The Louisiana Purchase Bicentennial Series in Louisiana History*, ed. Glenn R. Conrad (Lafayette: Center for Louisiana Studies, University of Louisiana at

Lafayette, 2004), 235–45; Gloria T. Hull, "Shaping Contradictions: Alice Dunbar-Nelson and the Black Creole Experience," in *Louisiana Literature and Literary Figures*, ed. Mathé Allain, vol. 17 of *The Louisiana Purchase Bicentennial Series in Louisiana History*, ed. Glenn R. Conrad (Lafayette: Center for Louisiana Studies, University of Louisiana at Lafayette, 2004), 250–55; Carolyn E. Ware, *Cajun Women and Mardi Gras: Reading the Rules Backward* (Urbana: University of Illinois Press, 2007); Martha Ward, *Voodoo Queen: The Spirited Lives of Marie Laveau* (Jackson: University Press of Mississippi, 2004); Ina Johanna Fandrich, *The Mysterious Voodoo Queen, Marie Laveaux: A Study of Powerful Female Leadership in Nineteenth-Century New Orleans* (New York: Routledge, 2005); Emily Clark, *Masterless Mistresses: The New Orleans Ursulines and the Development of a New World Society, 1727–1834* (Chapel Hill: Published for the Omohundro Institute of Early American History and Culture by the University of North Carolina Press, 2007); Emily Clark, "'By All the Conduct of Their Lives:' A Laywomen's Confraternity in New Orleans, 1730–1744," *William and Mary Quarterly* 54 (October 1997): 769–94. For Schafer, see note 1 above.

6. Wilma King, ed., *A Northern Woman in the Plantation South: Letters of Tryphena Blanche Holder Fox, 1856–1876* (Columbia: University of South Carolina Press, 1993); Kate Stone, *Brokenburn: The Journal of Kate Stone, 1861–1868*, ed. John Q. Anderson (Baton Rouge: Louisiana State University Press, 1995); Kimberly Harrison, introduction, in *A Maryland Bride in the Deep South: The Civil War Diary of Priscilla Bond*, ed. Kimberly Harrison (Baton Rouge: Louisiana State University Press, 2006), 1–44; Charles East, ed., *The Civil War Diary of Sarah Morgan* (Athens: University of Georgia Press, 1991); Sara Brooks Sundberg, "A Female Planter from West Feliciana Parish: The Letters of Rachel O'Connor," *Louisiana History* 47 (Winter 2006): 39–62; Carolyn Delatte, *Lucy Audubon: A Biography* (Baton Rouge: Louisiana State University Press, 1982); Allie Bayne Windham Webb, ed., *Mistress of Evergreen Plantation: Rachel O'Connor's Legacy of Letters, 1823–1845* (Albany: State University of New York Press, 1983); Giselle Roberts, ed., *The Correspondence of Sarah Morgan and Francis Warrington Dawson, with Selected Editorials Written by Sarah Morgan for the Charleston News and Courier* (Athens: University of Georgia Press, 2004).

7. Parr, *A Will of Her Own*, 102–4; Lee Sartain, "'Local Leadership': The Role of Women in the Louisiana Branches of the National Association for the Advancement of Colored People, 1920–1939," *Louisiana History* 46 (Summer 2005): 311–31; Lee Sartain, *Invisible Activists: Women of the Louisiana NAACP and the Struggle for Civil Rights, 1915–1945* (Baton Rouge: Louisiana State University Press, 2007).

8. More and more historians are integrating women into their histories. Kent Germany's recent book on the War on Poverty in New Orleans is a good example, as he covers the activities of African American women's groups as well as individual women leaders in the predominantly black areas of the city (*New Orleans after the Promise: Poverty, Citizenship, and the Search for the Great Society* [Athens: University of Georgia Press, 2007]).

9. New Orleans served as the capital again after the pro-Union state government took over in 1864. It remained the capital during Reconstruction, and in 1879, the capital was moved back to Baton Rouge. Algiers's population at that point was 5,816. Neighboring Jefferson had 5,107 inhabitants. Shreveport, on the Red River in north Louisiana, was the fifth-largest city with a population of 2,190 (Bennett H. Wall et al., *Louisiana: A History*, 5th ed. [Wheeling, Ill.: Harlan Davidson, 2002], 139–40, 163; Charles Robert Goins and John Michael Caldwell, *Historical Atlas of Louisiana* [Norman: University of Oklahoma Press, 1995], 51).

Marie Thérèse Coincoin
(1742–1816)

Cane River Slave, Slave Owner, and Paradox

ELIZABETH SHOWN MILLS

❀ ❀ ❀

Born a slave on the western fringe of the struggling, underpopulated French colony of Louisiana, Marie Thérèse Coincoin became the storied owner of land and slaves in a rich plantation belt. Her life has been the source of historical controversy and a great deal of myth—showing how historical portrayals depend on the perspectives of those who interpret the past. A woman of ability but obscurity in her own lifetime, she became a twentieth-century legend, reflecting diverse social agendas, economic interests, and family pride. This essay focuses on Coincoin's life as a window on eighteenth-century issues of gender, race, slavery, and sex and corrects many misperceptions about her and the National Historic Landmark with which she is most associated, Melrose Plantation.

The confluence of the many cultures into which she was born in 1742 shaped Coincoin's identity. Her master, French-Canadian Louis Juchereau de St. Denis, commandant of the outpost at Natchitoches, presented her for christening under the European saint name "Marie Thérèse," while her African parents gave her the African name "Coincoin." As a Creole—one born in the colony of parents from elsewhere—she would employ both European and African customs and laws in a life strategy that compartmentalized rather than hybridized their differences.[1] Assigned to sexual servitude, she used her lot to secure her freedom. As an aging freedwoman, she embraced slavery as a means by which she could improve the lives of her offspring but spurned community and church expectations that slaveholders should proselytize newly arrived Africans. A pharmacologist, a small-scale farmer, and an entrepreneur, she lived an unpretentious life that honored thrift, industry, and family.

Interpreting this woman who bridged two centuries and at least two cultures is problematic. To many, Coincoin is an archetype of women of African descent whose strength enabled their families to endure.[2] For others, notably the contemporary church, she was a source of shame. Branded a "concubine" by a Capucin zealot determined to morally reform Louisiana, she was criminally prosecuted for living with an unmarried white male and treated as a moral canker to be excised from the public's soul. In the twentieth century, she was portrayed by anthropologists as a racial stain on her family, one whose blackness supposedly led her offspring to excise her from their memory. Scholars have characterized her as both an astute businesswoman and a simpleton.[3]

As a woman of African descent in a slave regime, she was both victim and victimizer. She was the product of a society with complex needs and often warring values, a layered hierarchy structured by race, class, and gender. As a black woman and a slave, she weighed the limited options available and internalized the values that would enable her and her offspring to shuck off the shackles of oppression into which they had been born.

The borderland region that produced Coincoin was a hybrid of cultures and ethnicities. When Coincoin's parents arrived in the mid-1730s, Natchitoches was a rudimentary village, clustered around the perennially rotting walls of a fort expected to hold French Louisiana's western bounds against both the Spanish and Native Americans. The family of its commandant occupied quarters almost as crude as those of the three dozen Africans and Indians they held in slavery. The settlement, on a branch of the Red River, was one that survived by cultural accommodation and that was ruled more by the dictates of that commandant than laws emanating from Paris or New Orleans. Coincoin's master, who founded the post and governed it for three decades, sought stability through trade with those who were his rivals for colonial domain. The prosperity Cane River achieved during Coincoin's lifetime was based on the barter of skin: profits from the peltry sent to the intercontinental market at New Orleans were reinvested into slaves, a trade that Coincoin and other freed slaves would participate in, complicitly and implicitly.[4]

The law that governed French Louisiana's slaves, the Code Noir of 1724, reflected beliefs ingrained in French culture. It recognized the Catholic Church as its spiritual mother and promoted the sanctity of marriage and family. It forbade the separation of enslaved husbands and wives, as well as mothers from prepubescent children. Moreover, it decreed harsh penalties for the sexual exploitation of slave women by their masters. However, the Code Noir also reflected cultural mores that conflicted with church dogma, particularly in the code's proscription against marriage between black and white or slave and free. That injunction was rooted not so much in race as in long-standing continental

MELROSE PLANTATION MANOR, ISLE BREVELLE
Built 1832–33 by Louis Metoyer and his son Jean Baptiste Louis,
free men of color. Courtesy of John C. Guillet,
Guillet Photography, Natchitoches, La.

concepts of class and traditional tolerance of sexual partnerships not formal-
ized by marriage. In a society whose members expected its offspring to choose
spouses who would advance the family fortune or its social rank, illicit relationships enabled affluent males to enjoy intimate companionship that pleased
them, prior to marriage or after. In France, concubines were generally of the
same race as the men; in the American colonies, however, the prevalence of
African and Indian women offered alternatives to the "moral corruption" of
white females.[5]

Indubitably, sexual obedience and subservience was, fundamentally and historically, "a woman's lot." In exchange for granting exclusive rights to the use
of their bodies (without exclusive right to that of their partners), wives and
mistresses theoretically received financial support and "protection" from potential abuse by other males. However, both Coincoin and the owner who controlled her adult life had a radically different view of a "woman's place." Gender
disparities, racial oppression, and the economic impact of both were uncom-
monly open issues within the household of her last mistress, Marie des Neiges
de St. Denis, who was also Coincoin's godmother and childhood companion.
St. Denis challenged both the church and the Code Noir and ferociously battled
gender and racial exploitation. The code influenced Coincoin's life less than
French folkways and her mistress's example.[6]

The Natchitoches outpost that the St. Denis clan ruled was surrounded by indigenous tribes and situated just thirty miles from the capital of Spanish Texas.
Isolated from other French settlements, it syncretized the cultures of diverse
Europeans, Africans, and especially Native Americans. By 1803 half the "white"
population was of Indian extraction, and half of those were the children, grandchildren or great-grandchildren of Indian slaves. African culture had the least
impact, because French Louisiana effectively ended the importation of African
slaves in 1731. One shipload was brought to New Orleans in 1743, but after that,
four decades passed before the new colonial overlord, Spain, reinstituted the
trade.[7] As the original Africans died, from indigenous diseases but rarely old
age, the new Afro-Creole generations were decidedly French in culture.[8]

In the winter of 1735–36, four years after the suspension of the slave trade, a
newly arrived male in the St. Denis household (likely acquired from in-laws in
Spanish Texas) was presented for baptism and then wed to another St. Denis
slave.[9] Although local records identify some fellow Africans under their tribal
names, this couple would be known only as François and Marie Françoise, European saint names bestowed on them at baptism by the masters who compelled their conversion. However much they accepted the proselytizing, they
stand as a singular example at Natchitoches of African resistance to European

supplanting of their culture. To their firstborn, baptized as Gertrude, they gave the name "Dgimby" (var. "Dhimby," "Jimbi," "Gimbeau"). The sons baptized as François and Jean Baptiste were named "Choera" (var. "Kiokera," "Quioquira") and "Chocra" (var. "Chucha") by their African-born parents, and the daughter baptized as "Hyacinthe" answered to "Yandon" ("Yancdose"). Most revealing is the tribal name of their secondborn daughter, "Coincoin." Contemporary records, significantly, spell the name in various ways suggesting an inflectional difference in the syllables—"Coin Quin," "Kuen Kouin," "Qoin Quin," "Quoin Quoen," and as her son wrote the name in 1806, "Coin Quoin." One authority in African linguistics links that name to the Glidzi dialect of the Ewe people of coastal Togo, contending it was the customary name for secondborn daughters; however, more recent (but as of yet unpublished) work suggests other possible derivations.[10] In any event, the practices of Coincoin's family at Natchitoches stand out; the family is the only one in the Natchitoches area that retained African names past the first generation—and, apparently, African medicinal knowledge as well. In New Orleans, by contrast, sheer force of numbers enabled Africans to create a community that preserved African religion, craftsmanship, and culinary and medicinal skills.

The cultural skills preserved by Coincoin's family earned them privilege among St. Denis slaves. When the commandant's succession was settled in 1756, the widow St. Denis chose François, Marie Françoise, and their children as her personal lot. Their value to her enabled their family unit to remain more or less intact in the estate's division. However, across three days in April 1758, the widow, François, and Marie Françoise all succumbed to a plague that centered on the St. Denis compound. Coincoin and her nine surviving siblings, aged eight days to twenty years, were then parceled out among the five heirs. Most, however, would be brought back together within the household of the youngest St. Denis daughter—Coincoin's godmother, Marie des Neiges, wife of Antonio de Soto Bermudes.[11]

In the de Soto household, the sixteen-year-old Coincoin became nurse to a mistress who was herself plagued with intermittent paralysis. There, within months, Coincoin bore the first of five children by a mate family tradition identifies as Native American. Church and civil records are silent on the issue of their paternity, and that silence reflects a major shift in local attitudes toward the sanctity of slave families. Marriages between slaves at Natchitoches, which had been the dominant pattern under the St. Denis regime, virtually ceased with the death of the widow St. Denis. Exceptions occurred only sporadically when a new resident priest would encourage slave marriages before local opposition squelched his efforts. Few baptismal entries in Natchitoches for nonwhites past midcentury take note of the fact that slave infants had fathers as well as mothers.[12]

The lack of marriage opportunities for slaves ushered in a century of widespread *métissage* (interracial sexual unions) including both short-term and lifelong liaisons that spawned Cane River's unique multiracial community. Coincoin, perhaps unwittingly or perhaps by choice, would become the symbol of the open attitude toward interracial unions in the thinly populated hinterland. During her servitude to the de Sotos, her mistress fell into debt. Several of their slaves were sold in the mid-1760s, including two of Coincoin's young children. Amid those events, and despite evidence of favoritism toward Coincoin by her mistress, Mme. de Soto rented out Coincoin to "keep house" for a newly arrived bachelor merchant from the port of La Rochelle, Claude Thomas Pierre Metoyer. From that point forward all of Coincoin's children would be half-white.[13]

Events of the years to come attest that Coincoin and Metoyer entered into a long-term, committed relationship. He provided for her, attempted to defend her against persecution and prosecution, freed her and several of their children, and showed concern for her in numerous other ways. On her part, she remained with him for a decade after she became a free woman. Theirs appears to have been a relationship grounded in some degree of affection and respect, but it was a relationship of unequals. How Coincoin negotiated this inequality is not known. Arguably, like numerous counterparts throughout Louisiana who entered into *plaçage* arrangements, she valued the relationship. Perhaps she understood it was the best option she had. Indisputably, she availed herself of the opportunities Metoyer's attentions offered.[14]

Across the next twenty years, Coincoin bore ten half-white children at regular intervals of roughly two years. For the first decade, their cohabitation went unchecked, but in 1778 the Capucin firebrand, Luis de Quintanilla, targeted them in his attack on moral laxity at the post. Armed with a mandate he had sought from his bishop ("In case these concubinages do not cease after apostolic counsel, the concubines must deliver themselves to the Royal Court of Justice to be coerced and punished"), Quintanilla branded Coincoin a "public concubine" and demanded that she be returned to her mistress, who must "bring no further similar sins upon herself." Reinforced by a Spanish regime that had abandoned much of the French Code Noir, he also gave Metoyer an option to avoid legal prosecution—an option the Code Noir had specifically forbidden. Metoyer and Coincoin should, Quintanilla insisted, "make use of the apostolic means . . . to sanctify their bad concubinage by the union of matrimony."[15]

Metoyer rejected that option, at which point the commandant ordered Coincoin—but not Metoyer or Coincoin's owner—to suffer the "proscribed" but unnamed punishment. The applicable law was the commandant's own decree governing the behavior of blacks and slaves, issued in January 1770 as his first act of office. By its terms, the pregnant and near term Coincoin would be subjected to public humiliation and harassment on the "wooden horse," followed by a flogging. Although the Natchitoches ordinance did assert that "whites base enough to addict themselves to the shameless prostitutions . . . of negresses whose libertinage has created scandal . . . should be chastised according to the law in such cases," that provision was not invoked here. At Natchitoches, as in Europe and throughout its colonies, women bore the brunt of punishment in cases of fornication. The commandant's failure to impose punishment on the male is understandable in this case; both he and his sons fathered multiracial children and the commandant himself suffered from gonorrhea at his death.[16]

Neither the priest nor the penance ended the relationship that had already resulted in seven children and that would produce three more. Instead, Metoyer purchased Coincoin, their children, and the last child she had borne prior to their affair. Then, in a private document witnessed by friends but not notarized, he manumitted Coincoin and their newborn child.[17]

Coincoin was then legally free but not unfettered. Leaving the relationship with Metoyer was not a realistic option. By that time, Metoyer owned eight of her twelve children. Two of her first set of children had been sold years before to distant owners. Another two soon would be taken away even farther, when the de Sotos moved south to Opelousas. Leaving Metoyer would have meant forfeiting the right to nurture any of her offspring, and antagonizing him could lessen the likelihood of his eventually freeing those he still owned. Coincoin's decision was foregone. In all regards and above all else, her actions and choices demonstrate a commitment to her offspring and the betterment of their lot.

Moreover, financial survival as a free woman was a grave concern, given the limited employment opportunities available in her era for women of any color without male support. In a contemporary case in New Orleans, where considerably more economic options existed, a woman of color was convicted of conspiracy in theft charges brought against her sister because, the cabildo decreed, she must have known that her sister could not honestly earn enough money to pay for her rent, much less her "food, clothing, candles, firewood, soap, and other necessities."[18] For colonial women, freedom from servitude or marriage meant limited chances for survival.

During the second decade Coincoin spent with the increasingly prominent Metoyer, she bore three children and buried one. By a will she likely knew nothing about, filed in 1783 with a New Orleans notary to avoid stoking the fires of local gossip, Metoyer promised freedom to all the "mulâtres" born to Coincoin, together with a quarter of the land the Crown had granted him and a third of all else remaining after his debts were paid. The bequest to the children carried a caveat: "the express condition that their mother is to have the enjoyment and use of [this inheritance] for the rest of her life."[19] That 1783 will would never be probated, and neither Coincoin nor the children would receive an inheritance. Even so, the provision attests Metoyer's emotional attachment to Coincoin and the children she bore him.[20]

The preface to that will also seems to suggest paternal callousness. After commending his soul to God and begging forgiveness for his sins, Metoyer explicitly stated: "I declare I am a bachelor and *have no children*" (emphasis added). That declaration was not a denial, however; it was a legal fiction necessary to ensure that his wishes remained within the law. The Code Noir that had governed French Louisiana expressly forbade whites to make any bequest or donation to slaves or free people of color. Its Spanish successor, the Siete Partidas, had liberalized that provision but still circumscribed paternal bequests to illegitimate children. Only by denying paternity could Metoyer hope to ensure that Coincoin and their offspring received a share of what they had labored to accumulate.[21]

In October 1788, Metoyer set Coincoin aside and took a legal wife. Reason suggests that the severance agreement Metoyer and Coincoin executed, five days before his marriage, was one he dictated and Coincoin perhaps only consented to. By the terms of that accord, he gave her a tract of eighty arpents (sixty-seven acres) carved from his plantation. To that donation, he added the promise of an annual stipend of 120 livres, because, as he would state in the 1801 will that was probated at his death, he "anticipated" she would have difficulty supporting herself and her children.[22]

In these documents, Metoyer skirted the issue of paternity entirely. However, the marriage contract he executed immediately thereafter with the new Marie Thérèse in his life specifically set aside Coincoin's children from the future "community of goods" and reserved his right to free them when he pleased.[23]

As a free woman of color, Coincoin likely faced all the hardships Metoyer foresaw. Local lore has created a character cloaked in trappings admired by Euro-Americans of the mid-1900s—beauty, talent, and industry showcased in a luxurious lifestyle, complete with a mansion house, plantation empire, and an abundance of slaves. Still, one long-standing claim about her appears quite probable: that she was highly skilled in pharmacology and nursing. Indeed, those were family skills handed down through generations of her female offspring. Coincoin's daughter Susanne was midwife for Metoyer's plantation and nursed both his wife and youngest son. Coincoin's daughter Thérèse, as nurse to the paralyzed Mme. de Soto, was considered so indispensable that—despite Spanish laws guaranteeing a slave's right to self-purchase or third-party purchase for manumission—de Soto consented to sell Thérèse to her mother, only on condition that Thérèse remain with her until her death. Moreover, court records show that Coincoin's younger sister Marie Louise Mariotte bought her own freedom and then supported herself by manufacturing medicine. That Coincoin, like her sister, might have followed the same profession is entirely plausible.[24]

Some writers also speculate that Coincoin might not have prospered without Metoyer's support. To the contrary, she displayed considerable entrepreneurial skills, engaging in a variety of activities by which she could have supported herself and her children. She trapped bears and wild turkeys, selling their meat at the post. On the sixty-seven acres Metoyer provided to support their freeborn offspring, she planted tobacco—a labor-intensive crop—with apparent success. A surviving passport from 1792 notes her dispatch to the New Orleans market of a barge loaded with tobacco, hides, and bear grease.[25]

Despite popular accounts that credit her with vast lands, fifty or a hundred slaves, and a mansion house, Coincoin invested her earnings in something of far more value: the freedom of her offspring. She clearly had a source of income prior to Metoyer's 1788 donation of the land and his payment of the first annuity. In 1786, she purchased her firstborn daughter, paying slightly below market value because Marie Louise had been crippled in a gunshot accident. For her daughter Thérèse, a skilled nurse valued together with Thérèse's nine-year-old multiracial son at seven hundred piastres, Coincoin made two trips to the prairies south of Opelousas, where her former mistress promised their freedom on the basis of a fifty-piastres down payment. For her eldest son, Nicolas Chiquito, sold away to Spanish Texas, she sent her Metoyer son Augustin to Nacogdoches with three hundred pesos to free Nicolas and bring him back to Cane River. After her Metoyer son Louis fathered a child by a slave woman, Coincoin saved for four years to liberate him since although he was an adult he was not permitted to marry as a slave. Of all her pre-Metoyer children, the only one she failed to free was her daughter Françoise, sold as a child to a neighbor who moved her to a new settlement downriver. Françoise, like her mother, was sexually tied to the white men who owned or otherwise had control of her. Perhaps she had extended relationships with them, or perhaps she was their sexual prey. In any case she bore eleven mixed-race children, two of whom would eventually become free.[26]

As Coincoin's half-French sons passed through their twenties, Metoyer manumitted them, apparently waiting until he felt each was mature enough to live and prosper within societal constraints on free people of color. The daughter Susanne, however, was kept under his wing until his death when she was forty-seven. In the meanwhile, Coincoin's children by Metoyer lived as quasi-free long before their manumissions. When the twins Augustin and Susanne, at age nine, served as godparents to a cousin enslaved by Commandant de Mézières, the new priest called both of them "free mulattoes." A tax roll of February 1794 assessed Coincoin and her sons Augustin and Pierre consecutively, identifying each as free; then Pierre's name was crossed out after his slave status was made known to the assessor. The public works roster of 1792–94, itemizing those who contributed labor or slave labor to work on the roads, levees, and bridges, lists not only Coincoin and her freed son Augustin but also Pierre as a "mulâtre libre," and this time, he was not struck from the list. Coincoin's son Louis, who was freed with Pierre in 1802, applied in 1795 for a grant of land from Commandant Louis DeBlanc, a St. Denis grandson who awarded Louis the requested order of survey and settlement. Louis's slave status at the time of the concession would later be an issue in lengthy court proceedings during the American regime. Coincoin's daughter Susanne, whom Metoyer made a *statu liber* in 1802 but kept in slavery until he died in 1815, twice bought a slave from itinerant traders, despite the fact that she was still herself enslaved.[27]

Central to the legends about Coincoin's "vast" lands and slaveholdings is a myth that she founded the plantation known today as Melrose—a myth whose origin is traceable to the 1950s writings of local colorist Francois Mignon.[28] Historical site documentation work in the 1970s, however, disproved the lore. All known documentation for the plantation identifies Coincoin's son Louis as the recipient of the colonial grant, the entrepreneur who developed it, and its sole proprietor until his death sixteen years after that of his mother. Similarly, all known documentation for Coincoin places her homestead on the sixty-seven-acre tract Pierre provided at their parting. Still, both economic interests and community pride nurture the Melrose myth. Speaking for family members, one descendant wrote the author in the 1970s to say, "I know you proved that Coincoin did not build Melrose, but when I take people there, I still tell them that she did because I want them to be proud of her."[29]

The reality is that Coincoin was, at best, an enterprising farmer of modest means, living not in a pillared mansion but in the *bousillage* cabin common to her era. By 1794, she had mustered enough cash to commission a survey of the sixty-seven acres Pierre Metoyer had cut off for her from his own concession, so the grant could be finalized and a patent issued. The imperfect title Metoyer gave her rested on his 1786 petition for a concession and a 1787 order of survey and settlement by the local commandant. Because no surveyor was available, his concession and her title—like all others locally—went unfinalized until a surveyor arrived sometime around the winter of 1793–94.[30]

Prior to completing the terms for this patent, Coincoin also applied to the commandant for a concession in her own name: the standard eight hundred arpents available to household heads willing to make the required "improvements." She did not, however, request farmland; she lacked the hands to expand her planting operation beyond the sixty-seven acres she already had. Instead, she sought pine-hill land to the west of Old River, where cattle could forage, and hired a Spaniard to tend the herd of a hundred or more head each grantee had to own.[31]

No issue surrounding this Afro-Creole woman is more controversial than her ownership of slaves. Some free people of color—in Louisiana, as elsewhere— bought family members whom they could not legally manumit, thereafter serving as their protectors. Others, including freed men and women at Natchitoches, bought slaves for labor. Among their ranks, Coincoin appears to have been the first on Cane River to buy slaves she did not free; and she accumulated the largest number—at least sixteen of them. Indisputably, she bought them for profit; at issue is her motivation.[32]

Coincoin's bravura in buying several offspring simultaneously on installment, knowing that a downturn in revenue could cause her to lose her money and her children, was severely tested by the financial demands of land surveys and taxes. For five years, her debt to de Soto went mostly unpaid. Coincoin was, by this time, in her fifties—her body undoubtedly suffering a host of "female troubles" that fifteen childbirths would have wrought on her internally and externally. For women who labored physically, prolapsed wombs, spinal problems, joint stress, urinary incontinence, and hemorrhoids meant a serious decrease in productivity. This was the stage at which Coincoin likely realized that her mission to free her offspring would fail without slaves for labor.[33]

Her acquisitions—one woman and two men—were all African born. Like many slaveholders, she chose to buy a woman first: Marguerite, Congolese (aged about twenty-five—extrapolating her age from the 1816 document—at the time Coincoin acquired her), supplied labor while producing ten children of her own. She and Coincoin buried one of those infants, and Marguerite's teenaged daughters had begun a new generation by the time Coincoin divided the family among her own children. The two males, Harry, a Quissay aged fifty in 1816, and Louis, a Congolese, aged thirty-five that year, are known only from the documents by which Coincoin passed them to her sons. Unlike many contemporary male slaves, neither of these men appears in church records as a baptismal sponsor for slave infants.[34]

Those sacramental registers, and their silences, provide crucial insights into Coincoin's character. In contrast to African American women in New Orleans, who avidly embraced Catholicism and were central to its growth, Coincoin exhibited no such fervor. Although her multiracial children became religious leaders and founders of the first U.S. church built by and for African Americans, there is little evidence that Coincoin, as a free woman, was a practicing Catholic. She served as godparent to no infants, slave or free, other than three grandchildren in 1793 and 1795.[35]

Surviving records do suggest a woman who respected the African faiths of her children, lived up to one core principle shared by Africans and Christians (the rite of presenting infants to their God), and had compassion as a mother and slave owner. The records do not document her acting as an agent of the Catholic Church and catechizing among the unchurched, slave or free. In this regard, she was likely influenced by the social structure of the Natchitoches outpost, which fostered freedom in the individual exercise of conscience and faith. By this era, most parishioners lived on plantations distant from the church. Their priest regularly complained of their laxity and indifference and about the dereliction of masters in bringing even their own children to Mass and instruction. Coincoin's farm lay eleven miles from the parish church, along a rudimentary road and a river that had to be forded many times along that eleven-mile route. When a priest passed by on the river, typically once or twice a year, Coincoin took Marguerite's newest infant to whatever home the priest used for baptisms. But when Marguerite's infant Zenon died in October 1797, Coincoin made the trip into town to have him buried in sacred ground.[36]

White slaveholders along the river, as well as Coincoin's sons, did routinely present newly acquired Africans for baptism. Of the three whom Coincoin owned, however, the Congolese Louis was not baptized until two years after he arrived at the post, Marguerite was not baptized for at least twelve years, and the Quissay Harry was never baptized at Natchitoches. From the evidence, one might argue that when Coincoin purchased adults newly arrived from Africa, she respected them as people and honored their own religious beliefs. When and if they wanted to convert, she arranged it. But—unlike her Catholic neighbors—she did not feel an obligation to force their conversion.[37]

Whatever Coincoin's spiritual beliefs, it would not be surprising if there was an emotional distance between her and Catholic orthodoxy. Personal integrity and good citizenship do not require subscription to organized religion. Coincoin's prosecution by the priest and the painful, disfiguring punishment ordered by a commandant who indulged his own temptations with slave women (and whose bachelor son had just begun his own lifelong *plaçage* with a slave) likely diminished her respect for both the church and state. Moreover, given the extent to which Mme. de Soto and her powerful father had battled church officials, a respect for religious authority was likely not inculcated into Coincoin at all. However, tax records demonstrate that she was a good citizen who paid her assessments on time, in an era when the delinquent rolls included many prominent neighbors, and contributed her labor to the maintenance of the parish infrastructure.[38]

The last fifteen years of Coincoin's life saw marked changes in her livelihood and lifestyle. In 1802, Pierre agreed to free the last of the children they had together—provided Coincoin renounced the annuity he had promised in 1788. Those free children, he asserted, should see that their mother did not want for necessities. Coincoin concurred, partially. Her renouncement forfeited all claims to what he had promised *"except for that which concerns my habitation."*[39] Those sixty-seven acres on which she had labored for fifteen years she obviously considered *hers*—that she should be able to keep the land seems like a reasonable expectation in light of the labor she had invested into it.

Around 1806, Coincoin abandoned both farming and her homestead. Tradition holds that she went to live with one or another son and died in the home of Augustin. Supporting that tradition, the first American census taken in Louisiana in 1810 does not count her as a head of household. In the interim, her sixty-seven acres were assumed by her son Pierre, who is identified as its owner in federal land records from 1806 to 1816 and in deeds executed by neighbors in 1810. In her family's pursuit of her U.S. title to the Old River *vacherie*, her own witness stated that the land had gone unattended since 1807, the year that she invested in a tract adjoining her sixty-seven acres and turned the new land over to her youngest son Toussaint. After her son Pierre acquired other land in 1816, Coincoin sold the sixty-seven acres to a long-time neighbor. She clearly had no need for it. The resurvey of her homestead, made that year by the U.S. government, omits the customary sketch of the claimant's house, suggesting that it no longer stood on the property. Although the known evidence can support the tradition that Coincoin spent her last years with either her son Louis or her son Augustin, none of the evidence suggests that the aging freedwoman was ever the "mistress" of Louis's plantation that is now the National Historic Landmark known as Melrose.[40]

The March–April 1816 deeds by which Coincoin transferred her slaves to her Metoyer offspring mark the last records for her. Although those sales generated $5,250 in cash (some $80,000 in 2007 currency) and she died in possession of her eight-hundred-arpent *vacherie*, her offspring opened no succession to settle her affairs. Her daughter Thérèse, who had remained at Opelousas as Thérèse

Don Manuel, would sell her share of the *vacherie* to her Cane River kin. In the twentieth century, south Louisiana offspring of Thérèse would discover that the *vacherie* remained unpatented and apply for title, presenting a mangled genealogy that merged Marie Thérèse Coincoin and her daughter Thérèse into a single woman.[41]

Lore, be it oral history or family tradition, is typically flawed in many details. Yet there is often a core of truth. In Coincoin's case, both branches of her offspring and an endless parade of reporters, colorists, novelists, and scholars have painted verbal portraits with little resemblance to the real Coincoin. Even so, two core truths remain. First, her offspring recognized that the freedom they enjoyed before the Civil War was earned by the sacrifices of "the woman who started it all," even though personal memories faded as generations passed. Second, Coincoin's era was one in which single women, slave or free, had limited opportunities and little hope of achieving anything of substance. For slave women especially, interracial liaisons often represented the only way to escape the physical, sexual, moral, social, and economic degradation of enslavement.

Coincoin personifies the challenges women of African descent faced in colonial Louisiana. The institution of slavery shaped her life in both bondage and freedom. Torn between the values instilled by her African parents and the dictates of the society in which she had to survive, she navigated the system by using her assets as a woman. The records both she and Metoyer created attest that their relationship—whatever the basis on which it began and despite its imbalance of power—developed into one of mutual respect, if not love. She bore the brunt of the punishment meted out for that illegal relationship across color lines, but she parlayed the pain into freedom for herself and, ultimately, her children. Her slaveholding, like that of other free people of color in Louisiana, is a paradox—one demonstrating how hierarchies of power in slave societies ensnared virtually everyone, including former slaves themselves. That she held slaves for their labor, and not for humanitarian purposes, stands alongside the doggedness with which she pursued freedom for her offspring.

Like most historic figures, Coincoin was a complex and multidimensional person, a black woman struggling to survive in a society that measured worth by skin color. A successful entrepreneur, farmer, and medicine woman, she set an example of thrift, courage, and industry that helped her children not just prosper but navigate the barrage of legal and economic challenges that engulfed free people of color for generations thereafter. That example—not a plantation empire, a mansion house, or a romantic story of love across forbidden lines—is Coincoin's legacy.

NOTES

1. The term "Creole" in the eighteenth century applied to colonials born in the colony, whether of European or African extraction. The term was not racialized until much later.

2. A sampling of the literature follows, arranged by subject. ART: Cedric Dover, *American Negro Art* (Greenwich: New York Graphic Society, 1960). ARCHAEOLOGY: University College London Institute of Archaeology, "Cane River African Diaspora Archaeological Project—Research Design (2004)," http://www.ucl.ac.uk/archaeology/project/cane-river/research-design.htm. DANCE: Carrie Gaiser, "Caught Dancing: Hybridity, Stability, and Subversion in Dance Theatre of Harlem's Creole *Giselle*," *Theatre Journal* 58 (May 2006): 269–89. LITERATURE: Norman German, *No Other World* (Thibodeaux, La.: Blue Heron Press, 1992); Elizabeth Shown Mills, *Isle of Canes: A Historical Novel* (Provo, Utah: Ancestry, 2004). HISTORY: Gary B. Mills, *The Forgotten People: Cane River's Creoles of Color* (Baton Rouge: Louisiana State University Press, 1977). LIVING HISTORY: Blake Hayes and Katie Boarman, "Meatpies, Magnolias and Murals: A New Interpretation Plan for Melrose Plantation," Association for Living History, Farm and Agricultural Museums, *Interpreting Multiculturalism in the Modern Museum Setting*, http://www.alhfam.org/pdfs/15-Hayes_Boardman.pdf. GENEALOGY: Elizabeth Shown Mills and Gary B. Mills, "Slaves and Masters: The Louisiana Metoyers," *National Genealogical Society Quarterly* 70 (September 1982): 163–89.

3. For Coincoin's prosecution, see *Rex v. de Soto*, document nos. 1227–28, Natchitoches Colonial Archives, Clerk of Court's Office (hereinafter cited as NCA). For polar interpretations of her character, see Mills, *Forgotten People*, esp. chapter 2, and Frances Jerome Woods, *Marginality and Identity: A Colored Creole Family through Ten Generations* (Baton Rouge: Louisiana State University Press, 1972), esp. 45–46.

4. Elizabeth Shown Mills, "Family and Social Patterns on the Colonial Louisiana Frontier: A Quantitative Analysis" (senior thesis, New College, University of Alabama, 1981), chapters 1 and 2 (Mills Collection, Cammie G. Henry Research Center, Northwestern State University, Natchitoches [hereinafter cited as CHRC]).

5. For the Code Noir, see "Louis XV's edit concernant les nègres esclaves à la Louisiane, March 1724," *Louisiana Historical Society Publications* 4 (1908): 75–90. For French concepts of marriage and family, see François LeBrun, *La vie conjugale sous l'ancien regime* (Paris: A. Colin, 1975), and Jean-Louis Flandrin, *Familles: Parenté, maison, sexualité, dans l'ancienne société* (Paris: Hachette, 1976). For colonial concubinages, see David W. Cohen and Jack P. Greene, eds., *Neither Slave nor Free: The Freedmen of African Descent in the Slave Societies of the New World* (Baltimore: Johns Hopkins University Press, 1972), Thomas Marc Fiehrer, "The African Presence in Colonial Louisiana: An Essay on the Continuity of Caribbean Culture," in *Louisiana's Black Heritage*, ed. Robert R. Macdonald et al. (New Orleans: Louisiana State Museum, 1979), 3–31, and Gwendolyn Midlo Hall, *Africans in Colonial Louisiana: The Development of Afro-Creole Culture in the Eighteenth Century* (Baton Rouge: Louisiana State University Press, 1992), esp. 39–40, drawing from Pére Jean Baptiste Labat, *Nouvelle rélation de l'Afrique occidentale*, 5 vols. (Paris: G. Cavelier, 1728), 2:208–33.

6. Virginia Meacham Gould, "In Full Enjoyment of Their Liberty: The Free Women of Color of the Gulf Ports of New Orleans, Mobile, and Pensacola, 1769–1860" (PhD diss., Emory University, 1991), chapters 5 and 6; Elizabeth Shown Mills, "Marie des Neiges Juchereau de St.-Denis," in *Dictionary of Louisiana Biography*, ed. Glenn R. Conrad, 2 vols. (Lafayette: Louisiana Historical Association, 1988), 1:449–50, 55.

7. At the time importation was suspended, few settlers had the wherewithal to purchase black

labor, but the less affluent might acquire Native American captives through the Spanish post at Los Adayes or from the tribes themselves.

8. Elizabeth Shown Mills, "Social and Family Patterns on the Colonial Louisiana Frontier," *Sociological Spectrum* 2 (July–December 1982), 233–48, esp. 238, and Mills, "Family and Social Patterns on the Colonial Louisiana Frontier," esp. 39–45. For the African slave trade, see Hall, *Africans in Colonial Louisiana*, 86–95 and 139–40.

9. Elizabeth Shown Mills, *Natchitoches, 1729–1803: Abstracts of the Catholic Church Registers of the French and Spanish Post of St. Jean Baptiste des Natchitoches in Louisiana* (New Orleans: Polyanthos, 1977), entries 11 and 13. For the other church from which this paper is drawn, see Mills, *Natchitoches, 1800–1826: Translated Abstracts of Register Number Five of the Catholic Church Parish of St. François des Natchitoches* (New Orleans: Polyanthos, 1980), and Mills, *Natchitoches Church Marriages, 1818–1850: Translated Abstracts from the Registers of St. François de Natchitoches, Louisiana* (1985; rpt., Bowie, Md.: Heritage Books, 2004).

10. The names of Coincoin's siblings and their variants come from local notarial and church records, colony-level judicial files, materials sent from the colony to Spain (maintained as the Papeles Procedentes de Cuba at the Archivo General de Indias, Seville (hereinafter cited as PPC), and records generated in the confirmation of colonial land titles by the U.S. government. Coincoin's name derivation was determined by Jan Vansina, Africanist, anthropologist, and historian at the University of Wisconsin, in a letter from Vansina to Gary B. Mills, May 12, 1973 (letter in author's possession). Vansina had not been told that Coincoin was, indeed, the secondborn daughter in her birth family. Other possible origins of the name "Coincoin"—together with the sibling names uncovered by the author—are being pursued by the Africanist Kevin MacDonald at the Institute of Archaeology, University College London (MacDonald to Elizabeth Shown Mills, February 19, 2008).

11. Partition of St. Denis slaves, document no. 176, 203–5, NCA, and Louisiana State Archives microfilm Natchitoches F.T. 565, "Miscellaneous Archive Records, 1733–1820," particularly frames 232–50; burials of the widow St. Denis, François, and Marie Françoise, parish of St. François des Natchitoches, register 2, unpaginated, April 1758. For analysis of the St. Denis succession and the fate of its slaves, see Elizabeth Shown Mills, "Which Marie Louise Is 'Mariotte'? Sorting Slaves of Common Name," *National Genealogical Society Quarterly* 94 (September 2006): 183–204; and Elizabeth Shown Mills, "Jeannot Mulon *dit* LeBrun, f.m.c., Colonial Natchitoches, Louisiana," research report, December 8, 2005, Board for Certification of Genealogists, http://www.bcgcertification.org/skillbuilders/extendedreport.pdf.

12. Local attitudes toward slave marriage and interracial sex are extensively explored in Mills, "Quintanilla's Crusade: 'Moral Reform' and Its Consequences on the Natchitoches Frontier," *Louisiana History* 42 (Summer 2001): 277–302, and Elizabeth Shown Mills and Gary B. Mills, "Missionaries Compromised: Early Evangelization of Slaves and Free People of Color in North Louisiana," in *Cross, Crozier, and Crucible: A Volume Celebrating the Bicentennial of a Catholic Diocese in Louisiana*, ed. Glenn R. Conrad (Lafayette, La.: Archdiocese of New Orleans, 1993), 30–47, esp. 33–40. For Mme. de Soto's health issues, see *De Soto v. Diard*, 1779, document no. 1434, "Miscellaneous Archive Records, 1733–1820," frames 373–74, and Marie St. Denis to Marie Thérèse Coincoin, 1796, document no. 2804, 4, NCA.

13. For the sale of Coincoin's children, see Marie St. Denis and Antonio Gil y Barbo, document no. 757, and Marie St. Denis to Delissard Jouhannis, document no. 765, NCA. Document no. 757 erroneously identifies the sold child, Nicolas, as son of Coincoin's sister Gertrude. His correct identity as Coincoin's son is proved by (1) proceedings by which her son Augustin purchased Nicolas's free-

dom from the seized estate of Lieutenant Governor Gil y Barbo in 1793 (*Translations of Statistical and Census Reports of Texas, 1782–1836,* and *Sources Documenting the Black in Texas, 1603–1803,* 3 rolls [San Antonio: Institute of Texan Culture, 1979], roll 3, frames 826–29); (2) 1813 testimony on behalf of Nicolas in his private land claim (*American State Papers: Documents, Legislative and Executive, of the Congress of the United States,* class 8, Public Lands, 8 vols. [Washington, D.C.: Gales and Seaton, 1832–61], 3:199); and (3) 1838 testimony of Antoine Prudhomme in the district court suits *Roubieu v. Metoyer* and *Metoyer v. Roubieu* (bundle 59, no. 1395, and bundle 74, no. 1473, Clerk of Court's Office, Natchitoches). For most *métissages* in which the Cane River community is rooted, see Elizabeth Shown Mills, "(De) Mézières-Trichel-Grappe: A Study of Tri-Caste Lineages in the Old South," *The Genealogist* 6 (Spring 1985): 3–84, Gary B. Mills, "Monet-Rachal: Backtracking a Cross-Racial Heritage in the Eighteenth and Nineteenth Centuries," *The American Genealogist* 65 (July 1990): 129–42, and *Isle of Canes,* passim, but especially the eight introductory charts.

14. See pages 15–17 and 57–59 herein for more information about the institution of *plaçage*.

15. Quintanilla to de Mézières, *Rex v. de Soto,* document no. 1227, NCA. The multiracial slave children Coincoin bore were Nicolas Augustin and Marie Susanne, twins, January 22, 1768; Louis, ca. 1770; Pierre, ca. 1772; Dominique, ca. 1774; Eulalie, 1776 (d. 1785–88); and Antoine Joseph, 1778. The last three children (Marie Françoise Rosalie, 1780; Pierre Toussaint, 1782; and François, 1784) were born free.

16. De Mézière's Black Ordinance of 1770, document no. 652, NCA; Mills, "(De) Mézières-Trichel-Grappe: A Study of Tri-Caste Lineages in the Old South"; St. Louis Cathedral, register M3, "Libro Primero de Matrimonios de Negros y Mulatos . . . ," p. 10, for Juan Francisco Messiere; Governor Domingo Cabello y Robles to Carlos Francisco de Croix, October 19, 1779, vol. 88, box 2C36, and October 20, 1779, vol. 89, box 2C37, series 1, Bexar Archives (translations held at the Center of American History, University of Texas at Austin).

17. For the purchases, see Marie de St. Denis to Metoyer, May 31, 1776, document no. 1161, July 29, 1778, document no. 1312, and April 7, 1780, document no. 1473, NCA. Sketchy details of Metoyer's manumission of Coincoin and son Antoine Joseph appear in his unprobated 1783 will, Acts of Leonardo Mazange, vol. 7, pp. 187–91, Notarial Archives Research Center, New Orleans.

18. *Rex v. Cesario,* Fran[cis]co Christoval, "Noel, y la Negra Margarita," document no. 1777-03-13-01, folder 3671, Judicial Records of the Spanish Cabildo, Louisiana State Museum Historical Center, New Orleans.

19. Metoyer's 1783 will.

20. Some published accounts of Coincoin's life, striving to "realistically" appraise her achievements, assert that even her children's accomplishments would have been far less had they not received bequests from their white father. However, the children received no such bequests, and some achieved greater financial wealth than Pierre's legitimate sons who did inherit his sizable estate.

21. Hans W. Baade, "The Law of Slavery in Spanish Luisiana, 1769–1803," in *Louisiana's Legal Heritage,* ed. Edward F. Haas (Pensacola, Fla.: Perdido Bay Press, 1983), 43–86; Louis Moreau-Lislet and Henry Carleton, trans., *The Laws of Las Siete Partidas Which Are Still in Force in the State of Louisiana,* 2 vols. (New Orleans: James M'Karaher, 1820), esp. 210, articles 10, 12, and 14.

22. The Historic American Buildings Survey disputes Metoyer's land donation to Coincoin and erroneously identifies the origin of the tract she patented in 1794. Contrary to what the survey reports, Pierre himself petitioned for the land in 1786 and received the concession in 1787, but the final patent was not issued until surveys were made in 1794. Because the land had, meanwhile, been divided between them, two patents were issued in 1794: one to Coincoin for the eighty ar-

pents and one to Pierre for the remainder of his concession. See Historic American Buildings Survey, in cooperation with Cane River National Heritage Area et al., "Coincoin-Prudhomme House (Maison de Marie Therese)," HABS no. LA-1295, National Park Service, http://www.nps.gov/ hdp/samples/habs/coincoin/history.pdf. The original deed of gift from Pierre to Coincoin has strayed from the courthouse. The "Index to French Archives," located in the Clerk of Court's Office, Natchitoches, and created when the United States took control, identifies document no. 2119 as "Pierre Metoyer to Marie Thérèse, free negress, *Donation of Land.*" The index entry notes no date, but Pierre and Coincoin's 1802 abrogation of some terms of the donation (recorded in Misc. Book 2:206–7, NCA) dates it at October 8, 1788. Also relevant is Metoyer's 1801 will (folder 728, Melrose Collection, CHRC).

23. The marriage contract is missing; terms relating to Coincoin's children are reiterated in the 1801 will. Metoyer's personal copy of his marriage contract with Marie Thérèse Buard, the widow Pavie, has survived in private possession; copy in Mills Collection, CHRC.

24. Metoyer's 1801 will discusses Susanne's midwifery. Document no. 2804, NCA, covers Thérèse's conditional manumission. Mariotte's practice is revealed in *Rex v. La Costa,* document no. 1788, NCA, and in the case as it was carried on in New Orleans (translated in Laura Porteous, "Index to Spanish Judicial Records of Louisiana," *Louisiana Historical Quarterly* 26 [December 1943]: 897–906). Edwin A. Davis, *Louisiana: A Narrative History* (Baton Rouge: Louisiana State University Press, 1961), 134, more generally notes significant activity at Natchitoches in the manufacture of medicine.

25. "État de la Cargaison d'un . . . Gabarre a Marie Thérèse," April 20, 1792, microfilm roll 1, Jack D. L. Holmes Collection (transcripts from Papeles de Estado, Archivo Historico Nacional, Seville), Northwestern State University, Natchitoches. See also comments about Coincoin's economic enterprises in the 1801 will of Metoyer.

26. For the manumission of Marie Louise, see Pierre Dolet to Marie Thérèse Coincoin, September 9, 1786, Old Natchitoches Data, 2:289, Melrose Collection, CHRC, and Marie Thérèse Coinquin [*sic*] to Marie Louise, Liberty, January 29, 1795, document no. 2596, NCA. For the manumission of Thérèse, see document no. 2804, NCA. For the manumission of Nicolas, see *Translations of Statistical and Census Reports of Texas, 1782–1836,* roll 1, Gil y Barbo to Metoyer, 1793. For the manumission of Catiche, see Marguerite LeRoy to Marie Thérèse Coincoin, document no. 2550, and Marie Thérèse Coincoin to Catiche, document no. 2552, NCA. For the sale of Françoise, see Marie de St. Denis to Jouhannis, December 17, 1772, document no. 756, and Jouhannis to Jn Bte. Dupré, May 27, 1772, document no. 771, NCA. Françoise's daughter Marie Louise LeComte (fathered by her mistress's brother) was eventually freed by the son Marie Louise bore their next owner, Louis Monet—after Monet's widow petitioned the legislature for Louis's manumission. Some of these details appear in Mills, *Forgotten People,* 90. For Louis's purchase of his mother, see folder 396, Cane River Creole Collection, ms. no. 182, Historic New Orleans Collection. Françoise's youngest son François Nicolas Monet(te), also fathered by her master, achieved manumission before 1835, when he bought and freed his own daughter Marie Zelia; Misc. Book 18:412, Clerk of Court's Office, Natchitoches.

27. Manumission of Nicolas Augustin, August 1, 1792, document no. 2409, NCA; manumission of Dominique, January 15, 1795, document no. 2584, NCA; manumission of Louis, Pierre, and Marie Suzanne [*sic*], May 28, 1802, Misc. Book 2:208–11, Clerk of Court's Office, Natchitoches. For their treatment as free while still enslaved, see: Mills, *Natchitoches, 1729–1803,* entry 2304 (for evidence that at the baptism ceremony godparents Nicolas Augustin and Susanne were described as free mulattoes); 1793 tax roll (drawn February 1794), folder 703, Melrose Collection, CHRC; public works roster, n.d., folder 1, Natchitoches Notarial Acts, 1734–83, Natchitoches Parish Records Collection,

Louisiana State University Archives, Baton Rouge; Louis Metoyer private land claim certificate B1953 (sections 17 and 94, Township 7 North, Range 6 West), RG 49, General Land Office, National Archives; Louis Mettoyer [sic] claim for 883.60 acres, OPEL: May 1796, Opelousas Notarial Records; file B1953, Louis Metoyer, Louisiana State Land Office, Baton Rouge; *Boissier v. Metayer* [sic], 5 Mart. (O.S.), 678 (1818); Thomas Parham to Marie Susanne [sic], 1810, miscellany book 1:225–26, Clerk of Court's Office, Natchitoches; Robert Bell to Marie Suzanne [sic], 1811, miscellany book 2:94, Clerk of Court's Office, Natchitoches.

28. Coincoin's promotion by Francois Mignon, who spent his last three decades at Melrose under the patronage of the plantation's owners, may be explained by a local belief that he is her descendant, born surreptitiously to young Clothilde Chevalier by John Henry Sr. (letter from Lee Etta Vaccarini Coutii to Elizabeth Shown Mills, October 4, 1980, citing a statement by the late Joseph Henry, son of John, acknowledging Mignon as his half brother). Prior to Mignon's writings, accounts credited Melrose to "Louis Metoyer, former native of Santo Domingo" or to Augustin Metoyer, origin unstated. See "Melrose Manor on Cane River Stands as Relic of World's Strangest Empire," *Hammond (La.) Progress*, March 25, 1938, Herman de B. Seebold, *Old Louisiana Plantation Homes and Family Trees* (Baton Rouge: Pelican, 1941), 361–63, and Harnett T. Kane, *Plantation Parade: The Grand Manner in Louisiana* (New York: William Morrow, 1945), 265–67. The Coincoin myth emerged by 1953, when Mignon "informed" reporters that "a black lass from the Congo" named Marie started the plantation and passed it to her son Augustin, whose own son built the manor house; see "Melrose: Home of Famous Louisiana Authors," *Louisiana* REA *News*, July 1953, 11, and D. Garber, "History of Melrose Plantation Like Turning Pages of Novel," undated clipping from unidentified Texas newspaper, whose internal evidence dates it in the early 1950s. By 1958, Mignon had refined his account, asserting that the "first mistress of Melrose" was "Marie Therese Coin-Coin, a Congo-born slave girl" who built the first houses on the land in 1750 ("The Story of Melrose," in *Natchitoches: Oldest Settlement in the Louisiana Purchase* [Natchitoches: Association for the Preservation of Historic Natchitoches, 1958], 48–52).

29. Coutii to Elizabeth and Gary Mills, October 23, 1974. For the correction of local lore, see the Mills and Mills essays and monographs of the 1970s and 1980s cited in note 2.

30. File A1679, Marie Thérèse, free *negresse*, Louisiana State Land Office, and OPEL: May 1796, Opelousas Notarial Records.

31. Francis P. Burns, "The Spanish Land Laws of Louisiana," *Louisiana Historical Quarterly* 11 (October 1928), 557–81; C. Richard Arena, "Landholding and Political Power in Spanish Louisiana," *Louisiana Historical Quarterly* 38 (October 1955): 35; file B2146, Marie Thérèse Metoyer, State Land Office, particularly the testimony of Gaspard Bodin, December 14, 1812; claim B2146, Marie Thérèse, free Negro, OPEL: May 1794, Opelousas Notarial Records; serial patent 437,269, Marie Thérèse Metoyer, RG 49, General Land Office, National Archives.

32. For a sampling of the literature on slaveholding by blacks, see Larry Koger, *Black Slaveowners: Free Black Slave Masters in South Carolina, 1790–1860* (Jefferson, N.C.: McFarland, 1985), Michael P. Johnson and James L. Roark, *Black Masters: A Free Family of Color in the Old South* (New York: Norton, 1984), Edwin Adams Davis and William Ransom Hogan, *The Barber of Natchez* (Baton Rouge: Louisiana State University Press, 1954), and Virginia Meacham Gould, *Chained to the Rock of Adversity: To Be Free, Black, and Female in the Old South* (Athens: University of Georgia Press, 1998).

33. The October 10, 1795, census of slaveholders (leg. 201, PPC) is the first to credit her with slaves. Three of the five tallied that year should have been her enslaved sons Pierre and Louis and the African-born Marguerite, who had two children by 1797.

34. Marie Thérèse Coincoin to [various offspring], Conveyance Book 3:524–38, Clerk of Court's

Office, Natchitoches. Harry was likely the African *nègre* of that name (a rare one at Natchitoches) whom Coincoin's son Augustin purchased from a Virginia slave trader in 1810 (Archibald Phillips to Augustin Metoyer, miscellany book 1:98, Clerk of Court's Office, Natchitoches).

35. Mills, *Natchitoches, 1729–1803*, entries 2130 (1793), 2764 (1795), and 2791 (1795). On African American women and Catholicism, see Emily Clark and Virginia Meacham Gould, "The Feminine Face of Afro-Catholicism in New Orleans, 1727–1952," *William and Mary Quarterly* 59 (April 2002): 409–48.

36. Commentaries in 1795–1801 annual statistical censuses by Pierre Pavie, published in Elizabeth Shown Mills, *Natchitoches Colonials: Censuses, Military Rolls, and Tax Lists, 1722–1803* (Chicago: Adams Press, 1981), 115–23; also Mills, *Natchitoches, 1729–1803*, entry 3305 (burial).

37. Mills, *Natchitoches, 1800–1826*, entry 2060 (joint baptism of Louis and Marguerite).

38. Mills, *Natchitoches Colonials*, 68–110 (tax records). Emphasis added.

39. Misc. Book 2:206–7, Clerk of Court's Office, Natchitoches.

40. Elderly descendants in the 1970s reported that Coincoin's death in Augustin's home was recounted to them by Augustin's daughter-in-law, Perine Metoyer Metoyer (d. 1935), the community's "memory keeper" after Augustin's death. For Coincoin's absence as a head of household, see the 1810 U.S. census, Natchitoches Parish, Louisiana, National Archives microfilm publication M252, roll 10. For the federal land records, see the survey dated February 26, 1816, by Joseph Irwin, file A1679 (Marie Thérèse), and testimony of Gaspard Bodin, December 14, 1812, file B2146, State Land Office. For the local transactions, see: Louis Verchere to Dominique Rachal, document no. 3768, NCA; Jean Lalande to Marie Thérèse, June 5, 1807 [original documents], Conveyance Book 42, document no. 501; Marie Thérèse Coincoin to Toussaint Metoyer, September 17, 1814, Conveyance Book 3:308; Marie Thérèse Coincoin to Jean Baptiste Ailhaud St. Anne, March 9, 1816, Conveyance Book 3:522; Jean Lalande to Toussaint Metoyer, April 21, 1821, Conveyance Book 10:41, Clerk of Court's Office, Natchitoches.

41. Affidavit of Dennis J. Victorin, June 30, 1914, in file for Marie Thérèse Metoyer, serial patent 437,269.

The Baroness Pontalba

(1795–1874)

A Peculiar Drama

CHRISTINA VELLA

❀ ❀ ❀

Everyone who met the baroness Pontalba had an emphatic opinion of her, it seems, after her father-in-law shot her, and many who never knew her at all nevertheless opined about her freely, as people tend to do when they talk about a person at the center of a rancid scandal. Prosthetic stuffing and her clothes hid her shattered breast, but her mangled hand was hard to conceal. One bluish finger, until it was finally amputated, dangled alongside the grotesque stubs of other fingers that had been completely shot away. Having only one useful lung, she breathed deeply and frugally, was fast and blunt in speech, and rarely squandered her energy being excessively polite. By the time she returned to America in 1849, she was beyond caring what anyone thought of her. During the years she spent in New Orleans constructing the Pontalba Buildings, Mme. de Pontalba (she generally dispensed with her title) was a "character," too wealthy to be the object of ridicule but too striking to be ignored. Though she might be small, nervous, and dowdy, to many a gruff businessman, she was utterly intimidating.

Even before her "incident," as she always referred to it, she had not been beautiful. But she must have had immeasurable beauty within her to turn the ugly Place d'Armes, with its muddy field and squalid cottages, into an arabesque of iron and color. How sparkling her mind must have been to have conceived the Hôtel Pontalba in Paris, a poem of glass and gardens that is now the U.S. Embassy residence. To the Americans and Frenchmen who daily pass under the portals of her buildings, her architecture seems to reflect the dignity of a well-ordered nineteenth-century life, a life of polished marble, florid monograms, and protected assets. But there was nothing protected in the life of the baroness

Pontalba. She grew up with the burden of a great fortune, married into misery, and was disfigured as much by the hatred directed against her as she was by the physical attacks that laid bare her private unhappiness.

❀ ❀ ❀

Micaela Almonester de Pontalba was born in New Orleans in 1795 with no title but with a ponderable inheritance and a stiff will.[1] Louisiana was then a Spanish colony, its Iberian population amiably outnumbered by the descendants of the original French settlers. The little town, though the capital of the huge colony, was a shabby pesthole floating on swamp, a stinking, drenched community where women went barefoot to the opera, their slaves carrying lights and gowns over wooden sidewalks surrounded by swamp and alligators. Citizens threw their garbage into the streets to be purified by the air and fought yellow fever epidemics by praying and shooting cannon into the atmosphere.[2] Micaela's father, Andrés Almonester, was a Spaniard, old and rich by the time of her birth, and famed in the New World for his philanthropies. He built two charity hospitals, as well as schools, chapels, and storage buildings, and a grand cathedral, presbytere, and town hall on the square where Micaela would one day raise the Pontalba Buildings. He died when Micaela was three and he was seventy. Her mother was young, French, and poor before her marriage but famed afterward for marrying Micaela's father.

Micaela's husband, Célestin, was French, also born in New Orleans. His father, Joseph Xavier Delfau, later Baron Pontalba, was a brooding, obsessive man, morbidly devoted to his son, although in later years he developed a sincere attachment to Micaela's money. When little Célestin was five, the Pontalbas left Louisiana and moved to France. "Tin-Tin" and his mother sailed first, causing the elder Pontalba to fall into an excruciating depression over the separation. He dreamed, for example, of monsters throwing boiling liquid into the child's face, eating the child's eyes away to the bone.[3] When the Pontalbas were reunited in France, the father bought a country estate. Célestin, still idolized by his parents, became a page to Napoléon and eventually aide-de-camp to Marshal Michel Ney. In 1811, the elder Pontalba took the most fateful step of his life: he wrote to Micaela's mother in New Orleans proposing a match between her fifteen-year-old daughter and his twenty-year-old Célestin.

Money was not the main reason Pontalba sought the marriage. It was the only reason. But in an age when marriage was seen as a means of securing wealth as well as affection, a contract made on behalf of two young strangers, each the sole heir to a fortune, was hardly remarkable. Célestin and his mother traveled

MICAELA ALMONESTER, THE BARONESS PONTALBA

Circa 1840. Courtesy of the Collection of the Louisiana State Museum.

to New Orleans, and the couple were introduced. Micaela's future husband was handsome in his army uniform, and he promised to show her Paris. They were married on the Place d'Armes—Jackson Square—in the St. Louis Cathedral that her father built and was buried in. The service was in Spanish, which neither Micaela nor Célestin could understand, since they both spoke French, but everyone agreed that the groom was beautiful and the bride rich. Then, with both mothers in tow, they sailed away to France to live unhappily ever after.[4]

Micaela did not go to Paris but to the Pontalbas' rural estate. Château Mont-l'Évêque was fifty miles from the capital, near the provincial town of Senlis, a carriage journey of eight hours or eight days, depending on the state of the ruts that served the scanty traffic.[5] Micaela's new home was an ancient castle, a deeply shadowed fortress where, in parapets moist since the Middle Ages, she settled in with Célestin's parents.

Xavier de Pontalba had expected the marriage of Micaela and Célestin to be a business merger that would transfer the Almonester wealth into his possession, with the bulk of the fortune coming in Micaela's dowry. He was stunned, therefore, to discover that the dotal contract his wife had made in New Orleans gave him outright only forty thousand dollars from Almonester's vast estate.[6] There was more to the dowry, to be sure, but it was to be disbursed by Micaela's mother over several years and under specific rules. The more Pontalba ruminated on the dowry, the more fault he found with his daughter-in-law, who, he averred, had arrived "despoiled." He filled his son's pliable ears with talk of the insult the family had suffered because of the contract. For both the Pontalba men, the dowry soon became the only serious matter in the marriage. It was a stain on Micaela's existence, spreading and deepening with the passage of time, so that even after the birth of five children, even after Micaela's mother had handed over massive amounts of money, and after Micaela and Célestin were themselves grandparents, Célestin was still seeking redress in the courts for a dotal contract in which, he insisted, his family had been grievously cheated.

As an only child, Micaela would eventually inherit all of her parents' fortune, but that did not satisfy the Pontalba father and son. In the first place, they resented the inconvenience of having to wait for Micaela's mother to die. In the second place, a dowry, both in France and Louisiana, was exclusively controlled by the husband, whereas in Louisiana, his wife's inheritance was out of his eager hands.[7] Therefore, a large dowry from Micaela was preferable to a large inheritance.

The elder Pontalba thus set about coercing Micaela's mother to correct the marriage contract. First, he sued Mme. Almonester in Louisiana, claiming that she had no right to share in her husband's estate and that, moreover, she was squandering Micaela's inheritance.[8] Far from misspending Micaela's money, the mother was in fact buying remarkably successful rental property in Paris, houses that would eventually sustain several generations of Pontalbas in comfort.

Then Pontalba was inspired with a more effective stratagem. He would not permit his daughter-in-law to see her mother, who was living in Paris, even during the pregnancy and birth of Micaela's first son.[9] That child died after sixteen months. Micaela was pregnant again even as she stood at the cemetery in Mont-l'Évêque at the grave of the baby her mother had never seen. The Pontalbas did not have to imprison Micaela to keep her away from her mother. As they demonstrated many times during the marriage, they had only to order the coachman not to leave the grounds of Mont-l'Évêque. The France of 1814 was vast; the roads were infested with brigands. A young girl could make no journey to Paris alone. With her daughter pregnant a second time, Micaela's mother gave in. She agreed to increase the dowry with an entire block of houses in New Orleans, that is, one side of the Place d'Armes. The Pontalbas now collected the rent on sixteen houses, in addition to the rental income they had already been awarded in the original dotal contract.

The Pontalbas were not admired for these machinations. Marrying the wealthiest heiress one could find, getting a fine settlement, insisting on the dowry payments—all that was common enough in both Europe and America. But confiscating the girl's inheritance before both her parents died was an attack on the established customs that made even Xavier's friends uneasy. Still, people were accustomed to tolerating intolerable spouses; both the law and society discouraged premature exasperation. Despite all the wrangling over money, Micaela traveled with her husband in the next years, had children with him, and made over more of her fortune to him. Moreover, the documents of their lives indicate that, although Micaela was terrified of her father-in-law, she genuinely loved her husband; he in turn loved her, though not as passionately as he loved her money.[10] Micaela never expressed any physical fear of Célestin. She apparently thought she could manage him well enough if she could get him away from his parents. But Célestin would not hear of setting up a household of their own. Only after Micaela conceded more of her property to him was she permitted to move into one of her mother's apartment buildings in Paris, a house that she managed and maintained herself.[11] Célestin remained with his parents in the cold, underfurnished rooms of the Château Mont-l'Évêque. In this manner, they formally remained husband and heiress for several years.

In 1825, however, Micaela lost her only protector when her mother died. In her will, Mme. Almonester tried in every legal way imaginable, and in the strongest language possible, to prevent Célestin and his family from seizing the fortune she was leaving to Micaela.[12] Within hours of her mother's death, Célestin shouted at Micaela that he would revoke the will, just as he had succeeded in revoking the hated marriage contract.[13] But the Pontalbas did not have to resort to clever legal schemes. One week after her mother's funeral, Micaela turned over all of her property in New Orleans to the Pontalbas—the remaining side of the Place d'Armes and hundreds of acres of land near Bayou Road—property that her husband was not entitled to, even under French law, and that certainly was outside of his authority in Louisiana. In return, Célestin "allowed" Micaela to collect the rent from the houses her mother had purchased in Paris.[14]

Why did Micaela commit this act of notarized masochism? Was she unsure of her rights? Was she still so much under her husband's sway that, after fourteen years of marriage, he could still manipulate her into doing whatever he wanted? No. Micaela forfeited rents of forty thousand dollars a year in return for the privilege of remaining in Paris away from his parents. French law did not permit divorce. A husband could separate from his wife simply by sending her away, so long as he continued to provide for her. But a wife was required to take on her husband's nationality and live with him wherever he chose. If she ran away or refused to follow him wherever he ordered her, she could be charged with desertion, a criminal offense, and he could seize all her income, whether dotal or inherited. A separation would have been available to Micaela only if Célestin had forced her to live with his concubine. The law did not allow the least relief from having to live with his father. Micaela brought Célestin to court several times to force him to provide her with a home of their own. The few times she was granted a hearing, she was denied the right to sue. She appealed the judgment, at great expense, and lost again.[15]

Appeased by the monthly banquet of revenues he received from New Orleans, Célestin, always following his father's directives, agreed to extend his and Micaela's estrangement for another two years. It was one of the happiest periods of the marriage. Peace was not to last, however, and Micaela eventually consulted a lawyer who advised her that the Pontalbas had no legal right to any of her property in New Orleans except the rents awarded to them in the original dotal contract. The lawyer counseled Micaela to go to Louisiana at once and reclaim her income. In 1830, therefore, Micaela wrote to her three sons, who were in a military boarding school where their grandfather had placed them, explaining her plans. Then, without getting her husband's permission to leave the country, which she was legally required to do, she set sail for New Orleans.[16]

In 1811, Micaela had left a French city where Americans were still regarded as a foreign element. When she returned in 1830, New Orleans was a U.S. metropolis full of new businesses and speculators in sugar and cotton. The courts still operated in both French and English, and in both languages a judge ruled that Micaela could take back all of her inherited property, especially the two sides of the Place d'Armes. At that time, Micaela tried to obtain a Louisiana divorce, although it would have had no legal force in France. But the Pontalbas had connections to the governor of Louisiana, and Micaela's petition never received a hearing. She believed, however, that she had to wait several months for the court proceedings to begin. For the first time in twenty years, she was free from her father-in-law's glowering supervision; Mont-l'Évêque was an ocean away. She decided to take a steamboat tour of the United States (the western boundary was then Missouri). Along the way, she wrote to her beloved aunt in New Orleans, Victoire de Lino de Chalmette. Micaela's letters to this "dear little aunt," as she called Victoire, had always been rambling, formless, and flushed with tenderness. But now they were full of wonder as she described a new country and a new sensation: relaxation.

Micaela was as unprepared as any European for the emptiness of the land. She complained of going endless miles between steamboat landing and stagecoach depot without seeing a dozen houses. An extraordinary effort was required, she noted, to travel to the scattered cities of the United States, and then, on finally reaching a population center, she found few people. "I arrived here on the 2nd," she wrote from Philadelphia, "and already I know the whole community."[17] Everywhere she went, people made a fuss over Almonester's daughter. The governor of Quebec showed her around the countryside. In Washington, President Andrew Jackson sent his carriage and the secretary of state to fetch her. It was, after all, on her aunt's plantation that he had won the Battle of New Orleans, devastating the plantation as well as the British.

And it was to her "dear little aunt" that Micaela described a certain Monsieur Guillemin, a man who was her companion for over a year. J. N. François Guillemin was a gentleman of fifty-four, a respected French consul in New Orleans, long widowed, when he became friendly with Micaela, aged thirty-five.[18] Either by chance or design, Guillemin and Micaela found themselves on the same tour of the East Coast, heading for Niagara Falls, although Guillemin's new consular post was in the opposite direction, in Havana. Wherever the steamboat stopped, the two went sightseeing together. The boat reached New York and was bringing them back to New Orleans when Micaela decided to go out of her way to visit Pensacola with Guillemin, "so as to know the country better."[19] Judging from the scant population of Florida in 1831, country was indeed all there was to know. Once back in New Orleans, where she and Guillemin were to part, she revised her plans again and accompanied him to his new assignment in Havana. She spent two months with him in Cuba.

We do not know what Guillemin looked like. Four years later, Micaela's lawyer protested to a French court that if the judges "could only see a portrait of the gentleman," they would understand that the idea of an improper relationship was absurd.[20] But by then, Guillemin was dead and Micaela, herself disfigured, could hurt no one by disparaging his attractions.

On board the vacation boat, Micaela and Guillemin spent their endless leisure time together chatting with fellow passengers, eating, or simply roosting on deck, according to the two letters in which she wrote of him in detail. "Monsieur Guilmin is taking as good care of me as anyone could ask," she assured her aunt, misspelling Guillemin's name, as she did everyone's. "Right now, he is writing on one side of the table and I on the other."[21] One can picture them in the comfortable old clothes that all French travelers wore, swatting each other's mosquitoes as they floated into the dusk.

Célestin did not have access to Micaela's letters. Mailed from points in the United States to her aunt in New Orleans, they never crossed the Atlantic. He did, however, have agents whom Micaela dealt with during her trip, and he was not ashamed to ask them for reports. From a few drops of information squeezed out of two informants, Célestin's lawyer was able to draw for a French tribunal the lurid outline of an affair, which, he said, exhibited every form of lasciviousness and shocked people "on three continents," from Canada to Cuba and also in France, where they, too, heard about it.[22] No doubt the lawyer could have created a hair-raising story if he had ever got his hands on one particular letter Micaela wrote to her aunt. For what the lawyer did not know or could not prove was unclearly written in Micaela's own scrawl, as she described her travels with Guillemin: "He stays with me at the inn, where we get on marvelously, and tells me that he will not go away to the consulate until I leave the country. . . . Since my arrival, my room is never empty. . . . Here are the details, dear little aunt, that I believe will give you pleasure, I tell them to you because I know you love me."[23]

A shipboard romance was necessarily a serious affair for a married Frenchwoman. If found guilty of adultery, she was subject to a mandatory prison term and other unpleasant penalties, regardless of the location of her crime or the ugliness of her partner.[24] But adultery is a difficult activity to document. Despite diligent efforts, the Pontalbas never succeeded in proving anything about Guillemin except that Micaela kept company with him for fifteen months. There was no hard evidence offered during the trial that Guillemin had even held her married hand, and there remains none today. Micaela's letter, to an objective reader, admits everything and nothing. Yet it is true and unarguable that she remained with Guillemin for over a year while her husband and children were across the ocean.

Micaela knew that Célestin would pounce on the chance to prosecute her for what was then called "a criminal liaison." Though she might have invited a male friend to accompany her in public, she was probably too guarded to bring a lover. Nor was it likely that she would effuse about shared lodgings and bedroom visitors to her good Catholic aunt, unless Guillemin were indeed nothing more than a platonic admirer. She did not behave like a woman with a guilty conscience. On the other hand, there is one strong indication that she was having a well-deserved and potent romance: when the time came for Guillemin to depart for his new consular post, Micaela left her relatives and servants in New Orleans "and followed his caravan to Cuba," as Célestin's lawyer energetically pointed out.[25] It is a fact that cannot be dismissed.

Guillemin was worthy of an intelligent woman's love. He was a refined and reflective man who deliberated earnestly over the burning issues of his day. Alexis de Tocqueville, who interviewed him in New Orleans, remarked that Guillemin's courteous manner "concealed an ego which prefers monologue to conversation."[26] Nevertheless, Tocqueville recognized that "Monsieur Guillemin is an able man and, I think, someone of means. . . . He has been living in New Orleans some fifteen to seventeen years." Guillemin remarked that the Creoles of Louisiana were no match for the Americans as entrepreneurs. "How much acrimony is there between Creoles and Americans?" Tocqueville asked.

"Each criticizes the other," Guillemin answered, "They do not see each other much. But at bottom, there is no real hostility, since there is enough prosperity to go around." While denigrating Louisiana politicians, Guillemin delighted Tocqueville by remarking that he had no use for democracy in America. Finally, he gave a long sermon to Tocqueville about the inhumane treatment blacks received in Louisiana.

This was the man—bright, kindly, and perhaps a bit didactic—who did not leave Micaela's side for some fifteen months, in New Orleans, in New York, and finally, at the beginning of 1832, in Havana. Whatever we wish to think about their relationship, it is clear that Micaela enjoyed Guillemin's company, even going as far out of the way as Cuba was in those days to be with him. No letters remain from Micaela's trip to Havana, and we do not know precisely what she did there. She probably stayed with Guillemin at the consulate rather than in the inns in the capital, which one writer described as "distinguished only for their filth."[27] Cubans had windows without panes and beds without mattresses, according to some reports, because in January, the heat was so intense that lying on a mattress was unbearable. But Guillemin's residence was well appointed, the best of all the diplomatic accommodations in Cuba. The idyll, if that is what it was, lasted until March 12, 1832, when Micaela, now thirty-six, returned to New Orleans, alone for the first time in many months, the sole passenger on a cargo vessel. Leaving Guillemin perhaps extinguished some fragile light in her: the captain of the cargo boat judged her age as "about forty."[28]

When she got back to New Orleans, Micaela discovered that Célestin had filed suit to reclaim her French Quarter properties—an action she had expected. But he had gone further. He obtained a judgment in France that found her guilty of desertion. The French courts ordered her back to Mont-l'Évêque. Until she had lived with him six months, Célestin was authorized "to seize and stop any income of his wife," regardless of its source.[29] As an abandoned husband, he was entitled to the rents Micaela had recovered from New Orleans, as well as the rents from her mother's property in Paris.

The Pontalbas knew that Micaela had traveled with Guillemin; judging from the cruelty they inflicted on her in the next years, they intended to prosecute her for adultery if they could wring a confession from her. Célestin had always been dominated by his father in any matter regarding Micaela, notwithstanding his resilient attraction to her. But now his pride had been injured, first by her leaving France without his permission and filing for divorce and then, more grievously, by subjecting him to public ridicule by going off with Guillemin. It was easy for him to be persuaded that she deserved the harshest treatment.

In June 1834, Micaela returned to Mont-l'Évêque. She knocked at the door of the château and was faced with her father-in-law, who read out the rules by which she would now live. She was to be isolated in one small room of the Little Château, the guesthouse a few yards behind the castle, since she would now be in the position of "a caller staying too long in the family circle."[30] No servant was to be allowed in her room. She would be permitted at the family table in the main château, but no one would speak to her, not even servants, and her own conversation would fall on deaf ears. Even visitors to Mont-l'Évêque were soon made to understand that their welcome would end if they acknowledged her presence.

Long after she had escaped this ignoble penance, the memory of evenings at Mont-l'Évêque haunted Micaela like a bizarre dream: "If I am in the salon, no one speaks to me. If visitors come, they do not greet me. All in the gathering sit whispering in each other's ears until I am compelled to withdraw to my room." Life at the château, she wrote to her cousins, was but "miserable existence."[31] As for Célestin, he talked to his wife when his father was not around—but his father was nearly always around. Even during the worst of times, Micaela reported to her lawyer that there were "tender moments" between her and her husband, and the possibility, she thought, of true reconciliation. But the elder Pontalba also noticed the stubborn affection between his son and his enemy and blocked it by making sure they were never alone.

Early on, Micaela's lawyer perceived that there was a strategy underlying the peculiar drama at Mont-l'Évêque. Micaela had been called back to France in the hope that she would not come, opening the way for Célestin to seize her property permanently. "If she were so indiscreet as to answer the summons," her lawyer said, "if she failed to understand, they would make her life intolerable. . . . They would drive her to rebellion, since her rebellion was necessary in order to confiscate her income."[32]

The Pontalbas allowed Micaela to go to Paris to make repairs on her mother's property though they, and not Micaela, were still collecting the rents from that property. But each time, they made it harder for her to return. She was not permitted to bring a carriage into Mont-l'Évêque, so that she had to leave her coachman at the gates, to find his own lodging, while she walked to the château. Her lawyer suggested that she challenge the rules, that she show up with all her carriage horses, for example, or sit down at the head of the table in the father-in-law's usual place. But Mont-l'Évêque was a large estate surrounded by wilderness, where every person within screaming distance was a dependent of old Pontalba. It was not the lawyer who had to face the snarling men behind the château wall. Micaela filed petition after petition to the courts, appeal after appeal, but every hearing went against her. She was, moreover, epileptic. As she became increasingly agitated, her seizures became more frequent and severe. Finally, her despairing lawyer advised her to sacrifice her rents in Paris, to let Célestin garnish them while she got out of Mont-l'Évêque.[33] She was still covertly receiving money from New Orleans. She could live thriftily on that income. By 1835, therefore, Micaela was again domiciled in Paris.

The Pontalbas put harsh restrictions on her contacts with her three children, restrictions against which each of the sons rebelled in turn. Célestin, the eldest, was eighteen when he ran away from his military school just before graduation and demanded to live with his mother. After settling with her in Paris, he began getting into minor scrapes until one day he assaulted a hapless stranger on the Champs-Élysées and found himself in court. His grandfather disowned him; his father refused to see him. Micaela, upset that her son was being dragged into her quarrel with the Pontalbas, made up her mind to meet privately with her husband to discuss their son and possibly to reconcile the marriage, if Célestin would agree to live in Paris. "I know my husband loves me," she had written during one of their most bitter periods. Perhaps she hungered for reassurance. Perhaps she was a nineteenth-century woman in love with love. But, judging from the events of the succeeding months, it seems more likely that she knew him. Thus, in October 1834, a few days before their twenty-third anniversary, she set off once more for Mont-l'Évêque to meet with Célestin.[34]

That meeting and its aftermath is a long chapter in her story, a complicated chapter that ended tragically with her father-in-law's murderous attack on her. Finding that she was still alive after the shooting, the old man—he was eighty—committed suicide, one of the more productive acts of his morose life. Let us skip over the fateful night at Mont-l'Évêque, skip over the surprising relationship that developed between Micaela and her husband after the shooting, as she endured months of pain and a slow, agonized recovery. That relationship took several sharp turns, but in the end, her mind confused by heartrending memories, Micaela went back to her apartment in Paris, the object of everyone's gossip. Célestin went back to court, filing suits against her in both Louisiana and France to continue dispossessing her, as if nothing had happened to alter his projects.

Micaela's lawyer thought one good thing might come out of the shooting. Micaela at last had obvious proof of her mistreatment by the Pontalbas. Perhaps she could now win what the French termed "a separation of body and belongings," which would allow her to live apart from Célestin without yielding him control of her assets. In May 1835, a trial was held before a Senlis tribunal of three judges, the same magistrates who for twenty years had been quashing Micaela's petitions against the Pontalbas. In his presentation, Micaela's lawyer reviewed the hateful marriage from the beginning up to old Pontalba's attack. Then Célestin's lawyer reviewed the marriage from his client's point of view. Each barrister spoke for many hours. The tribunal's terse judgment was that, despite the shooting, Micaela would be denied a separation. Célestin was authorized to continue confiscating her income.[35]

How was such an outrage possible? First, because although Micaela's desire to control her separate property was considered reasonable in Louisiana, it was not in France. Under French law, all property belonged to the family, not to its individual members, and the husband alone was charged with the duty of keeping it intact for the benefit of his heirs. More importantly, in both Louisiana and France, women were removed by law from public life, the assumption being that their husbands were their protectors. They were in the legal position that children occupy in U.S. courts today. A woman needed her husband's permission to take a job, to be a witness in a criminal trial, to acquire a passport, open a bank account, enroll her child in school, obtain credit, make a contract, or keep her earnings.[36] Micaela was at a grave disadvantage from the moment she entered the courtroom.

But that was not all. In his pleadings, Célestin's lawyer treated the court to a brilliant, supple, vicious portrait of Micaela; anyone listening might have thought that she, and not old Pontalba, had been the killer in the family. She was painted as a spendthrift who wildly squandered "the family's resources"—never mind that she always spent her own money, and wisely at that. French judges had little notion of a woman's "own" money. But the main issue that destroyed Micaela's chances for a separation, the one burning issue at the center of the trial, was Guillemin. Micaela was accused again and again of humiliating the Pontalba family by her "shameless" affair with Guillemin. She had "followed that worthy gentleman" all over the globe, misrepresenting him as a fatherly escort. The deceased Guillemin was a decidedly defenseless corespondent to these accusations. There were clever insinuations that Micaela had pressed her uninvited attentions on many others, too.[37] By the time the judges heard it all, they were probably convinced that the intractable woman deserved to be shot.

Célestin was naturally pleased with the results of the trial, so pleased that he had the oral pleadings published—not all the pleadings, only those of his own lawyer, and not the entire argument, only those parts that were most damaging to Micaela. He gave out the printed copies first to his friends, then to Micaela's friends, and then to the entire Chamber of Peers—five hundred copies in all, each in an aesthetic rose binder.[38] The brochure with its lies attracted as much attention as the trial itself and caused nearly everyone who knew Micaela to shun her. Micaela was too sick anyway for social life. She spent most of her time in bed, attended by doctors. Her chest was oozing; part of her hand had to be amputated; and she could not walk more than a few steps at a time before she was out of breath. "I am not surprised my husband tells people I am doing well and in fine fettle," she wrote to her aunt. "He would like people to believe the balls in my chest improved me."[39] Nevertheless, she was bitterly hurt when she saw old friends turn their backs on her, people who should have known better than to believe the calumnies in a nasty little brochure.

Célestin's spite was finally his undoing, however, for in exposing his wife to public contumely, he violated his legal duty to protect her. In 1836 Micaela acquired a new lawyer who again petitioned the Senlis court for a separation. He went through the record of the first trial line by line and showed the judges that everything they had heard the previous May had been lies. This time, the judges, probably as much from fatigue as from conviction, took Micaela's side. They granted her a legal separation—the right to be let alone at last. To her cousin, Micaela described her joy as "indescribable."[40]

Célestin did not give up. He contested Micaela's control of the Place d'Armes property for several more years, until the Louisiana Supreme Court ruled against him definitively in 1839. That finally ended the dowry issue that had destroyed the family and shattered the happiness of the children. The year that Micaela and Célestin became grandparents, four lawsuits between them were settled; there was peace at last.[41]

❀ ❀ ❀

Micaela staggered away from the marriage with nothing she had not brought to it, except the balls in her chest. Still, she had a lot of money. The Senlis court that granted her a division of property granted her a fortune—her fortune—to manage for the first time. She knew exactly what she wanted to do with it: build. Her mother had been a builder, sponsor of a palatial townhouse in New Orleans. Her father had directed nearly every public construction undertaken in New Orleans in his lifetime. Real estate was in Micaela's blood.

She was in her forties by this time and had spent years thinking about her building plans. When she finally broke ground for the Hôtel Pontalba in Paris, she was like one of those late-talking children whose first words are compound sentences. Her first attempt at construction was an impressive four-level mansion that spread over three addresses on rue St.-Honoré, the faubourg where the new Napoleonic aristocrats like her were making common cause with France's newly rich industrialists. Tourist guidebooks even as late as the 1860s were wont to describe the magnificent Hôtel Pontalba as the largest private residence in Paris, second only to the Élysée Palace a block away.[42] That was probably never true, for one does not have to look far in Paris to find houses dating from the 1840s and 1850s that seem larger by far than Micaela's. But the boast shows that the Hôtel Pontalba was considered an important building even when the capital sparkled with big, new construction.

Micaela wanted the house as much as she ever wanted anything tangible. She modeled it after a townhouse on rue de Lille, the Hôtel d'Havré. She bought the old mansion, dismembered it, and prepared to use the accouterments—elaborate doors, intricately carved and decorated panels, wainscoting, shutters, mantelpieces, balustrades, even an entire ceiling—in her new dream house.[43] Then she hired a promising architect, L. T. J. Visconti, to draw all the plans and supervise construction of the house she could already see in her mind.

Visconti was a few years older than Micaela, the son of the wealthy and eminent curator of the Louvre. He is remembered today mainly as the architect of the Invalides and the initial architect of the New Louvre. But in 1838, when Micaela first talked to him, Visconti was known mainly for being his father's son and a specialist in designing fountains. The Hôtel Pontalba was his first large private commission. His career was still ahead of him, whereas the tragedies of her life were but recently behind her. He was overworked, arrogant, careless, and brilliant. She was intense, suspicious, bursting with ideas and demands—a wounded creature with an obsession.

Micaela's problems began when the workers used a soft stone of inferior quality for the foundation. She caught the mistake. The foundation had to come up and the project begun again. Micaela had expressly asked that Visconti use the doors, ceilings, and windows from the Havré house, all of which she had reverently entrusted to him. However, after the walls and openings were framed, she realized that the first floor elevation was too low to accommodate the accessories. Visconti's remedy was to raise the floor, but without altering the exterior elevation.[44] That meant that the ground floor was no longer at ground level; anyone inside who stepped out through the floor-to-ceiling windows fell out of the house.

The second floor caused even more problems, as evidenced by Micaela's furious scrawling over the plans. It was now June 1840, and tensions were rising along with the window frames, which again did not fit the Havré glass. Micaela's expenses enlarged with her problems. She had wanted a door in the middle of her bedroom, providing a view of the garden below. Instead, the contractors put the bedroom door in a sidewall, providing a clear view of the alley next door. When she directed the workers to close up that opening and cut a new one according to the plans, they sawed through an enormous support beam; the house had to be shored up from top to bottom. Visconti placed three amazing fireplaces in the sloping walls of the attic, where lighting a hearth would have meant setting the roof on fire, but he put no fireplaces at all in the frigid basement rooms. Micaela herself discovered most of the problems, halted the work, and figured out many of the solutions.[45] After Micaela and Visconti cracked heads, Micaela hired several contractors to finish the construction. She wound up in lawsuits with all of them, for by this time, she was not in the least shy of litigation. Her main suit with Visconti, which promised to be a landmark case, was eventually settled out of court.[46]

Despite all the trouble the Hôtel Pontalba caused her, it is no wonder that Micaela loved it. The interior of the house is a flowing brightness stippled with gardens that seem to spill in through the great panels of glass. We must give Visconti his due: nothing that was later done to the mansion, not the decorations imported from the Samuel Bérnard house in subsequent years, nor the elimination of columns on the facade, nor the addition of wings to each side, changed Visconti's basic plan of a building that is cloistered from the busy street at the same time that its main rooms look out on flowers, trees, and seclusion.[47]

Micaela did not build the house to impress her acquaintances or elicit the envy of people who had lately snubbed her. In the France of 1840, society people knew she had money, with or without a mansion, just as they knew who among them had made a fortune in stocks and how recently, who lived off an inheritance, and whether the inheritance represented old or new wealth. The members of her set were interconnected by marriage, and they knew the same things about their relatives that we know about ours. Besides, for most of Micaela's lifetime, wealth was not the crucial issue in determining whom to spurn, since the basis of class divisions was not money but family. Money enabled people of humble origin to marry into good families; but it was their new family affiliations, not money alone, that gained them acceptance in the roosts of the faubourgs.

Chances are that Micaela commissioned all her houses because she loved building, just as she would have ordered paintings if she had loved art. One has only to look around either France or Louisiana to realize that nineteenth-century people considered extravagant building to be an estimable and patriotic way to spend money. Architecture, even private townhouses or plantation mansions, needed no more justification than music or poetry. In fact, it pained Micaela to spend money on anything except houses. She rarely wore jewelry. Her clothes were a mess of housecoats, worn-out day dresses, and a single pair of sensible shoes that stayed on her feet through her journey to the next life. She loved music but cared nothing for literature or philosophy. She may never have immersed herself completely in either a book or a bath. But she spared no expense in making each of her buildings extraordinary.[48]

She lived at 41 rue St.-Honoré for much of the rest of her life, shifting her assets, selling off some parcels of her New Orleans land and speculating with others. Her life was mundane, as one's own existence always is. She rose early, worked twelve hours a day, and took time off only to be sick. By 1848, her business affairs were in order and she was eager to launch a massive new building project in New Orleans. While Paris shivered with revolution, Micaela and her sons Alfred and Gaston fled to the provincial safety of Louisiana.

❀ ❀ ❀

New Orleans in 1849 was among the five largest cities in the United States. Nevertheless, it was the capital of mildew and malaria, with a decaying French Quarter at the center of town. Micaela's plan was not merely for a house but for two magnificent blocks of houses that would surround and revitalize the dilapidated Place d'Armes. St Louis Cathedral, the Presbytere, and the Cabildo at the center of the square were also to be renovated before the project was completed. The fresh, new plaza, renamed Jackson Square, was even furnished with a statue of Andrew Jackson on his horse, partly paid for by Micaela.

When completed, the Pontalba row houses were the biggest residential buildings most people in New Orleans had ever seen. With their mixture of styles—

Greek revival, French, Spanish, and Creole—they did not look like the rest of New Orleans architecture. They appeared to have been transported from somewhere else. And in fact, they were mail-order buildings, monuments to the new notion that things could be ordered from one place and assembled in another. With their iron lace galleries and thirty-two identical houses, the Pontalbas reflected the then fashionable preference for exact duplication, a vogue made possible by manufacturing. Indeed, the exquisite rhythm of the buildings, the predictable repetition of certain forms, has protected them from later architectural vagaries.

Carriage drivers in New Orleans like to tell tourists that the Pontalbas were the first apartment buildings in the United States. Of course, this is nonsense. The houses were not redesigned as apartments until their renovation in the 1930s. They were row houses, that is, separate residences of three stories each, connected by a common facade. On the outside, the twin blocks have the structure of cleverly decorated Greek revival buildings. Each pediment with its pointed arch is separated by a recessed wing—the basic plan of a Greek temple. But instead of having the plain expanse and thick columns of a typical Greek revival design, the Pontalbas are swathed in iron lace.

New Orleans builders had long used decorative iron on balconies, but it was usually wrought iron and relatively simple. The Pontalba Buildings display intricately curved cast iron, and on a massive scale. The black iron lace covering the bright red brick of the sweeping buildings remains dazzling even today, when the square is surrounded by other tall structures and when elaborate cast ironwork is commonplace in the neighborhood. The iron decorations made the buildings light and pretty, gay rather than oppressive. Because of their iron webs on the facades, the buildings are as open and yet private as the faces of people protecting an interior life.

Inside, the Pontalbas were much like the raised Creole cottages seen throughout Louisiana. Each front door was for a ground floor shop to be rented out independently. The entrance to the houses was through a passageway at the rear. The salon, dining room, and reception rooms of each house were in the second story. The third story was for bedrooms or private sitting rooms. Slave quarters or storage space was in the finished attic.

No one knows who designed the Pontalba Buildings. Micaela had the plans with her when she arrived from France via New York. She brought these plans to a contractor, Samuel Stewart, who, in his labored but elegant Irish phrasing, worked out a detailed contract with her.[49] He was to supply the working drawings based on the plans she had shown him. As the work began, Micaela inspected all the drawings and the work, bravely choosing the accessories for all the houses from simple black and white drawings in pattern books. However, the architectural plans Micaela showed Stewart did not take into account the conditions of the local ground. Land in New Orleans is highest at the levee and descends several feet as one goes away from the river. Therefore, the Pontalbas, which stretched out for a block and were perpendicular to the levee, sat on higher ground at one end than at the other. That little oversight caused Stewart plenty of tribulation. Micaela exasperated the poor Irishman even more by asking for many changes. In fairness, her alterations were of the sort every owner makes to a building as he sees it going up. But she did not endear herself to Stewart by frequently remarking that she was a pretty good architect herself and that he could learn a thing or two from her.[50]

Micaela had no university degree; neither did Stewart, and neither did most architects of the time. But she was a lay genius in building. She scrambled up the scaffolding high above the square to solve the problem of fitting the roof. She, not the contractor or any architect, decided that the houses would have slender, graceful columns instead of the usual fat pillars. She gave the houses their modern interior shutters that disappear into the wall when opened, and she chose the mantelpieces, fireplaces, chandeliers, and locks. She decided that the floor joists ought to be reinforced with cross bridging. She knew enough about building to be a significant nuisance to Stewart and to supervise him in every detail, even though Stewart was himself something of a wizard in construction.

Most impressive, she authored the magical AP monogram that was worked out by her son Gaston after many trial drawings.[51] The AP that echoes through the long railings is a masterpiece of design in buildings full of brilliant details. The letters are perfectly clear and perfectly unobtrusive; they give a focal point to the patterns without detracting in the least from the diffused loveliness of the iron tracery. The monograms vanish into the delicate weaving of the galleries as soon as one stops thinking about them, letting the balconies again become a flowing panorama. In the monogram, Almonester and Pontalba are united in iron as they never were in life.

The result of Micaela and Stewart's testy collaboration was an architectural complex of imperishable grace. In the dancing galleries and red expanse of the Pontalba Buildings, Micaela captured what eluded her in life: the predictable, the lyrical, the lighthearted.

She timed the opening of the buildings so that the celebrated soprano Jenny Lind could live in them during the singer's month-long tour of New Orleans. Opera stars in midcentury drew as much attention as rock stars do today, especially in New Orleans, which was then the center of opera in the United States. Thousands of people gathered at the dock to see Jenny Lind's arrival by steamboat and to converge on her carriage as it tried to travel the few hundred yards to her quarters in the Pontalbas.[52] By the time Jenny Lind had completed her thirty sold-out performances, she had made the Pontalbas the most publicized buildings in town. Micaela, who was sentimental only about money, auctioned off everything the singer had used in the house, including her chamber pot.

Micaela left New Orleans in March 1851, and never saw the Pontalba Buildings again. She wanted to get out of the city before the yellow fever season. There were business affairs to take care of in France, grandchildren she had not seen, and faces waiting to greet her. Among them, astonishingly, was her husband, Célestin.[53]

❀ ❀ ❀

He was waiting for her as soon as she landed, a lost soul unable to cope with their eldest son and desperate for her help in saving what remained of his property. Fifteen years after her hard-won separation, Célestin took steps no court had ever been able to coerce from him. He left Mont-l'Évêque, moved permanently to Paris, gave her complete power of attorney over his assets, and offered himself to her, together with his debts and depressions. Micaela, who had fought with her life for the right to manage her own money, was soon managing all of his. Within a year, Célestin had a physical and mental breakdown and was "losing more of his mind by the minute," according to Micaela.[54] She was afraid to leave him alone. She cared for him for twenty-three difficult years, until her own death, a sacrifice that at least saved her children's inheritance from being distributed to creditors.

She remained an early riser, a hard worker, and a poor breather for the rest of her life. She was penny-pinching about everything except her houses, especially her mansion in Paris, where every wall and ceiling shimmered with décor.[55] Micaela lived out her last, vigorous, willful years in her beautiful hotel. She did not subscribe to any newspaper, owned no books except her account books, used no slippers, wore no underwear, and spoke her mind about everything. Judging from her will, she learned to spell rather well before she died. She assigned to her sons her property in New Orleans, her apartment houses in France, and the estate of Mont-l'Évêque. She directed that the Hôtel Pontalba was to be sold at her death; it eventually was purchased by the United States and became the residence of the U.S. ambassador to France.[56]

Micaela died in her bed on rue St.-Honoré in 1874, at the age of 79. Her husband, Célestin, was still formally alive, though he could not attend her funeral. His sons had to procure a "certificate of life" to verify that, although pallid as a fresco and completely demented, he was indeed a sentient being. Having outlived most of life's inclemencies, he nearly outlived all his caretakers. He remained in Paris in a house Micaela had rented for him, supervised by servants until his death in 1878 at the age of 87.[57]

Once the Guillemin scandal had passed, Micaela's name was never again involved in any rumor of romance. Had she really had an affair with him in those languid weeks while their steamboat breathed its way up and down North America? If Guillemin was only a friend, Micaela paid as stinging a price for his companionship as if he had been a lover. She might as well have shocked people "on three continents," for she was punished at home and publicly scorned as if her "lasciviousness" had been the true source of all her marital conflict. The true sources of the bitterness were, first, the mercenary actions of the Pontalbas, father and son, in trying to deprive her of her property and, second, the domestic laws and traditions in France that made it easy for them to make her life unbearable. Whether the interlude with Guillemin had been an affair or not made little difference in the end.

After all the fury and pain, Micaela and Célestin came back to each other, not reconciled exactly, but like veterans of a war that both sides lost. They remained legally separated during their last decades when they were most together, their relationship demonstrating that marriage is sometimes an awkward container for love. The baroness in the end fulfilled all of her ambitions, with Pontalbas' properties as well as her own. Her lovely buildings stand as the legacies of a woman who, through persistence and enormous suffering, survived her father-in-law's vicious calculations and the blind injustice of the law.

NOTES

1. For a complete biography, see Christina Vella, *Intimate Enemies: The Two Worlds of the Baroness de Pontalba* (Baton Rouge: Louisiana State University Press, 1997).

2. Amos Stoddard, *Sketches, Historical and Descriptive, of Louisiana* (Philadelphia: Matthes Carey, 1812), 154; C. C. Robin, *Voyage to Louisiana: 1803–1805*, abridg. and trans. Stuart O. Landry Jr. (New Orleans: Pelican, 1966); Minter Wood, "Life in New Orleans in the Spanish Period," *Louisiana Historical Quarterly* 22 (July 1939): 642–737; "Auto de Buen Gobierno de Don Manuel Gayoso de Lemos, 1798," in Special Collections, Howard-Tilton Memorial Library, Tulane University; Laura Porteous, trans., "Sanitary Conditions in New Orleans Under the Spanish Regime, 1799–1800," *Louisiana Historical Quarterly* 15 (October 1932): 612.

3. Letters of Baron Joseph X. Pontalba to his wife, manuscript letter diary in Pontalba Family Papers, WPA translation, Louisiana Historical Center, New Orleans (hereinafter cited as LSMHC).

4. *Le Moniteur de la Louisiane*, October 26, 1811. Almonester's remains were later removed to the cemetery behind St. Louis Cathedral.

5. "Inventaire après le décès de Mme. la baronne de Pontalba," April 30, 1874, III, coté cinquième,

and VI, annexes, Records of A. L. Massion, Étude XXXIV/1333, Archives Nationales, Paris; Eugène Miller, *Senlis et ses environs* (Senlis: n.p., 1896), 103ff., 150–53.

6. *Pontalba v. Pontalba*, Eastern District, docket no. 2856, April 1839, document M, p. 81, Louisiana Supreme Court Records, Department of Archives and Manuscripts, Earl K. Long Library, University of New Orleans (hereinafter cited as SCR); *Gazette des Tribuneaux*, October 10–14, 1835.

7. H. D. Lewis, "The Legal Status of Women in the Nineteenth Century in France," *Journal of European Studies* 10 (June 1980): 181; *Pontalba v. Pontalba*, docket no. 2856, April 1839, "Petition of Plaintiff," 6, and "Judgment" by the lower court magistrate, SCR; *Code civil*, articles 384, 374, 375, and especially articles 1549 ("Le mari seul a l'administration des biens dotaux pendant le marriage") and 1428 ("Le mari a l'administration de tous les biens personnels de la femme. . . . Il ne peut aliener les immeubles de sa femme sans son consentement"). A wife could, however, handle her own inheritance even in France, if it came to her through a will stipulating that the money or property was solely for her use—a will such as Micaela's mother eventually made.

8. Edouard de Pontalba to J. W. Cruzat, October 20, 1902, April 10, 1908, "Correspondance de baron Edouard de Pontalba, 1902–1914," in Cruzat Family Papers, Special Collections, Howard-Tilton Memorial Library, Tulane University; "Vente," March 5–6, 1816; Études XIV/624, 642, 643, "Bail," August 11–12, 1820, Records of L. H. Breton, Étude XIV/622, Archives Nationales, Paris.

9. "Registre de l'état civile de Mont-l'Évêque 1813 ê 1822," ms. in mayor's office, Mont-l'Évêque, France; "Acception de donation," December 9, 1817, série M. C., RE, Records of L. H. Breton, Étude XIV/632, Archives Nationales, Paris.

10. Letters of Micaela, Alfred, and Gaston de Pontalba, Special Collections, Howard-Tilton Memorial Library, Tulane University.

11. Records of L. H. Breton, Étude XIV/644, 64723, August 1820, Records of A. J. Fourchy, Étude LVIII/692, 15; April 1822, Records of L. H. Breton, Étude XIV/644, 647, Archives Nationales, Paris.

12. *Pontalba v. Pontalba*, docket no. 2856, document O, p. 91, SCR.

13. "Court Action between the Baron and Baroness de Pontalba," Tribunal of Senlis, May 11, 1835, WPA trans., LSMHC.

14. *Pontalba v. Pontalba*, docket no. 2856, document P, p. 97, SCR.

15. Abrogated in 1816 during the post-Napoleonic reaction, divorce was not reinstated in France until 1885. The grounds for divorce under Napoleonic law became, after 1816, the grounds for legal separation (the wife's adultery or, more rarely, extreme cruelty on either side). A *cour de cassation* on August 9, 1826, stated: "Le mari dont la femme refuse d'habiter avec lui peu l'y contraindre manu militaire" (H. D. Lewis, "Legal Status of Women," 180–81, 187). See also Claire Goldberg Moses, *French Feminism in the Nineteenth Century* (Albany: State University of New York Press, 1984). For a discussion of how the courts interpreted these laws, see the "Affaire Daloz," in *Plaidoyers de Philippe Dupin: Discours et pieces divers*, ed. Philippe-Simon Dupin and Eugene Dupin (Paris: Cotillon, 1868), 1:249–400.

16. "Passenger Lists of Vessels Arriving at New Orleans, 1820–1902," March 8–December 28, 1830, list. nos. 44–250, Louisiana Collection, New Orleans Public Library; Records of L. T. Caire, March 10, 1828, Notarial Archives Research Center, New Orleans (hereinafter cited as NARC); *Pontalba v. Pontalba*, docket no. 2129, February 2, 1831, SCR.

17. Micael de Pontalba to Victoire de Lino de Chalmet, New York, May 1831, and Saratoga, July 25, 1831, and Micael de Pontalba to Azélie Chalmet, Philadelphia, 1831, Letters of Micaela, Alfred, and Gaston de Pontalba, Howard-Tilton Memorial Library, Tulane University. For Micaela's efforts to petition for divorce in Louisiana, see Sebastiani to Pontalba, Paris, June 23, 1831, quoted in *Gazette des Tribuneaux*, October 14, 1835.

18. Guillemin's wife, Caroline Pieray, died in 1817 (burial records, Historic New Orleans Collection).

19. Micael de Pontalba to Victoire de Lino de Chalmet, Saratoga, May 1831, Letters of Micaela, Alfred, and Gaston de Pontalba, Howard-Tilton Memorial Library, Tulane University. There was a lively debate about Guillemin's age during the separation trial between the Pontalbas in 1836 (*Plaidoyers de Philippe Dupin*, 1:14); "Court Action between the Baron and Baroness de Pontalba," 103–4, Tribunal of Senlis, May 11, 1835, WPA trans., LSMHC.

20. *Gazette des Tribuneaux*, October 14–15, 1835.

21. Micael de Pontalba to Victoire de Lino de Chalmet, Saratoga, May 1831, Letters of Micaela, Alfred, and Gaston de Pontalba, Howard-Tilton Memorial Library, Tulane University. Her misspelling should not be taken as an indication of her closeness, or lack of it, to Guillemin. She also misspelled the name of the street where she lived in Paris, du Houssaie.

22. *Gazette des Tribuneaux*, October 14–15, 1835.

23. Micael de Pontalba to Victoire de Lino de Chalmet, Saratoga, July 25, 1831, Letters of Micaela, Alfred, and Gaston de Pontalba, Howard-Tilton Memorial Library, Tulane University.

24. "La femme adultère sera condamnée par le même jugement, et sur la requisition de ministère public, à la reclusion dans une maison de correction, pour en temps determiné qui ne pourra être moindre de trois mois, ni exéder deux années" (quoted by H. D. Lewis, "Legal Status of Women," 81).

25. "Court Action between the Baron and Baroness de Pontalba," 105ff, Tribunal of Senlis, May 11, 1835, WPA trans., LSMHC.

26. Alexis de Tocqueville, *Journey to America*, trans. George Lawrence (New Haven: Yale University Press, 1959), 103ff. and 380ff. The synopsis of Guillemin's interview is also taken from Tocqueville's untranslated notes that appear at the end of the book.

27. Eugène Ney, "Visite rècente à l'île de Cuba," *Revue des Deux Mondes* 12 (January 1831): 424–50.

28. She sailed on March 12, 1832 (report of Captain Torres of the *Brez Locorro*, U.S. Bureau of Customs, "Supp. Index to Passenger Lists of Vessels Arriving at Atlantic and Gulf Coast Ports, 1820–1874," Louisiana Collection, New Orleans Public Library).

29. *Pontalba v. Pontalba*, docket no. 2856, documents M, N, O, and P, SCR. He could impound her income at its source, but in France only. Célestin could not require that U.S. authorities enforce French law regarding her property. Once her New Orleans rents arrived in France, however, he could legally take them away from her. See also articles 105 and 106, *Code of Practice in Civil Cases for the State of Louisiana* (New Orleans: n.p., 1824), 34.

30. Micael de Pontalba to Azélie Chalmet, August 27, 1834, November 26, 1833, Letters of Micaela, Alfred, and Gaston de Pontalba, Howard-Tilton Memorial Library, Tulane University.

31. Ibid.

32. *Gazette des Tribuneaux*, 10, October 12, 1835.

33. Ibid.

34. Monsieur Dupoux [writing for Micaela] to Victoire de Lino de Chalmet, Paris, November 12, 1834, Letters of Micaela Alfred, and Gaston de Pontalba, Special Collections, Howard-Tilton Memorial Library, Tulane University; *Gazette des Tribuneaux*, October 10, 12, 1835; for reaction in France to the shooting, see Lettres d'Edgard, comte Ney à sa mere, dossier 13, to de Napoléon, prince de la Moskowa, dossier 4 (6), to de la ducesse d'Elchingen, November 9, 1834, and to d'Aloys, duc d'Elchingen, dossier 10, Archives du Maréchal Ney, Archives Nationales, Paris.

35. The entire trial is reported in *Gazette des Tribuneaux*, October 10–14, 1835.

36. H. D. Lewis, "Legal Status of Women," 81–84.

37. "Court Action between the Baron and Baroness de Pontalba," Tribunal of Senlis, May 11, 1835, WPA trans., LSMHC, is the best source for the pleadings of Célestin's attorney.

38. *Plaidoyers de Philippe Dupin*, 2:4–41.

39. Micael de Pontalba to Azélie Chalmet, April 6, 1836, and Micaela to her cousins, Paris, July 8, 1835, Letters of Micaela, Alfred, and Gaston de Pontalba, Special Collections, Howard-Tilton Memorial Library, Tulane University. Doctors' reports quoted in *Gazette des Tribuneaux*, October 14, 1835, and *Plaidoyers de Philippe Dupin*, 2:30.

40. Micael de Pontalba to Azélie Chalmet, April 6, 1836, Letters of Micaela, Alfred, and Gaston de Pontalba, Special Collections, Howard-Tilton Memorial Library, Tulane University.

41. "Transaction entre M. le baron et Mme. la baronne de Pontalba," June 16, 1836, Records of Ch. A. F. Berçeon, Étude LVIII/747, Archives Nationales, Paris.

42. Charles Simond, *Paris pendant l'année 1859* (Paris, n.p., 1900), 2:86.

43. "Vente par le mandatoire de M. le duc d'Havré à Mme. de Pontalba," December 17, 1838, Records of Ch. St.-Ange Berçeon, Étude II/1000, Archives Nationales, Paris.

44. "Note adressèe á Mssrs. les experts, par Made. la baronne de Pontalba," n.p., n.d., manuscript in Special Collections, Howard-Tilton Memorial Library, Tulane University; Visconti Papers, private collection of the late comte Hervé du Périer de Larson of Paris.

45. Visconti Papers, private collection of the late comte Hervé du Périer de Larson of Paris.

46. See the case involving Micaela de Pontalba, Leroy, Texier, and Benois, October 28, 1841 (D2U332027), Tribunal de Commerce, Archives de Paris, Annexe à Villemoison, and *Baronne de Pontalba c. Vivenel*, May 18, 1843, Tribunal de Commerce, Archives de Paris, Annexe à Villemoison, and *Tencè c. de Pontalba et Vivenel*, April 23, 1842, Tribunal Civil de la Seine, December 26, 1842, Cour d'Appel, November 20, 1843, Cour d'Appel, and registre 131 (1843), 2e chambre, Archives de la Seine (D1U9, 131), Archives de Paris.

47. Visconti Papers, private collection of the late comte Hervé du Périer de Larson.

48. "Inventaire après le décès de Madame la baronne de Pontalba, April 30, 1874," Records of Augustin-Louis Massion, Étude XXXIV/1333, Archives Nationales, Paris.

49. For Micaela's plans for the square, see New Orleans First Municipality Council minutes, October 12, 1839, December 16, 1844, September 7, 1846, January 15, 1852, and June 7, 1853, Louisiana Collection, New Orleans Public Library; "Building Contract, Samuel Stewart and Agents of Mrs. M. L. A. de Pontalba," January 6, 1852, Records of A. Ducatel, NARC. The contract was obviously filed with the notary some time after it was made.

50. *Stewart v. Pontalba*, testimony of Allen Hill, Joseph Jewell, H. Lathrop, and Richard Rice, Rare Manuscripts Department, New Orleans Public Library.

51. W. A. Tallen to Samuel Stewart, New Orleans, September 25, 1849, in *Stewart v. Pontalba*, testimony of Allen Hill, Joseph Jewell, H. Lathrop, and Richard Rice, Rare Manuscripts Department, New Orleans Public Library; Notebooks of Gaston de Pontalba, Graphics Collection, LSMHC.

52. *New Orleans Weekly Delta*, September 16, 1850; *New Orleans Commercial Bulletin*, February 2, 1851; *New Orleans Bee*, February 2, 1851; *New Orleans Daily Delta*, February 12, 16, 1851; C. C. Rosenberg, *Jenny Lind's Tour of America and Cuba* (New York: Stringer and Townsend, 1851).

53. Micael de Pontalba to Azélie Chalmet, Paris, August 16, 1852, Letters of Micaela, Alfred, and Gaston de Pontalba, Howard-Tilton Memorial Library, Tulane University.

54. Ibid.; "Procuration," April 30, 1852, March 5, 1854, Records of Ch. St.-Ange Berçeon, Archives Nationales, Paris.

55. "Inventaire après le décès de Madame la baronne de Pontalba," Records of Massion, Archives Nationales, Paris.

56. The mansion was purchased by Edmond de Rothschild and remained in the Rothschild family until the Second World War and the German occupation. After the liberation, the United States government purchased it from the Rothschilds ("Consentement à execution du testament de Mme. la baronne de Pontalba" [contains will], August 26, 1874, Records of Massion, Étude XXXIV/1337; "Succession of M. L. A. Pontalba," August 7, 1874, 2nd District Court, docket no. 37.182, Louisiana Collection, New Orleans Public Library).

57. "Certificat de vie," May 31, 1875, Records of C. A. Moquard, Étude LXVIII/17, numéro 1279, Archives Nationales, Paris; death certificate of J. X. C. de Pontalba in Pontalba Family Papers, LSMHC.

Marie Laveau

(1801–1881)

A New Orleans Voudou Priestess

CAROLYN MORROW LONG

❀ ❀ ❀

Marie Laveau, known as the "Voudou Queen of New Orleans," dominates the public imagination as a near mythical figure.[1] She has been the subject of newspaper articles, popular histories, three novels, a film, an opera, and a play. A Web search for "Marie Laveau" produces over ten thousand hits. Tour guides offer their spiels at the site of her home on St. Ann Street and her tomb in St. Louis Cemetery no. 1. Laveau has also drawn the attention of serious scholars in the fields of religious studies, anthropology, and history.[2]

With each generation, the Laveau legend has evolved and transmuted. Influenced by the social and political milieu of the time, perceptions of Marie Laveau have cycled from benevolent provider to she-devil to mother goddess. Most, but not all, of the obituaries published at the time of Laveau's death depicted her as a saintly woman and a devout Catholic who nursed the sick, provided for the poor, and ministered to prisoners. During the late nineteenth and most of the twentieth century, journalists and popular historians characterized her as a fraud, the "procuress" for a prostitution ring, and an evil sorceress. In recent years the New Orleans Voudou community has accorded her the status of a *lwa*, or Voudou deity.[3] Behind this continually evolving narrative is a real—and considerably less flamboyant—individual whose family history affords a view into the personal and spiritual lives of women of African descent.

In Louisiana, each generation of Marie Laveau's female relatives became more European and less African in phenotype. Her grandmother and mother typify the ways in which women of African descent escaped slavery through self-purchase and voluntary manumission. They also, like many women of African descent, gave birth to children of mixed race.

Marie Laveau's kinswomen illustrate, too, the ways New Orleans Afro-Creoles inhabited the permeable boundary between official Catholicism and traditional West African religions, moving easily between the two as the occasion required. Laveau's public embrace of her African heritage distinguished her from her female relatives and most other women of her race and class. Through her combination of spiritual power, clairvoyance, healing abilities, beauty, charisma, showmanship, intimidation, and shrewd business sense, she assumed leadership of a multiracial religious community as New Orleans's most celebrated Voudou priestess.

❀ ❀ ❀

Marie Laveau's great-grandmother, called Marguerite, was probably born in West Africa around 1736 and sold into slavery as a child, arriving in New Orleans on the last French slave-trading ship in 1743. She is likely to have been a Wolof from present-day Senegal, a people noted for their trading and marketing skills and considered to be extraordinarily intelligent and handsome. Wolof women were in great demand as domestic servants.[4] Twenty-year-old Marguerite and her daughter Catherine, age two, were listed in the 1756 property inventory of the white Creole Henry Roche *dit* (known as) Belaire, a master shoemaker and a man of some wealth. Catherine later identified her father as a black man called Jean Belaire.[5]

At some point Marie Laveau's enslaved grandmother Catherine and perhaps her great-grandmother Marguerite became at least nominally Catholic. The Ursuline nuns, an order dedicated to advancing Catholicism through the catechesis of women, directed pious matrons not only to instruct their own families but also to proselytize their slaves and encourage baptism, confirmation, and godparenting.[6]

Catherine and Marguerite may have been baptized at St. Louis Cathedral through the efforts of Roche-Belaire's neighbor, Madame Piquery, or the enslaved women of her household. The register for slaves and free people of color records the 1754 baptism of an enslaved infant named Catherine, natural daughter of Marguerite, and the 1756 baptism of a group of adult slaves, including a negress named Marguerite. In both cases the baptisands and their godparents were designated as slaves of Madame Piquery. One can conjecture that Henry Roche-Belaire, a widower occupied with his own business, allowed Madame Piquery to take Catherine and Marguerite to the cathedral along with her own slaves. The priest would not have made the distinction in ownership when recording the baptism in the sacramental register.[7]

ARTIST'S CONCEPTION OF MARIE LAVEAU

By Carolyn Long, 2005. Courtesy of Carolyn Long.

Marie Laveau's grandmother Catherine spent the first thirty years of her life in the Roche-Belaire household. During that time she gave birth to two mulatto children who may have been fathered by Henry Roche. New Orleans's population of biracial *gens de couleur libres*—free people of color—was the result of such sexual encounters between white masters and enslaved women. Some were clearly cases of rape or coercion, and some were long-lasting consensual relationships. Many men freed their enslaved concubines and acknowledged and provided for the future security of their offspring, but no such solicitude was bestowed on Catherine. Rather than liberating her, Henry Roche *dit* Belaire sold Catherine and her son Joseph while retaining ownership of her daughter Marguerite.[8]

After enduring two more owners and giving birth to two more mulatto children, in 1784 Catherine became the property of the free woman of color Françoise Pomet.[9] Slave ownership by free people of African descent was not unusual in late eighteenth- and early nineteenth-century New Orleans. Some purchased their relatives and loved ones in order to free them, but others bought and sold slaves for the same reasons as whites.[10] Catherine was not a kinswoman or friend of Françoise Pomet. Pomet was a successful entrepreneur who owned several other female slaves. She may have been engaged in the common practice of deploying her bondswomen to sell merchandise and foodstuffs on the street or in the city's markets, extracting a portion of their earnings and allowing the slaves to keep the balance.[11]

When the Louisiana colony passed from French to Spanish rule in 1769, laws regulating the emancipation of slaves became more liberal. Through a practice known as *coartación*, slaves could purchase their freedom for a price agreed on with their owners.[12]

In 1795, at the age of forty-two, Catherine paid the formidable sum of six hundred pesos in cash to her mistress Françoise Pomet and thereby became a free woman. She subsequently took the surname Henry, derived from Henry Roche *dit* Belaire, her first owner and the possible father of her children.[13] In 1798 Catherine Henry bought a piece of property on the uptown side of St. Ann Street between Rampart and Burgundy, and here she built a small cottage that would become famous as the home of Marie Laveau.[14] In the 1820s the census and the city directory listed her as a trader, or *marchande*.[15]

Catherine Henry died in 1831 and was buried with the full rites of the Roman Catholic Church. A receipt filed with her succession papers shows that the funeral cost $29.50; that covered two priests, two cantors, three choir boys, and one *suisse* (an usher employed by the church to keep order) as well as the *droits et bénéfices de la fabrique* (a fee paid to the wardens for use of the church).[16]

Catherine Henry's daughter Marguerite was voluntarily released from slavery in 1790.[17] By 1795 she had become the concubine of the Frenchman Henri D'Arcantel, with whom she had four quadroon children. Her name appears as Marguerite D'Arcantel in official records. In his 1817 will, D'Arcantel left a five hundred dollar bequest to Marguerite and their surviving son and daughter.[18] The sexual relationships between masters and enslaved women were by definition exploitative, but white men and free women of color formed liaisons that, although unlawful, were agreeable to both. These domestic partnerships were a fact of life in colonial Louisiana and continued to be so under the American administration. Some women of color became the concubines of white men strictly for financial security, and some men chose cohabitation with a woman of color over marriage to a white woman because it was more convenient; others entered into these relationships out of mutual love and respect.[19]

Marguerite's alliance with Henri D'Arcantel may have been motivated more by a desire for financial support than by affection. Women of color are usually depicted as being scrupulously faithful to their white "protectors." Marguerite, however, challenges that image. In 1801, she gave birth to her famous daughter, Marie Laveau, the result of a brief affair with Charles Laveaux, a prosperous free mulatto businessman who traded in real estate and slaves. Laveaux subsequently married another free woman of color.[20] Marie and her maternal and paternal half siblings were the first generation of this family to be born free. She was baptized at St. Louis Cathedral, with her grandmother Catherine serving as godmother.[21]

Some free women of color, instead of forming domestic partnerships with white men, entered into legal marriage with men of their own caste. Marie Laveau and both of her half sisters made this choice.[22] Charles Laveaux accompanied eighteen-year-old Marie to the notary's office to enact her marriage contract with Jacques Paris, a free quadroon who had immigrated to New Orleans from Haiti. As a dowry, Laveaux give his daughter a piece of property in the Faubourg Marigny, the new suburb below the original French settlement. Marie and Jacques were married by the Spanish priest Fray Antonio Sedella (known as Pére Antoine) at St. Louis Cathedral on August 4, 1819. The couple had two daughters, who apparently died during childhood.[23] By 1824 Jacques Paris had vanished; whether he died or simply deserted his wife remains unknown. No documentation of his death has been discovered, but Marie Laveau was henceforth known in official records as the widow Paris.[24]

Rather than remaining single or marrying another free man of color, Marie Laveau entered into a domestic relationship with Louis Christophe Dominic Duminy de Glapion, a white Louisiana native of noble French birth.[25] Marie and

Christophe were unable to wed because of Louisiana's antimiscegenation law. They nevertheless lived together for thirty years in Catherine Henry's old cottage on St. Ann Street. Marie and Christophe were the parents of seven children; of these, only two daughters, Marie Heloïse Euchariste and Marie Philomène, survived to adulthood.[26]

Christophe Glapion speculated in stocks, money lending, real estate, and slaves. Laveau and Glapion were themselves slave owners, buying and selling eight slaves between 1828 and 1854.[27] Like most racially mixed couples, they socialized with Laveau's family and friends within the free colored community and chose them as godparents for their children. Glapion maintained at least some contact with his mother and sisters, although Laveau and their quadroon children would not have been acknowledged by his kin, and especially not by his female relations. Glapion died in 1855.[28]

Both before and after Glapion's death, Marie Laveau engaged in various acts of charity and community service. She was renowned for nursing yellow fever and cholera victims during the city's frequent epidemics.[29] She sponsored the education of an orphaned boy, referred to as her protégé, at the Institution Catholique des Orphelines Indigents (Catholic Institution for Indigent Orphans).[30] On several occasions she posted bond for free women of color accused of minor crimes.[31] She visited condemned prisoners, built altars in their cells, and prayed with them in their final hours.[32]

Marie Laveau was undoubtedly a lifelong Roman Catholic. She was deeply connected to St. Louis Cathedral, where she received the sacraments of baptism and marriage, attended mass, and presented her children for baptism. She served as godmother for her nephew and her granddaughter, demonstrating that she met the canon law requirement that godparents be baptized in the Roman Catholic faith and demonstrate a commitment to the church. When she died, her funeral was conducted by a priest of St. Louis Cathedral.[33]

Marie Laveau never abandoned her devotion to Catholicism. But rather than using her spiritual gifts to exercise leadership within the church, as did some other women of color, Laveau chose the vocation of Voudou priestess. Unlike most free women of color, who lived unremarkable lives as wives/domestic partners and mothers, participated in church activities, and engaged in occupations such as seamstress, hairdresser, boardinghouse keeper, or market entrepreneur, Marie Laveau became a public figure. She was beloved by many and despised, feared, and ridiculed by others. These attitudes cut across boundaries of race, class, and condition of servitude.[34]

New Orleans Voudou is the only indigenous North American example of the New World Afro-Catholic religions common to the Caribbean and South

America. When enslaved Africans were exposed to Catholicism, they found many elements to which they could relate. The supreme being common to most African belief systems was analogous to God the Father, and the African deities and ancestors who serve as intermediaries between men and the supreme being became identified with Mary the Blessed Mother and the legion of saints. The rituals, music, vestments and miracle-working objects of the Catholic Church seemed intrinsically familiar to Africans, whose religious ceremonies stressed chanting, drumming, dance, elaborate costumes, and the use of spirit-embodying amulets. Through a process of creative borrowing and adaptation, they reinterpreted Roman Catholicism to suit their own needs, the result of which was the evolution of Haitian Vodou, Cuban Santería, Brazilian Candomblé, and New Orleans Voudou.[35]

In the early years of the nineteenth century, there were still some Africans among New Orleans's slaves and free blacks. In addition, many enslaved and free Africans had arrived in New Orleans from Haiti at the turn of the nineteenth century. These African-born community elders retained elements of their traditional religions, and women took responsibility for initiating their daughters into these traditions. Laveau's great-grandmother, grandmother, and mother could have served the Voudou spirits in addition to God the Father, Jesus, and the saints of the Roman Catholic Church. Any or all of these neighbors and kinswomen might have trained the young Marie in the religion of her ancestors. Laveau would have perceived Catholicism and Voudou as different, but not conflicting, ways of serving the spiritual forces that govern the world.[36]

There is an extensive scholarly literature on the present-day Afro-Catholic religions of the Caribbean and South America, but truly reliable documentation of early New Orleans Voudou is scarce.[37] From the 1820s through the 1890s, numerous Voudou-related articles appeared in New Orleans newspapers, which described Marie Laveau as "the head of the Voudou women," "the Queen of the Voudous," "her majesty," "the celebrated Marie Laveau," "the Priestess of the Voudous," or "the ancient queen," indicating that her exalted position was widely recognized.[38] Voudou themes were also popular in national publications such as *Appleton's Journal, Harper's Weekly*, and *Century*.[39] Between 1936 and 1941, fieldworkers with the federal Works Progress Administration Louisiana Writers' Project interviewed elderly New Orleanians who remembered the Voudou traditions of the later nineteenth century.[40] Their unpublished eyewitness accounts provide a valuable counterpoint to the highly sensationalized stories generated by white journalists and popular historians. From these sources we can derive some idea of the religion embraced by Marie Laveau and her followers.

New Orleans Voudou was characterized by a complex theology and a pantheon of deities and spirits. The goal of Voudou worship was to achieve a spiritual balance among the individual, the community, the natural environment, and the deities. Voudou had no central organizational authority. Individual priestesses, and a few priests, ministered to racially diverse, mostly female congregations that met for services in the homes of their leaders. Marie Laveau's cottage on St. Ann Street served this purpose.[41]

Marie Laveau's front room was filled with altars laden with candles, images of the saints, flowers, fruit, and other offerings. Here she presided over weekly Friday night meetings, which were attended by "more white than colored." A core group of her closest followers was always present to assist her. A chorus of young singers, accompanied by an old man who played the accordion, supplied the music. All present were dressed in white. Herbs, food, liquor, candles, and coins were arranged on a white cloth on the ground or the floor, in accordance with a custom referred to as "spreading a feast for the spirits." The service began with Catholic prayers, such as the Hail Mary and the Our Father. Laveau would pour out libations of water or wine, saluting the four cardinal directions, and rap three times on the ground "in the name of the Father, Son, and Holy Ghost." Afterward the participants would chant and dance. All of these rituals were intended to call the spirits to enter the bodies of the faithful and provide counsel to the congregation. A shared meal followed the religious portion of the service.[42]

In addition to holding regular services for her followers, Marie Laveau also gave consultations and performed ceremonies for individual clients. Louisiana Writers' Project narrators told of rituals to attract and control a lover, bring about a marriage, improve business, and win in court as well as those for negative purposes.[43] According to the obituary published in the *New York Times* after her death, Laveau received "Louisiana's greatest men and most distinguished visitors[.] . . . [L]awyers, legislators, planters, and merchants all came to pay their respects and seek her offices."[44]

The most important of the Voudou ceremonies took place on the Eve of St. John the Baptist (June 23) on the shore of Lake Pontchartrain. St. John's Eve coincides with the summer solstice, which in pre-Christian Europe was believed to be a time when the human and spirit worlds intersected. Men and women responded by lighting bonfires to attract good spirits and drive away bad ones, protect livestock and people from disease, and ensure a successful harvest. Believers also immersed themselves in sacred bodies of water supposed to be endowed with magical and medicinal virtues. The Roman Catholic Feast of St. John was grafted onto this night of pagan religious observance.[45] The celebration of St. John's Eve was probably introduced into Louisiana by French and Spanish colonists, and at some undetermined time it was adopted by people of African descent.

According to both printed sources and oral testimony, Marie Laveau led this celebration from sometime in the 1830s until the early 1870s. These accounts vary considerably, but all describe bonfires, drumming, singing, dancing, ritual bathing, and a communal feast.[46]

Although many white people attended Marie Laveau's ceremonies and sought her advice, the dominant society never accepted Voudou as a valid religion. In order to justify slavery, "civilized" whites necessarily distanced themselves from the dark and "savage" peoples whom they strove to enslave. They scorned all things of African origin: personal adornment, language, music, dance, and religious beliefs. Nevertheless, the French and Spanish colonial governments and the Catholic Church were reasonably tolerant of Voudou. But the Protestant Anglo-Americans who poured into New Orleans after the Louisiana Purchase of 1803 saw Voudou as a potential breeding ground for slave rebellion and a threat to public safety. They also considered this African practice to be an offense against Christian morality—a horrifying brew of sorcery, devil worship, interracial fraternization, and sexual license.[47]

Before the Civil War, newspaper accounts focused on police raids of private Voudou ceremonies and the arrest of the participants for "unlawful assembly" of enslaved and free persons. The earliest such article, titled "Idolatry and Quackery," reported in 1820 that a house in the Faubourg Tremé (the neighborhood behind the French Quarter) had been "used as a temple for certain occult practices and the idolatrous worship of an African deity called Vaudoo. . . . Many slaves and some free people repaired there of nights to practice superstitious, idolatrous rites, to dance, carouse, &c."[48] These raids became more frequent in the 1850s as the debate over slavery escalated and the United States began its inexorable progress toward civil war.[49]

In the later nineteenth century, as the idealistic goals of Reconstruction gave way to Jim Crow segregation and racism, journalists shifted their attention to the more accessible St. John's Eve celebrations, using the occasion to ridicule people of African descent. An 1869 article observed sarcastically that "June is the time devoted by the voudou worshipers to . . . their most sacred and therefore most revolting rites. Midnight dances, bathing and eating, together with other less innocent pleasures, make the early summer a time of unrestrained orgies for the blacks." This newspaper announced that "the celebrated Marie Laveau" was planning to retire. Taking a poke at the newly freed slaves, the writer quipped that now "a more youthful hand puts up love philters and makes fetishes for the intelligent freedmen, who elect governors and members of Congress out of their own number."[50]

Despite their avowed abhorrence of these African-based practices, journalists and the reading public were obviously fascinated by it and Marie Laveau. Even after Laveau ceased to appear in public, reporters still trekked out to Lake Pontchartrain on St. John's Eve, hoping to see the Voudou Queen, and published their ever more extravagant "orgy stories" of bonfires, bloody animal sacrifice, savage drumming, chanting, dancing, drunkenness, nude bathing, and interracial fornication. The title of an 1896 article provides the most flagrant example of this sensationalism: "Dance of the Voodoos—Outlandish Celebration of St. John's Eve—A Living Cat Eaten by the Voodoo King—Unparalleled Scenes of Savagery in the Pontchartrain Swamps."[51]

By the turn of the twentieth century, New Orleans Voudou, as an organized religion, had been forced underground. Journalistic descriptions of naked, drunken orgies bolstered claims that people of African descent were unfit to vote, hold office, or associate with white people. Following the abolition of slavery, the prohibition against "unlawful assembly" could no longer be used as an excuse for breaking up Voudou services and arresting the participants. Instead, the police harassed the Voudou community by means of newly instituted laws against disorderly conduct, exposing the body in public, practicing medicine without a license, and fortune-telling.[52]

Anti-Voudou sentiment was not confined to white New Orleanians. African American clergy and educators moralized against Voudou as superstition and devil worship—the dark opposite of Christianity—that was not only sinful, but also an impediment to racial progress. Such attitudes caused many Voudou devotees to fear and deny their former beliefs.[53]

As Marie Laveau became incapacitated by old age, she retired to her cottage on St. Ann Street and was cared for by her daughter Philomène. Laveau died at home on June 15, 1881. Her funeral was attended by a racially diverse crowd of devotees and curiosity seekers that blocked the streets around her home and followed her cortege to the cemetery. The newspaper reported that "the most prominent and the most humble joined in paying their last respects to the dead."[54]

All of New Orleans's English-language dailies and even the *New York Times* carried obituaries and remembrances. Most rejected the idea that Marie Laveau was actually a Voudou priestess, portraying her instead as a woman of great beauty, intellect, and charisma who was pious and charitable as well as a skilled herbal healer. Two newspapers took the opposite view. The *New Orleans Democrat* described Laveau as "the prime mover and soul of the indecent orgies of the ignoble Voudous," and the *New Orleans Times* announced that the spirit of Marie Laveau would be "propitiated by midnight orgies on the Bayou."[55]

Although the obituaries and official cemetery records attest that Marie Laveau was interred in her family tomb in St. Louis Cemetery no. 1, some people believe that her remains rest in a wall vault in St. Louis Cemetery no. 2, known as the "Wishing Vault." Today devotees visit both gravesites to leave offerings of coins, fruit, candy, flowers, Mardi Gras beads, or holy cards and to draw cross marks on the marble slab.[56]

According to popular legend, as Marie Laveau grew older, she was gradually and secretly replaced by her daughter, referred to as "Marie II," creating the illusion that one woman of imperishable beauty reigned as queen of the Voudous until the 1890s.[57] Nineteenth-century newspaper articles cited various women as having replaced or succeeded Laveau, but nowhere do we find any suggestion that either of her surviving daughters, Marie Heloïse Euchariste or Marie Philomène, became the new Voudou Queen.[58] The archival evidence and the oral testimony of the Louisiana Writers' Project informants argue against the possibility that Heloïse or Philomène assumed this role. Heloïse died at age thirty-five in 1862.[59] Philomène continued to live in the Laveau-Glapion cottage until her death in 1897; by all accounts she was a very strict Roman Catholic who detested Voudou.[60] There may have been a "Marie II," but if so, her identity remains a mystery. The original Marie Laveau and this other, younger woman—maybe even several others—have merged to form a single persona, the legendary Voudou Queen.

Other Voudou priestesses lived and practiced their vocation in nineteenth-century New Orleans, but their names have been forgotten. How can we explain the enduring celebrity of Marie Laveau? By all accounts, in addition to her genuine spiritual gifts she possessed extraordinary beauty, a magnetic personality, and a flair for showmanship. Even during her lifetime she had become a cult figure. Although feared by some people, she developed a following not only among people of color but also among upper-class white New Orleanians and visitors to the city, who were welcome at her ceremonies and numbered among her clients. Her reputation may have been augmented by the deeds of her successors.

Earlier journalists and popular historians could not reconcile the idea of Marie Laveau as a virtuous and exemplary Christian with her leadership of the Voudou congregation. If she were indeed good, she could not have been a Voudou priestess; if she were a Voudou priestess, she could not have been good.

In recent years, Voudou has experienced a revival and attitudes toward it have changed from fear, condemnation, and derision to tolerance, interest, and reverence. Contemporary priests and priestesses have established temples that serve a middle-class, mostly white, community of believers. Marie Laveau is honored as a Voudou deity.[61]

Our present understanding of the Voudou religion enables us to see that there is no conflict between the kind and charitable Marie Laveau who appears in the sacramental registers of St. Louis Cathedral as baptisand, bride, mother, and godmother and was buried with the full rites of the Roman Catholic Church and the Marie Laveau who was Queen of the Voudous. Her fame endures as her legend continues to evolve.

Marie Laveau was renowned in nineteenth-century New Orleans as a pious and charitable Roman Catholic free woman of color who was also the city's most prominent Voudou priestess. Her life illustrates important aspects of New Orleans culture, where racial identity, gender roles, and religious beliefs were fluid. The experiences of her maternal ancestors were not unusual in New Orleans. These women made the transition from enslaved to free, from African to mixed race; they were equally comfortable with Voudou and Roman Catholicism; they were able to take advantage of the opportunities for slaves and free persons in the thriving commercial economy of New Orleans. Marie Laveau built on the foundation established by her female ancestors and surpassed other women of her race and class through her compelling personality, her many capabilities, and her authentic spirituality.

NOTES

1. During the nineteenth century the name of this religion was usually spelled "Voudou." "Voodoo" is an Americanized spelling that has taken on the negative connotation of meaningless mumbo-jumbo, as in "voodoo economics" or "voodoo science," and is considered offensive by some people.

2. The newspaper articles about Voudou are too numerous to list, but selected other sources follow, ordered according to genre. POPULAR HISTORIES: George Washington Cable, "Creole Slave Songs," *Century Magazine* (April 1886): 807–28; Henry Castellanos, *New Orleans as It Was: Episodes of Louisiana Life* (1895; rpt., Gretna, La.: Pelican, 1990); Herbert Asbury, *The French Quarter: An Informal History of the New Orleans Underworld* (New York: Garden City Publishing, 1938); Robert Tallant, *Voodoo in New Orleans* (1946; rpt., Gretna, La.: Pelican, 1983). NOVELS: Robert Tallant, *The Voodoo Queen* (1956; rpt., Gretna, La.: Pelican, 1983); Francine Prose, *Marie Laveau* (New York: Berkley, 1977); Jewel Parker Rhodes, *Voodoo Dreams: A Novel of Marie Laveau* (New York: Picador, 1995). FILM: Steven Hank, director, *The Widow Paris*, UNO Productions, 1991. OPERA: John Joseph Carbon, "Marie Laveau: A Full-Length Voodoo Opera" (PhD diss., University of California, Santa Barbara, 1983). PLAY: Daniel du Plantis, "Gris-Gris," 1998. WEB SITES: http://www.loyno.edu/history/journal/1984-5/brouillette.htm; http://www.themystica.com/mystica/articles/l/laveau_marie.html; http://www.csicop.org/sb/2001-12/i-files.html; http://weeklywire.com/ww/03-20-00/austin_cols

_ventura.html; http://www.prairieghosts.com/laveau.html (all Web sites were accessed September 12, 2007). SCHOLARLY WORKS: Rachelle Sussman, "Conjuring Marie Laveau: The Syncretic Life of a Nineteenth-Century Voodoo Priestess in America" (master's thesis, Sarah Lawrence College, 1998); Ina Johanna Fandrich, "Mysterious Voodoo Queen Marie Laveaux: A Study of Spiritual Power and Female Leadership in Nineteenth-Century New Orleans" (PhD diss., Temple University, 1994); Martha Ward, *Voodoo Queen: The Spirited Lives of Marie Laveau* (Jackson: University Press of Mississippi, 2004); Ina Johanna Fandrich, *The Mysterious Voodoo Queen, Marie Laveaux: A Study of Powerful Female Leadership in Nineteenth-Century New Orleans* (New York: Routledge, 2005); Carolyn Morrow Long, *A New Orleans Voudou Priestess: The Legend and Reality of Marie Laveau* (Gainesville: University Press of Florida, 2006).

3. "Death of Marie Laveau," *New Orleans Daily Picayune*, June 17, 1881; "Wayside Notes—The Death of Marie Laveau," *New Orleans Daily City Item*, June 17, 1881; "Recollections of a Visit on New Year's Eve to Marie Laveau, the Ex-Queen of the Voudous," *New Orleans Daily States*, June 17, 1881; "The Dead Voudou Queen," *New York Times*, June 23, 1881; "Marie Laveaux—Death of the Queen of the Voudous Just before St. John's Eve," *New Orleans Democrat*, June 17, 1881; "A Sainted Woman," *New Orleans Democrat*, June 18, 1881; "Voudou Vagaries—The Spirit of Marie Laveau to be Propitiated by Midnight Orgies on the Bayou," *New Orleans Times*, June 23, 1881; Castellanos, *New Orleans As It Was*, 90–101; Asbury, *The French Quarter*, 254–83; Tallant, *Voodoo in New Orleans*, 51–74; Sallie Ann Glassman, *Vodou Visions: An Encounter with Divine Mystery* (New York: Villard Books, 2000), 52–53.

4. If Marguerite were African born, she would have been transported to Louisiana in 1743 on the *St. Ursin*, after which the French ceased to import slaves to Louisiana. The previous ship, the *St. Louis*, had left the Senegal Concession on Gorée Island in 1730, before Marguerite was born (Gwendolyn Midlo Hall, *Africans in Colonial Louisiana* [Baton Rouge: Louisiana State University Press, 1995], 29–55. Table 2 in Hall [60], "French Slave-Trade Ships from Africa to Louisiana," gives the names of the ships, year and port of embarkation, and number of slaves landed). Although only one-third of the Africans brought to Louisiana by the French were women, almost all of those women were Wolofs (Gwendolyn Midlo Hall, "African Women in French and Spanish Louisiana: Origins, Roles, Family, Work, Treatment," in *The Devil's Lane: Sex and Race in the Early South*, ed. Catherine Clinton and Michele Gillespie [New York: Oxford University Press, 1997], 248–49).

5. Marguerite and her daughter Catherine were listed in a 1756 property inventory included in the marriage contract of Henry Roche-Belaire and Catherine Laurandine, February 24, 1756, document no. 748, file 3432, box 40, Judicial Records of the Spanish Cabildo, Louisiana State Museum Historical Center, New Orleans (hereinafter cited as LSMHC). This document identifies his occupation and lists his real estate holdings, household furnishings, tools, and slaves, valued at 5,349 French livres. Marguerite was simply described as "a negress," with no indication of her birthplace. Catherine identified her parents as Marguerite and Jean Belaire in her will, Acts of Octave de Armas, March 19, 1831, 10:359–60, act 213, Notarial Archives Research Center, New Orleans (hereinafter cited as NARC).

6. Emily Clark and Virginia Meacham Gould, "The Feminine Face of Afro-Catholicism in New Orleans," *William and Mary Quarterly* 59 (April 2002): 416–18.

7. Thanks to Emily Clark for advice on whether Catherine and Marguerite might have been baptized along with the Piquery slaves. Baptism of Catherine, September 26, 1754, vol. 3, pt. 1, p. 28, act 294. This Catherine was born on August 29, 1754, a date consistent with the age of Marie Laveau's grandmother. Baptism of Marguerite and other adult slaves, April 17, 1756, 3:56, act 675.

St. Louis Cathedral (hereinafter cited as SLC) records were accessed at the Archdiocesan Archives (hereinafter cited as AA), and all are from the registers for slaves and free persons of color (hereinafter cited as S/FPC). The priests recorded baptisms, marriages, and funerals in the sacramental registers in their native language. The Spanish-speaking priests rendered French names in Spanish: "Maria" for "Marie," "Francisco" for "François," etc., and they often substituted "b" for "v," resulting in "Labeau" instead of "Laveau." I have used the person's French name in the text but have cited the source exactly as it was spelled in the original document.

The census for the Villars district of New Orleans for 1763 and 1766 shows Roche and Piquery living near or perhaps even adjacent to each other (census taken by Sieur Villars, captain of militia, from *Archivo general de Indias, audencia de Santo Domingo, legajo 2595*, in Jacqueline K. Voorhies, *Some Late Eighteenth-Century Louisianians, Census Records 1758–1796* [Lafayette: University of Southwestern Louisiana, 1973], 5).

8. For the emancipation of slave concubines, see Judith Kelleher Schafer, *Slavery, the Civil Law, and the Supreme Court of Louisiana* (Baton Rouge: Louisiana State University Press, 1994), 180–200. Sale of Catalina and two-year-old son Josef by Henrique Roche to Bartholemé Magnon, Acts of Raphael Perdomo, September 30, 1784, 4:426, NARC.

9. Sale of Catalina and son Josef by Bartolomé Magnon to Joseph Viscot (Bizot), Acts of Raphael Perdomo, October 5, 1784, 4:430; sale of Cathalina by Josef Visot (Bizot) to Francisca Pomet, f.w.c., Acts of Raphael Perdomo, August 12, 1788, 12:354, NARC. Bizot retained ownership of Catherine's son Joseph.

10. Leonard C. Curry, *The Free Black in Urban America* (Chicago: University of Chicago Press, 1981), 44–45, tables C-5 through C-8, "Free Black Slaveholding (New Orleans)," 270–71.

11. For evidence of Pomet's slave ownership, see Spanish census of 1791 and 1795: enumerated in the household of Francisca Pomet, free woman *sangre mezclada*, were three enslaved negresses (1791 Spanish census, New Orleans Public Library [hereinafter NOPL]); 1795 Spanish census, *Databases of Household Censuses for New Orleans, Mobile, and Pensacola*, compiled by Virginia Meacham Gould, in Gwendolyn Midlo Hall, *Databases for the Study of Afro-Louisiana History and Genealogy, 1699–1860*, CD-ROM (Baton Rouge: Louisiana State University Press, 2000). For Pomet's purchases and sales, see Francisca Pomet to Don Juan Bautista Pomet, power of attorney to sell slave, Acts of Pedro Pedesclaux, April 8, 1788, 3:465; trade of slave Alcira for slave Ursula by Pedro Muchau to Francisca Pomet, October 31, 1791; sale of slave Ursula by Francisca Pomet to Maria Pradeau Hognon, November 2, 1793; sale of slave Maria by Francisca Pomet to Jose Vincente Gonzales, December 1, 1801. All citations are from Hall, *Databases for the Study of Afro-Louisiana History and Genealogy*. Benjamin Henry Latrobe recorded his observations of the Afro-Creole market women in his 1819 journal (*Impressions Respecting New Orleans: Diary and Sketches 1818–1820*, ed. Samuel Wilson Jr. [New York: Columbia University Press, 1951], 100–102). One of the best known of these entrepreneurs was Eulalie Mandeville, who ran a very successful dry-goods business during the first half of the nineteenth century, using enslaved and free black women as vendors (2nd District Court records for *Nicolas Théodore Macarty v. Eulalie Mandeville, f.w.c.*, docket no. 626, Supreme Court Historical Archives, Louisiana and Special Collections, Earl K. Long Library, University of New Orleans).

12. Louisiana actually passed from French to Spanish ownership in 1763 but was not effectively governed by Spain until 1769. For more on the Spanish Codigo Negro and the practice of *coartación* (slaves' right to self-purchase), see Kimberly Hanger, *Bounded Lives, Bounded Places: Free Black Society in Colonial New Orleans, 1769–1803* (Durham, N.C.: Duke University Press, 1997), 25–26, 42–44.

13. Emancipation of Catarina by Francisca Pomet, Acts of Carlos Ximines, January 13, 1795, 9:12, NARC. In subsequent documents, Catherine's surname was usually given as Henry or Henri, but sometimes as Pomet.

14. Sale of lot on St. Ann Street by Miguel Meffre to Cathalina Pomet (Henry), Acts of Pedro Pedesclaux, March 23, 1798, 31:185–86, NARC.

15. United States census for New Orleans 1820, Catherine Henry, *marchande*, Rue Ste. Anne, sheet 72, line 11, National Archives and Records Administration; Catherine Henry, trader, John Adem Paxton's *New Orleans Directory and Register* for 1822.

16. Funeral of Catherine Henry, SLC, funerals of S/FPC, June 18, 1831, vol. 9, pt. 1, p. 137, act 709, AA.

17. Catherine's daughter Marguerite remained enslaved in the Roche-Belaire household until the death of Henry Roche *dit* Belaire. She was then sold to François Langlois, who freed her gratis a year later (sale of Margarita from the succession of Enrique Roche, March 23, 1789, document no. 2062, file 2334, p. 30, Judicial Records of the Spanish Cabildo, box 53, LSMHC; emancipation of Margarita by François Langlois, Acts of Pedro Pedesclaux, October 16, 1790, 11:720, NARC).

18. The Spanish census of 1795 lists Henri D'Arcantel as sharing his home with a free mulatress named Marguerite (*Databases of Household Censuses for New Orleans, Mobile, and Pensacola*). Of Marguerite's four children with Henri D'Arcantel, Marie Louise and Antoine survived to adulthood (will of Henri D'Arcantel, October 22, 1817, will book 3:65–66, microfilm, NOPL).

19. For early antebellum travelers' accounts of interracial concubinage (*plaçage*), see Paul Alliot, "Historical and Political Reflections on Louisiana," in *Louisiana under the Rule of Spain, France, and the United States 1785–1807*, ed. and trans. James Alexander Robertson (1910, rpt. Freeport, N.Y.: Books for Libraries Press, 1969), 1:85–87, 103, 111; François-Marie Perrin du Lac, *Voyage dans les deux Louisianes*, in *Louisiana under the Rule*, 185, 205; Jack D. L. Holmes, "Do It! Don't Do It!: Spanish Laws on Sex and Marriage," in *Louisiana's Legal Heritage*, ed. Edward F. Haas (New Orleans: Louisiana State Museum, 1983), 23; Christian Schultz, *Travels on an Inland Voyage* (New York: Isaac Riley, 1810), 2:193–94.

20. For more on Charles Laveaux's occupation, prosperity, and education, see Long, *Voudou Priestess*, 23–24, 31–32. Marriage of Charles Labeau and Maria Francisca Dupart, SLC/S-FPC, August 2, 1802, 1:21, AA (these sacramental records use the Spanish forms of French names—for example, "Labeau" for "Laveaux" and "Maria" for "Marie"). Their children were Marie Dolores and Laurent Charles (baptism of Marie de los Dolores Labeau, SLC/S-FPC, June 2, 1804, vol. 7, pt. 3, p. 245, act 1771; baptism of Lorenzo Labeau, SLC/S-FPC, November 30, 1805, vol. 8, pt. 2, p. 167, act 760, AA).

21. Perhaps because both parents were committed to other partners, Charles Laveaux's name did not appear in the baptismal record for Marguerite's daughter (baptism of Maria, SLC/S-FPC, September 16, 1801, vol. 7, pt. 1, p. 41 verso, act 320, AA). Ina Fandrich, who discovered this document, argues convincingly in her article "Birth of New Orleans' Voodoo Queen," *Louisiana History* 46 (Summer 2005): 294–309, that this is indeed the baptismal record of Marie Laveau, stating that a search of baptismal entries between 1780 and 1810 revealed that only this one described a free mulatto infant named Marie, daughter of Marguerite, free mulatress, and goddaughter of Catherine, free negress.

22. Marie Laveau's maternal half sister, Marie Louise D'Arcantel, married the free man of color Louis Foucher (marriage of Luis Foucher and Maria Luisa D'Arcantel, SLC/S-FPC, April 4, 1815, 1:49, act 490, AA). Laveau's paternal half sister Marie Dolores Laveaux married François Auguste, also a free man of color (marriage of Francisco Augusto and Maria Labeau, SLC/S-SPC, October 7, 1818, 1:58, act 244, AA).

23. Marriage contract between Santyaque Paris and Marie Laveaux, July 27, 1819, Acts of Hugues Lavergne, vol. 1, act 5, NARC; marriage of Santiago Paris and Maria Labeau, SLC/S-FPC, August 4, 1819, 1:59, act 256, AA. The marriage record identifies Paris as a "native of Jeremie on the Island of Santo Domingo" (now Haiti). Baptism of Marie Angèlie Paris, February 14, 1823, 18:2 verso, act 13; baptism of Felicité Paris, November 17, 1824, 18:170 verso, act 857, AA. The two girls subsequently disappeared from the archival record, meaning that they probably died as children.

24. Fantastic scenarios about the disappearance of Jacques Paris are found in the novels of Robert Tallant (*The Voodoo Queen*, 75), Francine Prose (*Marie Laveau*, 107–24), and Jewell Park Rhodes (*Voodoo Dreams*, 360–68).

25. Christophe Glapion was the grandson of the Chevalier Christophe de Glapion, Sieur du Mesnilgauches of Normandy, France, and the legitimate son of Denis Christophe Duminil de Glapion and Jeanne Sophie Lalande Ferrier. For more on Glapion's lineage, see Long, *Voudou Priestess*, 51–53.

26. Baptism of Marie Heloïse, August 19, 1828, 21:220, act 1232; baptism of Marie Louise (Caroline), September 10, 1829, 22:56, act 317; funeral of Caroline, December 9, 1829, vol. 9, pt. 1, p. 2, act 8; funeral of Christophe, May 21, 1831, vol. 9, pt. 1, p. 129, act 848; funeral of Jean Baptiste, July 12, 1832, vol. 9, pt. 2, p. 274, act 1730; baptism of François, May 13, 1834, vol. 23, pt. 3, p. 403, act 2715; funeral of François, May 18, 1834, vol. 10, pt. 3, p. 301, act 2019; baptism of Philomène, unnumbered volume, May 31, 1836, act 363; baptism of Archange Edouard, unnumbered volume, May 7, 1839, act 438. All are in the baptism or funeral records of S/FPC, SLC, AA.

27. Christophe Glapion's business transactions are recorded in numerous notarial acts and court cases; see Long, *Voudou Priestess*, 63–65, 79–83. For the slave-trading activities of Glapion and Laveau, see: sale of Eliza by John Woolfolk to Christophe Glapion, Acts of Carlisle Pollock, March 14, 1828, 24:178; sale of Eliza by Glapion to Pierre Monette, f.m.c., Acts of A. E. Bienvenu, April 26, 1854, vol. 5, act 62; sale of Peter by Arnold Bodin to Christophe Glapion, Acts of Joseph Lisbony, April 12, 1848, vol. 3, act 84; sale of Peter by Glapion to P. M. Mervoyer, Acts of Jean Agaisse, October 24, 1849, 7:220, act 1090; sale of Molly and her son Richard by Pierre Tricou to Marie Laveau, Acts of Carlisle Pollock, February 7, 1838, 60:19; sale of Molly and younger son Louis by Glapion to Philippe Ross, f.m.c., Acts of A. E. Bienvenu, April 26, 1850, vol. 5, act 63; sale of Molly's older son Richard by Glapion to Elihu Creswell, Acts of S. H. Lewis, March 8, 1850 (missing from notarial book; recorded in Conveyance Office book 51:475); sale of Irma by P. O. Peyroux to Marie, f.w.c., widow of Santiague Paris, Acts of Louis T. Caire, August 10, 1838, 66A:235–36, act 594; sale of Irma and her son Armand by widow L. Paris to Demoiselle C. Peyroux, Acts of L. T. Caire, October 21, 1839, act 676; sale of Juliette by Pierre Monette, f.m.c., to Marie Laveau, November 15, 1847, Acts of Paul Laresche, act 223; sale of Juliette by Laveau to Sanité Couvreure, f.w.c., Acts of Jean Agaisse, April 27, 1848, 6:79–80, act 42, NARC.

28. For more on the domestic and social lives of mixed-race couples, see Virginia Meacham Gould, "In Full Enjoyment of Their Liberty: The Free Women of Color of the Gulf Ports of New Orleans, Mobile, and Pensacola, 1769–1860" (PhD diss., Emory University, 1991), 149–54, 220, and Caryn Cossé Bell, *Revolution, Romanticism, and the Afro-Creole Protest Tradition in Louisiana 1718–1868* (Baton Rouge: Louisiana State University Press, 1997), 112–14, 134. Death certificate for Christophe Glapion, June 26, 1855, 17:42, microfilm, NOPL; he is buried in the "widow Paris" tomb in St. Louis Cemetery no. 1.

29. Marie Laveau's nursing activities, her care for orphans, and her prison ministry are mentioned in the obituaries and remembrances that followed her death and in an interview with her daughter Philomène ("Death of Marie Laveau—A Woman with a Wonderful History, Almost a

Century Old, Carried to the Tomb Thursday Morning," *New Orleans Daily Picayune*, June 17, 1881; "Wayside Notes—The Death of Marie Laveau," *New Orleans Daily City Item*, June 17, 1881; "Flagitious Fiction," *New Orleans Daily Picayune*, April 11, 1886).

30. "Journal des seances, Institution Catholique des Orphelines, 47eme seance du 3 septembre, 1852," 109, AA.

31. *State of Louisiana v. Julia Evans, f.w.c.*, 1st District Court, September 4, 1850, docket no. 5410; *State of Louisiana v. Elizabeth Martel, f.w.c.*, 1st District Court, January 11, 1858, docket no. 13416; *State of Louisiana v. Ophelia Garcia, f.w.c.*, 1st District Court, December 3, 1860, docket no. 14840, NOPL. Thanks to Dr. Judith Schafer for calling my attention to these cases.

32. "The Condemned—The Decorations of the Altar," *New Orleans Daily Picayune*, May 10, 1871.

33. For the record of Marie Laveau's baptism and marriage and the baptisms and funerals of her children, see notes 21, 23, and 26. Her godparenting is recorded in the baptism of Eugene Foucher, legitimate son of Marie Laveau's half sister, Marie Louise D'Arcantel, and the free man of color Louis Foucher, SLC/S-FPC, July 20, 1820, 16:213, act 1157, AA; baptism of Marie Glapious [*sic*], natural daughter of Marie Laveau's daughter Heloïse with the free man of color Pierre Crocker, SLC/S-SPC, July 9, 1850, vol. 32, pt. 3, p. 454, AA. Marie Laveau's funeral was conducted by Father Hyacinth Mignot of St. Louis Cathedral, burial book for St. Louis Cemetery no. 1 (January 17, 1881–January 8, 1883), 467, AA.

34. Of the twenty-eight Louisiana Writers' Project (hereinafter cited as LWP) informants who actually knew Laveau as a neighbor, friend, relative, or spiritual leader, eleven had a favorable opinion, nine simply conveyed information without making value judgments, and eight expressed fear or disapproval. Of those who had no personal knowledge of Laveau, four made positive statements, twenty-two were neutral, and five had a negative opinion. White informants were no more likely than African Americans to condemn Marie Laveau. Only one of the six white interviewees expressed a negative view; the others were either neutral or positive. These attitudes are reflected in the nineteenth-century newspaper articles cited elsewhere in this essay.

35. For Haitian Vodou, see Donald Cosentino, ed., *Sacred Arts of Haitian Vodou* (Los Angeles: University of California Fowler Museum of Cultural History, 1995). For Santería, see George Brandon, *Santería from Africa to the New World: The Dead Sell Memories* (Bloomington: Indiana University Press, 1993). For Candomblé, see Roger Bastide, *The African Religions of Brazil* (Baltimore: Johns Hopkins University Press, 1978). For the evolution of New Orleans Voudou, see Carolyn Morrow Long, *Spiritual Merchants: Religion, Magic, and Commerce* (Knoxville: University of Tennessee Press, 2001), 37–70, and Long, *Voudou Priestess*, 93–118.

36. Clark and Gould, "The Female Face of Afro-Catholicism," 5; Long, *Voudou Priestess*, 100–102.

37. The literature on Vodou, Santería, Candomblé, and other Afro-Catholic New World religions is vast; some examples have been cited above. The few published sources on eighteenth-century New Orleans Voudou are Antoine-Simon Le Page du Pratz, *Histoire de la Louisiane* (1758, English translation, *The History of Louisiana*, London: Beckett, 1774), 377; and Laura Porteous, "The Gri-Gri Case, A Criminal Trial in Louisiana during the Spanish Regime, 1773," *Louisiana Historical Quarterly* 17 (January 1934): 48–63. Later nineteenth-century sources (not necessarily reliable) have been cited elsewhere in this essay.

38. "Curious Charge of Swindling," *Daily Picayune*, July 3, 1850; "Local Intelligence—Recorder Long's Court," *New Orleans Daily Crescent*, July 12, 1859; "Voodooism," *New Orleans Commercial Bulletin*, July 5, 1869; "St. John's Eve—The Voudous," *New Orleans Daily Picayune*, June 24, 1873.

39. See, for example, Marie B. Williams, "A Night with the Voudous," *Appleton's Journal* 13,

March 27, 1875, 403–4; Lafcadio Hearn, "The Last of the Voudous," *Harper's Weekly Magazine*, November 7, 1885, 726–27; Charles Dudley Warner, "A Voudoo Dance," *Harper's Weekly Magazine*, June 25, 1887, 454–55; George Washington Cable, "Creole Slave Songs"; George Washington Cable, "The Dance in Place Congo," *Century Magazine* (February 1886): 517–32.

40. lwp. The interviews are located in the Federal Writers' Collection, Cammie G. Henry Research Center, Northwestern State University, Natchitoches. Many are quoted in Long, *Spiritual Merchants*, 48–52; and Long, *Voudou Priestess*, 108–11, 116–18, 130–33, 135–36.

41. Long, *Voudou Priestess*, 93–118.

42. Descriptions of small, private ceremonies at the home of Marie Laveau come from Marie Deed (b. 1866), interview by Robert McKinney, n.d.; Raymond Rivaros (b. 1876), interview by Hazel Breaux, n.d.; Charles Raphael (b. 1868), interview by Hazel Breaux and Jacques Villere, n.d.; Oscar Felix (b. 1868), interview by Edmund Burke, March 14, 1940, folder 25, lwp. Newspaper accounts come from "Idolatry and Quackery," *Louisiana Gazette*, August 16, 1820; "Great Doings in the Third Municipality," *New Orleans Daily Picayune*, June 29, 1850; "A Singular Assemblage," *New Orleans Bee*, June 29, 1850; "A Mystery of the Old Third," *New Orleans Daily Crescent*, June 29, 1850; "Another Voudou Affair," *New Orleans Daily Crescent*, July 4, 1850; "The Rites of Voudou," *New Orleans Daily Crescent*, July 31, 1850; "The Voudous in the First Municipality," *Louisiana Courier*, July 30, 1850; "Unlawful Assemblies," *New Orleans Daily Picayune*, July 31, 1850; "More of the Voudous," *New Orleans Daily Picayune*, July 31, 1850.

43. Laura Hopkins (b. 1878), interview by Maude Wallace, February 9, 16, and 21, and March 4, 1940, and by Wallace and Henriette Michinard, April 1940, folder 43, lwp; Joe Landry (birth date unknown), interview by Zoe Posey, July 18, 1939, folder 25, lwp; John Slater (birth date unknown), interview by Cecile Wright, n.d., folder 25, lwp.

44. "The Dead Voudou Queen," *New York Times*, June 23, 1881.

45. James George Frazer, *The Golden Bough: A Study in Magic and Religion* (1922; rpt., New York: Macmillan Company, 1951), 724. St. John's Eve is still celebrated in France and Spain, in French Quebec, and in the former French and Spanish colonies of Latin America and the Caribbean.

46. Descriptions of St. John's Eve celebrations come from lwp interviews: Oscar Felix, Charles Raphael, and William Moore (b. 1864), interview by Edmund Burke, March 1, 1940, folder 25, lwp; James Santana (birth date unknown), interview by Zoe Posey, July 10, 1939, folder 25, lwp; Joseph Alfred and Eugene Fritz (birthdates unknown), interview by Robert McKinney, n.d., folder 25, lwp; "Pops" (b. 1859), interview by Robert McKinney, n.d., folder 25, lwp. Newspaper stories include "The Voudous' Day," *New Orleans Times*, June 25, 1870; "The Vous Dous Incantation," *New Orleans Times*, June 28, 1872; "Voudou Vagaries—The Worshipers of Obeah Turned Loose," *New Orleans Times*, June 26, 1874; "Fetish Worship—St. John's Eve at Milneburg—A Voudou's Incantation—Midnight Scenes and Orgies," *New Orleans Times*, June 25, 1875; "St. John's Eve—After the Voudous—Some Singular Ceremonies—A Night in Heathenness," *New Orleans Daily Picayune*, June 25, 1875.

47. For more on whites distancing themselves from anything of African origin, see Rosan Jordan and Frank de Caro, "Race, Class, Identity, and Folklore Studies in Louisiana," *Journal of American Folklore* 109 (Winter 1996): 38–42. There is no evidence that the colonial government or the Catholic Church made any official attempt to suppress Voudou. For Anglo-Protestant attitudes toward Voudou, see, for example, John Adem Paxton, introduction to the *New Orleans Directory and Register* for 1822, 40–41, and Cable, "Creole Slave Songs," 815.

48. "Idolatry and Quackery," *Louisiana Gazette*, August 16, 1820.

49. Newspaper accounts of police raids from the 1850s are cited in note 41.

50. "Voodooism," *New Orleans Commercial Bulletin*, July 5, 1869.

51. "Dance of the Voodoos," *New Orleans Times-Democrat*, June 24, 1896.

52. New Orleans city ordinance no. 3046, passed May 7, 1879; New Orleans city ordinance no. 7086, passed May 17, 1881; state law against practicing medicine without a license, Louisiana House of Representatives, 1887; New Orleans city ordinance no. 13,347, passed May 23, 1897; typed copies in folder 44, LWP.

53. For an example of African American condemnation of "superstition," see *Southern Workman* 7 (April 1878): 30–31. Some of the LWP informants who were former Voudou adherents stated that they had "gotten religion" (meaning they had joined the Baptist or Methodist Church) and given it up. See, for example, Mary Washington (b. 1863), interview by Robert McKinney n.d., folder 21, LWP.

54. Death certificate for Marie Glapion born Laveau, June 16, 1881, 78:1113, microfilm, NOPL. Recollections of Marie Laveau's funeral were provided by Rose Legendre (b. 1868), interview by Maude Wallace, March 20, 1940, folder 25, LWP; Laura Hopkins (b. 1878), interview by Maude Wallace, March 4, 1940, folder 43, LWP. The quotation is from the *New Orleans Daily Picayune*'s obituary.

55. "Death of Marie Laveau," *New Orleans Daily Picayune*, June 17, 1881; "Wayside Notes—The Death of Marie Laveau," *New Orleans Daily City Item*, June 17, 1881; "Recollections of a Visit on New Year's Eve to Marie Laveau, the Ex-Queen of the Voudous," *New Orleans Daily States*, June 17, 1881; "The Dead Voudou Queen," *New York Times*, June 23, 1881; "Marie Lavaux—Death of the Queen of the Voudous Just before St. John's Eve," *New Orleans Democrat*, June 17, 1881; "A Sainted Woman," *New Orleans Democrat*, June 18, 1881; "Voudou Vagaries—The Spirit of Marie Laveau to be Propitiated by Midnight Orgies on the Bayou," *New Orleans Times*, June 23, 1881.

56. For more on the practices associated with both these gravesites, see Carolyn Morrow Long, "Voodoo-Related Rituals in New Orleans Cemeteries and the Tomb of Marie Laveau," *Louisiana Folklore Miscellany* 14 (1999): 1–14.

57. Lyle Saxon introduced the notion that the original Marie Laveau was replaced by her daughter in *Fabulous New Orleans* (1928; rpt., Gretna, La.: Pelican, 1988), 243. Catherine Dillon of the LWP first coined the names "Marie I" and "Marie II" (unpublished "Voodoo" manuscript, chapter 11, "Marie the Mysterious," folder 317, LWP), and Robert Tallant carried this idea to fruition in *Voodoo in New Orleans*, 52, 73–74.

58. "St. John's Eve—The Voudous," *New Orleans Daily Picayune*, June 4, 1873; "Fetish Worship," *New Orleans Times*, June 25, 1875; "A Voudou Dance," *New Orleans Times-Democrat*, June 24, 1884.

59. Succession of Eloise (Heloïse) Euchariste Glapion, November 28, 1881, Parish of Orleans Civil District Court, judgment no. 4597, original in NOPL. In this document her son Victor Pierre Crocker and her sister Philomène testified that Heloïse had died in June 1862.

60. "Flagitious Fiction," *New Orleans Daily Picayune*, April 11, 1886; "Voudooism—A Chapter of Old New Orleans History," *New Orleans Daily Picayune*, June 22, 1890; Alice Zeno (b. 1867), interview by Hazel Breaux, n.d., folder 25, LWP; Anita Fonvergne (b. 1860), interview by Hazel Breaux, April 13, 1937, folder 25, LWP; Martha Gray (birth date unknown), interview by Henriette Michinard, n.d., folder 25, LWP.

61. In 1999 the contemporary New Orleans Vodou priestess Sallie Ann Glassman announced that the spirit of Marie Laveau had "entered her own body the evening before during a ceremony on Bayou St. John" (Douglas MacCash, "Midsummer Rite," *New Orleans Times-Picayune*, June 30, 1999). Glassman's book, *Vodou Visions*, is a series of "visions" of the Haitian Vodou deities called *lwa*. Glassman salutes Marie Laveau as a "historical *lwa* of New Orleans; Vodou Queen; strong, intelligent, wise and powerful woman. . . . Hear her drum rhythms pulsing like blood. It is the ongoing passage of the bloodline in the eternal feminine" (52–53).

Sarah Katherine (Kate) Stone

(1841–1907)

The "Agony and Strife" of Civil War Louisiana

MARY FARMER-KAISER

❀ ❀ ❀

Sarah Katherine Stone, affectionately known to her family and friends as Kate, came of age during the Civil War. Twenty years old when the war erupted, the young lady from northeast Louisiana had anticipated a splendid "bellehood," the time in a southern woman's life between finishing her education and marriage filled with visiting, parties, beaux, and courtship. Instead, in winter 1861, her "joyous future" gave way to "woeful changes" in the "agony and strife" of war. War, Confederate defeat, and emancipation turned the young belle's world on its head. "We cannot bear to think of the past, and so dread the future," she confided in her wartime journal. Gone were the wealth, status, and privilege that her place in the planter, slaveholding class once ensured. Indeed, she asked in April 1865 as the Civil War ended, "If the Negroes are freed, we will have no income whatever, and what will we do?" The future was fraught with the unknown.[1]

The war Kate Stone so passionately supported transformed her from a carefree belle to a resilient young woman who, for the first time in her life, worried about her family's safety, fortunes, and future. The war took men, land, slaves, and wealth from the South—and from the Stone family more personally. Although Kate bitterly condemned the physical loss of all that defined her planter-class lifestyle, the young belle worked to preserve her antebellum status and sense of worth in a world turned upside down by war. In so many ways, the Civil War and Confederate defeat led Kate to reshape her identity. To a considerable degree she continued her bellehood during the first year and a half of war by enjoying days of visiting and evenings of "chess, music, singing, gossip, and fruit," but by late 1862 and 1863 that proved increasingly difficult. The war forced

SARAH KATHERINE (KATE) STONE

Date unknown. Courtesy of John Q. Anderson Manuscript Collection,
MSS 2162, Louisiana and Lower Mississippi Valley Collections,
Louisiana State University Libraries, Baton Rouge, La.

more responsibility on the young woman and brought about the loss of family and friends, Yankee occupation, and finally, after a harrowing series of events in spring 1863, refugee life in Texas. Reading, an increasingly rare luxury, and writing in her diary offered Kate an escape from war, an escape that at times seemed the only way she could preserve her antebellum status and identity. Confederate surrender, however, thrust Kate into a struggle to rebuild the shattered southern society that surrounded her and her own place in it. In the years to come, she would be forced to reconstruct white southern womanhood as she understood it. Like other women of her race and class, Kate ultimately embraced an identity that went well beyond the one that emphasized adherence to principles of proper feminine behavior that were taught to southern belles in the antebellum years. Modifying the Victorian ideal that confined women to a private sphere where they were expected to be dutiful wives and devoted mothers, Kate assumed a public role that sought to honor the Confederate cause, reconstruct white southern manhood, and preserve the racial and class hierarchies of the antebellum South.[2]

Born to William Patrick Stone and Amanda Ragan Stone in 1841, Kate enjoyed the life of a planter's daughter in one of Louisiana's well-to-do slaveholding families.[3] Although William Stone died unexpectedly in 1855, the family prospered under the direction of Kate's widowed mother—a woman Kate described admiringly as "a brave resourceful woman."[4] In 1860, Amanda Stone moved the family to Brokenburn Plantation, "a handsome property" of 1,260 acres just a few miles north of Milliken's Bend along the Mississippi River not far from Vicksburg, Mississippi. There, the thirty-seven-year-old mother oversaw a vast plantation, built a sawmill, and amassed a fortune in fertile, flat land, cotton, and slaves. That year, Carroll Parish census takers recorded her worth at $215,000 in real estate and personal assets. Thus, with much productive land, some 150 slaves in a time when prime field hands brought between $800 to $1,200 each, and a cotton crop in 1861 expected to do away with the family's debt as well as leave a surplus, the Stone family anticipated an idyllic, comfortable future. "Life seemed so easy and bright before us," the young belle remembered about the days just before war. "Hereafter," she predicted, "we would have nothing to do but enjoy ourselves."[5]

Kate took great pleasure in the lifestyle and activities of her class. Self-described as thin and tall with "an irregular face, a quantity of brown hair, [and] a shy, quiet manner," she was the eldest daughter of ten children. She graduated from the Nashville Female Academy, a ladies' "finishing school," and continued her education at home by studying French. Kate also read ferociously—during the war she read anything she could get her hands on, ranging from William

Shakespeare to, in her words, "several trashy novels." She especially enjoyed her neighborhood of large plantations where there "was always something going on—formal dining, informal 'spend the days,' evening parties, riding frolics." Kate also enjoyed being the indulged belle of the household. Her mother, with the aid of overseers, her two young brothers, and her sons, carried out the managerial responsibilities of Brokenburn, and slaves attended to the needs of the family, household, and fields. Kate, however, eschewed domestic duties. As her mother prepared the house for a hot Louisiana summer in 1861, for instance, the young lady escaped the "dusty and disagreeable" surroundings by retiring to her room "with a new novel and a plate of candy." But war would require much more of Kate. By 1864, she would declare forthrightly: "I doubt that I was ever intended for a poor girl. Deprivations go hard with me." Certainly, the young belle much preferred the activities of her class prior to war when she eagerly anticipated visits to the city, entertaining guests, and gossiping about beaux, books, and fashion.⁶

Still, "rumors of war" loomed over Kate's serene antebellum life at Brokenburn, and wartime realities soon sobered her "easy and bright" days. In January 1861, Louisiana seceded from the Union and became part of the Confederate States of America from its founding in early February. Two months later, the fighting erupted at Fort Sumter, South Carolina, and men across the South hurried to join the action. William R. Stone, Kate's older brother by fifteen months, was one such man. It was on his departure, along with that of one of her young uncles, that the Confederate belle began recording the momentous events that overwhelmed her life. William "is wild to be off to Virginia," she recounted in her wartime diary, and "so fears that the fighting will be over before he can get there." No one foresaw a war of four long years. Like most, she expected a short engagement in which courageous young soldiers fought gallantly for a noble cause and "glorious victory."⁷

As men left for war and battles materialized in distant places, Kate, like other white southerners, exhibited a passionate—if somewhat naive—confidence in the new nation. God had after all, she believed, given the Confederacy "wise rulers, brave and successful generals, valiant and patriotic men, and a united people." The young belle steadfastly opposed all who questioned the new nation, secession, or war. At least in the abstract, she demanded the most from her countrymen. "How much better to burn our cities," Kate wrote decidedly in May 1862 as the Yankees advanced on nearby Vicksburg, "than let them fall into the enemy's hands." Kate demonstrated a fervent belief that secession and war was in the best interest of all southerners. To the neighbor who thought the "whole affair" was "a grand humbug," Kate responded impatiently: "He cannot appreciate the earnestness and grandness of this great national upheaval, the throes of a Nation's birth." Her unbridled enthusiasm exposed, she proclaimed: "We should make a stand for our rights[;] . . . a nation fighting for its own homes and liberty cannot be overwhelmed." "Our Cause is just and must prevail," Kate concluded.[8]

Kate disliked being left behind, unable to demonstrate fully her own support for the Confederacy. Frustrated, she asked in the days following William's departure, "what can women do but wait and suffer?" Kate wanted to be a part of it, confiding to her journal: "Quietly our days are passing, when the whole planet is in such a state of feverish excitement. . . . Oh! to see and be in it all." "I would eat my heart away," she declared in 1862, "were I a man *at home* [during] these troublous times." At least, Kate asserted, men fighting had "constant excitement to buoy them up and the consciousness of duty done." She had a fierce patriotism of her own, but she pictured herself living in domestic isolation far from the hostilities.[9]

Kate's "weary days of watching and waiting" would soon end, for war—and ultimately defeat—came early to Louisiana. Although not the first region of the Deep South to endure an extended Yankee presence, the delta area surrounding Vicksburg experienced the loss of provisions and finery with the Union blockade of the Mississippi River, Yankee depredations, and the disintegration of slavery long before other parts of the South. While planters in the path of Union general William Tecumseh Sherman's march to the sea faced Yankee destruction and plunder in late 1864, the Louisiana and Mississippi delta encountered it in 1862 and 1863. Indeed, the "busy world outside," once so far away, closed in on the Mississippi River in 1862 and on Brokenburn by early 1863.[10]

Both Union and Confederate forces understood the strategic importance of the Mississippi River and its tributaries. "Whatever nation gets control of the Ohio, Mississippi and Missouri Rivers will control the continent," Sherman once asserted. John Beauchamp Jones, a Confederate war clerk in Richmond, similarly understood, writing: "If they get possession of the Mississippi River, it will be a sad day for the Confederacy." By mid-February 1862, the Union had commenced its offensive down the Mississippi River. That month, Kate wrote: "The general impression is that Nashville and Memphis are doomed, and the Yankee gunboats will then descend the Mississippi." Union victories over the following months bolstered northern efforts to split the Confederacy. The mighty river was open from the north as far as Fort Pillow, Tennessee. The end of April brought the Yankee capture of New Orleans—"the greatest City of the South," according to Kate—and by mid-May the hated enemy occupied the state capital and reigned over the Mississippi River southward from Natchez to the Gulf of Mexico. By July, Confederates retained control over only one major city on the river—Vicksburg. Over the next year, enemy forces struggled to take that river port—a city just across the Mississippi, some thirty miles, from the Stones. "Fair Louisiana with her fertile fields of cane and cotton, her many bayous and dark old forests," Kate wrote, "lies powerless at the feet of the enemy." The "boom of cannon" became a common sound as the "strife and din of war" drew "fearfully near." The Yankees had arrived. "They are polluting the waters of the grand old Mississippi," Kate recorded in June 1862. And the family lived in a state of anxiousness for soon, on June 25, Union troops appeared, and they remained in the area for the next year. Enemy gunboats moving toward Vicksburg seemingly overran the Mississippi River. Many families in the Stones' plantation neighborhood began seeking refuge elsewhere. "Some of the plantations have been deserted by the owners," Kate reported uneasily in July, while others had been "molested" and "burned by the Yankee bands." Christmas night brought Sherman and thirty thousand Union troops to nearby Milliken's Bend. With no Confederate forces in the area, the Yankees confiscated property with no resistance for months to come. Between summer 1862 and spring 1863, the young belle recounted tale after tale of enemy troops "all around us but not on the place" as well as pleas from soldiering brothers who begged the family "to secure a place in the back country and move to it." At least for now, however, the family remained. No longer isolated from the ravages of war, Kate's beloved "fair Louisiana" was the frontline. [11]

As the enemy threatened Louisiana, Confederate women like Kate and her mother answered the call to defend their new nation. Confederate patriotic womanhood clearly assigned a wartime role to the new nation's women. Linked to white southerners' patriotism and sense of nationalism was a call for women to sacrifice for the cause. Perhaps most important, Confederate womanhood called on women to "give up" sons, fathers, and husbands to their country. It was women's duty to urge men to join the fight. The Stone women did just that. As brothers and sons traipsed off to battle, the Stone family recognized their "consciousness of duty" and attached the "future glory for our name" to the soldiers' wartime endeavors. Courage and bravery in battle demonstrated soldiers' worth as well as brought honor and status to their families. Likewise, "shirking stay-at-homes," as Kate called the "coward souls" who refused to volunteer, brought disgrace. By war's end, the young woman had watched four brothers and one uncle head off to war. [12]

The Confederate cause called on its women to sacrifice more than their men. Certainly, the call to sacrifice all things for the Confederacy took its toll on Kate. For even as she thanked God for the opportunity "to show my devotion to my

Country," the belle complained despondently of not having a dress "that will do," bemoaned the absence of ribbons and books, and declared—after a day as "commander-in-chief" of "pickle making" and weaving in 1862—that "keeping house" was "horrid work." Thus as the early days of excitement gave way to wartime scarcities of flour, cloth, coffee, shoes, and more, Kate supplemented fervent patriotic declarations with a reluctance to relinquish all that had been lost. Whatever her contributions to the Confederate cause, the young belle was among the many elite southern white women who, in the face of war, were all too often "better at noble pronouncements than personal hardship." Looking forward to visitors arriving at Brokenburn in early 1862, Kate especially regretted the exacting "war footing"—cornbread, "home-raised meal," milk, butter, and tea—on which the family lived. It seemed odd to be expecting company, she noted, and have "no flour or any 'boughten' delicacy to regale them on." Similarly, Kate complained, "Clothes have become a secondary consideration." Just as store-bought delicacies vanished, so too had elaborate dresses. "No frills . . . for us," she lamented, telling herself that "fashion is an obsolete word." Planter-class women had long relied on fashion to demonstrate their social status, and Kate very much felt this particular "hardship" endured by southern "ladies." Perhaps more serious to Kate, however, was the absence of reading materials. "Not a book or paper in the house," the avid reader grumbled in spring 1863. Unable to obtain delicacies for visitors, silk for dresses, and books to pass away the time, Kate was distraught. She detested sacrificing the things in life that she had long regarded as the essentials of her existence. Living in diminished conditions, her elite, planter-class identity crumbled with every day the war persisted.[13]

The war also called on Confederate women to demonstrate their support for the cause through "domestic patriotism." This role beckoned women to go beyond sacrifice and to broaden their household duties to include supplying soldiers with clothing, bedding, and even tents. When the president of the nearby Natchez sewing society came to visit in summer 1861, Kate was astounded at the quantity of garments the group had made for soldiers after only three months. She also noted somewhat uncomfortably that the "eager, enthusiastic" woman "was horrified" when Kate and her mother acknowledged they "had not taken a stitch in the Cause." Properly reprimanded, the Confederate belle joined the soliciting committee of a sewing society in her community. The Stone women henceforth made gloves, shirts, uniforms, undergarments, socks, comforters, tobacco bags, and canteen covers for southern soldiers. As the war proceeded, the leisure that bellehood had long guaranteed eroded, and Kate kept busy with the "unaccustomed work" of sewing, knitting, and weaving.[14]

Wartime realities also demanded that planter-class women take on more responsibility and assume roles heretofore thought improper. The cause demanded that they cast aside antebellum femininity for assertive action. Even before the enemy approached northeast Louisiana, Amanda Stone took precautions to protect her family and possessions. Just one day after the departure of her eldest son and brother, the widow initiated wartime adjustments. First came growing different crops. Cotton, suddenly, was not as important, or as profitable. "Mamma is having quantities of peas, potatoes, and all things eatable planted, as our only chance for anything from this time until the close of war will be to raise it ourselves," wrote Kate in May 1861. The promise of these "abundant crops" led the Confederate belle to conclude steadfastly that summer: "The North cannot starve us, try as they may." At least at Brokenburn, it seems Kate was correct. For unlike many southern households that rightly feared starvation, the Stones—despite Kate's many complaints about living in reduced circumstances—remained pleasantly supplied into 1863. Beyond fruit and "vegetables of all kinds," the pantry included sugar and molasses, eggs, peanuts, chickens, and game.[15]

As the realities of war neared and the Yankees arrived in Louisiana, the Stones also made adjustments to their labor force. Planters like Amanda Stone rightly feared the loss of slaves as Union troops neared. Both slaves and slave owners understood that their presence opened the way to black liberation. "The Negroes are eager to go leaving wife and children and all for freedom promised them," Kate recorded in summer 1862. Early the next year she would record matter-of-factly: "A great number of Negroes have gone to the Yankees from this section." With the enemy nearing, Amanda Stone thus increasingly worried about her slave property. In summer 1862, she informed her slaves, "If the Yankees c[o]me on the place each Negro must take care of himself and run away and hide." Perhaps somewhat naively, Kate reported: "We think they will." Eventually, however, the widow moved her valuable human chattel. Keeping 30 slaves, including the house servants, at Brokenburn, Amanda Stone sent 120 slaves away, first in January 1863 to Delhi, then in March to the salt works near Winnfield, and finally in May to Lamar County, Texas. Foreseeing the inevitable, she hoped to minimize additional financial losses by moving her property before they could escape to, or be seized by, Union troops. "The place looks deserted now with its empty cabins and neglected fields," Kate reported after the slaves departed, and, she added gravely, "the scene is the same wherever we go."[16]

The war exacted more than cotton and slaves from the Stone family, and with no end to the war in sight, 1862 demanded more adjustment and sacrifice from the family. That year brought the departure of two more Stone men. In March, Coleman, Kate's younger brother who had turned nineteen just that month, headed off for the "glorious fight for fame and honor." A "high spirited, reckless boy," brother "Coley" told his sister that "chains could not hold him at home." In October, Walter, at the time a boy of seventeen who had never been away from home but was "wild to be off," left his mother and sister with tear-filled eyes. Although supportive, Kate closed her diary entry the day Walter departed wearily: "It is late and I am frightened." Before war's end, the cause would draw away yet another brother. In August 1864, James, by then seventeen years old, joined an independent cavalry regiment despite his mother's reservations. With "heavy hearts," the family said goodbye to brother "Jimmy."[17]

By 1864, Amanda Stone had good reason to want to "keep [Jimmy] a while longer." The war had by that time claimed the lives of two of the Stone men— Walter in February 1863 and Coley in September that same year. Although supportive of the call of duty that the Stone brothers answered, the Stone women nonetheless grieved their loss. Thus, like so many others, the family longed for, but also dreaded, news of the war. Kate vented her frustration as the family awaited word from William after the Battle of Seven Days in Virginia in 1862: "[M]y heart leaps to my lips and I turn sick with apprehension whenever I hear a quick step, see a stranger approaching, or note a grave look on the face of any of the boys coming in from a ride." Although William escaped harm, with every military engagement came renewed worries about loved ones lost. But death came not only from battle. Brother Walter died of pneumonia. "He was but a boy and could not stand the hardships of a soldier's life," lamented Kate. "Four months of it killed him," she bemoaned. The death of Coley left the family similarly mournful. Injured when his horse fell and crushed his shoulder and arm, Coley "crossed the Dark Valley" after fever set in. Yet even as the brothers' deaths left the family grief stricken, the Stones recognized they were not unique in their sacrifice. "Not to us alone has God sent trouble and sorrow," Kate wrote in December 1863. With news of death frequent, she testified to a difficult truth: "Nearly every household mourns some loved one lost."[18]

With men away at battle or, worse, lost to the war, Confederate women left on the home front–turned–battlefield assumed ever more responsibility as they sought to preserve family property and position. Increasingly, it was the ever more defiant and bold slaves that planter-class southerners came to fear most. At Brokenburn, the Stone women felt especially vulnerable. Without male protection—Kate's other young uncle succumbed to swamp fever in 1861, and the overseer and her brothers were all away—only the young belle, her mother, an aunt and niece, and sister remained. "We have heard such horrible stories of the outrages of the Yankees and Negroes," Kate wrote in fall 1862. "We are in a helpless situation," Kate acknowledged in spring 1863. "Three ladies and two little girls and not a white man or even a gun on the place, not even a boy until Johnny gets back."[19]

Although unwilling or unable to admit it, Kate was witnessing the very collapse of slavery. By spring 1863, planters in northeast Louisiana had long surrendered hopes of working their fields. In "low spirits," one neighbor complained that his slaves would "not even pretend to work." Other neighbors watched slaves simply leave. "The slave women marched off in their mistresses' dresses," she noted in disbelief. With increasing frequency, Kate recorded confrontation between masters and slaves. "Mrs. Hardison's servants have behaved worse than anyone's," she insisted. Having used "very abusive language," they had "done everything but strike her." Indeed, while visiting the Hardison plantation just days after penning these words, Kate encountered slave resistance firsthand. Trembling in a corner, Kate watched as "three fiendish-looking" black men "with their guns leveled" raided the house and threatened their owners. "I was never so frightened in my life," she remembered. Scenes like this were repeated across the South in the months and years that followed. The foundation of slavery crumbled as slaves claimed freedom for themselves with both bold acts such as these and more subtle steps that owners rendered mere "trouble" with the servants.[20]

Kate came to fear slaves as much as, if not more than, the Yankee enemy. In so many ways, insolent slaves—especially unfamiliar runaways—represented a foe far more frightening and powerful than Yankees. In the family's own quarters, she recorded seeing "strange" slaves who "looked at us and grinned" in such a way that "terrified us more and more" in March 1863. Noting that their looks "held such a promise of evil," Kate's fear was manifest. Insurrection was a terrifying reality that had come home. One particularly startling dispute between two slave women that same month ended in violence when Aunt Laura's cook, Jane, cut "a great gash" in the face of "Aunt Lucy," the Stones' head house servant. When Amanda Stone responded to the incident by calling Jane "to interview her on the subject," the woman whom Kate described as "nearly six feet tall and . . . as black as night . . . with a fearful temper" arrived "with a big carving knife in her hand and fire in her eyes." Perhaps unsurprisingly, Kate reported that her mother "did not say much" to the woman. Later that night Jane departed with her children in tow. Although Kate was "only too thankful to get rid of her," she nonetheless worried Jane might return. "We would not have been surprised to have her slip up and stick any of us in the back," Kate noted anxiously in her journal. The fear that the slave might return was short lived, however. Not long after Jane's departure, Kate reported that she and her children had drowned. "A short space of freedom for them," Kate added unsympathetically. Before long, however, the Confederate belle would be forced to acknowledge just how little control whites had over slaves who, essentially, were free. "It is only because the Negroes do not want to kill us that we are still alive," she admitted in September 1864.[21]

Direct confrontation with Yankees followed on the heels of the standoff with the slaves. Not long after the alarming row with Jane, two "most villainous-looking" Yankees arrived determined to seize Kate's horse, Wonka. For days the horse had been kept in the cane fields to conceal it from nearby troops. Indeed, it had been brought from the mosquito-ridden fields only minutes before the soldiers appeared. Although Kate "begged them not to take the horse" and her mother offered to pay them, it was not enough. In hopes of saving her beloved pet, she "called to one of the Negroes to open the gate, thinking it would give Wonka a chance to escape." When the slave "seemed afraid" to do so, Kate rose to defend her family's honor and property herself. She ran to open the gate. But the incident quickly turned dangerous. One of the men called for her to stop. Kate did not. She threw the gate open only to have the soldier dash up and point a pistol to her head. Kate responded to the soldier's abuse by defiantly opening another gate. With Louisiana succumbing to Union troops all around, it seemed too much for the young Confederate to give up her horse—and all that it stood for—without struggle. However, Kate's efforts proved futile. The soldiers captured Wonka. After crying "the rest of the day and half of the night," the young lady realized how dangerous her actions had been. "This country is in a deplorable state," Kate later wrote, concluding gravely: "The outrages of the Yankees and the Negroes are enough to frighten one to death."[22]

At last, convinced in large part by the horrific events of that month, the Stone family decided in March 1863 that it was time to leave Brokenburn. "The life we are leading now is a miserable, frightened one," Kate confided, "living in constant dread of great danger, not knowing what form it make take, and utterly helpless to protect ourselves." Thus the family hastily prepared to depart on what Kate called "our journey to the unknown." As they did so, and to no one's surprise, the slaves proved exceedingly helpful. "You could see it was only because they knew we would soon be gone," Kate wrote about the slaves during the last days at Brokenburn, insisting: "Two days longer and we think they would all have gone to the Yankees, most probably robbing and insulting us before they left." Only two slaves agreed to join the family on its trek west. "So passes the glory of the family," Kate commented scornfully about the others.[23]

On a moonless night, the family left Brokenburn for what would turn out to be an exile of more than two years. The journey was difficult and took the party of nine—including Kate, her mother, two youngest brothers, sister, an aunt and niece, and two slaves—first by horse to Delhi, then by train to Monroe where they spent seven weeks, and finally by way of a small, slightly improved farm wagon to northeast Texas. In their hurried departure, the Stones lost much. Even before reaching Delhi, the family encountered floodwaters, which forced them to leave behind everything from undergarments to family treasures. Personal belongings lost, they feared losing still more. Beyond the nearly thirty slaves left behind, the family also expected that the house and everything left in it would be lost to renegade Yankees. The house and its possession were indeed lost—one of Kate's younger brothers had gone back to Brokenburn to try to retrieve the slaves who had stayed behind, and he discovered that some of the slaves had joined the Union army and others had taken control of the homestead. "Our house," the young lady wrote in the midst of travel in May 1863, was "stripped of furniture, carpets, books, piano, and everything else, the carriage, buggy, harness, and everything of that kind." Although they regretted going, "nearly everyone," a more mature Kate reminded her mother, had long departed.[24]

It was not the Yankees, as Kate had feared, who ravaged Brokenburn, however. It was the Stones' slaves who assumed control of the plantation and, in so doing, dismantled the household from within and stepped closer to a future of freedom for themselves. With the family's departure, these masterless servants acted to appropriate what years, perhaps even generations, of labor had made possible for others. Webster, the family's dining room servant and coachman—once called by Kate "our most trusted servant"—claimed Brokenburn as "his own." "Aunt Lucy" took her place as "mistress," and capered around in Amanda Stone's clothes while drinking the family's "most fragrant coffee." William claimed Mrs. Stone's room for his family. The Brokenburn left behind was "a place of abundance"—a comfortable homestead, clothes to be "quarreled over," a yard "alive with poultry," a garden "stocked with vegetables," and a bed of strawberries "red with fruit"—and even Kate admitted "it would have been foolish" for slaves to leave. To these slaves, however, remaining was much more than a wise decision. Brokenburn, the lands and other remaining possessions, represented the slaves' past and, at last, provided them a future. Left "to protect" the Stone homestead, the slaves instead "divided up" the family's belongings and claimed Brokenburn as their own.[25]

The Stones had become refugees in their own homeland. In need of "everything," the family found themselves without the possessions and security their planter-class status once ensured. Fortunately they had escaped with a "great bag" of gold carried by Kate around her waist, but they still struggled to make do. They bought secondhand clothes at exorbitant prices and searched for "anything else buyable." And while the family ate a diet of cornbread, fat bacon, and sassafras tea, Kate—refusing these "stern realities of life" and clinging desperately to her antebellum status and identity—rejected that "coarse" and "common" fare and chose instead to "nearly starve," in her overstated words, on bread and milk. The family also relied on others for quarters, which Kate steadfastly protested were "uninviting" at best. To Kate's dismay, the situation did not improve once in Texas. After weeks of hard travel across some 275 miles, the Stones reached Lamar County—"the dark corner of the Confederacy," according to Kate—in July 1863. To say the belle was unimpressed with her new home would be an understatement. "There must be something in the air of Texas fatal to beauty," she wrote upon her arrival. Certainly, that the family was staying "right out on the bare prairie in a rough two-room shanty" with the overseer and his family did not help matters. Kate disliked living "*en famille*" with the overseer, noting derisively in her journal, "their ways are not our ways." The young lady clung desperately to entrenched beliefs that her planter-class status could outlast difficult times.[26]

Once in Tyler, a town Kate found more "civilized" than the Texas prairie, the Stone family spent the next two years in relative safety as refugees. It was an existence that Kate initially disliked immensely. She found the place unfriendly, claiming that they lived as "*renegades*" in a community where locals exhibited a "prejudice" against planter-class refugees. Although dressed in remodeled, homespun, and even secondhand clothing herself, Kate often resorted to fashion to distinguish her own social status from that of lower-class locals. "Hoops"—"the awkward, ungraceful cages" that she and her mother had long abandoned—she remarked, "are just coming in with full fashion [in Tyler]." "Nothing looks funnier than a woman walking around with an immense hoop—barefooted," she scoffed. Wartime realities and Confederate womanhood may have dictated that the belle forgo hair ribbons, pretty bonnets, lace stockings, French slippers, and silk dresses, but Kate's disparaging accounts of what Texas women were and were not wearing made clear her unwillingness to abandon prewar notions of the southern feminine ideal or antebellum understandings of class.[27]

Kate longed for the contentment and commotion of Brokenburn. She missed the leisure, the entertaining, the finery, and the security of her antebellum life and planter-class status. She especially hated that her family continued to struggle to obtain better accommodations, better food, and better clothes. Kate persisted in complaining about disagreeable quarters and lamented having "so little to eat." Despite the cushion provided by the gold she had managed to escape Brokenburn with and the family's income from renting slaves, the Stones found that there was only so much that could be bought. Able to obtain only flour, sugar syrup, and "rusty, rancid bacon," Kate recognized the absurdity of having "two fine cooks and two dining-room servants" with "such fare." The young lady also continued to be disappointed that beautiful, reasonably priced dresses and shoes were nowhere to be found. "Everything is so enormously high," she reported after her mother returned from Shreveport with "five or six dresses" that had cost nearly one thousand dollars. Generally trying to combat "ennui," she filled her days in Texas with reading—although books were a scarce luxury—remodeling dresses and bonnets, writing in her journal, visiting other refugees, and longing for "pleasure jaunts" to Louisiana. Unhappiness over unremitting hardship—that is, to her, having servants but less than desirable food for them to serve and paying exorbitant prices for new dresses—had seemingly come to replace the more immediate fear of the enemy.[28]

Although deprivations persisted, after almost a year in Tyler, Kate finally confessed that they were "having the most enjoyable life" in exile. The Stones had reestablished, albeit temporarily, some of the social status they had lost with the war's onslaught. Life was busy again. Recording days of "riding, sewing, singing, receiving visitors, and playing," the young belle took pleasure in the bustling refugee community and found acceptance with local residents. In a new home, the Stones entertained frequently. They also headed efforts to raise money for a soldiers' home. Reclaiming prewar notions of leisure time and entertaining as well as exercising the benevolence expected of planter-class families, Kate—like "the nobility of France in the days of the French Revolution"—henceforth committed herself to "thrusting all the cares and tragedies of life aside and drinking deep of life's joys while it lasted."[29]

Mounting news of Confederate defeat tested Kate's efforts to "live only in the present" and her hope that her planter-class status could survive the war. Vicksburg had fallen. Word arrived that William had been wounded at Gettysburg, and that Confederate general Robert E. Lee had failed in the Pennsylvania countryside. Soon Atlanta and then Savannah fell. It was all becoming too much. "All our coast cities have passed out of our hands," she reported in spring 1865. Indeed, Richmond was threatened. "God spare us from this crushing blow," she cried passionately, "and save our dying country!" Just days later, Kate reported that "all" spoke of surrender. "I cannot bear to hear them talk of defeat," the young Confederate exclaimed. Unlike her fellow countrymen who sought peace even if it meant conquest, Kate longed for a Confederate rally. Defeat, rather than another stand, descended on the South. "*Conquered, Sub-*

mission, Subjugation are words that burn into my heart," Kate lamented upon receiving news of the Confederacy's demise.[30]

The Stones had sacrificed dearly for the Confederate cause. They had given their men, two of whom had forfeited their lives to the now lost cause. Forced to flee their home, they had lost crops, slaves, clothing, furniture, and other possessions. "The degradation seems more than we can bear," Kate proclaimed resentfully in May 1865. "Our glorious struggle of the last four years, our hardships, our sacrifices, and worst of all, the torrents of noble blood that have been shed for our loved Country—all in vain," she grieved. Like so many others, Kate struggled to reconcile the deaths of her brothers with defeat. Engulfed by hopelessness, the refugees decided it was time to make the "sad journey to the old scenes."[31]

Although it no longer "seemed the same place," Brokenburn again became home to the Stones in November 1865. The place, Kate reported, was "in better repair than most," but remained saturated with memories of those now gone. "But if the loved ones who passed through its doors could be with us again," she yearned longingly, "we might be happy yet." A more mature Kate knew better. "We must bear our losses as best we can," the hardened twenty-six-year-old told herself. "Nothing is left but to endure." Despondent and exhausted, Kate refused invitations to see old friends and new neighbors. "I felt like I did not want to see anybody or ever dance again," she later remembered. Grieving her lost bellehood, she added, "I felt fully forty years old." For the next three years, Kate, her mother, three remaining brothers, younger sister, and uncle tried to restore the once lucrative plantation.[32]

For Kate Stone and other women of the planter class, Confederate defeat and emancipation destroyed more than their economic position. Union victory and Reconstruction for these women meant finding a new place for themselves and their families. No longer a carefree belle of the planter class, Kate spent the years after the war assuming ever more responsibility and continuing to worry about her family's fortunes and future. She also struggled to reconcile her antebellum expectations of white southern womanhood with the destruction of southern society as she knew it. The war and the immediate postwar years demonstrated her resilient wherewithal as well as her embrace of the increasingly flexible public identity available to elite southern white women.

Hardship continued to plague the Stones. After their return to Brokenburn, everything seemed to be "going to rack and ruin," and Kate worried much about the family's financial outlook. During these years of "long silence"—Kate abandoned her journal between the autumns of 1865 and 1867—the young woman endeavored with her family to raise a crop while also fighting "hired labor, high water, and cotton worms."[33] With levees gone, yet another casualty of the war, the family battled flooding with every rise of the Mississippi River. More difficult than overflow, pests, and crop failure was the struggle to accept the new position of former slaves and the now costly labor system. For almost the next decade, and much to the alarm of white families like the Stones, elected officials in the area were overwhelmingly black or else "carpetbagger" Republicans. Moreover, although some freedpersons in the area continued working for former masters, that was not the case at Brokenburn. Only a few of the slaves left behind in 1863 remained, and Kate did not expect those brought back from Texas to stay long.[34] And though Kate happily reported that the family had "generally managed" to keep a cook—as "that" was "new and disagreeable work to us all"—the "old hands" were gone and the Stones turned to distant places like New Orleans for workers. Even more troublesome was that former slaves demanded wages—and, according to Kate, "high wages" at that.[35] The Stones' future seemed bleak. "We made about twenty bales of cotton," Kate reported of the family's 1867 cotton crop, "and spent $25,000 doing it." "We are worse off," the young woman cried more than two years after war's end, "than even in Texas." By the next year, much to Kate's dismay, her three brothers were working the fields themselves, and continued flooding and crop failure led to the family's loss of Brokenburn.[36]

Living in the Reconstruction-era South, Kate worried incessantly about the changing status of her ex-Confederate family and exhibited special distress about the fate of the Stone men. Planter-class men had indeed endured multiple losses—military, political, and economic—with Union victory, and ex-Confederate women like Kate were to play a critical role in, as historian LeeAnn Whites maintains, the "reconstruction" rather than "further deconstruction" of their manhood. William, Kate apprehensively recorded, continued to try his hand at farming in both Louisiana and Mississippi despite setback after setback; Jimmy refused to return to study medicine; and, more alarming, Johnny had been "sent away" after fighting and "near killing" a freedman. She fretted too over her brothers' marriage prospects, lamenting that if they "only had money" the girls who had once been "great belles in the neighborhood" would have long been members of the family.[37]

Reclaiming white southern womanhood for herself was an additional concern for Kate. Despite having once insisted that marriage was "a dreadful risk for any woman," she nonetheless remained attentive to potential suitors and expressed the desire to marry well. In 1869, Kate married Henry Bry Holmes, a young Confederate lieutenant she had met in Tyler, Texas. In the years to come, she supported his efforts to reestablish himself as a planter and, once southern white Democrats reclaimed control from Republican hands by the 1880s, as the Madison Parish clerk of court and, later, as sheriff. Kate also became a mother, giving birth to four children, two of whom would live to adulthood.

Beyond the Victorian roles of dutiful wife and devoted mother, Kate also came to embrace a new civic role for herself. In particular, Kate played a prominent role in her community's efforts to "restore" the South in a way that rehabilitated, and indeed vindicated, the Confederacy and the race and class hierarchies it embodied. Kate participated in these efforts most noticeably by founding the Madison Infantry Chapter of the United Daughters of the Confederacy and remaining an active member of the organization until her death in 1907. Demonstrating her unremitting commitment to the Confederacy and desire to commemorate its dead, she worked in particular for the erection of a Confederate monument that still stands in Tallulah's courthouse square.[38] Almost fifty years after her death, upon the publication of her wartime journal, Kate would be honored as "a leader in the civil, social, cultural, and religious life" of the city. With widespread coverage and great fanfare, Tallulah celebrated "Kate Stone Day" on March 17, 1955. Ceremonies on the courthouse steps, an open house at the local book club, and an extravagant parade of colorful floats and hundreds of costumed men, women, and children reenacting the years before, during, and after the Civil War officially commemorated her efforts to honor the Confederacy, its cause, and its men.[39]

Working to reclaim a southern white womanhood for herself that emphasized antebellum notions of domesticity and femininity, Kate Stone had demonstrated a new kind of southern womanhood. Kate had consented, albeit at times reluctantly, to the expanded responsibilities and expectations thrust on her by war and Confederate defeat in a way that blended the old with the new. Even in the face of wartime shortages, reduced income, Yankee occupation, and rebellious slaves, she endeavored to preserve her antebellum sense of self. In exile, she worked to reestablish, at least temporarily, some of the family's antebellum social status even as the Stones lived in diminished circumstances. Meeting head-on the postwar hardships of crop failure, overflow, dramatically increased labor costs, exhausted financial resources, and the need to help the Stone men reconstruct their own diminished manhood, Kate—now a more mature, resilient southern woman much like the plantation mistresses of old—assumed greater responsibilities and worries. Finally, as white southerners worked to rebuild a New South in the image of the antebellum South, she accepted a public presence as a way to defend the Confederate cause she had so fervently championed. Like other women of the former slaveholding class, Kate Stone not only changed what it meant to be a southern lady but did so in a way that upheld the ideals of white southern manhood and womanhood in the process.[40]

NOTES

The author would like to thank Giselle Roberts, the editors, and the press's readers for their careful reading of this essay and insightful critiques.

1. Kate Stone, *Brokenburn: The Journal of Kate Stone, 1861–1868*, ed. John Q. Anderson (Baton Rouge: Louisiana State University Press, 1995), 11, 12, 293, 335; Drew Gilpin Faust, "Introduction: Writing the War," in Stone, *Brokenburn*, xxx.

2. Stone, *Brokenburn*, 136. Anya Jabour's *Scarlett's Sisters: Young Women in the Old South* (Chapel Hill: University of North Carolina Press, 2007), Giselle Roberts's *The Confederate Belle* (Columbia: University of Missouri Press, 2003), and Victoria Ott's "When the Flower Blooms in Winter: Young Women Coming of Age in the Confederacy" (PhD diss., University of Tennessee, 2003) offer the best descriptions of how young, elite, southern white women responded to and were transformed by the Civil War. For other treatments of the Civil War as a watershed event for southern women, see Jane Turner Censer, *The Reconstruction of White Southern Womanhood, 1865–1895* (Baton Rouge: Louisiana State University Press, 2003); Laura F. Edwards, *Scarlett Doesn't Live Here Anymore: Southern Women in the Civil War Era* (Urbana: University of Illinois Press, 2000); George C. Rable, *Civil Wars: Women and the Crisis of Southern Nationalism* (Urbana: University of Illinois Press, 1989); Anne Firor Scott, *The Southern Lady: From Pedestal to Politics, 1830–1930* (Chicago: University of Chicago Press, 1970).

3. Drew Gilpin Faust notes in her introduction to the 1995 edition of *Brokenburn* that the family's slave ownership placed Amanda Stone "among the most elite slaveholders in 1860" (xxxii). Although certainly true, among their neighbors in Louisiana's Madison and Carroll Parishes, the Stones were not the most elite planters. Rather, according to 1860 census data (see note 4), they were typical among slaveholders in the state's Mississippi River cotton parishes where the "average slaveholding on large plantations was about 100" (Joseph Karl Menn, *The Large Slaveholders of Louisiana—1860* [New Orleans: Pelican, 1998], 33).

4. Stone, *Brokenburn*, 70. The 1850 census slave schedule reports that the Stone family owned only 21 slaves. Over the next decade, that number increased to at least 77, as recorded in the 1860 census slave schedule, and, according to Kate, to 150 slaves in 1861 ("Schedule 2: Slave Inhabitants in the Western District in the Parish of Madison . . . Louisiana," August 22, 1850, 1850 federal census; "Schedule 2: Slave Inhabitants in . . . the Parish of Carroll . . . Louisiana," July 11, 1860, 1860 federal census; Stone, *Brokenburn*, xvii).

5. Stone, *Brokenburn*, 3, 11, 12; Faust, "Writing the War," xxxi–xxxii, John Q. Anderson, introduction, xvi–xvii, in Stone, *Brokenburn*; "Family," folder 17, box 3, John Q. Anderson Papers, 1954–73, mss. no. 2162, Louisiana and Lower Mississippi Valley Collections, Louisiana State University Libraries, Baton Rouge (hereinafter cited as Anderson Papers); "Schedule 1: Free Inhabitants in Ward No. 1 in the Parish of Carroll . . . Louisiana," July 11, 1860, 1860 federal census; Helen Spann Murphy, "Life Story of 'Kate' As Told by Mrs. Murphy," *Tallulah (La.) Madison Journal*, March 11, 1955.

6. Stone, *Brokenburn*, 35, 280, 4, 136, 13, 285; Murphy, "Life Story of 'Kate.'" Three Stone children died before the war. On education, see Christie Ann Farnham, *The Education of the Southern Belle: Higher Education and Student Socialization in the Antebellum South* (New York: New York

University Press, 1994), and Jabour, *Scarlett's Sisters*, 49–82. On the changing role of the belle in planter-class households, see Jabour, *Scarlett's Sisters*, 263–70, and Roberts, *Confederate Belle*, 54–75, 172–76. On the wartime role of plantation mistresses, see Edwards, *Scarlett*, 77–79, Drew Gilpin Faust, "Trying To Do a Man's Business: Slavery, Violence, and Gender in the American Civil War," *Gender and History* 4 (Summer 1992): 197–214, Rable, *Civil Wars*, 112–21, and Scott, *The Southern Lady*, 81–102.

7. Stone, *Brokenburn*, 12, 13, 39. On secession and war in Louisiana, see *The Louisiana Purchase Bicentennial Series in Louisiana History*, vol. 5, *The Civil War in Louisiana, Part A: Military Activity*, ed. Arthur W. Bergeron Jr. (Lafayette, La.: Center for Louisiana Studies, 2002).

8. Stone, *Brokenburn*, 79, 101, 27, 19; Edwards, *Scarlett*, 66–67, 71–74; Jabour, *Scarlett's Sisters*, 249–56; Roberts, *Confederate Belle*, 35–53. Early works examining southern white women and the war underscored their unqualified support for the Confederacy; see Mary Elizabeth Massey, *Women in the Civil War* (1966; rpt., Lincoln: University of Nebraska Press, 1994). More recent studies question their unconditional loyalty to the Confederacy and support for the war; see Joan E. Cashin, *Our Common Affairs: Texts from Women in the Old South* (Baltimore: Johns Hopkins University Press, 1996), 22–26, Drew Gilpin Faust, "Altars of Sacrifice: Confederate Women and Narratives of War," *Journal of American History* 76 (March 1990): 1200–1228, Drew Gilpin Faust, *Mothers of Invention: Women of the Slaveholding South in the American Civil War* (Chapel Hill: University of North Carolina Press, 1996), and LeeAnn Whites, *The Civil War as a Crisis in Gender: Augusta, Georgia, 1860–1890* (Athens: University of Georgia Press, 1995).

9. Stone, *Brokenburn*, 24, 87, 17, 92. Faust, "Altars," 1206–7; Jabour, *Scarlett's Sisters*, 255–63; Roberts, *Confederate Belle*, 41–53, 134.

10. Stone, *Brokenburn*, 17, 87. Bergeron, *Civil War in Louisiana*.

11. General Sherman quoted in Roberts, *Confederate Belle*, 110; John Beauchamp Jones quoted in *Voices of the Civil War*, ed. Richard Wheeler (New York: Thomas Y. Crowell, 1976), 56; Stone, *Brokenburn*, 91, 100, 138, 122, 128, 169, 154; Wheeler, *Voices*, 223, 328–29, 471–72. On the Yankee arrival at Milliken's Bend, see Wheeler, *Voices*, 165, and John Q. Anderson, "Review of *Brokenburn: The Journal of Kate Stone*," 7–9, unpublished paper delivered at the Texas State Historical Society, [April 30, 1955], folder 12, box 2, Anderson Papers.

12. Stone, *Brokenburn*, 109, 138, 121, 103. On the Confederate ideology of sacrifice and patriotic womanhood, see Faust, "Altars," Roberts, *Confederate Belle*, 5, 42–47, 76–87, and Catherine Clinton, *Tara Revisited: Women, War, and the Plantation Legend* (New York: Abbeville Press, 1995), 58–59.

13. Stone, *Brokenburn*, 110, 161, 109, 86, 109, 155, 193; Edwards, *Scarlett*, 67. On planter-class women and shortages, see Merton E. Coulter, *The Confederate States of America, 1861–65* (Baton Rouge: Louisiana State University Press, 1950), 219–39, Edwards, *Scarlett*, 74–76, Rable, *Civil Wars*, 91–111, Roark, *Masters Without Slaves: Southern Planters in the Civil War and Reconstruction* (New York: Norton, 1977), 48–54, and Roberts, *Confederate Belle*, 58–61. On wartime fashion, see Edwards, *Scarlett*, 75–76, Faust, *Mothers*, 221–26, Rable, *Civil Wars*, 92–96, and Roberts, *Confederate Belle*, 79–84.

14. Stone, *Brokenburn*, 39, 146. On domestic patriotism, see Roberts, *Confederate Belle*, 47–53. On women's contributions to Confederate soldiers, see Rable, *Civil Wars*, 139–44, Faust, *Mothers*, 24, 46–48, and Massey, *Women in the Civil War*, 147.

15. Stone, *Brokenburn*, 18, 31, 109. Roberts, *Confederate Belle*, 125–47; Edwards, *Scarlett*, 74–75. On agricultural adjustment, see Roark, *Masters Without Slaves*, 39–41, and Roberts, *Confederate Belle*, 55–56.

16. Stone, *Brokenburn*, 128, 173, 125, 169, 172. On slaves' escape to Union lines, see Edwards,

Scarlett, 77, 103–4, Litwack, *Been in the Storm So Long: The Aftermath of Slavery* (New York: Knopf, 1979), 30–36, and Stephen V. Ash, *When the Yankees Came: Conflict and Chaos in the Occupied South, 1861–1865* (Chapel Hill: University of North Carolina Press, 1995), 160–69.

17. Stone, *Brokenburn*, 139, 94, 140, 282.

18. Ibid., 282, 262, 133, 187, 259–64, 164–65.

19. Ibid., 137, 175, 191; Roberts, *Confederate Belle*, 161–64; Edwards, *Scarlett*, 78–79.

20. Stone, *Brokenburn*, 175, 185, 195–97. In 1935, W. E. B. Du Bois first argued that the demise of slavery came well before war's end and illustrated the pivotal role slaves played in bringing about emancipation (*Black Reconstruction* [New York: Free Press, 1998], 55–127). See also Ira Berlin et al., *The Destruction of Slavery*, series 1, *Freedom: A Documentary History of Emancipation, 1861–1867* (New York: Cambridge University Press, 1985), 1:1–56, Edwards, *Scarlett*, 78–79, 104–6, 112–15, Litwack, *Been in the Storm*, 104–66, and Roark, *Masters Without Slaves*, 68–108.

21. Stone, *Brokenburn*, 197, 170–73, 180, 298; Litwack, *Been in the Storm*, 27–30, 59–63; Roberts, *Confederate Belle*, 161–64.

22. Stone, *Brokenburn*, 182–84, 166.

23. Ibid., 185, 188, 198, 203.

24. Ibid., 203. For the family's escape, see 197–203.

25. Ibid., 193, 209, 210. Even Kate admitted the slaves seemed to "think it is all to help them" (37). On slave expectations and seizure of masters' possessions, see Litwack, *Been in the Storm*, 17–27, 113, 145, and Edwards, *Scarlett*, 113–14.

26. Stone, *Brokenburn*, 202, 200, 193, 211, 237, 223–25. On Confederate refugees, see Joan E. Cashin, "Into the Trackless Wilderness: The Refugee Experience in the Civil War," in *A Woman's War: Southern Women, Civil War, and the Confederate Legacy*, ed. Edward D. C. Campbell Jr. and Kym S. Rice (Richmond, Va.: Museum of the Confederacy; Charlottesville: University Press of Virginia, 1996), 29–53, Jabour, *Scarlett's Sisters*, 263–64, Roberts, *Confederate Belle*, 70–75, and Mary Elizabeth Massey, *Refugee Life in the Confederacy* (Baton Rouge: Louisiana State University Press, 1964).

27. Stone, *Brokenburn*, 238, 225, 223, 225. On the class dimensions of refugee life, see 226, 232, 234, 237–38, 249, 275. On clothing and planter-class women, see Roberts, *Confederate Belle*, 83–84, Edwards, *Scarlett*, 76, Faust, *Mothers*, 221–26, and Elizabeth Fox-Genovese, *Within the Plantation Household: Black and White Women of the Old South* (Chapel Hill: University of North Carolina Press, 1988), 212–16, 223–24.

28. Stone, *Brokenburn*, 258, 267, 193, 290.

29. Ibid., 321, 295, 293.

30. Ibid., 293, 330–31, 333, 334, 339; John D. Winters, *The Civil War in Louisiana* (Baton Rouge: Louisiana State University Press, 1963), 186–205.

31. Stone, *Brokenburn*, 340, 364.

32. Ibid., 364, 369.

33. Ibid., 372, 368.

34. Those slaves who had "taken over" in 1863 were not among the slaves mentioned by Kate after her return to Brokenburn. See Stone, *Brokenburn*, 362–66. On former slaves' use of mobility to assert freedom, see Litwack, *Been in the Storm*, 292–335, and Peter J. Kolchin, *First Freedom: The Responses of Alabama's Blacks to Emancipation and Reconstruction* (Westport, Conn.: Greenwood Press, 1972), 3–23. On the struggle of African Americans to assert freedom and the ways in which others restricted it, see Eric Foner, *Reconstruction: America's Unfinished Revolution, 1863–1877* (New York: Harper and Row, 1988), 77–123. On Reconstruction in Louisiana, see C. Peter Ripley, *Slaves*

and Freedmen in Civil War Louisiana (Baton Rouge: Louisiana State University Press, 1976), Joe Gray Taylor, *Louisiana Reconstructed, 1863–1877* (Baton Rouge: Louisiana State University Press, 1974), and John C. Rodrigue, *Reconstruction in the Cane Fields: From Slavery to Free Labor in Louisiana's Sugar Parishes, 1862–1880* (Baton Rouge: Louisiana State University Press, 2001).

35. Stone, *Brokenburn*, 373, 368. On planter-class women and postwar housework, see Censer, *Reconstruction of White Southern Womanhood*, 51–90, and Edwards, *Scarlett*, 171–77. Kate reported that freedmen expected twenty to twenty-five dollars plus rations of food (*Brokenburn*, 368). See also Litwack, *Been in the Storm*, 308–9, 411–12, 438–39.

36. Stone, *Brokenburn*, 369; Murphy, "Life Story of 'Kate.'"

37. LeeAnn Whites, *Gender Matters: Civil War, Reconstruction, and the Making of the New South* (New York: Palgrave Macmillan, 2005), 86; Stone, *Brokenburn*, 368, 371; Laura F. Edwards, *Gendered Strife and Confusion: The Political Culture of Reconstruction* (Urbana: University of Illinois Press, 1997); Faust, *Mothers*.

38. Stone, *Brokenburn*, 367; Anderson, introduction, xvii–xxviii; Edwards, *Scarlett*, 179, 181–82; Murphy, "Life Story of 'Kate'"; Censer, *Reconstruction of White Southern Womanhood*, 153–206; Jabour, *Scarlett's Sisters*, 281–83. On elite southern white women's efforts to support southern white manhood and "rehabilitate" southern patriarchy see Whites, *Civil War as a Crisis in Gender*, 160–208, Whites, *Gender Matters*, 85–111, LeeAnn Whites, "'Stand By Your Man': The Ladies Memorial Association and the Reconstruction of Southern White Manhood," in *Women of the American South: A Multicultural Reader*, ed. Christie Anne Farnham (New York: New York University Press, 1997), 133–49, Karen L. Cox, *Dixie's Daughters: The United Daughters of the Confederacy and the Preservation of Confederate Culture* (Gainesville: University of Florida Press, 2003), and Faust, *Mothers*, 247–57.

39. Anderson, introduction, xxviii. For coverage of "Kate Stone Day," see *Tallulah (La.) Madison Journal*, February 4, 10, 20, and 25, 1955, and March 5, 17, 25, 1955, *Vicksburg (Miss.) Evening Post*, March 8, 13, 16, 18, 1955, and *Vicksburg (Miss.) Herald*, March 18, 1955.

40. Censer, *Reconstruction of White Southern Womanhood*; Edwards, *Gendered Strife*; Jabour, *Scarlett's Sisters*, 281–83; Whites, *Civil War as a Crisis in Gender*.

Eliza Jane Nicholson

(1843–1896)

New Orleans Publisher

PATRICIA BRADY

❀ ❀ ❀

Eliza Jane Nicholson was the first woman newspaper publisher in the South, running the *New Orleans Picayune* for twenty years. In that capacity (unique then, still rare today), she became a promoter of reform and change in the city of New Orleans, across the state of Louisiana, and throughout the South. Inheriting a staid provincial paper—dense with received political opinion, shipping news, crime reports, and out-of-date international intelligence, she created a new kind of newspaper—lively, dynamic, and well written, with feature stories, literature and book reviews, signed columns, a woman's page, and illustrations. She was committed, moreover, to employing women journalists at the paper and to promoting their careers. Readers eagerly looked for their bylines, and a few of these pioneering women became national celebrities.

Forsaking a nearly forty-year history during which the paper's turgid pages could easily have been stamped "for men only," the new *Picayune* appealed to a wide audience, especially the dramatically growing numbers of educated women readers and their families. Nicholson's innovations caught rival New Orleans papers flat footed, as the *Picayune*'s sales took off. If imitation is truly the sincerest form of flattery, she should have been complimented indeed as the other dailies rushed to copy her style—expanding coverage, establishing literary departments, and hiring women reporters. Nicholson revolutionized the newspaper business in New Orleans during the two decades of her career.

Beginning at a young age, Eliza Nicholson displayed an interest in learning and soon a willingness to defy convention by seeking a career away from home. She had the strength of character to marry the man she chose despite family objections and later to set for herself the unprecedented goal (for a woman) to manage successfully a major newspaper in one of America's most important cities. When she married a second time, she took care to enter into a prenuptial contract to preserve her control over the business and property she had inherited from her first husband. Having enjoyed the support of an older woman writer when she first arrived in New Orleans, she later mentored several younger women writers and reporters. She was a talented, ambitious, determined woman who utilized those characteristics to succeed beyond all expectations in her chosen career, and she did this in a culture where and era when women of her class were expected to confine their talent and ambition to the family realm.

❀ ❀ ❀

Born near Pearlington in southern Hancock County, Mississippi, on March 11, 1843, Eliza Jane Poitevent was the third of eight children of Mary Amelia Russ and William Poitevent. Her father was a very successful timberman and saw-mill owner with a small fleet of ships delivering lumber to customers through-out the southern United States and Latin America. Because of her mother's ill health, sometime in the 1850s Eliza was sent to live with Mary Amelia's younger sister on a large farm a few miles away from the Poitevent home. Jane Potter Russ Kimball was a childless, vital woman in her twenties who was devoted to her nieces. Her husband, Leonard Kimball, one of Hancock County's earliest settlers, was a wealthy lumberman and longtime friend of William Poitevent. The Kimballs informally adopted Eliza, and she used the surname Kimball dur-ing her childhood and adolescence.[1]

Adoptions by family members were commonplace in eighteenth- and nineteenth-century America; both Martha and George Washington and Rachel and Andrew Jackson adopted the children of family members.[2] As in these more famous cases, Eliza remained close to her parents, brothers, and sisters, but her aunt Janie and uncle Leonard brought her up.

Her adoption was crucial to Eliza's future as a writer. Hundreds of acres of pine woods on Hobolochitto Creek, a tributary of the Pearl River, gave her the space to wander in the forest and along river banks, musing and dreaming. As the Kimballs' only child, she grew up a solitary, introspective girl with a fervent love of nature and the outdoors, of animals, of poetry and literature. Her aunt taught her at home, and Eliza read widely in the family library. She began writ-ing early and perhaps began to dream then of publishing her poetry.

PEARL RIVERS
(ELIZA JANE POITEVENT HOLBROOK NICHOLSON)

1890s. Courtesy of the Historic New Orleans Collection,
Museum/Research Center, acc. no. 81-93-L (2) MSS 219, f. 447.

Unlike an earlier generation of southern women, however, she enjoyed the opportunity of higher education. She attended the Amite Female Seminary in Liberty, Mississippi, as a boarding student. Incorporated by a Baptist minister in 1855, the seminary was one of a new wave of schools for girls in the Deep South. A combination of high school and finishing school, such seminaries and academies had long been common in the East but had come late to Mississippi. Although Eliza made many friends, she later scoffed at the level of education there, being sent, she said, "to learn—I must say nothing that has been of much use to me as a woman."[3]

After graduation in 1859, Eliza returned to the Kimballs, where she remained until after the Civil War. For intelligent, talented elite women, the antebellum years had offered almost no socially acceptable employment opportunities. At war's end, things changed. The depressed economy, plantation failures, a drastic decrease in the number of marriageable men, and their own sense of pride and independence stemming from wartime experiences led many women to seek work. Still, violating taboos that had a long history carried a stigma. Teaching and writing were the only occupations that were considered proper for ladies, and staying at home was still the ideal of southern womanhood.[4]

With the lumber business flourishing, however, Eliza's family continued to prosper after the war. Poverty didn't force her to seek work, and the Kimballs provided a loving home. Several local men courted the attractive young lady, but she didn't find anyone to suit her taste. By the late 1860s, then in her mid-twenties, Eliza found country life as a literary spinster unsatisfying. Despite the vehement opposition of her parents, both adoptive and natal, she decided to pursue a career as a writer—and "to be paid for it!" Her talent and ambition would no longer allow her to remain an ornamental member of rural Mississippi society, writing verse as a hobby. In 1867, she sent poems to John Overall, editor of *The South*. His encouragement and suggestions for stylistic improvements emboldened her to begin submitting poems for publication elsewhere.[5]

Like many women writers, she adopted a pseudonym—"Pearl Rivers," reflecting warm affection for her Mississippi homeland. Her poetry too reflected this devotion to "that happiest of places, the home of my childhood." On March 22, 1868, her first published poem appeared in the *Picayune*, called "A Chirp from Mother Robin," and she became a regular contributor. Her essay, "A Week with Pearl Rivers," described life in Mississippi. Other poems were published by the *New York Home Journal* and the *New Orleans Times*.[6]

To her family's further horror, she soon decided to leave home for the metropolis of the Gulf South—New Orleans. There she would attempt to become a professional writer. She did at least agree to live with her maternal grandfather,

Samuel Potter Russ, on Clio Street in the American sector, instead of staying in one of the downtown boarding houses that were the lot of most beginning journalists.

To a sheltered country girl, New Orleans had everything—sophisticated residents, endless parties and social events, balls, theaters, circuses, an opera house, ballet, book stores, coffee houses, grand hotels, and elegant restaurants. Of course, to rural Mississippian parents like the Poitevents and Kimballs, the city had everything they dreaded—a large influential black population (including officeholders and policemen), radical politicians, a Reconstruction government, crime, and endless temptations. Eliza's grandfather, who had moved to the city before the war, introduced her to many of the important personages of New Orleans. Among them was Colonel Alva Morris Holbrook, the proprietor of the *Picayune*, who had accepted her poems for publication.[7]

In 1870, Holbrook hired her as the paper's literary editor—at twenty-five dollars a week. As a poet, Eliza had written in the privacy of her home, protected from the hustle and bustle of commercial life. Now she was venturing into strange territory. Nineteenth-century newspapers were purely masculine preserves infused with an air of clubby, unbuttoned bonhomie and manned by hard-drinking, cigar-smoking reporters. It took real nerve for a young single woman to join an editorial office where the highest compliment she might expect was to be considered "one of the boys."

As the journalist Catherine Cole later wrote, "The prejudice against working women was extreme." Poetry was one thing, journalism another. As the first woman in the city to work for a newspaper, Eliza endured gossip and criticism so stinging that, in Cole's view, "she was to no small degree a martyr."[8]

She must have been a startling sight to the men of the *Picayune*. At twenty-seven, she was a very small woman; taking after her "little mama," she was barely five feet tall with tiny childlike hands. Her large gray eyes, curly Titian red hair, and turned-up nose (which she referred to as her "pug nose") were complemented by a captivating smile, a birdlike tilt to her head, and a charm of manner that attracted both men and women until her death. Completely without editorial experience, she adjusted slowly to her new position; her own poetry became a feature of each Sunday's edition.[9]

Owing to limited leisure time and her socially suspect position as a paid employee, female friends were hard to come by. A devoted exception was the poet Mary Ashley Townsend. Eleven years Eliza's senior, she was a native New Yorker who had moved to New Orleans with her husband in 1860. Mary was well established socially but nevertheless submitted poetry for payment to the *Picayune* and other papers, generally under the pseudonym "Xariffa." The new literary editor very much admired Xariffa and regularly featured her poems. They became fast friends as the leading literary women of the city.[10]

Redefining her life when she came to New Orleans, Eliza Jane Poitevent assumed a new persona as "Pearl Rivers," even going so far as to have personal stationery printed with an entwined P and R. Although her family members continued to call her Eliza or Liza Jane, for the rest of her life her close friends and intimates called her Pearl. She also took a step very common among nineteenth-century women. She dropped a few years off her age, a deception aided in her case by her small size and youthful appearance.

According to their biographies, most lady writers began writing as children, published in their teens, and became successful by their early twenties—or at least that became the official story after they altered their birth dates. Pearl dropped six years from her age, telling everyone that she was born in 1849. Shortly after her arrival at the *Picayune*, the paper reported that she was "a maiden of hardly adult years." The incorrect date appears in every reference work and article on her career; only family genealogical files and school records reveal her true age.[11]

Within a few months of her employment, Alva Holbrook began to take a sentimental interest in his young protégée. Then sixty-three, he was married to a violently unstable woman, Jennie Bronson Holbrook. Their public quarrels were a byword. Holbrook filed for divorce in November 1871; the divorce became final in January 1872. He promptly proposed marriage to Pearl, and the oddly assorted pair were married quietly at her grandfather's house on May 18, 1872. Her parents were aghast that she was marrying a divorced man, not to mention a man who was six years older than her father. An announcement was sent to the newspapers after the Holbrooks left on their wedding trip. As the *Picayune* reported, "Quite a sensation was created . . . in literary circles" by the news.

At the same time that he divorced his first wife and remarried, Holbrook also divested himself of the heavy responsibility of editing a daily newspaper. He sold the *Picayune* in 1871 to a consortium of local men and retired to enjoy life with his new "help-meet and . . . God-send." They lived uptown on Constance Street, where Pearl began work on a collection of her poems for publication.

But scandal dogged the newlyweds. Although Jennie Holbrook had written to a friend that she was delighted to be rid of her former husband's "vile old carcass," she sued—unsuccessfully—for alimony in June 1872. Holbrook's attorney argued that the couple was "being plagued and tormented by [Jennie Holbrook], knowing the torture which must result from her course to a gentle-minded woman."

Enraged by her failure in court, the divorcée came to the Holbrooks' home in her ex-husband's absence and tried to kill his new wife, shooting at her twice with a revolver, neither bullet finding its target. Jennie then tried to brain Pearl with a bottle of bay rum, but the Holbrooks' Irish maidservant seized the assailant, and, streaming with blood, Pearl ran away to take refuge with neighbors. Her attacker started chopping up the furniture with an axe. After being arrested, tried, and confined to the parish prison, Jennie Holbrook apparently left town. When the news hit the papers—"Violent Assault with Intent to Kill," the nightmare dreaded by her family when the writer set out for the big city became reality.[12]

Jane Kimball hated all the talk; it nearly killed her to have her adopted daughter's reputation discussed publicly. Pearl's many friends at home, who refused to believe that she had been involved with a married man, helped her bear all the trouble. Pearl held her head high but she too found the talk hard to bear. She wrote of "what deep humiliation I suffered when I was dragged down from my high estate and *stoned* as it were! It was terrible."[13]

There was nothing to be done but live through it, so she continued working on her book, selecting poems from among her old work and writing new ones. In 1873 J. B. Lippincott, a major publishing house in Philadelphia, accepted the poems and published a slim volume (131 pages) called *Lyrics by Pearl Rivers*; the book was dedicated to "Three Singers"—Dr. William Henry Holcombe, a distinguished homeopathic physician; John W. Overall, who first encouraged Pearl's literary aspirations; and Mary Ashley Townsend, sister poet and dearest friend.

Most of the poems were simple and naturalistic, their subjects usually the woods, streams, and wildlife. In "The Singing Heart," however, she wrote of her recent difficulties, "The world has bruised the singing heart, / It has wept tears like dew; / And Slander, with a poisoned dart, / Has pierced it through and through. / But singing hearts are hard to kill, / And God made mine with wings." The book didn't make a great stir in the national literary world, but it was favorably reviewed and was a lifelong source of pride to the author.[14]

Alas for Alva Holbrook's dreams of cozy retirement, the new owners of the *Picayune* soon ran the paper into the ground. The lingering effects of a torpid postwar economy meant that the nationwide depression of 1873 hit the South especially hard. Having two warring state governments in Louisiana (one Democratic, one Republican) didn't help the situation. Running a successful daily newspaper in New Orleans had become hard going indeed.

In May 1874, the Mississippi River overflowed its banks from the Gulf of Mexico to above Memphis, Tennessee. The paper published a full-page map showing the extent of the deluge. Flooding in New Orleans was severe, the inundated areas coinciding almost exactly with those of 2005's Hurricane Katrina. Then, however, construction in the city was confined to higher lands near the river levee. Economic losses were heavy, but the dissipation of floodwaters into the unpopulated cypress swamps at the back of town lessened the human tragedy.

In September the White League, a conservative white supremacist organization, attacked and defeated Republican loyalists and the Metropolitan Police, largely black, in the Battle of Liberty Place. Federal troops arrived almost immediately, however, and put the Reconstruction administration back in power. Congressional investigations of the violence in Louisiana didn't make New Orleans any more attractive to national investors. In December, Holbrook finally repurchased the paper for one hundred thousand dollars, putting twenty thousand down, and set to work.[15]

Before he could make much progress, however, he died. He passed away on January 3, 1876, leaving his entire estate to his widow. She found herself "with nothing but a big, unwieldy newspaper, almost swamped in a sea of debt": the *Picayune* was hardly a prize. Pearl's family urged her to let the paper die a decent death and return home. After declaring bankruptcy, she would have been allowed to keep a thousand dollars. Independent as always, however, she spent about three months considering her options before deciding to take over and resuscitate the ailing paper.[16]

The consortium of men who had owned the paper may not have known what they were doing, but the longtime senior managers of the *Picayune* were sound newspapermen who supported the new proprietor. The business manager, George Nicholson, was an Englishman from Leeds who had come to New Orleans in 1842 and worked his way up from counter clerk; he had managed the financial affairs of the paper for years. Nicholson, whom Pearl called "Uncle Nick," became her chief advisor; he was a comfortably situated man of fifty-six who had such faith in the *Picayune* that he bought a quarter interest in the paper to provide needed operating capital.[17]

Once she had made the decision to take over, the young proprietor went down to the newspaper office on Camp Street to speak with the assembled staff. She planned, she said, to be a hands-on editor who would actively guide the future of the paper. She went on, "I am a woman. Some of you may not wish to work for a woman. If so, you are free to go, and no hard feelings. But you who stay—will you give me your undivided loyalty, and will you advise me truly and honestly?" A few of the men did leave, but most of them stayed. Pearl inspired enviable devotion in her staff. When a city newspaper sneered in print at the idea of a lady editor, José Quintero, the Cuban-born chief editorial writer at the *Picayune* and a noted duelist, visited the offices of all the papers to let them know that he would personally resent their publishing any further insults to his employer.[18]

On Sunday, March 26, 1876, the masthead, which had previously read "Holbrook & Company," was changed to "E. J. Holbrook and Company" with a second line clarifying, "Mrs. A. M. Holbrook." A notice in the paper ("To the Public") described the new ownership and outlined the plans to make the *Picayune* a family paper. It was a huge gamble to take, and Pearl pretended a sangfroid that she didn't possess. She confessed "how frightened [she was] on the first morning when the staff brought copy to her for her approval." She wrote, "I never felt so little, so weak, so inadequate as in the first days when I realized the task I had before me." She worked long, hard hours, learning everything about running a successful daily and steadily paying off Holbrook's and the *Picayune*'s debts as well as fighting various suits and claims, which wouldn't be finally settled in her favor for another ten years. One of her greatest sources of pride was that, no matter how hard the times or tenuous the paper's finances, those who worked for the *Picayune* were always paid. As one of her editors later wrote, "The child poet had become a business woman, and the singer a heroine."[19]

Her social life as a widow was restricted. She lived simply, her loneliness somewhat assuaged by the companionship of cages of birds and a tiny white puppy named Mat (perhaps a Jack Russell terrier, a popular breed among New Orleans ladies of the period). She wrote of this beloved pet in a poem entitled "Only a Dog": "Ah if you knew / How true a friend a dog can be / And what a friend he was to me, / When friends were few!" She commented that "I like dogs better than I do people—as a race."[20]

On a vacation trip back to Mississippi, she wrote to George Nicholson about Jane Kimball's advice on her social life. Because of the gossip that had attended Pearl's marriage to Holbrook, her foster mother wanted her to be especially circumspect as a widow. A minimum of two years' mourning was expected, and Pearl chafed at that fact. In her early thirties, she was interested in remarrying, mentioning various eligible Mississippi bachelors who were assiduous in their attentions. As she put it, "I don't know how I happened to cut all the other ladies out—it *must* be my red-head."[21]

George Nicholson was a married man with four grown children; his wife, Sarah, died in early 1877 after a long illness. He was a tall, attractive man with sandy hair streaked with gray and a well-trimmed beard. He loved reading, especially English poetry, and often quoted from his favorites—William Shakespeare, Ben Jonson, and Thomas Gray. Good humored and witty, hospitable and kind hearted, he was very popular among a large group of friends.

Friendship and mutual admiration soon turned to love, and the two began a quiet courtship. The warmth of their love shines through their writings. He wrote "Serenade, a poem per se for *Somebody*," which declared "Queen of my life thou art" and "I'll bask in the light of eyes / That smile for me alone!" From Mississippi, she wrote "If ever you saw a lonely girl it is this one! I miss you so much. . . . I often wonder how a man of your age having lived in the City among 'men of the world' so long can be so fresh and youthful in feeling. You do not seem at all like an old man to me!" They were married at St. Paul's Episcopal Church on June 27, 1878. She was thirty-five; he was fifty-eight; and this time, her father gave her away.[22]

Before the ceremony, Pearl and George signed a marriage contract in which she maintained her separate financial property. She owned three-quarters of the newspaper to his one quarter, and its buildings, property, and equipment remained hers. He owned a considerable number of lots and houses in the city and sold her a large piece of property in the Garden District where they planned to build their home. The notary public was José Quintero of the *Picayune*.[23] With the uncertainty over the paper's future, the difference in their ages, and his adult children, this arrangement seemed most likely to protect everyone's financial future.

The *Picayune* was the center of their married life. Every day, they went down to Camp Street, where they worked long, long hours. Pearl was the heart of the editorial effort, deciding the policies and direction of the paper in consultation with her staff. Everyone understood that hers was the last word; she didn't hesitate to make difficult decisions. She later wrote about the anxieties that debt and newspaper management caused, lamenting that they took up "many weeks and years" that should have been happier.[24]

The summer that the Nicholsons married, the city's improving economy stuttered for a few months. For the second time since the Civil War, yellow fever attacked New Orleans, spreading well up the Mississippi River valley. George had written to a friend that "New Orleans was especially familiar with death" because of its epidemics. Church bells ceased to toll for funerals, barrels of tar were burned on street corners, and carbolic acid was abundantly spread as a disinfectant—all unavailingly. Many fled the city, its population dropping to about half its normal size. The epidemic finally died out with cold weather in late November. More than four thousand people in the city died, but the Nicholsons remained on the job. Although some issues of the *Picayune* had fewer pages than usual, the paper appeared regularly throughout those frightening months.[25]

From the time she took command at the newspaper, Pearl always worked to expand the *Picayune*'s coverage and to make it appealing to a wider circle of readers. The enlarged Sunday edition's circulation leaped. Book reviews, under the uninspired title Recent Publications, sometimes ran as long as two and half columns. Besides books, popular magazines were briefly surveyed. Half a dozen poems were typically published, as well as three or four short stories or sketches by some of the nation's well-known writers, including Mark Twain, Bret Harte, and Joel Chandler Harris. Humorous reprints from other papers added some spice, and Louis Winterhalder, the new staff artist, provided cartoon drawings.[26]

The society column (a boon to the social historian) was called the Society Bee, and the proprietor wrote it herself for several years. Modeled after similar reportage in eastern papers, the column was at first resented as intrusive and then embraced by the city's socialites. At thirty-six, Pearl portrayed herself as "the old lady" of the *Picayune* to whom a stingless bee (no scandal or innuendo allowed here) reported all that was going on socially.[27]

Eventually the paper published a dozen or more original columns on specialized subjects of the sort that today would be bought from syndicates. The *Picayune*'s Family Physician gave medical advice. Household Hints gave housekeeping advice but also included menus and general information of interest to women. Sports, women's and men's illustrated fashions, business, agriculture, industry, shipping, and the arts were all covered extensively. The *Picayune*'s Telephone printed consumer complaints about streets and public services. Green Room Gossip reported on the city's numerous theaters and their programs and performers, both local and traveling. On Sundays, a whole page, In Lilliput Land, catered to children's interests with stories, short poems, and illustrations. The Weather Frog, a jaunty cartoon character accompanying weather reports, was a popular innovation.

Numerous illustrations (some of them two columns wide) brightened both feature and news stories. Besides employing a staff artist, on Pearl's suggestion the paper began regularly ordering three or four cuts, that is, illustrations, a week from a national source. Stockpiling images of famous people, such as Queen Victoria and Kaiser Wilhelm, they added others as celebrity struck. By the 1890s, special carnival editions with lithographs of each krewe's floats regularly sold out.[28]

Still as great an animal lover as when she was a girl, Pearl used the paper to attack the cruelty of dog and cock fights, the beating of horses and mules by their drivers, and the general mistreatment of animals. She instituted another weekly column, Nature's Dumb Nobility, and she and George were among the founders of the New Orleans branch of the Society for the Prevention of Cruelty to Animals. She also contributed to such practical projects as placing watering troughs throughout the city.[29]

Editorially the *Picayune* was staunchly pro-Democratic. It promoted honest local government, strong public education, improved public works, economic development in the city, and modern transportation and communication. It was tepidly supportive of black education and economic improvement without committing itself to any idea of equal rights or, conversely, campaigning for white supremacy. Undoubtedly in favor of women's education, employment opportunities, and legal reforms, editorials encouraged girls to get practical training for real-life jobs so they wouldn't have to face poverty. The paper unceasingly advocated higher teachers' pay, job security, and the appointment of women school board members. Pearl supported the pioneering work of Sophie B. Wright in educating the poor and infirm. But although it covered the activities of Louisiana suffragists, particularly of Caroline Merrick, founder of the state's first women's suffrage organization, the paper never took a strong editorial stand in favor of women's right to vote.[30]

Pearl not only earned the devotion of established *Picayune* staff members but also showed an instinctive flair for hiring talented new writers. To the disgust of many diehard secessionists, she hired two experienced northern newspapermen when the pro-Union *Republican* went out of business shortly after federal troops left the city—Henry Robinson and Nathaniel Burbank. The latter was a jolly three-hundred-pound giant with a curled moustache and a booming voice. As managing editor, he was invaluable, even chivvying the proprietor into meeting deadlines. His admiration for Pearl shows in a thank-you note for Christmas hankies: "It is sweet to be remembered. To be remembered by you—my 'boss'—is honey."[31]

Thomas E. Davis, from Texas, first worked as a reporter and later became editor in chief. His wife, Mollie Moore Davis, a published poet, became another of Pearl's friends. Mollie contributed poetry, travel, and semiautobiographical pieces to the *Picayune*. Her association with the paper was key to her later national success as a short story writer and novelist. Her salon on Royal Street in the French Quarter was the place where the Nicholsons and the local literati gathered on Fridays for coffee and good talk.[32]

Among the women whose careers Pearl fostered was Martha Smallwood Field, a widow with a small daughter to support, who joined the *Picayune* in 1881. As "Catherine Cole" she wrote a weekly column and other articles; she was also sent as the paper's special correspondent all around the United States and to Europe. Whenever she had gone for some time without seeing her "dear old lady," as she jokingly called Pearl, she felt lonely and begged her to allow her to come back and become "one of us boys" again.[33]

Another discovery was Elizabeth Meriwether Gilmer, whom Pearl encouraged by publishing a short story and then hiring her as an editorial assistant. Gilmer developed an inimitable style with her Sunday Salad column and later headed the women's department of the paper. After the Hearst papers lured her away, she became the most famous woman journalist in the nation as "Dorothy Dix." Elizabeth appreciated Pearl's having shown her "the wide plains of knowledge," avowing "I am but one of the multitudes that love you."

Among the many reasons these women reporters had for loving and admiring Pearl was her determined insistence on equal pay for male and female staff members—truly radical in a time when women routinely received considerably less pay than men doing the same job.[34]

The offices at the *Picayune* were comfortable and dumpy; little renovation or redecoration took place during the next twenty years. After encountering a mahogany desk downstairs where business was done, visitors frequently got lost in the meandering corridors leading to offices furnished with a random assortment of battered old desks, tables, and chairs. When the first telephone book was published in December 1879, the *Picayune* was among its ninety-nine subscribers. The *Picayune* had one telephone that served all departments of the paper throughout the Nicholsons' tenure. No sense wasting money on frivolities like another phone line. Electric lights followed a few years later. When the building next door was connected to provide additional office space, it was joined on the upper floor by a simple metal walkway between two office windows.[35]

For years Pearl wrote at a table in Nathaniel Burbank's busy office, where the office boy stacked high the books and magazines sent to her for review. In 1888 she finally bought herself a new cherry-wood desk. Delighted with her acquisition, she began an occasional column of personal commentary—A Busy Hour at My Desk or An Idle Hour at My Desk.[36]

The Nicholsons readily spent money, however, on improvements to keep ahead of the competition and run an up-to-date paper. At a considerable cost, the *Picayune* subscribed to the new Associated Press, receiving thousands of words daily hot off the telegraph. Headlines became snappier and more eye catching over time. Typefaces were updated every few years, and the paper eventually purchased fifteen linotypes. Office typewriters followed as typesetters refused to continue working from handwritten copy. New presses (a huge capital expenditure) were a source of pride; the Nicholson's ultimate purchase, the Hoe Presto Perfecting Press, printed on huge rolls of paper.[37]

Readership was the basic scale used to gauge newspaper success, and the *Picayune*'s masthead proudly boasted "Largest Circulation in the Southwest."[38] Pearl kept close tabs on circulation and constantly worked to enlarge the paper's readership in adjoining areas, employing (for a small sum) newspaper vendors and checking on them wherever she traveled. Small-town Louisiana and Mississippi stringers (part-time reporters, paid by the story) and a Washington bureau enlarged the paper's reach. She dreamed of regional, perhaps even national, circulation at a time when the possibilities of such effective distribution were still very limited. Her paper's success drove its major rivals, the *Times* and the *Democrat*, to merge and to copy her innovations. By the 1890s the *Picayune* boasted sales of nineteen thousand copies daily and thirty thousand for the Sunday edition, always tidily ahead of its closest competitors.

Good writing was Pearl's passion, but she knew that the paper had to stay in business to publish anything at all. Advertising was the lifeblood of a newspaper; with its increasing circulation, the *Picayune* raked it in. Salesmen made trips as far afield as St. Louis and Baltimore and successfully sold ads there. To encompass all the new features and the growing number of ads, the paper expanded in length. By the 1890s, the daily had sixteen pages and the Sunday edition, thirty-two pages, printed in three sections. The front page of the Sunday edition was completely covered with advertisements large and small.[39]

Surprisingly and somewhat frighteningly, in 1880 the busy executive discovered that she was pregnant. Nearly thirty-eight was an advanced age to become a first-time mother in those days, and Pearl was afraid. Just before the baby's birth, she wrote in a panic to her older friend, Mary Ashley Townsend, the mother of three. Mary wrote back soothingly— "Now my darling *don't get blue*." At the cost of only a few hours of physical torture came the greatest joy of a woman's life. Don't forget, she wrote, "anesthetics are the glory of the age."[40]

What Pearl's sufferings were we don't know, but her joy overflowed in January 1881, when she gave birth to a son named Leonard Kimball Nicholson. Two years later, shortly after Pearl turned forty, Yorke Poitevent Nicholson was born. The birth of these robust blond boys changed the Nicholsons' routine drastically. During the first years of their marriage, without the leisure to build or decorate their own home, they had rented houses, once living for a year at the St. Charles Hotel. Now they made the time to build a large, two-story house on Pearl's property on Jackson Avenue in the fashionable Garden District. With a wide gallery and gardens, it made a comfortable family home. She no longer went to the office so often. Copy was delivered to her at home uptown, and she sent it back meticulously marked up.[41]

One of the greatest contributions Pearl made to the cultural life of New Orleans was her stout support through the *Picayune* of the World's Industrial and Cotton Centennial Exposition. Celebrating the first shipment of American cotton to England in 1784, the exposition was intended to trumpet the city's postwar economic recovery, attract new business, and perhaps make a profit for the shareholders. The paper continued to be a major backer as more than two hundred acres of Upper City Park (today's Audubon Park), stretching from St. Charles Avenue to the Mississippi River, came to house a fantasy city, including a vast crystal horticultural hall, all lit by the incandescent magic of electricity. Streets leading to the site were paved, a street railway on St. Charles Avenue and docks on the riverside were built, and the *Picayune* trumpeted the opening of the exposition on December 16, 1884, with an eleven-and-a-half-column story.[42]

Unfortunately, a national financial panic, extensive flooding in the Ohio River valley, foul weather in New Orleans, and inept management caused the exposition to end heavily in debt. But for Pearl and her friends, it was a huge intellectual boon. While they were in town covering the fair, a dozen newspaperwomen organized the Women's National Press Association, electing Pearl the first president. Mary Ashley Townsend was chosen official poet of the exposition, and Martha Field wrote a series of stories for the paper. Everyone who attended enjoyed the exhibitions, the band concerts, and other entertainments.[43]

Under the direction of the redoubtable Julia Ward Howe of Boston, the Woman's Department was one of the fair's greatest successes. Many New Orleanians grumbled at the selection of the abolitionist author of "The Battle Hymn of the Republic," but she soon made fast friends with Pearl Rivers and other women writers. She frequently entertained, introducing locals to the poet Joaquin Miller and other literary visitors, such as Richard Watson Gilder, editor of the *Century*, and Charles Dudley Warner, literary critic for *Harper's*. Her borrowed house was the place for intellectual conversation, and New Orleans women reveled in the opportunity.[44]

Another new friend for Pearl was Mrs. Frank Leslie, publisher of several journals, including *Frank Leslie's Illustrated Newspaper*. Born Miriam Follin in New Orleans, she too had inherited a publishing business heavily in debt and had proved herself a masterful executive. For a time in the 1880s, they corresponded regularly, making a pact as women journalists to support each other, publishing each other's work, and running admiring sketches in their respective papers.[45]

The increasing financial stability of the *Picayune* and the dependability of its managers and reporters allowed the Nicholsons an easier life. They began summering out of town—often on the Mississippi Gulf Coast—to avoid the city's crushing heat and danger of yellow fever. In 1887, they built a second home on the beach in Waveland, Mississippi, only fifty miles away from New Orleans and easily reached in two hours by the Louisville and Nashville Railroad. They called this large, raised, center-hall cottage "Fort Nicholson," and for the next six years, it became the principal residence of Pearl and the boys, with George joining them on weekends. The final settlement in their favor of the various suits against the *Picayune* also made their lives much easier. Triumphant telegrams to Pearl celebrated: "Ten years of heroic struggle!" and (from George) "A Waterloo victory for us."[46]

Over on the coast, Pearl regained many of the pleasures of her girlhood. She never replaced Mat, the lapdog who had been such a comfort in her widowhood. Instead, she took in numerous stray and neglected dogs. She began riding again—"I used to be a sort of cowboy in petticoats." Now she used a proper sidesaddle, but she was still an exceptional rider. A devoted mother, she taught her sons reading, writing, nature, typewriting (Leonard saved samples of his work on "this wise little instrument"), and whatever else struck their fancy.

She made several scrapbooks for her sons as entertainment and as a teaching tool. One special book was filled with clippings and handwritten information about her life and career. She wrote: "The *personal* things that you will find in this book have not been pasted here through a spirit of vanity, but with the sweet thought that perhaps my little boys will some day be glad and proud to read the kind things that have been said about the little Mama who loves them so well."[47]

Pearl never gave up direction of the newspaper, however. When she was in Mississippi, manuscripts, letters, and notes were brought to her daily by train; urgent matters were communicated by telegram. Her secretary went frequently to type correspondence, and one staff member or another came almost daily to work with her and enjoy a fish dinner. Her "watchful care" infused every detail of the publication.[48]

In October 1893, a major storm swept the Mississippi coast, much like 1976's Hurricane Camille. More than fifteen hundred people were killed, and Fort Nicholson was destroyed. The *Picayune* chartered a relief boat that carried food, clothing, and medical supplies into the devastated areas. The Nicholsons moved back to their house in New Orleans full-time.[49]

The responsibility of the newspaper, marriage, and motherhood had absorbed Pearl's energy for years. In the 1890s, however, she returned to creative writing with two long dramatic monologues about women of the Old Testament.

Despite painful arthritis that twisted her hands like little bird's claws, she continued to write in pencil on a pad. She wrote from the point of view of Abraham's cast-off concubine Hagar and of Leah, the unloved first wife of Jacob. Both were published in the prestigious *Cosmopolitan* literary magazine in 1893 and 1894, respectively. She considered them her finest work.[50]

Pearl and George Nicholson remained romantically devoted to each other throughout their marriage. Martha Field wrote a sketch in *Godey's Lady's Book*, which described George as "a husband who is still a lover," and Mrs. Frank Leslie was fascinated with Pearl's life "with the lover-husband." He sent notes embellished with hand-drawn garlands "To my sweet wee Wife" and "love to my little Wife." He sometimes signed himself "Darling old Fellow."[51]

Then in the cold February of 1896 George Nicholson fell ill with "la grippe"—influenza. Although he was seventy-five, he was a hale and physically active man. But his condition soon worsened, and he died in the afternoon of February 4, 1896. His sudden death was a shock to the entire city. A distraught Pearl was supported throughout the ordeal by her aunt Janie and George's widowed daughter, Annie Nicholson Reed.[52]

Pearl's death was even more unexpected than George's. Shortly after his funeral, she too went to bed with flu, which shortly turned to pneumonia. She retained her faculties until the end, seeing her friends and family and making plans for her adolescent sons. Counting on their friends at the *Picayune*, she and George had named Thomas Rapier, the paper's manager, to be the guardian of the boys and their very large estate. Now Pearl decided that they would continue to live in the family home on Jackson Avenue under the care of Annie Reed.[53]

Shortly before Pearl's death, as she was making these final arrangements, she told her friend Martha Field: "I am not afraid to go, for long since I have had my money's worth." She died on Saturday morning, February 15, 1896, eleven days after George and less than a month before her fifty-third birthday.[54]

Her funeral was at 3:30 in the afternoon at their home. Her simple casket was in the library surrounded by flowers. A sheaf of red roses was placed on her breast, representing her devotion to her sons. There was barely room to hold the huge crowd who came to pay their final respects. The pallbearers were all staff members of the *Picayune*.[55]

In the history of American literature, Pearl Rivers barely receives a footnote. Her talent was minor, typical of many nineteenth-century semiprofessional poets; even her later dramatic monologues, though deeply felt, are rather wooden. It is as a pioneering and successful newspaperwoman and businesswoman that she made her mark.

Ambition, competence, and determination were the hallmarks of her career.

Loving her family, she nonetheless flouted their deepest feelings in pursuing a newspaper career in New Orleans. As the first woman in the South to work for a major daily, she was the object of gossip and criticism. Like other literary ladies of the Gilded Age, she underplayed her steely ambition and emphasized her own domesticity and femininity in her writings. But in reality, public scandal, personal loss, and financial hardship only made her more resolved to pursue her course.

Despite her love for George Nicholson and sincere appreciation of his contributions to the *Picayune*, three-quarters of the paper was always hers. She determined to make *her* newspaper number one in the Southwest—and she did.

Eliza Nicholson was in a sense a working feminist who never became a political activist. Although she had great power as a publisher, she never joined a suffragist organization, campaigned for women's voting rights, or used the *Picayune* to advocate suffrage. The causes for which she worked—animal rights, honest government, improved public education—were not particularly controversial. But through the paper's editorials, she stoutly supported the right of women to employment, to equal pay, to success and respect, and she backed up her ideas through hiring women writers and promoting their careers. Her own career was a shining example of one woman's ability to succeed.

֍ ֍ ֍

The *Picayune* and other New Orleans newspapers have long since been bought by a national publishing chain, the old Camp Street offices demolished to make way for a high rise. Pearl Rivers's memorial in New Orleans is a lagoon at the front of City Park, thickly bordered with wild swamp iris.[56]

NOTES

1. Nicholson Family Papers, ms. no. 219, folders 476, 481, Historic New Orleans Collection (hereinafter cited as HNOC).

2. Patricia Brady, *Martha Washington: An American Life* (New York: Viking, 2005), 147.

3. Nicholson Papers, folder 501, boxes 13, 16, HNOC; James Henry Harrison, *Pearl Rivers: Publisher of the* Picayune (New Orleans: Department of Journalism, Tulane University, 1932), 9.

4. Patricia Brady, "Literary Ladies of New Orleans in the Gilded Age," *Louisiana History* 33 (Spring 1992): 148.

5. Nicholson Papers, folder 501, HNOC. Overall published *The South* as a weekly newspaper in New Orleans. Ida Raymond [Mary T. Tardy], "Eliza Poitevent," in *Southland Writers: Biographical and Critical Sketches of the Living Female Writers of the South* (Philadelphia: Claxton, Remsen, and Haffelfinger, 1870), 2:637.

6. Raymond, "Eliza Poitevent"; W. Kenneth Holditch, "'A Creature Set Apart': Pearl Rivers in the Piney Woods," in *Mississippi's Piney Woods: A Human Perspective*, ed. Noel Polk (Jackson: University Press of Mississippi, 1986), 103.

7. B. H. Gilley, "A Woman for Women: Eliza Nicholson, Publisher of the New Orleans *Daily Picayune*," *Louisiana History* 30 (Summer 1989): 234–35.

8. Nicholson Papers, folder 501, HNOC.

9. Nicholson Papers, folders 370, 443, 481, 501, HNOC.

10. Brady, "Literary Ladies," 147.

11. Nicholson Papers, folder 476, boxes 13, 16 (scrapbook), HNOC.

12. Ibid., folder 345, box 16 (scrapbook), HNOC; Gilley, "A Woman for Women," 235–36.

13. Nicholson Papers, folder 378, HNOC.

14. *Lyrics by Pearl Rivers* (Philadelphia: J. B. Lippincott, 1873); Holditch, "'A Creature Set Apart,'" 119.

15. Thomas Ewing Dabney, *One Hundred Great Years: The Story of the* Times Picayune *from Its Founding to 1940* (Baton Rouge: Louisiana State University Press, 1944), 225–37, 256–57.

16. Nicholson Papers, box 13, HNOC.

17. Ibid., folders 476, 513, HNOC.

18. Ibid., folder 501, HNOC; Holditch, "'A Creature Set Apart,'" 107; Gilley, "A Woman for Women," 236.

19. Harrison, *Publisher of the* Picayune, 17, 22; Nicholson Papers, folders 501–2, 513.

20. Nicholson Papers, folder 37, box 16 (scrapbook), HNOC.

21. Ibid., folder 378, HNOC.

22. Ibid., folders 378, 481, 486, 491, box 16 (scrapbook), HNOC.

23. Inventory of the succession of George Nicholson, 48–595, Parish of Orleans Civil District Court; inventory of the succession of Eliza Jane Nicholson, 48–749, Parish of Orleans Civil District Court.

24. Gilley, "A Woman For Women," 237.

25. Dabney, *One Hundred Great Years*, 268–70; Khaled J. Bloom, *The Mississippi Valley's Great Yellow Fever Epidemic of 1878* (Baton Rouge: Louisiana State University Press, 1993), 88–89, 98, 102–3, 107–8, 125, 142, 280.

26. Harrison, *Publisher of the* Picayune, 45–46; Holditch, "'A Creature Set Apart,'" 106.

27. Harrison, *Publisher of the* Picayune, 31.

28. Ibid., 30–37, 40–44; Dabney, *One Hundred Great Years*, 313; Nicholson Papers, folder 3, HNOC.

29. Holditch, "'A Creature Set Apart,'" 116.

30. Harrison, *Publisher of the* Picayune, 25; Nicholson Papers, folder 40, HNOC; Gilley, "A Woman for Women," 241–43.

31. Harrison, *Publisher of the* Picayune, 22; Nicholson Papers, folder 5, HNOC.

32. Dabney, *One Hundred Great Years*, 305–6; Brady, "Literary Ladies," 105, 155.

33. Harrison, *Publisher of the* Picayune, 24; Nicholson Papers, folder 92, HNOC.

34. Harrison, *Publisher of the* Picayune, 24; Lamar Whitlow Bridges, "A Study of the New Orleans Daily Picayune under Publisher Eliza Jane Poitevent Nicholson, 1876–1896" (PhD diss., Southern Illinois University, 1974), 299–300; Nicholson papers, folder 94, HNOC; Gilley, "A Woman for Women," 248.

35. Dabney, *One Hundred Great Years*, 246; Nicholson Papers, folder 443, HNOC; Bridges, "A Study of the *Times Picayune*," 287, 289.

36. Harrison, *Publisher of the* Picayune, 59–60; Nicholson Papers, folder 443, HNOC.

37. Harrison, *Publisher of the* Picayune, 26–27; Dabney, *One Hundred Great Years*, 288–89, 295–96, 314.

38. *New Orleans Daily Picayune*, May 6, 1895, 4.

39. Bridges, "A Study of the *Times Picayune*," 279–82; Harrison, *Publisher of the* Picayune, 26–27, 30.

40. Nicholson Papers, folder 132, HNOC.

41. Nicholson Papers, folder 476, HNOC; New Orleans city directories 1878–1884.

42. Dabney, *One Hundred Great Years*, 285–86.

43. Dabney, *One Hundred Great Years*, 287; Bridges, "A Study of the *Times Picayune*," 307; Harrison, *Publisher of the* Picayune, 27.

44. Brady, "Literary Ladies," 152.

45. Nicholson Papers, folders 136–45, HNOC.

46. Bridges, "A Study of the *Times Picayune*," 284; Nicholson Papers, folders 11, 13, box 13, HNOC.

47. Harrison, *Publisher of the* Picayune, 8; Nicholson Papers, folders 37, 443, boxes 13, 16 (scrapbook), HNOC.

48. Nicholson Papers, folder 501, HNOC.

49. Bridges, "A Study of the *Times Picayune*," 284; Dabney, *One Hundred Great Years*, 324.

50. Nicholson Papers, folder 443, HNOC; Harrison, *Publisher of the* Picayune, 28, 63; Holditch, "'A Creature Set Apart,'" 117.

51. Nicholson Papers, folders 24, 136, 353, 354, 360, 501, HNOC.

52. Nicholson Papers, folder 513, HNOC.

53. Inventory of the succession of George Nicholson, 48–595, Parish of Orleans Civil District Court; inventory of the succession of Eliza Jane Nicholson, 48–749, Parish of Orleans Civil District Court.

54. Holditch, "'A Creature Set Apart,'" 119; Nicholson Papers, folder 247, HNOC.

55. Nicholson Papers, box 13, HNOC.

56. Harrison, *Publisher of the* Picayune, 5.

Kate Chopin
(1850–1904)

Knowing What It Means to Miss New Orleans

EMILY TOTH

❀ ❀ ❀

"N. Orleans I liked immensely," Kate O'Flaherty wrote in her diary after her first visit in 1869. It was "so clean—so white and green. Although in April we had profusions of flowers—strawberries and even blackberries."[1]

It was nineteen-year-old Kate O'Flaherty's first visit to Louisiana, and like so many warm souls, she was enthralled. She spent one memorable evening in "a dear little house near Esplanade St." whose hostess was a former opera singer, and they "quaffed all sorts of ales and ices—talked French, and German—listened enchanted to Mrs. Bader's exquisite singing and for two or three hours was as gay and happy as I ever have been in my life."[2]

The ground was laid for her lifelong love of New Orleans, a common thread among Yankee visitors: even today, there are many people who "came for a weekend and never left." Kate O'Flaherty did leave, to go back to St. Louis, but she left much of her heart in New Orleans. She knew what it means to miss New Orleans, and her fascination with the city's ways shaped and colored—in fact, made possible—her literary career.

Kate O'Flaherty Chopin is the second most read woman writer from Louisiana. (The first is vampire novelist Anne Rice.) Chopin is usually called a Louisiana writer and even a southern lady. But in fact she was an urban Catholic from St. Louis, where she spent all but fourteen years of her life.

As we say in Louisiana, she was "not from here."

Kate O'Flaherty was born in St. Louis on February 8, 1850, the second child of Eliza (Faris) and Thomas O'Flaherty. It had been a marriage of convenience. Eliza, just sixteen, lovely and French speaking, brought a certain social status to the match: her Charleville ancestors had been among the first settlers in

St. Louis. Thomas, a thirty-nine-year-old widower with a small son, was an Irish immigrant, a wealthy self-made man who sold supplies to those trekking west to make their fortunes. He was a smart investor whose real estate holdings supported his daughter until the end of her life, half a century later.[3]

Young Katy may have been a bit of a brat—for she was sent off to boarding school, to the St. Louis Academy of the Sacred Heart, when she was only five years old. But a few months into the term, she was suddenly brought home on All Saints' Day, 1855. Her father, one of the "solid men" of St. Louis involved in building a new railroad bridge across the Gasconade River, had been on the inaugural train over the bridge. It collapsed, sending some thirty people to their deaths. Thomas O'Flaherty was among them.[4]

Nearly forty years later, his daughter Kate wrote of a similar reported death in a train crash, in her "Story of an Hour." In Kate Chopin's 1894 story, the new widow is at first grief stricken, and then more than a little happy, and then finally joyful at the thought that the rest of her life, spread out ahead of her, belongs to her alone. She needn't submit her will to anyone else's and she exults: "Free! Body and soul free!"[5] The fictitious wife's story ends ironically—but in real life, twenty-seven-year-old Eliza O'Flaherty was suddenly a rich widow. She never remarried. Nor had her mother and grandmother, both of whom soon came to live with her.[6]

And so Kate O'Flaherty grew up in a household of very independent women, where the only males were her brother, her half brother, and an elderly slave, freed when war came. The O'Flaherty-Faris-Charleville women controlled their own money, made their own decisions, and were healthier and lived longer than most women of their time. Kate's great-grandmother, Victoire Verdon Charleville, tutored Kate in French, music, and storytelling, sharing juicy tales from St. Louis history. Madame Charleville's own mother, Kate's great-great-grandmother, had been an illiterate battered wife who escaped from her husband and got the first legal separation in St. Louis. Four years later she gave birth to another child, said nothing about who might be the father, and founded a line of boats delivering goods up and down the Mississippi River. She was a Frenchwoman with an entrepreneurial spirit, and she was Kate O'Flaherty's most intrepid ancestor.[7]

Young Kate returned to the Sacred Heart school two years after her father's death and gained a lifelong friend in Kitty Garesché, a schoolmate whose family was banished from St. Louis for their southern sympathies during the Civil War. That happened the year Kate was thirteen, in 1863. That winter her half brother, a Confederate soldier, died of typhoid, and her great-grandmother died of pneumonia. After the Battle of Gettysburg that July, a celebrating group of

KATE CHOPIN

1876, in St. Louis. Kate Chopin loved to shock her neighbors with her
flamboyant riding habits. Reprinted by permission of the Missouri
Historical Society, St. Louis, IM 001-000870, acc. no. 1982.13.23.

Union soldiers invaded the O'Flaherty household with bayonets, forcing Kate's mother to raise a Union flag. This "outrage," as a neighbor called it, may have involved some kind of sexual abuse, since "outrage" often meant that in the nineteenth century.[8]

All we know is that Kate, like many abuse survivors, withdrew to the attic, where she read books and did not talk to anyone for at least several months. Finally a gifted and dedicated teacher, Madam Mary O'Meara, helped bring young Kate out of her melancholy and encouraged her to write. Kate O'Flaherty's "Commonplace Book," which she began in 1867, is the first piece of writing we have from her hand.[9] She became one of the best Sacred Heart students, honored for her intelligence and leadership and admired as a teller of engaging and marvelous stories.

Like most writers, and most women who are public achievers, Kate O'Flaherty showed an early promise and a drive that conflicted with the expectations for a young lady in society. As a St. Louis belle, after graduation, she continued taking piano lessons and attending the opera and concerts. She joined a German Reading Club, dutifully attended debutante functions, and complained about them in her "Commonplace Book" diary: "I dance with people I despise; amuse myself with men whose only talent lies in their feet."[10] She deeply regretted that "my dear reading and writing that I love so well have suffered much neglect."[11]

She was ready to break out of the St. Louis mold.

Oscar Chopin was not one of the men she'd known all her life. They may have been distantly related, with Louisiana cousins on both sides, but he was in many ways a Frenchman. Aurelian Roselius Oscar Chopin had been born in rural Natchitoches Parish in Louisiana on September 30, 1844. His mother had been a local heiress, just sixteen years old when she married his father, a French-born doctor, twenty-five and notoriously cruel to his slaves and his wife. His mother bravely ran away for several years at a time when few women left their brutal husbands, and her own mother had urged her to return—but her gentle son Oscar helped her. Oscar also ran away from home rather than serve as his father's slave overseer. (Kate Chopin would later link the treatment of wives and slaves in such stories as "Désirée's Baby" and "Athénaïse.")[12]

Then Oscar's parents were reconciled, the Civil War broke out, and Dr. Chopin moved the whole family to France to sit out the conflict. And so Oscar spent his young manhood in Château-Thierry, where he failed his baccalaureate while enthusiastically pursuing wine and young women.[13]

When the war ended, Dr. Chopin returned to claim his Louisiana land and made himself even more unpopular among those who had lost sons. That may be why he moved his wife and himself to the St. Louis Hotel in the French Quarter (Vieux Carré) of New Orleans, where he could fume all he liked about "the Americans." Oscar preferred to move to St. Louis, where he studied banking at his great-uncle's firm. He wrote to his cousin in France about the beauty of local young women and "the vast opportunity for love."[14] While he was in St. Louis, his mother died.

On June 9, 1870, Kate O'Flaherty and Oscar Chopin were married in St. Louis, then embarked on a three-month European honeymoon that was cut short by the Franco-Prussian War. The new Madame Chopin kept a diary in which she reveled in her freedom: she walked about alone, smoked cigarettes, enjoyed watching gamblers, and poked gentle fun at her new husband. She wrote little about love and less about sex: the diary was not locked, and women of the Victorian era were always discreet. (Her "headaches," which occur twenty-eight days apart in her diary, were evidently menstrual notations.)[15]

By the time Kate and Oscar Chopin settled in New Orleans that fall, Kate was already pregnant with their first child.[16]

When they arrived, New Orleans was still occupied by the hated Union soldiers in uniform. Although she spoke fluent French and came from a Confederate family, Kate Chopin was an outsider, a Yankee, and a symbol of the victorious North. New Orleans itself had surrendered in 1862, three years before the end of the war, but many New Orleans men had remained in the Confederate Army after the surrender, and there were tensions over who had fought in the war and who had not.[17]

There were also oppositions between the "French," hunkered down in their crumbling cottages in the French Quarter and smarting from the humiliations and lootings inflicted by the occupiers—versus the somewhat richer "Americans" in their Garden District homes on the other side of Canal Street. Kate, as a thoroughgoing "American," might have endured snubs and shunnings in the French Quarter, while Oscar, a native French speaker, might have been unwelcome in the Garden District. The young Chopins, also determined to distance themselves from Oscar's father, set up their first home in the neighborhood called the Irish Channel (now also called the Lower Garden District).[18]

Years later, in a story called "A Matter of Prejudice," Kate Chopin made fun of a grouchy old woman in the French Quarter who—like old Dr. Chopin—hates everything American. The character even has a unique theory (which may have been Dr. Chopin's, about his daughter-in-law named O'Flaherty) that "the Irish voice is distressing to the sick."[19]

The story ends with a happy reconciliation, thanks to a beloved daughter, and Kate Chopin's first biographer, Daniel Rankin, claimed that she charmed her crusty father-in-law with her music and her unwillingness to let him faze her.

In any case, he died just two months after Kate and Oscar settled into their first home on Magazine Street between Robin (now Euterpe) and Terpsichore (now the site of Jackson School).

In that house, on May 22, 1871, Kate Chopin gave birth to her first son, assisted by a quadroon nurse named Alexandrine, who wore hoop earrings and a high bandana *tignon*, the only decorative headdresses that servants of color were allowed to wear. The French-born obstetrician, Dr. Charles Jean Faget, had treated old Dr. Chopin in his last illness and was the model of a modern physician: he believed in giving women chloroform to ease the pain of childbirth. Twenty-three years later, Chopin wrote about the joys of holding her first son: "The sensation with which I touched my lips and my fingertips to his soft flesh only comes once to a mother. It must be the pure animal sensation: nothing spiritual could be so real—so poignant."[20] (Edna in Chopin's *The Awakening* is not a mother-woman and remembers childbirth much less happily: "an ecstasy of pain, the heavy odor of chloroform, a stupor which had deadened sensation.")[21]

Little Jean Baptiste Chopin soon had younger brothers: Oscar Charles, born September 24, 1873; George Francis, born October 28, 1874; Frederick, born January 26, 1876; and Felix Andrew, born January 8, 1878. In 1874 the Chopins moved into a house further uptown, at Pitt and Constantinople (the house no longer exists). In 1876 they moved again, to what is now 1413–15 Louisiana Avenue, between Prytania and Coliseum, a pretty double house surrounded by flowers. The Chopins rented their side (1413) from a sugar dealer, and their two servants, a cook and a laundress, lived in a one-story service building in the back. The Chopins' fifth and last son, Felix (always called "Phil") was born in that house, now a private home that still has the same acanthus-leaf ceiling medallions and fireplaces.[22]

All the Chopins' homes were in the "sliver by the river," the oldest, highest, and safest part of New Orleans, protected by the Mississippi River levee. The Louisiana Avenue house is not in the zone flooded after Hurricane Katrina in 2005, and the parts of New Orleans most devastated by the flood had been wetlands—lakes and swamps—when the Chopins lived there.

When she could, Kate Chopin loved walking about the city, exploring. But she was pregnant, not supposed to be seen in public, for much of the nine years the couple lived in New Orleans, and the weather was too hot for much strolling. Kate and the children often spent summers at Grand Isle, then emerging as a resort for "Creole" families. ("Creole" meant American-born but with pure French or Spanish ancestry; those with mixed racial ancestry were known in the Chopins' day as "Creoles of color.") At Grand Isle, among the Creoles, Kate

Chopin was a thorough outsider, and her character Edna's shock at the Creoles' open affections, risqué books, and freedom of speech about childbirth may all have been young Madame Chopin's own experiences.[23]

Oscar was sometimes alone in the city, especially when Kate visited her mother for months at a time—and in 1874, he got into trouble. In a corrupt election, two different governors had been chosen, and Oscar joined a quasi-military company associated with the White League. That September, in the Battle of Liberty Place, the White Leaguers—including Oscar Chopin—attacked the Metropolitan Police on Canal Street. The police had cannons; twenty-seven people died; and for years it was rumored that White Leaguers might be arrested and charged with treason.[24]

Kate Chopin, with three small children and only Oscar's income, could not have been pleased. Her later stories about war are always sad, without glory and with loneliness and never-ending grief ("Ma'ame Pélagie," "Beyond the Bayou," "A Wizard at Gettysburg"). Her characters are not enhanced by the war, but traumatized forever.[25]

But there were also pleasures in occupied New Orleans. The French Opera House was the first in the United States to stage *Lohengrin* and *Tannhäuser*. During the 1870s Mardi Gras evolved from street gangs and their mischief into elaborate parades and floats, some with satirical political messages. There were horse races like those Edna enjoys in *The Awakening*, and a writer for the New Orleans *Picayune*, George W. Cable, was beginning to publish Louisiana local color stories.[26]

Kate Chopin kept diaries, now lost, during her New Orleans years: writers always write. The only surviving lines are a short description of visiting a cotton warehouse with Oscar. She was fascinated by the men's world of business, so alien to the polite life of wives.[27]

Still, Kate Chopin came of age as an adult woman—no longer a schoolgirl, no longer a daughter—while she lived in New Orleans. She discovered sexuality as well as sensuality, and she saw so much, including the French Market (later in her story "Nég Créol"), St. Louis Cathedral ("A Sentimental Soul"), and Congo Square, where the slaves had danced before the war, with intricate drumming and rhythms unknown to the rest of the United States ("La Belle Zoraïde"). (That open field is now part of Louis Armstrong Park, honoring the origins of jazz.)

Young Madame Chopin saw the pretty houses along Bayou St. John, the waterway that curved through the city ("A Lady of Bayou St. John"). She saw old retainers, former slaves, slightly dotty spinsters, unregenerate French speakers who still refused to accept the "Americans," kind priests and indifferent priests, shopkeepers and would-be artists, and people of generosity and courage. Years later, in "Dr. Chevalier's Lie," she portrayed a doctor much like her own physician: careful, caring, discreet.

She also undoubtedly met the painter Edgar Degas, who spent five months in New Orleans, starting in the fall of 1872. Oscar, a cotton factor who was the middle man between growers and buyers of cotton, worked with Degas's uncle, and Degas's painting of the "Bureau de Coton" shows Oscar's workplace. The Degas family lived on Esplanade Street, where Léonce and Edna Pontellier have their cottage in *The Awakening*, and Degas—an avid gossiper—gave Kate Chopin the names for those characters, some twenty-six years before she actually wrote them. Degas's New Orleans neighbor, a stuffy businessman whose wife ran off with someone else, was named Léonce; Degas's French friend, a painter who gave up her art when she married, was named Edma Pontillon.[28]

In short, the New Orleans years were full of music, motherhood, discoveries, and small dramas. As the title figure says in Chopin's "A Lady of Bayou St. John"—"I have memories, memories to crowd and fill my life, if I live a hundred years!"[29]

But in 1878, the year after the Yankee occupation ended, there was a yellow fever epidemic that killed four thousand people. A year later, after several bad harvests and the loss of city property for unpaid taxes, Oscar was bankrupt and had to close his cotton factor business. The Chopins would have to leave New Orleans and live on his family lands in Cloutierville, in Natchitoches Parish. Kate Chopin would miss the rich, raffish ways of New Orleans for the rest of her life.[30]

The trek to Cloutierville was arduous, with five sons, Oscar's young sister Marie who was living with them, servants, and helpers—and Kate herself, pregnant with her sixth and last child. Their only daughter, Marie Laïza, always called "Lelia," was born on December 31, 1879, and baptized in Cloutierville's St. John the Baptist Church the following February.[31]

By then Kate Chopin knew that she had become even more of a foreigner. New Orleans, like St. Louis, was a big city where a young matron could wear flamboyant riding clothes and hats with plumes. She could smoke Cuban cigarettes and be considered rather chic.

That was not the case in Cloutierville, which—then and now—consisted of one long street of small houses facing each other, with farmlands and bayous behind them. The Chopins lived in a handsome white house, with an outside staircase, a lower story of brick, and an upper one of heart cypress. As was the custom, the family lived on the second floor, to evade mosquitoes and breathe cooler air. A cook and a laundress lived in the back.

Natchitoches Parish was an odd French outpost in mostly English-speaking north Louisiana. The town of Natchitoches itself, half a day's drive from Cloutierville, was the oldest white settlement in Louisiana, founded in 1714, and the whole Cane River area had a colorful history of marriages and misbehavings between white men and women of color. As in New Orleans, but nowhere else in Louisiana, there was a large population descended from the prewar "free people of color"—a lighter-skinned, third racial group between whites and blacks. The free people of color had their own settlement (Isle Brevelle) and their own church (St. Augustine) and generally did not consider themselves "Negroes." (Kate Chopin describes them in a sketch called "A Little Free-Mulatto.")[32]

Although there were only about seven hundred people in Cloutierville, there was a distinct caste system for the whites as well. The Chopins immediately became part of the ruling bourgeoisie, thanks to Oscar's land holdings and those of his brother Lamy (who named the post office, "Chopin, Louisiana," which still exists today). Dr. Samuel Scruggs and his wife, Lise DeLouche, put on fabulous feasts, and he was a grand raconteur whose stories were among those Kate Chopin pondered and used later. (Her first novel, *At Fault*, includes Dr. Scruggs's claim that Harriet Beecher Stowe visited Natchitoches Parish to gather material before she wrote *Uncle Tom's Cabin*. The proof was, of course, lost.) Also among the Scruggses' dinner guests were Mrs. Scruggs's daughter, Lodoiska ("Loca") Sampite and her husband, Albert—who would play a singular role in Kate Chopin's life.[33]

Cloutierville, meanwhile, had a certain natural beauty. In the summer the fields were bursting with life, and in the fall a lovely purple haze trembled over the forests. The weather was colder than it is today, and in December there would be snow and ice storms. There might be traveling circuses (as in Chopin's later story, "A Little Country Girl"), but there was no opera; there was no lending library; and there was little or no acknowledgment of Mardi Gras.

Although the richer residents often spent the winters, after the cotton harvest, buying fashionable clothes and visiting in New Orleans—Cloutierville was a simple country town. White ladies might take naps in the warm afternoons, but most people worked. Kate Chopin herself worked in Oscar's general store, which stocked clothes, supplies, and foodstuffs. (Chopin later described such a store in "Azélie.") Oscar was very generous and let everyone run up credit.[34]

The store attracted countless colorful characters, including Native Americans, wild-cowboy Texans, Chinese laborers, and "redbones," the offspring of African Americans and Native Americans. There were many poor and working-class whites, though few were "Cajun": most of their ancestors had come directly from France. (The Acadians, refugees from Canada in the 1760s, mostly settled in "Acadiana," or central Louisiana. In Kate Chopin's day the term "Cajun" was considered somewhat insulting, as she shows in her story "A Gentleman of Bayou Têche.")[35]

But all these people worked and toiled in the afternoons, wearing their work clothes—except for Kate Chopin.

There was at least one time when, in a hurry, she jumped on Oscar's horse bareback and flew galloping down the street. But mostly she was noted for her "promenades on horseback." In midafternoon, she would dress herself in her big-city finery—her lavender riding habit, her hat with the plume—and ride slowly down the town's one street, admiring and being admired. Everyone who was working stopped to gawk.[36]

On rainy days, or when the street dust was very high, she might walk. When she crossed the street, she would lift her skirt higher than was normal, displaying her ankles to all.[37]

She was considered a bold outsider and an "étrangère" (stranger), as well as something of a Yankee. Oscar was a social favorite; Kate was—not. They were not invited to be godparents for local babies, and rumors circulated about Kate Chopin's ineptitude—especially about the time when a servant failed to appear, and Kate had to figure out how to milk her own cow.[38]

Cloutiervillians made their own melodramas, with romances, feuds, and gossip, often at village dances (as in Chopin's "At the 'Cadian Ball" and "A Night in Acadie"). There was sadness, too, when one of Kate's cousins died in childbirth. By 1881, two years into their Cloutierville stay, Kate and Oscar were spending more and more time apart. She stayed with her mother for months in St. Louis, and Oscar traveled without Kate to Hot Springs, Arkansas, for his health. By the end of 1882 he had had several episodes of "swamp fever," evidently misdiagnosed by Dr. Scruggs, who did not give him the quinine needed for malaria until it was too late.[39]

On December 10, 1882, Oscar died. Kate was a thirty-two-year-old widow, her oldest child just eleven, and she was twelve thousand dollars in debt. She did what she had to do legally, which included petitioning to be the guardian of her own children—who, under Louisiana law, passed to the nearest male relative, Oscar's brother. She sold much of the property, ran the remaining businesses, and used the independent skills she'd learned in her mother's house.[40]

She also created a village scandal—with someone else's husband.

Albert Sampite ("Sam-pi-tay") was the richest planter in the area: it was said that one could ride all day just on his lands. He was handsome and charming, and a specialist in consoling widows. His wife, Loca, was considered a "plain country woman," and he spent little time at home: his signature appears on numerous legal documents, as he was a restless wanderer about town, available when anyone needed a witness. Apparently he gambled in the woods, or so Kate Chopin wrote in a later short story she significantly called "Loka": "Choctaw Joe and Sambite played dice every night by the campfire . . . and fought and slashed each other when wild with drink."[41] The real-life Albert Sampite drank a great deal but never seemed to be drunk.[42]

Later, his wife, Loca, told everyone that "Kate Chopin broke up my marriage." Exactly what transpired between Kate Chopin and Albert Sampite cannot be known, although he did involve himself with her money: descendants found some of her papers in the coffee can where he kept his financial records. Both liked horses and the night, silence and mystery. Their lands bordered each other's, and there were many secret places where people could meet during the dark, dark country nights.[43]

Still, Albert and Loca had two children. Divorce was impossible within the Catholic Church, and almost impossible outside it. Since Cloutierville had no high school, Kate's children would eventually have to go to boarding school, leaving her alone among people who hated her. Meanwhile, her mother was urging Kate to return home—and St. Louis happened to have the best public school system in the country.

Suddenly, about a year and a half after Oscar's death, Kate and the children abruptly moved—or fled—back to St. Louis.[44]

But the Cloutierville years (1879–84) were pivotal in Chopin's development as a writer. She moved outside the sphere of motherhood; she examined different modes of marriage; she studied rural life and compared it with the big city; she endured a degree of ostracism and social criticism she had never encountered before; and she learned that a tiny village can contain an entire world. As she wrote about the widowed Thérèse in her first novel, *At Fault*, widowhood "awakened unsuspected powers of doing."[45] Kate Chopin spent the last twenty years of her life in St. Louis, but much of her heart and her imagination remained in Louisiana. Those fourteen years had made her into a writer.

A year later, Eliza Faris O'Flaherty died of cancer. Most nineteenth-century women writers lost their mothers before they were ten years old, but Kate Chopin had had her mother with her for thirty-five years—sharing gossip, giving advice, promoting self-confidence and wisdom. After a long and painful period of grieving, Chopin cast about for ways to lift her spirits and improve her finances, and she turned to the way women have always communicated with each other: through telling stories.[46]

By 1889 Kate Chopin was publishing short stories in St. Louis magazines and newspapers; two years later she broke into national magazines. She wrote about a woman pianist who refuses to give up her art for love ("Wiser Than a God"), and about young lovers whose emotions ruin their careful life plans ("A Point at Issue!"). Her early stories were mostly romantic comedies in the American "genteel tradition" championed by most magazine editors. Stories should be published, editors thought, only if they were suitable for "the Young Person."[47]

Kate Chopin, a worldly woman who was no longer midwestern, did not fit in—especially once she read the stories of Guy de Maupassant, the amoral French writer whose detachment and treatment of adult themes (adultery, suicide, melancholy, and madness) thrilled her. Meanwhile, her early stories set in Missouri lacked wide appeal. They would not propel her into national magazines.[48]

Emboldened by Maupassant, and ambitious for literary success, Kate Chopin found her French roots. She turned to Louisiana for her material. She had a treasure in her past, in those fourteen years away from home.

Women's novels are often circular: the central characters leave home, go on adventures, but finally return to the nest. And so it was with Kate Chopin's life—except that her years in Louisiana had transformed her forever. In her 1894 diary she wrote that if her mother and her husband could "come back to earth, I feel that I would unhesitatingly give up every thing that has come into my life since they left it and join my existence again with theirs. To do that, I would have to forget the past ten years of my growth—my real growth."[49]

By then she had created a salon, the first in St. Louis. On Thursdays, she invited artists, journalists, and intellectuals to her home for spirited conversation, argument, and amusement. Chopin had also quietly publicized herself and become the first professional woman writer in St. Louis—and the first to join the national literary scene.[50]

Her breakthrough, "For Marse Chouchoute," contains the first-ever literary depiction of Cloutierville: "This little French village, which was simply two long rows of very old frame houses, facing each other closely across a dusty roadway."[51] *Youth's Companion*, based in Boston, accepted the story immediately.

But before "For Marse Chouchoute" appeared in print, Chopin did have some pointed grudges to settle in her first published novel, which is her first and longest comparison of Louisiana and St. Louis.

At Fault (1890) is the story of a woman who loves a man she should not love—because he has been married to another woman. But Chopin complicated the story, and made it less clearly autobiographical, by making the woman a Louisiana plantation owner (Thérèse) and the man a St. Louis businessman (David) who moves to the Cane River country in search of profits. He is divorced from his alcoholic wife, who remains in St. Louis among her silly, superficial friends.

Thérèse, an earnest Catholic, refuses to have a romance with a man she sees as still married—and Kate Chopin, in tackling divorce and female alcoholism, was dealing with two taboo subjects in 1890s fiction.

The story ends happily for Thérèse and David, but its greatest interest is the contrast between the Cane River country of Louisiana—which Kate Chopin was developing as her own private literary domain—and the world of status seekers in St. Louis. Some St. Louis characters are, indeed, recognizable satirical portraits of real figures, while the generous, emotionally direct characters are almost entirely Louisianians.

Chopin uses warm, lush language to portray Louisiana, from the descriptions of the wild bayou vegetation to the salty bits of French in the dialogue. St. Louis, in contrast, is gray, stolid, dull. Louisiana people are compassionate and funny, while St. Louisans are pompous and cliquish.

After *At Fault*, Chopin knew that Louisiana was her most salable and interesting material. In 1894 Houghton, Mifflin of Boston published *Bayou Folk*, her first collection, consisting of twenty-one short stories set in the Cane River country and two in New Orleans ("La Belle Zoraïde" and "A Lady of Bayou St. John").

Bayou Folk reviewers praised the collection for its "charm" and its unique portrayal of a world new to the reviewers, all of whom were in the Northeast. But most did not see what Kate Chopin was really saying, beneath the exotic veneer of local color.[52]

Some of the *Bayou Folk* stories are short and quirky vignettes: a pair of twins carry their new shoes rather than wearing them ("Boulôt and Boulotte"), a plain man fancies himself as grander than he is ("A Gentleman of Bayou Têche"), and a young woman is courted by two men, one of whom sacrifices to make her happy ("A No-Account Creole"). Some of the stories seem to be slight character sketches, but they actually explore deadly conflicts in loyalties ("The Bênitous' Slave," "For Marse Chouchoute"). Some are resolved with a woman character's making a heroic, life-changing sacrifice ("Beyond the Bayou," "Ma'ame Pélagie").

The stories are not about traditional happiness, as found in romance and marriage. Seven show fathers without wives; three husbands are brutal; two wives have absent husbands. Religious people are often uncharitable: a priest ignores a young girl's ties to her grandmother ("Love on the Bon Dieu"); a group of church ladies try to tame a Native American girl for whom they have more than a little disdain ("Loka").

Chopin, who grew up with slaves in her household, depicts the particular horrors of slavery for women. *Bayou Folk* includes a slave mother who goes insane when her mistress takes her child ("La Belle Zoraïde") and a slave master who is unspeakably cruel to his wife and child ("Désirée's Baby"). *Bayou Folk* ends with a story about young woman who is delighted to be a widow ("A Lady of Bayou St. John").

In her portrayal of Louisiana, Kate Chopin blended French sophistication—the spare, precise storytelling style of Guy de Maupassant—with American local color, popular stories in which provincial details of dress and manner were described piquantly to entertain readers in the Northeast who enjoyed portrayals of "others." The gatekeepers and cultural leaders of the Northeast—who controlled what was published and what was distributed—liked to showcase the "quaint" ways of rural people. Readers in New York and Philadelphia and Boston considered themselves more than a little superior to the poorly clothed, "simple" people in Louisiana, whose speech was often portrayed as an uneducated dialect. (Kate Chopin's dialect renderings are easier to read than most.)

Most of the most popular local color writers were women, and their writing—like Kate Chopin's—was usually a disguise for deep social criticism, even protest. Editors in the Northeast would not have accepted stories showing New York men being brutal to their wives—but when the husband in "Désirée's Baby" speaks cuttingly and "stab[s] thus into his wife's soul," he is no different from cruel husbands anywhere.[53] Kate Chopin used local color as a mask, to criticize powerful and cruel people of both sexes, including the slave-owning woman in "La Belle Zoraïde." Chopin did not claim that her stories were "universal"—but in an essay about another author, Hamlin Garland, she wrote that "Human impulses do not change and can not so long as men and women continue to stand in the relation to one another which they have occupied since our knowledge of their existence began[;] . . . social problems, social environments, local color and the rest of it are not *of themselves* motives to insure the survival of a writer who employs them" (Chopin's emphasis).[54]

Kate Chopin was definitely after more universal truths about women and men, especially their forbidden behavior. In "At the 'Cadian Ball," she more than hints at a sexual relationship between two characters who go off with others at the end, while in "In Sabine," she does something utterly unique.

Battered women's stories are not uncommon in American women's writings, as the prime short story researcher Susan Koppelman has shown.[55] The typical story depicts a woman who is isolated by her husband, who denies her any of her pleasures or her connections with family and friends. She has no money, often has small children, and endures brutality from her husband until she loses her mind or her life. "Tony's Wife," by the New Orleans writer Alice Dunbar-Nelson, would be published in 1899, but Kate Chopin had shown the powerlessness and self-delusion of a worn-out wife in the 1892 story "A Visit to Avoyelles." There, a kindly ex-suitor finds his formerly lovely sweetheart beaten down by caring for four small children in a dilapidated isolated house, living "as poorly as pine-woods people."[56] At the end, the suitor leaves sadly, while the wife gazes after her robust husband, at work in the fields.

A year later, in "In Sabine" (1893), Kate Chopin added details and emotional intensity to a similar scene: a former admirer, Grégoire, happens upon the dilapidated homestead where 'Tite Reine, once a saucy piquant "little queen," is now beaten and abused by her robust husband, Bud Aiken. Only the intervention of a black woodsman has kept Bud from killing her in a drunken rage. Grégoire gets Bud drunk, makes off with his horse, and gives 'Tite Reine his own fine young horse to make her escape—but they do not leave together. Kate Chopin was not after a traditional happy ending, with a rescuing prince. Grégoire rides off to Texas, while 'Tite Reine goes alone, back to the family that will save her.

"In Sabine" is the only American short story of its era in which a battered woman escapes.[57] "A Visit to Avoyelles," in which the wife stays wistfully with her husband, found a publisher immediately (*Vogue*), but magazines were not interested in "In Sabine." Chopin got it into print only by slipping it into her *Bayou Folk* collection at the last minute.

None of this was noticed by Kate Chopin's readers. Her exacting descriptions of nature—trees, plants, farmhouses—and her entrancing portrayals of dances, food, and courting customs seemed to lull her early readers. They noticed the squeaky fiddles, the spicy gumbos, the flirtatious patois—but did not notice that her local color stories are really tales of social protest in which women seek to be independent, free, and outspoken.

By setting her stories in Louisiana, Kate Chopin could speak out.

She also had one editor behind her. Josephine Redding, the outspoken editor of *Vogue* (a new fashion magazine), opposed the "intellectual asphyxiation" of the genteel tradition and eagerly published Chopin stories rejected by more conventional magazines such as the *Atlantic Monthly*.[58] *Vogue* was the first publisher for, among others, "Désirée's Baby," "La Belle Zoraïde," "A Lady of Bayou St. John," "Dr. Chevalier's Lie," and "The Story of an Hour." All of them are about women with hidden lives.

After *Bayou Folk*, Kate Chopin seems to have been wrestling with her Louisiana material. Her stories about children sold easily to *Youth's Companion*, which paid well, but by the mid-1890s she was in her mid-forties, with a great deal of knowledge about the complexities of human passions. She wanted to write more for adults, but the local color expectations—cute local customs, uneducated

Louisiana characters speaking in dialect—were constricting. The Louisiana she knew from her annual visits was much bolder and more colorful than what she could publish.

In 1891, for instance, Loca Sampite had finally gotten a legal separation from her husband Albert, who—according to her petition—isolated her from friends and family and beat her so badly with a leather strap that she could not work for a year. "All Frenchmen beat their wives" was a local saying, and it took great courage, and three years, for her to come forward to say "No." Her mother, Mrs. Scruggs, took her in. Later, when she had to see Albert to get child support, Loca would carry her black bullwhip.[59]

Albert moved on to another woman, his sister-in-law Maria Normand De-Louche (blonde, blue eyed, Cuban—much like Calixta in "At the 'Cadian Ball" and "The Storm"). They lived across a pasture from each other for the rest of his life, and he paid her bills for—it was said—the "fine sewing" she did for him.[60]

Kate Chopin had hardly forgotten Albert Sampite. Her violent, impetuous male characters all have names beginning with A, and those named Alcée (pro-nounced "Al-say," the same as "Al. S—e") share his passionate nature and charm, his love for horses and the night, as well as his dangerous side.

But some of the Louisiana that Kate Chopin knew had changed, been lost. An October 1893 hurricane destroyed some of Grand Isle and most of the smaller islands she had known, inspiring her to write an elegiac short story, "At Chênière Caminada," about an island fisherman infatuated with a New Orleans belle. That lost Grand Isle and Grand Terre also appear in *The Awakening*. (A century later, Grand Isle continues to disappear, pummeled by hurricanes and coastal erosion, and the tropical paradise Chopin described is now a spare fish-ing village, the water not safe for swimming.)

Her second, more mature short story collection, *A Night in Acadie* (1897), had even fewer conventional stories. Despite the title, the stories are not set in "Acadie" or Acadiana, the part of Louisiana roughly between Lafayette and Alexandria. Sometimes Chopin does use Acadian ("Cajun") names of people and places—but probably to deflect readers from thinking that everything she wrote was violating the privacy of real people.

The twenty-one stories in the *Night in Acadie* collection are mostly about character transformations. "Athénaïse," named for Chopin's grandmother, is about a runaway bride who changes her mind, while her husband learns not to force her to his will. In "A Respectable Woman," the protagonist has racy thoughts that she conceals; in "Regret," the central character, a grouchy single woman, learns that she loves children after all. In "Odalie Misses Mass," a thirteen-year-old white girl is proud of her new finery and wants to show it off in church—but instead chooses to spend the day with her best friend, a very old black woman. Their friendship is unique in American literature for the time, crossing racial and generational divides.

In *A Night in Acadie*, Chopin's women characters are eager and energetic, but the men are often gentle, bordering on being slackers, in such stories as "Polydore" and "Azélie." Yet they, too, can be generous across racial lines: in "Ozème's Holiday," a young white man gives up his vacation to do chores for an old black woman.

Chopin was mellowing, thinking about her five sons and what kind of men they would become. In 1897 Jean, the oldest, was twenty-six, and all of them except George, a medical student, still lived at home and resisted getting jobs. In late 1898 Chopin detached herself even more from Louisiana, finally selling her house in Cloutierville. She stopped in New Orleans long enough to attend writer Mollie Moore Davis's salon, where the guests often included such authors as Ruth McEnery Stuart, Catherine Cole, and Eliza Nicholson. And then Chopin went back to her own real life: her career as a St. Louis writer.[61]

Her editors had told Kate Chopin that she might have more success with a novel, and so she wrote, using her Louisiana material, the novel that became her fourth, last, and most famous book. She drew on Louisiana's natural, dreamlike loveliness, and its urban sophistication, and its tolerance—up to a point—for passion and rebellion.

The Awakening (1899) takes place entirely in Louisiana, beginning at the Creole summer resort, Grand Isle, where Edna Pontellier, mother of two, is a Kentucky-bred outsider who does not understand the affectionate, outspoken ways of the Creoles. She most admires the Creole "mother-woman," the beautiful Adèle Ratignolle, but she is also intrigued by the disagreeable pianist, Mademoiselle Reisz. Edna's stuffy husband, Léonce, is pompous and irritating. During the summer of her awakening, Edna learns to swim—feeling power in her body—and becomes infatuated with Robert, a Creole young man whose mother owns the island's cottages. Each summer, Robert devotes himself flirtatiously to a different female visitor, always a safely married woman. But this time he abruptly leaves for Mexico, and Edna is bereft.

Back home in New Orleans after the summer, Edna continues awakening to her discontent. Servants take care of her children, who eventually go for a long visit with their grandmother. When Léonce goes out of town, Edna refuses to go with him and moves out of his house into a little cottage of her own. She spends her days painting and thinking, and after awhile, her nights in an affair with a Creole roué, Alcée Arobin. She also carries on a continuing serious dialogue with her two friends, Adèle Ratignolle and Mademoiselle Reisz, about what manner of a woman she is. Is she an artist? A lover? Or a mother who's strayed from her primary duties?

Robert returns from Mexico and Edna declares her love for him, but then has to attend Adèle Ratignolle, who is giving birth. When Edna returns, Robert has abandoned her. After a sleepless night, Edna goes to Grand Isle and swims until her strength has gone.

The Awakening has much of the beauty of south Louisiana, and Edna, who turns twenty-nine, is the same age as Kate Chopin when she moved from New Orleans to Cloutierville. It is a critical age of self-discovery for women, even today, and often it means turning away from motherhood, from shaping one's life around others, and moving onto a new life path. Edna's two lovers, Alcée and Robert, both have parts of Albert Sampite's first name and his appeal, and *The Awakening* is the kind of story Kate Chopin had been observing all her life, among the many unfulfilled society women in Louisiana and St. Louis.

But she set her story in the lush paradise of Grand Isle, with acres of chamomile, the aroma of the sea, the calls of the gulls, and a hypnotic refrain: "The voice of the sea is seductive." Grand Isle, with its trembling prairie, casts a spell over Edna on hot summer nights. The little fort that she visits with Robert has wriggling snakes and blind sand crabs, and Robert entrances her with midnight stories of pirate gold.

New Orleans, too, is both symbolic and real. It is the wicked city, where rakes and secrets flourish, but also Léonce's place of business and keeping-up-with-the-Joneses. The Pontelliers live in a large, white and green double cottage on Esplanade, the boulevard where Degas stayed, and where young Kate O'Flaherty spent her marvelous evening with an opera singer on her first visit, thirty years earlier. Alcée Arobin takes Edna to the horse races and then out the shell road toward Lake Pontchartrain. Edna meets Robert in one of the many small cafés in a leafy garden in the suburbs, and the story ends on a crisp wintry, sunny day at Grand Isle, where the waves invite her. At the end, Edna is like the wounded bird she sees, circling the water before she goes under.

Kate Chopin knew what the gatekeepers would not publish in the United States. Although she translated Maupassant's writings about women with secret lovers, she knew that "guilty love" (adultery) was rarely permitted in American fiction. But after she turned in *The Awakening* to her publisher, she let her imagination run freely, back into her Louisiana past.

She wrote "The Storm" in St. Louis, in her diary, in 1898, and never attempted to publish it. She knew it was too hot for her contemporaries to handle.

The story takes place during a hot Louisiana afternoon in the Cane River country, with the lovers from "At the 'Cadian Ball" meeting again—five years later, each married to someone else. Calixta's husband is the sweet, bumbling Bobinôt; Alcée's wife is the pretty but prissy Clarisse.

Calixta is at her sewing machine when Alcée arrives on her porch during a rainstorm. The storm outside inspires a storm inside. The lovers gravitate toward the big white bed, filling the room like an altar, and the language is romantic and sensual: "Her lips seemed in a manner free to be tasted, as well as her round white throat and her whiter breasts. . . . And when he possessed her, they seemed to swoon together at the very borderland of life's mystery."[62]

Afterward, they laugh happily as he rides away. Calixta greets her husband and little son with great enthusiasm, while Alcée writes to his wife that she and their babies are welcome to stay at the Biloxi resort for as long as they like. "So the storm passed," the story concludes, "and every one was happy."

Calixta resembles Maria Normand DeLouche, Albert Sampite's mistress, who was the first woman in Cloutierville to own a sewing machine. Alcée resembles the romantic, passionate side of Albert Sampite—and we can only wonder whether something like "The Storm" ever took place in tiny Cloutierville where (most likely) everyone would have known about it.

By May 1899 everyone knew that Kate Chopin had published a new novel, *The Awakening*, and many reviewers were shocked and angry. They ignored some of Kate Chopin's smaller breaches of decorum, such as her description of a pregnant woman at a time when a woman with child was not to be seen in public. Unlike most women writers of her era, Kate Chopin was the mother of many children and raised as a Catholic. Depicting Madame Ratignolle as a beautiful and bountifully pregnant Madonna was not out of place for Kate Chopin.[63]

Reviewers did notice, and did not forgive, the fact that Edna in *The Awakening* commits adultery. Some fulminated that such a thing should not be mentioned, even though such things do happen; others inveighed against a wife and mother's having stray thoughts or urges. And yet . . . almost all the naysayers were men.[64]

The women of St. Louis wrote letters of praise to Kate Chopin and invited her to speak to their clubs. Her friends gathered round her, and although it was clear that her vision was too avant-garde—perhaps too French—for St. Louis in 1899, she was not alone.[65]

But at the turn of the century, there were other burdens that Kate Chopin was carrying alone. She was having trouble with her eyesight and with shortness of breath. St. Louis's air was very unhealthy, and she was a smoker. When her son Jean married—the first to do so—Chopin was delighted at the prospect of being a grandmother. Instead there was tragedy: her young daughter-in-law died in childbirth, along with her newborn baby. Jean had a nervous breakdown, from which he never fully recovered, and Chopin was tending him for the rest of her life.[66]

In the early 1900s she wrote half a dozen short stories, some of them children's sketches set in Louisiana, but her creative energies were mostly gone. Her third short story collection, *A Vocation and a Voice*, was canceled by the publisher (it was finally printed in 1991, ninety years after the original expected date).[67] Only three of its twenty-two stories are set in Louisiana, and one—"The Godmother"—is a strange and grim tale of a drunken young man, a social favorite among the student teachers in Natchitoches, who commits a murder. Kate Chopin was no longer a sunny writer of charming local color stories.

Still, she kept a lively curiosity. The St. Louis World's Fair of 1904 excited her, and she bought a daily pass. But after a particularly hot day at the fair, she suffered a cerebral hemorrhage and died, at age fifty-four, on August 22, 1904. She was buried in Calvary Cemetery in St. Louis.[68]

She was already being forgotten, and within a decade, most of her writings were out of print. Only "Désirée's Baby" remained in short story anthologies. It gives a very stark picture of Louisiana—slavery, violent tempers, an isolated plantation—and Désirée herself is submissive and almost silent, the kind of female figure who was favored for years in the American literary canon.

Kate Chopin was not entirely forgotten in Louisiana. At the Normal (teaching) School in Natchitoches (now Northwestern State University), students lived in Kate Chopin Hall, a dormitory that burned down in the 1970s, and they wrote adaptations of Chopin stories to perform with their drama club. In 1964 Mildred LaCaze McCoy of Cloutierville bought and restored the house that had been Kate Chopin's home, calling it the Bayou Folk Museum.[69]

But the national rediscovery of Kate Chopin turned out to have nothing to do with Louisiana. Per Seyersted, a Norwegian businessman who decided to become a literary scholar in his early forties, enrolled as a graduate student at Harvard University—where Cyrille Arnavon, a French professor, directed him to read Kate Chopin. Seyersted, whose mother was a women's rights leader in Norway, was hooked. Over nearly a decade, Seyersted doggedly traveled around the United States, collecting and copying (by hand) Chopin's forgotten stories and manuscripts. Finally he published them and a Chopin biography in 1969.[70]

Seyersted also promulgated the story that *The Awakening* had been banned and taken off library shelves in St. Louis. This was not true, but it served to attract scores of rebellious readers and feminists who wanted to read a banned book—and who were enthralled when they did.[71]

The Awakening, "Désirée's Baby," and "The Storm" are now the most widely read of Kate Chopin's Louisiana writings, although she is rarely considered a local color writer. Every September *The Awakening* sells more copies than it did during Chopin's lifetime, as students stock up for classes in American literature and women's studies. Most of the critical analyses and celebrations of her work come from outside Louisiana, and most often readers see her as a wise, mature recorder of women's lives, struggles, and passions.[72]

Still, it was Louisiana that formed Kate Chopin as a writer. At an impressionable age, she learned about sensuality, motherhood, music, marriage, and gossip in what was always an exotic and slightly foreign environment. In Louisiana she heard the stories and listened to murmured secrets, often in a unique French patois heard nowhere else in the world. She learned that much of life comes through hints, not through confrontations; through whispered words and carefully chosen silences.

Without Louisiana, Kate Chopin might have been an ordinary wife and mother in St. Louis. With Louisiana in her heritage and in her heart, she became what Edna in *The Awakening* is supposed to be: "The courageous soul . . . that dares and defies."[73]

In her small pocket of Louisiana, she created a universe.

NOTES

1. Kate Chopin, commonplace book diary, in Emily Toth, Per Seyersted, and Cheyenne Bonnell, eds., *Kate Chopin's Private Papers* (Bloomington: Indiana University Press, 1998), 85.

2. Toth, Seyersted, and Bonnell, eds., *Private Papers*, 85.

3. The source of all biographical information unless otherwise stated is Emily Toth, *Unveiling Kate Chopin* (Jackson: University Press of Mississippi, 1999). That book also draws on Emily Toth, *Kate Chopin* (New York: William Morrow, 1990).

4. Toth, *Unveiling Kate Chopin*, 9.

5. Kate Chopin, *The Complete Works of Kate Chopin*, ed. Per Seyersted (Baton Rouge: Louisiana State University Press, 1969), 353–54.

6. Toth, *Unveiling Kate Chopin*, 11.

7. Toth, *Unveiling Kate Chopin*, 11–14.

8. Toth, *Unveiling Kate Chopin*, 30–31.

9. Toth, Seyersted, and Bonnell, eds., *Private Papers*, 82.

10. Ibid.

11. Ibid., 64.

12. Toth, *Unveiling Kate Chopin*, 63–64.

13. Ibid., 52.

14. Ibid.

15. Toth, Seyersted, and Bonnell, eds., *Private Papers*, 100–121.

16. Toth, *Unveiling Kate Chopin*, 61.

17. Ibid., 65–67.

18. Ibid., 65.

19. Chopin, *Complete Works*, 285.

20. Kate Chopin, 1894 diary, in Toth, Seyersted, and Bonnell, eds., *Private Papers*, 183.

21. Chopin, *Complete Works*, 994.

22. Toth, *Unveiling Kate Chopin*, 71–72.

23. Ibid., 78–80.

24. Ibid., 76–77.

25. Ibid., 32–33.

26. Ibid., 67, 68, 130.

27. Ibid., 80.

28. Ibid., 73–75.

29. Chopin, *Complete Works*, 301.

30. Toth, *Unveiling Kate Chopin*, 81.

31. Ibid., 84.

32. Ibid., 82–84. See the chapters on Marie Thérèse Coincoin and Clementine Hunter in this volume for more information about the Natchitoches area.

33. Toth, *Unveiling Kate Chopin*, 89–90.

34. Ibid., 85.

35. Ibid.

36. Ibid., 86–87.

37. Ibid., 87.

38. Ibid., 86.

39. Ibid., 90–92.

40. Ibid., 92–93.

41. Chopin, *Complete Works*, 215.

42. Toth, *Unveiling Kate Chopin*, 95–99.

43. Ibid., 97, 99.

44. Ibid., 99–100.

45. Chopin, *Complete Works*, 741.

46. Ibid., 202, 105–6.

47. Ibid., 124, 159.

48. Ibid., 122–23.

49. Toth, Seyersted, and Bonnell, eds., *Private Papers*, 183.

50. Toth, *Unveiling Kate Chopin*, 128–30.

51. Chopin, *Complete Works*, 105.

52. Toth, *Unveiling Kate Chopin*, 148–50.

53. Chopin, *Complete Works*, 244.

54. Ibid., 693.

55. Susan Koppelman, ed., *Women in the Trees: U.S. Women's Stories about Battering and Resistance, 1839–2000* (New York: Feminist Press, 2000).

56. Chopin, *Complete Works*, 228.

57. Susan Koppelman, personal communication, October 31, 1997.

58. Toth, *Unveiling Kate Chopin*, 171.

59. Ibid., 140.

60. Ibid., 206.

61. Ibid., 207.

62. Chopin, *Complete Works*, 594–95.

63. Toth, *Unveiling Kate Chopin*, 220.

64. Ibid., 220–24.

65. Ibid., 224–27.

66. Ibid., 236–38.

67. Susan Koppelman, personal communication, October 31, 1997.

68. Toth, *Unveiling Kate Chopin*, 239–40.

69. Ibid., 242.

70. Per Seyersted, *Kate Chopin: A Critical Biography* (Baton Rouge: Louisiana State University Press, 1969), and Chopin, *Complete Works*.

71. Toth, *Unveiling Kate Chopin*, 243.

72. Ibid., 243–44.

73. Chopin, *Complete Works*, 946.

Grace King

(1852–1932)

New Orleans Literary Historian

MARY ANN WILSON

❀ ❀ ❀

Grace King was born in New Orleans in 1852 in the decade preceding America's bloodiest war, a war that would shape her sensibilities and inspire a fierce loyalty to her city and her region. When the war came ten-year-old Grace stood at an upstairs window of the King townhouse on Camp Street, watching the flames along the Mississippi levee destroying stores of cotton and supplies the Confederates were burning lest they come into the hands of the enemy.[1] Her family decided to abandon their New Orleans home and take refuge on a family plantation near New Iberia, Louisiana. Grace King never forgot this experience of loss and dispossession; in fact, she would begin her 1932 autobiography, *Memories of a Southern Woman of Letters*, with a dramatization of the scene. Her family would never recover its former wealth and position. This exile from home and her subsequent experiences in Reconstruction New Orleans reinforced King's innate conservatism and desire to preserve what could be salvaged from the city and its past.

In both fiction and history, Grace King set herself this grand task of preservation, believing that after catastrophic events it remains for the women who survive to document, chronicle, and often defend the past. To these ends, she wrote histories of Louisiana's colonial past. But she wrote fiction centered in her own time—the Civil War and Reconstruction—and focused on how these events profoundly affected the lives of women.[2] New Orleans became, in Grace King's mind and in the minds of post–Civil War Americans, a microcosm of the South, a city with a unique racial and political history and a mélange of ethnicities demanding its own story in the larger national narrative. Beneath the veneer of harmless local color fiction, in a writing career that spanned five

GRACE KING

From the oil sketch of King by Nell Pomeroy O'Brien, circa 1935.

Courtesy of the Historic New Orleans Collection, Museum/Research Center,

acc. no. 1987.178.1.

decades from the 1880s to the 1930s, Grace King asked questions about both black and white women's roles and functions that echoed larger questions of national unity and identity plaguing a country still reeling from a divisive civil war but on the cusp of a larger global destiny.

Unlike her contemporary Kate Chopin, Grace King never married. She more closely fits the common nineteenth-century stereotype of women writers: single and childless, she lived in the family home with her parents and siblings all her life; she began to write after her father's death and her favorite sister's marriage and published her first article anonymously. Grace King was also proficient and prolific in several genres—history, biography, and autobiography as well as fiction—much like the French women of letters she met on her European trips. This European model blended with her own evolving conception of a southern woman writer and with a newly emerging professionalism among women writers as a group in America. Unlike their early nineteenth-century sisters, these women were not always driven by economic necessity to write. Yet, particularly in the South, because the proper southern lady's behavior was culturally prescribed, they felt compelled to give public reasons for their work that had nothing to do with literary vocation or passion to express themselves.[3]

Grace King combined the economic motive—she began to write after her father's death, hoping to be financially independent—with an avowed desire to sustain an intellectual life through her writing. It may in fact have been this intellectuality that distanced her from the well-meaning but decidedly unintellectual and somewhat intimidated young men who might have been her suitors.[4] Her letters and journal entries reveal a woman passionate about being physically and financially independent, conditions marriage would inevitably threaten. She also makes some strong statements against southern males, pointing to the discrepancy between their outward chivalry and their private egotism, dissipation, and cruel treatment of their wives. Despite youthful suitors and curiosity about the intimacies of marriage, Grace King seems to have ultimately settled into a single literary life sustained from childhood by a clear and inspired sense of herself as a writer, observing wistfully only on occasion that marriageable men were scarce.

Living out her artistic vocation in a radically changed postwar American South, Grace King dramatized women's experience across the color line, capitalizing, as Kate Chopin did, on the northern appetite for stories about the South, a region deemed exotic, quaint, and still steeped in antebellum mythology. In a Gilded Age America masking the failures of Reconstruction, Grace King emerged as a representative voice of white New Orleans and Louisiana. She was a Protestant American championing an aristocratic Creole world in decline by uncritically heroicizing its patriarchal past in her histories.⁵ But despite herself she captured its complex racial and political dynamic in her fiction.

Grace King's writing career began with a challenge from the northern editor of *Century* magazine, Richard Watson Gilder, during the 1885 Cotton Centennial Exposition in New Orleans. Gilder had previously published the works of another New Orleanian, George Washington Cable, whose negative depictions of autocratic, cruel, mixed-race Creoles' treatment of their slaves in such works as *Old Creole Days* (1879) and *The Grandissimes* (1880) angered both King and the white Creole establishment of the city. At the same time that cities like New Orleans sought to rehabilitate their post–Civil War image and economy through such events as the exposition, individual southerners like Grace King were equally committed to such rehistoricizing. When Gilder challenged her to write better of Creoles than Cable had done, she set to work writing what would be her first major published work, "Monsieur Motte" (1886), the story of a freed quadroon slave's undying loyalty to the white daughter of her former master and mistress. Set against the background of Grace King's own experience during the 1860s as a student at the Institut St. Louis, a private school for girls, this is a story of surrogate motherhood in which the former slave Marcelite, hairdresser to the young girls, reveals herself to be the fictional "Monsieur Motte," who has been paying for the orphan Marie to attend the *institut*. But the self-abasing Marcelite is quick to clarify that Marie is indeed white. Stripped of her identity as "Monsieur Motte," Marcelite loses all her previous power and "she began to reproach God, and vaguely to rebel against the shadow on her skin as casting the shadow on her life."⁶ Like Kate Chopin's story, "Désirée's Baby," King's tale is a complex one of race, identity, and interracial maternal love whose larger issues the author manages to avoid. Dealing more easily with gender issues than racial ones, she gives us a look behind the walls of a Catholic girls' school with all its rituals and coming-of-age trials. The girls are like hothouse flowers, reared and sheltered from the world in an unnatural environment, ill prepared for the moral complexities waiting outside the convent walls. In uniting themes of maternity, racial identity, and the cloistered lives of young white girls and women, "Monsieur Motte" delineates the path of Grace King's future fiction and also reveals that she was perhaps more passionately—and certainly more straightforwardly—interested in writing about women than she was in writing about race relations in postbellum New Orleans.

In the expanded version of this story, her 1888 novel *Monsieur Motte*, King has the quadroon Marcelite walk Marie down the aisle and shed tears the night before on the bridal wreath, "the tears that only mothers shed on bridal wreaths of daughters, praying the prayers that only mothers pray on the wedding nights of daughters."[7] King creates a fairy-tale ending in the tradition of the sentimental novel, complete with restored plantation, a marriage of love and not of convenience, and an abject, fawning former slave who has redeemed herself in the eyes of the white world—everyone living together in harmony because of their mutual goodness. King's vision of a future Edenic South much like the plantation myth of earlier sentimental fiction hardly explores the deeper implications of its racial themes. Like many southern women of her generation, the author of *Monsieur Motte* seemed unable to imagine a relationship of equality between a black and a white woman, so even in the decades of the 1880s and 1890s, she typically reverts to the master-slave trope while tentatively granting her black characters their share of common humanity.

The world of *Monsieur Motte* was Grace King's adopted world, bequeathed to her from her parents: the distinguished attorney William Woodson King, with Georgia and Alabama roots, and the New Orleans-born Sarah Ann Miller—both Protestants who ultimately immersed themselves in Catholic Creole culture. Young Grace's bonds to white Creole culture were forged early in her childhood when, like her mother, she attended French-speaking Catholic convent schools in New Orleans, receiving there the best education to be had in the area during this time period. Despite their Anglo-Presbyterian heritage, the Kings and Millers had earlier assimilated easily into the sophisticated Creole and Roman Catholic New Orleans world of the 1840s, illustrating the gradual blending of two major groups making up nineteenth-century New Orleans.[8]

References to her mother frame Grace King's career, as maternal themes permeate her works. She dedicates her 1893 volume of short stories, *Balcony Stories*, to her mother, "whose balcony stories were the delight of my childhood"; and over forty years later, at the end of her career, Grace King pays tribute yet again to "that charming *raconteuse*," on the first page of *Memories of a Southern Woman of Letters*.[9] Sarah Miller King's verbal facility and her love of books clearly marked her imaginative daughter's formative years, attuning her to the nuances of female voice and experience and to the defining events of women's lives: education, marriage or the single life, work, motherhood. In the lyrical introduction to *Balcony Stories*, King invokes those "low, soft mother voices" that inspired the stories, thus providing an organizing metaphor for this collection of brief, impressionistic vignettes detailing the various fates of women, black and white: the decline of a spoiled, pampered beauty in "La Grande Demoiselle"; romantic illusion versus the reality of marriage in "Mimi's Marriage"; the reconciliation of two estranged women in "The Old Lady's Restoration"; the surrogate motherhood of a crippled, freed slave in "A Crippled Hope."

The most frequently anthologized short story from this collection is "The

Little Convent Girl," a tale of thwarted mother love and a daughter's tragic death—both motivated by the young girl's discovery that her mother is black. Like Marie Modeste, the little convent girl has been sheltered from life and its realities behind cloistered walls; but her fate is complicated by a racial identity she discovers only when she is released from the convent and put on a boat downriver to New Orleans, into the arms of the mother whose identity mirrors her own. Eighteen years old, on the cusp of womanhood, this innocent young girl is brought back to the boat a month later by her distraught mother to see the captain and his crew who had begun to show her the larger world outside the convent. The mother is desperate to divert her obviously morose daughter. But at the story's end, the little convent girl slips into the Mississippi River, petticoats fluttering. King's ambivalent ending—whether the drowning is intentional or an accident—nevertheless reads like a death wish: "Perhaps, as the pilot had told her whirlpools always did, it may have carried her through to the underground river, to that vast, hidden, dark Mississippi that flows beneath the one we see; for her body was never found."[10] King's heroine succumbs to the currents of race and region marking identity in the pre- and postwar South, as King herself dramatizes the fates of those marked by miscegenation.

While her mother's stories fed Grace King's literary imagination, she was concurrently developing a historical sense fueled by New Orleans's European heritage, its maternal roots in France and the city of Paris, which King would call "the mother of New Orleans."[11] At the age of sixteen, she met one of the major Creole intellectuals of his day, Charles Gayarré, the renowned historian of the Louisiana Territory. Gayarré was a significant influence on her life and sensibility, and the inspiration for her own historical imagination. His European-furnished country retreat outside New Orleans, his extensive library and intense love of the French language, his encouragement of King's burgeoning literary and historical interests—all combined to help shape Grace King's literary vocation. She would later dedicate her 1895 *New Orleans: The Place and the People* to his memory, concluding the book with an account of his funeral. Gayarré's library, transferred to the King home after his death, contained original copies of Spanish and French exploration narratives that would serve as seminal documents for her 1896 biography of the founder of New Orleans, Jean Baptiste le Moyne, Sieur de Bienville, and for her *De Soto and His Men in the Land of Florida* (1898).

But these historical works would come considerably later than the watershed year of 1885 when northern publisher Richard Watson Gilder issued his famous challenge to Grace King. It would be during that same year that King would meet the New England reformer Julia Ward Howe, who was in New Orleans at the invitation of the Centennial Exposition to direct its Women's Department. A hard-driving, energetic proponent of abolition and woman's suffrage, the sixty-five-year-old New York-born activist was, ironically, put in charge of showcasing New Orleans history at the centennial, which she apparently did successfully by assembling art objects and memorabilia from old Creole houses and displaying them for New Orleanians. Howe also resurrected a literary club called the Pan Gnostics, which held weekly meetings to discuss literature or to hear one of its members present a paper. Among the club's members was Eliza Poitevent Nicholson, who had become proprietor of the *New Orleans Picayune* after her husband's death in 1876. "Heroines of Novels," the paper Grace King presented, would become her first published article. Timid about writing and delivering it, King nevertheless took the opportunity to express herself as a fledgling literary critic who had read widely and thought intelligently about how women characters were portrayed in English, American, French, and German literatures. She concluded that none of these writers were true to the reality of women's lives, none probed their complex nature, but relied instead on flat domestic icons or soulless sensualists. Not surprisingly, she finds Charlotte Brontë and George Eliot most to her liking. Perhaps the ideas in King's first literary effort were less important than the fact that she overcame her timidity and read the essay before an enthusiastic and supportive group of intelligent and like-minded men and women—an early literary community that helped to focus her considerable intellectual energy, gave her an audience for her still-evolving literary aesthetic, and prepared her for the literary salons she would witness in Paris and the later vibrant gatherings of artists and writers she would hold in her New Orleans home on Coliseum Street.

Watching Julia Ward Howe orchestrate the Women's Department of the Cotton Centennial and spearhead this gathering of readers and writers inevitably gave Grace King a glimpse of a species of woman radically different from the demure, modest, and passive ideal, a vestige of prewar days in the South, still predominant in New Orleans. King's reaction to such a woman was characteristically ambivalent. Although she admired Howe's organizational skills and enterprising spirit, she deplored her lack of feminine grace. Writing to her sister May McDowell, King complained that Howe and her daughter Maud "literally 'grabbed' for food—and eat and drank like cormorants."[12] Clearly, Grace King appreciated the new vistas such protofeminists like Howe opened up to her but lamented the sacrifice of feminine modesty and propriety often accompanying such vision. In this respect, King was not unlike many other women of her time—North and South—caught in a transitional period that would spawn the New Woman and usher in an era of unprecedented and rapid change in the new century.

King's world continued to expand as she traveled to New England at the invitation of noted writer and editor Charles Dudley Warner in 1888. Warner was editor of the Hartford *Courant* and coauthor with his friend Samuel Clemens of the 1873 novel *The Gilded Age*, which ultimately gave the era its name. Warner introduced her to the residential community of Nook Farm in Hartford, Connecticut, where such luminaries as Warner, Samuel Clemens, feminist activist Isabella Beecher Hooker, and the by then aged Harriet Beecher Stowe lived and wrote. King's friendship with Olivia Clemens would remain a sustaining force in her life. "Livy," as she was affectionately called by her husband and close friends, was a woman described as "refined," and "domestic" rather than intellectual.[13] She thus accorded with the southern writer's ideas about proper feminine behavior.

But on another level, the friendship between Olivia Langdon Clemens and Grace King was a surprising one. Olivia was born to a wealthy abolitionist family, the Langdons, in Elmira, New York. As Susan K. Harris points out, the Langdons were social activists committed to human rights and were most likely financial backers of the Elmira branch of the Underground Railroad. Living in Hartford, Connecticut, among the literati of Nook Farm, Olivia Clemens was exposed to the major intellectual currents of her day in science and natural philosophy. Like Grace King, she was proficient in languages as well as an avid reader, and she pursued, at least before her marriage to Samuel Clemens, an intellectual life in keeping with the Victorian constraints of her day. Olivia eventually became her famous author-husband's editor and censor, reading many of his works in manuscript and shaping the text the public would read. Although from opposite ends of the political spectrum, Olivia Clemens and Grace King shared a love of reading and books, often discussing these in their letters. Robert Bush argues that Grace and Livy "were symbolic types of their respective regions, and both were representative of the American late nineteenth century."[14]

As young women from different sides of the sectional divide coming of age during a period of radical change in women's lives, Grace and Olivia embodied many of the same contradictions. They both believed in the importance of women's education and were lifelong readers. Both outwardly espoused and valued traditional feminine roles while admiring more militant and activist women in the public sphere. Grace and Olivia became confidantes from the early years of King's career, sharing their anxieties about family problems and reporting news of their European travels. Livy of course settled into Victorian domesticity with the volatile but loving man who would become Mark Twain, while Grace went on to become a public persona in the salons of Europe and New Orleans. The last letter Grace King wrote to Livy Clemens curiously combines her heartfelt sympathy on the death of the Clemenses' beloved daughter Susy with comments criticizing the affluent Hartford society she had witnessed on her New England trips. Calling Hartford a "most perfect expression of American Philistinism,"[15] King ungraciously attacks her former hosts in this intimate letter of consolation to her friend. Despite the personal relationship she had sustained with Livy Clemens, King could not resist essentializing and equating her with the opulence of postwar New England.

Indeed, throughout her northern travels, Grace King was alternately seduced and repelled by the prosperous Gilded Age mansions evoking memories of an impoverished South. She often felt her outsider status as the representative southerner at dinner parties and social gatherings. One memorable party given by Sam and Olivia Clemens found King seated beside the notorious Union general Lucius Fairchild who proceeded to denounce President Grover Cleveland's decision to return Confederate battle flags to the South. She wrote her sister Nan about her dinner with "the man I've been railing at like everything for a week. . . . He is a very good looking, sleek faced one-arm rascal. Hypocrite is written all over his face and drops from his tongue whenever he opens his mouth."[16] Although in some ways Grace King's southern conservatism intensified as a result of her New England sojourn, on this and subsequent visits to the region her feminist sympathies deepened—at least temporarily—as a result of meeting a new breed of women, northern feminists and autonomous creative women writers who gave her a new image of herself and of the future of women as a whole: Isabella Hooker, Olivia Clemens, Mary Wilkins, Annie Fields, Sarah Orne Jewett.[17] She never became a propagandist, a role she would have shunned, but King was an early advocate of woman suffrage. Susan B. Anthony, in 1888, in fact invited Grace King to speak on the suffrage question at a convention in Washington, but she declined. The issue of suffrage no doubt sensitized the southern author to the power dynamics influencing her life and the lives of all women. Like many women writers of her day, Grace King was still dependent on male editors for publishing venues and opportunities, but the example of these New England women who enhanced a sense of herself as a serious writer fostered her confidence in her abilities and talents.

This trip outside the confines of New Orleans and Louisiana became the first of many over the next decades to New York, New England, Canada, England, and to that mother of New Orleans, Paris. In France, she met two women— Madame Marie Thérèse Blanc, a sophisticated writer and critic acquainted with American literature and a protégée of George Sand, and Madame Blaze de Bury, doyenne of a literary salon attracting the leading artists and intellectuals of her day. After her return from Europe in 1892, Grace King assumed the role of hostess to prominent writers who visited New Orleans, carrying on the Parisian tradition of the salon she had witnessed and admired. Madame Blanc and Grace King knew each other's cultures well; later Blanc published an article on the work of Grace King, while King wrote a series of articles in *Harper's Bazaar* on Madame Blanc and her circle. Grace King's comments on Madame Blanc stress the French woman's innate morality, the absence of "French sins" in her novels and "blue-stockingism" in her salons.[18] These rather provincial and prudish observations contrast sharply with another incident stemming from King's European sojourns. Madame Blanc proposed that King translate and publish for an American audience some letters of George Sand to one of her paramours, Michel de Bourge. When she returned to New Orleans, King gave the letters to Charles Dudley Warner, her Hartford friend, wanting to give him a chance to read and comment on the prospects for publication. "He jumped away from them as from a fire," King recalls, "and wrote me a severe scolding for translating them. No magazine would publish such things, he wrote, and he was ashamed that I should even think of submitting them to an editor."[19] Although she admits to being shocked at the letters' erotic content, the southern spinster was perfectly willing to have them published. Warner's reaction, however, points to the residual genteel Puritan tradition that still reigned in turn-of-the-century America. Bowing to the will of her male editor, King abandoned this project after his rejection, lamenting the decision in her memoirs—if only she had completed it, she could have tried to publish it during the 1930s, when the literary climate had become more tolerant and enlightened.

The 1890s were a productive decade: King wrote two volumes of fiction, *Tales of a Time and Place* and *Balcony Stories*; the biography of Bienville; her *History of Louisiana* for schools; *New Orleans, the Place and the People*; and *De Soto and His Men in the Land of Florida*. Grace King was one of many American women writers, dating from the colonial period, who wrote histories, either anonymously or under their own names. This practice stemmed directly from female students' exposure to history in their antebellum curricula. Admittedly, most of these women were from New England and were initially spurred on by the drama of the Revolutionary War and its aftermath. The range of works was impressive, from histories of educational institutions to sacred histories to histories of famous men such as George Washington for use in schools. What if anything Grace King knew of these women writers and their works is unclear, but the fact remains that there was a female literary tradition in place for the writing of history in several genres, including poetry, drama, and prose fiction. Living in a city like New Orleans, whose colorful past witnessed the flags of France, Spain, the United States, and the Confederacy alternately flying; surviving a war that heightened her already-fertile literary and historical imagination; having access to the library of a prominent male historian of Louisiana—no doubt all of these factors contributed to King's foray into history writing. And the initial chapter of her first major published work, *Monsieur Motte*, shows us the girls of the Institut St. Denis competing for a recitation prize from "l'Histoire de France, par D. Lévi Alvares, pére."[20]

Grace King immersed herself in the wealth of data on colonial Louisiana history. She was inspired by her earlier talks with Charles Gayarré but wrote about these topics from her own unique perspective. She infused dull historical and geographical details with life by focusing on the personalities of the men she treated. With the fiction writer's eye, she saw the essential drama of events such as Iberville's first glimpse of the Mississippi River and the picturesque details of setting. She gave her reader a landscape grounded in factual detail but colored with imaginative flair. In the following selection, she takes us from the Gulf Coast of two centuries ago to her own view of it in the present:

> A railroad trestle now spans the deep embrasured little recess, and the eye of the speeding passenger can note on the eastern side the eminence upon which Iberville camped nearly two centuries ago. Now, as then, guns, planted upon it, would sweep three fourths of the limited horizon, arbitrarily commanding the channel in all its length and breadth. The channel now is ever white with sails of business or pleasure boats, and the fanciful gaudiness of summer villas studs the sombre, heavily-wooded beach. Opposite the island, under the wide-spreading branches of the great oaks where once the fishing and hunting parties of Indians lighted their fires and swung their cauldrons, a quaint assemblage of French and Spanish houses forms a town,—a town picturesque and redolent of an indefinable charm, despite the sordid vulgarities of competing summer-resort hotels.[21]

Perhaps the history that best captures Grace King's unique melding of historical data with fictive technique is her 1895 *New Orleans: The Place and the People*. In her dedication to the memory of Gayarré, she notes that his "recent death at the age of ninety . . . may have seemed the end of nineteenth-century Creole civilization."[22] Personifying the city as female, King seems in this work to be extending her fictional treatment of girls and women in transition to this protean city that has transformed itself over time but has never lost its essential French character. She romanticizes New Orleans's lack of competition with sister cities, its unenterprising nature, its sensuous, languid spirit, calling it neither a "Puritan mother, nor a hardy Western pioneeress."[23] In this respect, King was tapping into national discourses about Louisiana and New Orleans, represented in, for example, the 1870 series of articles called *The Great South* by journalist Edward King published in *Scribner's* magazine depicting Louisiana as "a paradise lost . . . its rich vitality dormant and passive, luxurious and unambitious, on the glorious shores of the tropic Gulf."[24] Embedded in the chapters on male explorers, conquerors, and statesmen are fascinating accounts of how shiploads of young women, potential wives for the young male colonists, arrived from the mother country France in the eighteenth century to domesticate the men and keep them from marrying Indian girls; how the Ursuline sisters came to New Orleans from Rouen to educate generations of young New Orleans women, black, white, and Indian; how three "secular" women dressed up as men so they could fight when their ship was attacked by pirates. Chapter 4, "The Ursuline Sisters," thus documents how women, secular and sacred, came to New Orleans. Throughout her narrative, Grace King makes observations with characteristic irony. For example, she notes that "the women here are extremely ignorant as to the means of securing their salvation, but they are very expert in the art of displaying their beauty," describing shortly after the procession of young schoolgirls, white and virginal, in honor of their patron, Saint Ursula.[25] In this lyrical, impressionistic history anchored in stories one might have heard from those mothers on balconies, the author articulates the essential civilizing nature of women and captures that elusive blend of sacred and secular that is New Orleans. She interprets data rather than merely reporting, making *New Orleans: The Place and the People* a feminized social history eminently readable even in our own time.

One section in particular of this unique history indicates Grace King's historical grasp of New Orleans's complex racial situation and reveals the largely unconscious, culturally conditioned, assumptions she made about race and caste. Chapter 14, "The Convent of the Holy Family," treats one of the city's established religious orders and the death of its mother superior. This death piques the natives' curiosity as to the identity of these women and the role they have played in the city's history. King uses the mother superior's death as an occasion to delineate the various racial hierarchies in the city—free people of color, both nativeborn and from the West Indies; mulattoes, quadroons, octoroons; and, at the bottom of the racial scale, Negro. The founders of the "colored sisters" of the Convent of the Holy Family, descended from free people of color, set up orphanages, asylums for the sick and aged, and generally ministered to those in need. From their remote, virginal convents, their contributions to the life of the community were uncomplicated and safe. But in this same chapter, King also

discusses the quadroon subculture of "almost white" women who would do anything to have their daughters pass for white and marry into the privileged class.
For these mothers and their daughters, viewed through the lens of a historian
whose patrician views of her city's origins and future often blinded her to the
deeper social and cultural realities of a society in transition, Grace King showed
little of the sympathy we see in her fiction. She sees them as "unscrupulous and
pitiless," "secretly still claiming the racial license of Africa." These women are, in
her mind, threats to "family purity, domestic peace, and household dignity, the
most insidious and the deadliest foes a community ever possessed."[26] For this
southern historian, whose 1921 *Creole Families of New Orleans* traced Creole
origins to distinguished white European bloodlines, the quadroon subculture
in New Orleans embodied racial ambiguities she could treat more subtly and
sensitively in her fiction where her sympathy for dispossessed and powerless
women often overcame her innate conservatism about race.

As the new century began, Grace King suffered the deaths of her mother and
brother Will and of her former mentor and publisher, Charles Dudley Warner.
Time and reflection and a lingering resentment of the riches and splendor she
saw in the New England mansions of her northern friends increased the emotional distance she felt from this earlier life. At the same time, she continued
her work with the Louisiana Historical Society, often serving as its official hostess for visiting dignitaries such as President McKinley and lecturing to history
teachers about Louisiana history. She was becoming not only a kind of representative New Orleanian, with all that this implied both locally and nationally,
but also the public image of intellectual southern womanhood. All of these factors, coupled with an invitation from the northern publisher of her New Orleans history to write a romance about the Reconstruction period in the South,
eventually resulted in her 1916 novel, *The Pleasant Ways of St. Medard*.

This novel hardly qualifies as a romance of Reconstruction, as King staunchly
resisted publisher requests for love stories of Federal officers and southern belles
like Thomas Nelson Page's 1898 *Red Rock* and Thomas Dixon's 1902 *The Leop-
ard's Spots*. These two writers and others like them had bowed to editorial pres-
sures to package the war's aftermath in palatable formula fiction, appropriate for
"genteel tradition" magazines. But life for Grace King in post–Civil War New
Orleans had often been grim and difficult and in her mind demanded serious
authorial treatment. She indeed always felt herself to be a realist "a la mode de
la Nlle Orleans" with "a mind sensitive to romantic impressions, but critical as
to their expression."[27] She did however rewrite *St. Medard* five times, trying to
please George Brett of Macmillan. The book languished on editorial shelves

until it was discovered in manuscript by critic Edward Garnett, who, assuming King's novel had already been published, wrote a glowing review of it, along with Willa Cather's *O Pioneers!* for the *Atlantic Monthly* in February 1916.

The Pleasant Ways of St. Medard, published by Henry Holt, tells the story of two families, black and white, in Reconstruction Louisiana, in the small town of St. Medard in St. Bernard Parish, southeast of New Orleans. Closely based on the King family's experiences after the war, *St. Medard* is a tale of dispossession and exile that shows the effects of the war on the economic, social, and psychological health of its characters. The novel dramatizes how slaves were inevitably separated from their former masters, how gender roles were destabilized after the war, how southern masculinity had to be nurtured and rehabilitated by women in the wake of defeat—and how all of these factors resulted in a society whose race, class, and gender boundaries became permeable and shifting. Grace King is remarkably clear sighted in observing how all the patriarchal structures suffered as a result of the war, and she bemoans a world turned upside down. Within these disintegrating structures, David Kirby maintains that "the true heroines of King's works . . . are typically strong and resourceful characters, female 'men of action,' to use King's phrase."[28]

The novel went into several small but respectable printings, but perhaps because America was caught up in 1916 in the war in Europe that soon would be its own war, *St. Medard* never received the wide critical exposure and acclaim it might have. In a letter to Edward Garnett, who enthusiastically endorsed the manuscript, the author relates that the book was a best seller in New Orleans and had been well received nationally. But she laments that southern newspapers were largely indifferent to it, which shows, she asserts, "that the South has been too well whipped to have any longer any individual pride."[29] King goes on to say, however, that the women she knows who have gone through Reconstruction claim the story as their own, as do the men. Clearly, King's novel struck a resonant chord with those whose fate it seemed to echo. Another generation of readers is presently rediscovering this "memoir thinly disguised as fiction"[30] and will no doubt situate it in the larger discourses about the Civil War and women that historians and literary critics are creating.

As America moved into the decade of the 1920s and yet another postwar period, Grace King was in her seventies holding court in the city she loved. She had been awarded an honorary doctorate of letters in 1915 by Tulane University and remained a driving force in the Louisiana Historical Society. She stood in the streets of New Orleans in 1918 celebrating Armistice Day in a scenario vastly different from her childhood Civil War experience in 1865. Her Friday afternoons of conversation and tea in the house on Coliseum Street attracted artists, writers, and critics. Among those who called were American writer Sherwood Anderson, author of *Winesburg, Ohio*; critic Edmund Wilson, whose memoir, *The Twenties*, documented his relationships with American writers both at home and abroad who were shaping a new generation of fiction; Lafcadio Hearn, a transplant to New Orleans who was writing sketches of Creole life for New Orleans newspapers; and Lyle Saxon, another chronicler of the city's past and present. Saxon would in fact dedicate his 1928 series of impressionistic vignettes of the city, *Fabulous New Orleans*, to Grace King. Inspired by her earlier exposure to the salons of Paris, these gatherings of writers and artists served as an important social and cultural thread in the rich tapestry that was literary New Orleans in the 1920s. In 1924 she helped found Le Petit Salon, a women's group that met to hear lectures given by various literary and artistic figures, and she gave receptions for the cast of Le Petit Theatre, a regional little theater group in the French Quarter. She served as the salon's president until her death in 1932. The salon continues today, though it no longer flourishes with a four-hundred-woman membership as it did in Grace King's day.[31]

By this time in her life, she had written thirteen books, eleven of which were concerned with New Orleans, and had achieved a position of some eminence locally, nationally, and internationally. The French government would decorate her with the gold palms of officier de l'instruction publique for her work on the history of Louisiana and its French roots and for her abiding interest in public education. She had humanized and feminized the process of historical research with her woman's eye for detail and artifact, making it clear that to her history lay just as much in "bits of old furniture, jewelry, glass, old miniatures, portraits, scraps of silk and brocade" as in the dusty volumes of historical archives.[32]

But Grace King's relationship with New Orleans was never uncomplicated. Like a loving but stern relative, throughout her career she had castigated the city for its intellectual apathy, its failure to buy her books, its excessive interest in balls and social functions at the expense of more artistic or intellectual endeavors. Echoing journalist Edward King's depiction of Louisiana and New Orleans as passive and languid, Grace King in *New Orleans: The Place and the People* criticized the city for its lack of ambition and competitiveness and its citizens for their self-indulgent appetites for food and festivity.

Commenting to a friend about local reception of her 1921 book, *Creole Families of New Orleans*, King wrote: "The price causes inevitable consternation. How capricious is the taste of extravagant people. Our rich ones who literally are casting money before swine, in the way of luncheons, teas, and country club frolics, are affrighted at the idea of paying six dollars for a book."[33] She even extended this criticism to the entire South, where she maintained that "books are of no account." Whether King's criticism merely masked her disdain for changing literary tastes or not, these private statements to sympathetic friends indicate the radical split between the public and the private Grace King. Like a good southern daughter, she extolled the virtues of her city and region in public documents while lamenting their flaws and shortcomings in private. The same impulse that led her to focus her energies on the history of colonial Louisiana rather than on times closer to her own also lies behind the last of Grace King's works, her 1932 memoir, *Memories of a Southern Woman of Letters*, published just a few months after her death.

Writing her memoirs was an act of self-assertion for Grace King but also of self-repression, illustrating what Kate Capshaw Smith describes as a "cosmetic impulse, a particularly southern strategy of evasion and denial."[34] Most of the chapters in this profile of a southern woman of letters in fact deal with her trips abroad and to Canada and her efforts to educate the English, the French, and those woefully ignorant northerners about the South and Louisiana. She dedicates a whole chapter to her French mentor Madame Blanc, praising her dedication to her writing, even in her last days. King details her efforts in all her travels to create an image of the South for public consumption. At the same time, she likewise tries to create a persona and voice for public consumption in this, her last book. Imagining a largely northern readership for *Memories* may have contributed to her efforts to minimize unpleasant conversations with northerners about the South and her own family's experiences while in exile during the war. As a "Who's Who" of local, national, and international celebrities, *Memories* is valuable; but conspicuously absent from this memoir are references to Grace King the artist, to the aesthetic and professional challenges she faced as a woman writer in a unique region of the South with its own peculiar gender and race dynamics. For these, the interested contemporary reader must turn to the voluminous journals Grace King left behind, only now being disseminated and edited by scholars.

Near the end of *Memories*, King remembers the tribute she received from the Louisiana Historical Society in 1923, complete with artfully worded tribute and loving cup. When asked to give a speech recounting the history of the organization, she recalls words that might describe her rambling, anecdotal style in the book that "I gossiped along in a leisurely way, forgetting, as ladies will in their talk, the passing minutes; nevertheless, the story came to an end with much kind applause, and the event of the evening, which I had been unconsciously delaying, took place, the presentation of a loving cup."[35] Grace King brings down the curtain on her extraordinary life with a shy, self-deprecating blush.

As a woman who never married and who considered herself a learned south-ern woman of letters with strong European influences, Grace King embodied many contradictions, her innate patrician conservatism often battling with her sympathetic views of women's socially and culturally constructed roles. Her fic-tion explores the shifting racial and gender identities of Reconstruction Amer-ica, localizing them in a New Orleans that many post–Civil War Americans saw as a microcosm of the South. But in the vein of a true woman of letters, Grace King was not only a fiction writer but a historian, a self-appointed chronicler of New Orleans and Louisiana history. Bilingual and widely traveled in Eu-rope and America, she became a kind of cultural ambassador for the region she called home. Her fiction and history became complementary aspects of a complex vision documenting not only a society in transition but a formative period in the lives of southern and American women. Understanding Grace King demands listening to both these voices and the legacy of public and private history she left behind.

NOTES

1. Robert Bush, *Grace King: A Southern Destiny* (Baton Rouge: Louisiana State University Press, 1983), 7.

2. Melissa Walker Heidari, introduction, in *To Find My Own Peace: Grace King in Her Journals 1886–1910*, ed. Melissa Walker Heidari (Athens: University of Georgia Press, 2004), xx.

3. Anne Goodwyn Jones, *Tomorrow Is Another Day: The Woman Writer in the South 1859–1936* (Baton Rouge: Louisiana State University Press, 1981), 47.

4. Bush, *Southern Destiny*, 41–42.

5. The term "Creole" for Grace King meant those born in Louisiana of pure French or Spanish stock, although she acknowledged the ambiguity of this term in *New Orleans: The Place and the People* (New York: Macmillan, 1895). An influx of Anglo-American immigrants, Acadian immi-grants, and free blacks from Santo Domingo complicated the Franco-Spanish designation.

6. Grace King, *Monsieur Motte* (1888; rpt., Freeport, N.Y.: Books for Libraries Press, 1969), 106.

7. Ibid., 236.

8. Ibid., 4.

9. Grace King, *Balcony Stories* (1893; rpt., Albany, N.Y.: NCUP, 1994), 1; Grace King, *Memories of a Southern Woman of Letters* (New York: Macmillan, 1932), 1.

10. King, *Memories*, 57.

11. Grace King to Branch King [her brother], November 29, 1891, in Grace King Papers, Louisiana State University, Baton Rouge, quoted in Robert Bush, introduction, *Grace King of New Orleans*, ed. Robert Bush (Baton Rouge: Louisiana State University Press, 1973), 18.

12. Grace King to May McDowell, March 4, 1885, quoted in Bush, *Southern Destiny*, 48.

13. Bush, *Southern Destiny*, 78.

14. Susan K. Harris, *The Courtship of Olivia Langdon and Mark Twain* (Cambridge: Cambridge University Press, 1996), 2; Bush, *Southern Destiny*, 91.

15. Grace King to Olivia Clemens, December 6, 1899, Bancroft Library, University of California, Berkeley, quoted in Robert Bush, "Grace King and Mark Twain," *American Literature* 44 (March 1972): 49.

16. Grace King, quoted in Bush, "Grace King and Mark Twain," 36.

17. Helen Taylor, "The Case of Grace King," *Southern Review* 18 (Fall 1982): 699.

18. Bush, *Grace King of New Orleans*, 350, 351.

19. King, *Memories*, 153.

20. Nina Baym, *American Women Writers and the Work of History, 1790–1860* (New Brunswick, N.J.: Rutgers University Press, 1995), 7; King, *Monsieur Motte*, 12.

21. Grace King, *Jean Baptiste Le Moyne, Sieur de Bienville* (New York: Dodd, Mead, 1893), 70.

22. Bush, *Grace King of New Orleans*, 22.

23. Grace King, *New Orleans: The Place and the People*, xvii.

24. Edward King, "Louisiana," in *The Great South*, ed. W. Magruder Drake and Robert R. Jones (Baton Rouge: Louisiana State University Press, 1972), and quoted in Taylor, "The Case of Grace King," 690.

25. Ibid., 66.

26. Ibid., 348.

27. Grace King to Fred Lewis Pattee, January 19, 1915, quoted in Bush, *Grace King of New Orleans*, 398.

28. David Kirby, *Grace King* (Boston: G. K. Hall, 1980), 110.

29. Grace King to Edward Garnett, quoted in Bush, *Grace King of New Orleans*, 401.

30. Bush, *Grace King of New Orleans*, 207.

31. Mary Gehman and Nancy Ries, *Women and New Orleans: A History* (New Orleans: Margaret Media, 1985), 103.

32. Grace King, *Creole Families of New Orleans* (Baton Rouge: Claitor's, 1971), viii.

33. Grace King to Warrington Dawson, quoted in Bush, *Southern Destiny*, 289.

34. Kate Capshaw Smith, "Conflicting Visions of the South in Grace King's *Memories of a Southern Woman of Letters*," *Southern Quarterly* 36 (Spring 1998): 136.

35. King, *Memories*, 397.

Louisa Williams Robinson, Her Daughters, and Her Granddaughters

(1855–1932)

Recognizing the Contributions of Three Generations of Coushatta Women in Louisiana

LINDA LANGLEY, CLAUDE OUBRE, AND JAY PRECHT

❀ ❀ ❀

The lives of Louisa Williams Robinson, her daughters, and her granddaughters illustrate the vital role women played in the survival of the Coushatta community into the twenty-first century. Robinson owned property, raised four daughters and five sons, and successfully navigated Louisiana's inheritance laws on two occasions. Her oldest daughter, Sissy Robinson Alabama (1873–1914), obtained the only federal trust lands in the Coushatta community before 1972. Ernest Stevens, acting commissioner of the Bureau of Indian Affairs, wrote to Emery A. Johnson, Indian Health Service director, in 1971 to acknowledge a past relationship between the federal government and the Coushattas in part based on Alabama's 160 acres, which her heirs held in trust until 1953.[1] Robinson's youngest daughter, Ency Robinson Abbey Abbott (1897–1956), became one of the last Coushatta women to practice traditional medicine, and her daughters continued the family legacy, working to support their families, weaving baskets, and passing Coushatta traditions to the next generation.

This chapter examines the economic and cultural roles of women in the Coushatta community by highlighting the contributions of three generations of women within one family. Although some of the accomplishments of Robinson, her daughters, and her granddaughters were unique, their overall efforts to help their family and community survive and flourish reflect similar contributions

LOUISA WILLIAMS, KOASATI (COUSHATTA) WOMAN
1908, weaving moss blanket, near Elton, La. Courtesy of the National Museum
of the American Indian, Smithsonian Institution, neg. 2744.
Photo by NMAI Photo Services staff.

made by numerous other Coushatta women. As an eighty-two-year-old Coushatta woman recently noted, "We were all poor. We helped each other, and we did what we had to do to survive."[2]

Many Coushatta women farmed, butchered animals, and made cane and longleaf pine-needle baskets to trade and sell. These contributions ensured the economic viability of both their families and their community. Perhaps more importantly, Coushatta women also functioned as tradition bearers. They taught their children traditional stories, songs, and beliefs, transmitting their language as well as their values to each new generation. As a result, the Coushattas today retain much of their traditional culture, including their language.

The story of Louisa Williams Robinson and her descendants illustrates historian Devon Mihesuah's contention that Native women "have been just as crucial to the economic, social, religious, and political survival of tribes" as Native men.[3] Today, Coushatta women provide visible political leadership. They sit on the tribal council and head tribal departments. The extent of women's roles in Coushatta decision making before the nineteenth century remains unclear. The Coushattas associated with the Creek Confederacy in the eighteenth century, and scholarship on Creek women suggests a central informal role, including significant influence over decisions of war and peace.[4]

Coushatta women also "became the custodians of traditional cultural values" strained by contact with Europeans and multiple relocations beginning in the sixteenth century. Spanish explorer Hernando de Soto encountered the Coushattas in 1540 and provided the first written account of their community on the Tennessee River. The Coushattas moved south from there, eventually settling near and affiliating with the Creek Confederacy. In the second half of the eighteenth century, the Coushattas increased their political power, culminating with the emergence of Alexander McGillivray, son of a Scottish trader and his Coushatta wife, who wielded previously unparalleled power within the Creek Confederacy.[5]

The majority of the tribe remained in the Upper Creek villages until the United States gained control of the territory through the Treaty of San Lorenzo in 1796. Faced with the imminent intrusion of settlers from Georgia, Red Shoes, the Coushatta chief and a relative of McGillivray, led approximately four hundred Coushattas to Spanish Louisiana.[6]

The vital social and economic contributions made by Coushatta women to their community permeate historical accounts. Europeans frequently visited Indian villages during the summer months, when travel was easiest, which was also when women's traditional economic work of gardening, gathering, and processing was at its peak. Some authors believe that this seasonal imbalance, as well as cultural bias, created the European myth of the "squaw as drudge."[7] Although the characterization of Coushatta women's work as drudgery was misguided, one should not underestimate the economic impact of their efforts. They raised children, farmed, gathered food, assisted male hunting parties by gathering firewood and water, cooked, butchered the animals, and smoked the meat, helping to ensure the survival of their community. As trade with Europeans transformed deer hunting into a commercial venture, men and women worked together to capitalize on the resulting economic opportunities. Men procured the marketable natural resource, and women added significant economic value by processing the deerskins. They also generated additional income by selling venison, honey, wild foods, and fresh vegetables to traders.[8]

The changes brought by the European trade affected women differently than men. Women continued to perform their traditional roles within their families and communities, but they also acted as cultural intermediaries through marriages to European traders. The Indian wives wielded such influence on their husbands that U.S. Indian agent Benjamin Hawkins forbade his assistants to marry Creek women. Also, the "mixed-blood" children of unions between Creek women and white traders often became powerful advocates for their mothers' families and the Creeks. Describing the unusual position of these women, historian Kathryn Holland Braund writes, "Creek women were central elements in a complicated cycle of cultural adaptation, change, and persistence that dominated Creek history in the late eighteenth century."[9]

Coushatta women continued to adapt and persevere in the nineteenth and twentieth centuries despite several additional relocations. After the Louisiana Purchase and the coming of more Americans into the area, the Coushattas moved farther westward into the large, irregularly patrolled, and often lawless Neutral Strip between the Calcasieu and the Sabine Rivers. The Coushattas remained there until after the Adams-Onis Treaty in 1819 established the west bank of the Sabine River as the western boundary of the Louisiana Purchase, thereby making the Neutral Strip part of the state of Louisiana. At that point, a large group of Coushattas, including Louisa Williams's parents, moved westward into east Texas, fleeing American encroachment and seeking sanctuary among the Spanish again. In Texas, the Coushattas became key trading partners with many non-Indians in their vicinity, including the pirate Jean Lafitte, who traded for provisions when docked at Galveston Island.[10]

Most likely, Coushatta women produced or helped produce the majority of the supplies traded by the tribe. The accounts of travelers and neighboring non-

Indians clearly highlight the continuing significance of Coushatta women during the tribe's years in Texas. German traveler Von Wrede commented on the work performed by Coushatta women after a journey through the state in 1841. He noted women making corn meal by "stamping corn in a mortar" and "sifting it through a number of sieves . . . until the finest meal was obtained," roasting whole corn, and "cooking peaches in iron pots."[11]

Attorney J. Feagin of Livingston, Texas, recalled Alabama and Coushatta women bartering moss rugs, reed cane baskets, and deerskins with his mother. Another observer from that time, known as Grandma Harrison, recalled, "No one brought more or better goods to Drew's Landing on packet days than did the Indians. The women were adept at basket making, weaving, pottery, and bead work, and were quite skilled in cooking, especially meats and vegetables."[12]

Coushatta women also continued to process deerskins. Texas traveler William Bollaert described the labor-intensive and often unpleasant process that involved soaking the skins in water, scraping the hair off, rubbing them with deer brains and water, and then drying them with smoke from the bark of trees. Skins processed by Coushatta women generated significant cash income. Bollaert noted that "a Coshatte can get $2 at least for a deerskin," which spoke to the exceptional quality of work done by Coushatta women in tanning the skins.[13]

When the Coushattas moved back to Louisiana in 1870 and ultimately settled north of Elton in the 1880s, the women of the community brought with them a long tradition of wielding economic and social influence. However, despite their importance, Coushatta women, like Native women in general, seldom appear in diplomatic and government documents created by European and American men, and when they do, the document's authors often attempt to fit these women into their Eurocentric worldviews. To counteract this effect, we draw on land and probate records, travelers' accounts, correspondence, the records of Indian agents, missionaries, and church officials, and local mercantile accounts in reconstructing these Coushatta women's lives. In keeping with Mihesuah's advice that writers who want to learn about past events in Native American history should "ask Indian women," we also draw on the oral accounts of Ency Robinson Abbey Abbott's three surviving daughters, Elizabeth Marie Abbott Thompson (1926–), Loris Abbott Langley (1928–), and Edna Lorena Abbott Langley (1933–), which provide insight and descriptive information about the lives of their grandmother, mother, and aunts.[14] Taken together, these sources paint a picture of women who not only survived against all odds but even thrived, as daughters, wives, and community members.

LOUISA WILLIAMS ROBINSON

Louisa Williams was born in 1855 in what is today part of eastern Texas, the oldest child of Suzanne Thompson and August Williams. Like many Indian tribes, the Coushattas trace their descent matrilineally. She, her mother, and her daughters and granddaughters are members of the Kawaknasi Bobcat clan.[15] No records have survived to document the specific events of Williams's childhood, although historical records do provide general descriptions of life in the Coushatta villages.

The recollections of Emma Haynes, an ordinary farmer's wife from Polk County, offer the only surviving descriptions by a woman from that time period. Her observations provide the most vivid details about life in Long King's Village, a Coushatta community on the Trinity River in the mid-1800s. According to Haynes, "The squaws did all the work. They tanned leather and made the clothes. They cultivated the corn, ground the meal with a pestle and mortar. . . . The women made baskets of all shapes and sizes and painted them all colors of the rainbow. They gathered long moss, boiled it, and whipped it in preparation for weaving into saddle pads."[16] Nearly a century later, the ethnographer Lydia Paz verified Haynes's observations in her documentation of the division of labor among the Coushattas in Louisiana.[17]

The Swiss-trained botanist Berlandier, traveling through present-day Texas in 1828, noted an unusually high level of marital devotion and companionship among Coushatta spouses. In his assessment of Coushatta wives, he wrote, "the wife becomes a comrade to her husband, willingly sharing his sorrows and his labors."[18] A few years later, the Spanish regional governor José Francisco Madero reported to the chief of Bexar on the conditions of the Coushatta people living on the east banks of the Trinity River, near the present-day town of Liberty, Texas. Madero's report supports earlier accounts, noting that the Coushattas were peaceful, family oriented, and proficient at both farming and hunting. He counted 120 families in three villages, as well as 82 single men and 104 single women, not including children. Echoing Berlandier's observation that men and women shared the farming chores, Madero noted that "each family plants for itself maize, beans, sweet potatoes and legumes, and what each harvests is sufficient for the year, and enough is left to sell to outsiders and to provide for passers-through."[19]

After successfully petitioning the Texas government for their own reservation lands in 1854, the tribe found that one league of the land promised to them was already settled.[20] At this point, some of the Coushattas joined the Alabamas to form what the U.S. government eventually called the Alabama-Coushatta

**LOUISA WILLIAMS ROBINSON AND WINNIE TEMPLE,
KOASATI WOMEN**

1908, near Elton, La. Courtesy of the National Museum of the American Indian,
Smithsonian Institution, neg. 2746. Photo by NMAI Photo Services staff.

Tribe of Livingston, Texas, creating the mistaken notion that the two tribes actually became one at some point in history.

Just as they had done throughout their history, a large group of Coushattas chose to strike out on their own rather than have their fate determined by another government. Accordingly, in the early 1870s, a group of Coushattas, including Louisa Williams and her parents, decided to move back into southwestern Louisiana where they settled on the banks of the Calcasieu River in a small community that would later become known as Indian Village.[21]

By the late nineteenth century, the majority of the Coushatta families in Louisiana had relocated again to slightly north of the present-day town of Elton in the Bayou Blue area of Allen and Jefferson Davis parishes where the tribal community is still located today. In the collective memory of the tribe, there are various explanations for the move from Indian Village to Elton, ranging from a red ant infestation to the encroachment of white settlers who coveted the prime lands occupied by the Indians.[22]

Most Coushatta tribal members used the Homestead Act of 1862 to obtain individually owned land, thereby bringing to an end the earlier practice of corporate land ownership as a tribal community. Only the Robinson estate was brought into trust by the federal government through the Indian Homestead Act of 1884. As a result, the federal government did not protect the natural resources (timber and oil) on most Coushatta homesteads, and local companies eventually gained rights to these resources.[23]

About the same time as the Coushattas moved to Bayou Blue, Williams entered a new phase of her life through marriage to Alex Robinson, the son of Sarko and John Robinson and a member of the Nita (Bear) clan. Both interviews with Robinson's descendants and the notes of ethnographer John Swanton indicate that the couple later separated, but local court records show they never legally divorced. Despite their eventual separation, they had nine children over sixteen years, four daughters and five sons, seven of whom survived into adulthood. Church records indicate that Louisa and Alex Robinson, all of their surviving children, and all of their future sons- and daughters-in-law became members of St. Peter's Congregational Indian Church, which was founded in 1901. Additionally, in 1902 the couple had two of their younger daughters, twelve-year-old Lucy and five-year-old Ency, baptized in the church.[24]

Beginning in the early twentieth century, the church played an important role in the Coushatta community not only as a house of worship but also as a location for community gatherings and a school for Coushatta children. Community members began accepting leadership roles in the church in 1906, and in 1913, Louisa's son Mark Robinson became an assistant pastor. The church also helped preserve the Koasati language as missionaries and linguists recorded Native-language sermons and parables and attempted to translate the Bible into Koasati. For example, Gene Burnham of the Summer Institute of Linguistics translated the Christmas story and New Testament parables into Koasati between 1979 and 1981, and Coushatta preacher Solomon Battise recorded two Koasati sermons in 1973.[25]

Born in Texas, Louisa Williams Robinson came of age planting and gathering corn, tanning deerskins, and cooking over an open fire. As a teenager, she moved to a new land, where she learned to deal with a non-Indian society in which people spoke French and English instead of Spanish, and overcame a variety of other situations typically faced by immigrants. While adjusting to these changes, she married, raised a large family of children, and provided for her family's livelihood by making and trading items locally. Robinson made these transitions so successfully that she was eventually able to navigate the challenges of two judicial systems to fight for her father's property after his death, to transfer forty acres of her own land to each of her children before her death, and to help take care of her grandchildren after her daughter died.[26]

These transfers took place on June 15, 1920, by which time three of Louisa and Alex Robinson's nine children had died. Louisa Robinson signed four of the conveyances, and Alex Robinson signed two. Each of the deeds handled by Louisa Robinson carries the phrase "I, Louisa Williams, wife of Alex Robinson, authorized by her husband," which is further evidence of the subordinate role of women in the eyes of early twentieth-century law and society. All of the documents signed by Louisa Robinson, including deeds, succession records, and even check endorsements, were done with an "X" notated as "Her Mark," indicating that she achieved this astonishing ability to navigate the U.S. and Louisiana judicial systems without ever learning to read or write English.[27]

It is remarkable that Robinson was willing and able to transfer property to her children during her lifetime, because a reduction in her landholdings necessarily reduced her own income and her status as a landowner. By giving each of her children forty acres of land, the minimum amount of land considered necessary to make a family economically independent, Robinson ensured that they could produce sufficient crops for subsistence plus enough to sell to purchase necessary supplies and pay taxes.

Robinson's three surviving grandchildren remember her as an incredibly intelligent woman who remained sharp and alert right to the end of her life. They especially credit her for the initiative she took in teaching her daughters how to work, raise a family, and become self-supporting despite facing prejudice as both a woman and an Indian. They also are glad that their grandmother taught them women's traditions used to protect the tribe before access to Western medicine, although they are hesitant to discuss these traditions in detail. Her husband, Alex Robinson, died of pneumonia on February 5, 1922; she lived an additional ten years before succumbing to the flu and dying on January 29, 1932, at the age of seventy-seven.[28]

LOUISA WILLIAMS ROBINSON'S DAUGHTERS
CARRY ON HER LEGACY

In 1932, Coushatta women still worked alongside men in carrying out almost all of the daily chores—plowing fields, planting crops, harvesting, and fishing—although the men still served as the primary hunters and the women still produced the principal trade items, longleaf pine-needle and swamp-cane baskets. Many of the older tribal women recall times when the sale or exchange of these baskets provided the main, or even the sole, household income.

Louisa's eldest daughter Sissy was one of the first Native women to receive land in Louisiana under the Indian Homestead Act of 1884. Sissy Robinson initiated her petition for land in 1891, when she reached the age of eighteen. The fact that Robinson, a single Native American woman, composed the necessary correspondence and completed all the legal steps of the homestead process is a testimony to the importance that Louisa, herself nonliterate in the English language, placed on education for her children. Sissy Robinson's homestead, the only land brought into trust by the federal government, played an important part in gaining federal services in the 1930s and 1940s and reestablishing the community's status as a federally recognized tribe in 1973.[29]

Sissy Robinson married Jackson Alabama, a man of the Hapi (Salt) clan when she was about twenty years old. They had eight children together, two of whom died in infancy. They baptized all of their surviving infants at the Indian church in the Coushatta community, where Sissy Alabama became the first woman ever to serve as a church officer, holding the position of Sunday school secretary and treasurer from 1909–11. Ten years passed before any other women held office in the church. In 1921 Sissy Alabama's two younger sisters, Lucy and Susie, served as deaconesses at St. Peter's, and her youngest sister, Ency, became church secretary.[30]

Sissy Alabama's life, although full and productive, was unfortunately cut short, and she never had the opportunity to see her first grandchild. Alabama died of tuberculosis on May 15, 1914, and her eldest daughter Mittie died of complications in childbirth two weeks later. The baby, Jane, survived. Tuberculosis also carried away Sissy Alabama's husband within a year, leaving the couple's five surviving children orphans.[31]

Sissy Alabama's oldest daughter, Annie Alabama, was just eighteen years old when her mother died, and not yet twenty when her father's death orphaned her and her younger brothers and sisters. The patriarchal Louisiana legal system in 1916 determined how the courts addressed the issue of caring for the Alabamas' minor children after their death. Within four months of her father's death, Annie Alabama filed suit in the Fifteenth District Judicial Court to be appointed as the guardian of her four younger siblings. The court initially appointed Mark Robinson, Louisa Robinson's son and the children's uncle, as dative tutor for the minor children, "there being no male descendants of lawful age"; however, the court did agree to convene a family meeting of friends and relatives of Jackson and Sissy Alabama to deliberate on Annie Alabama's request. Not surprisingly, and despite evidence of the key roles played by women in traditional decision-making processes, the court extended invitations to the family meeting to five Coushatta men but no women.[32]

Although there is no record of the court granting Annie Alabama's petition for legal guardianship of her minor siblings, court proceedings do indicate that she became the primary caretaker for the children. The inventory of Sissy and Jackson Alabama's estate shows that the couple owned 360 acres of land, forty-four head of cattle, twenty horses, and a mule at the time of their death. This estate, valued at $3,610 in 1916, was extremely large by the standards of the day. The inventory lists Sissy Robinson as the owner of 160 acres, twenty-four head of cattle, and thirteen horses. The court allowed Mark Robinson to sell timber from Sissy and Jackson Alabama's land in order to pay the costs of supporting the minor children. The court record itemized expenditures, which included six payments to Louisa Robinson totaling nineteen dollars to reimburse her for buying milk for the children as well as expenditures for a doctor's visit and ultimately a coffin for fifteen-year-old Nolan. One can only imagine how important it was to Louisa Robinson to provide for her grandchildren after her daughter Sissy Alabama's death and how hard she must have worked to generate sufficient cash to buy the milk they needed.[33]

Louisa Robinson's youngest daughter Ency also had a notable role in the Coushatta community. She married twice, first to Dennis Abbey, a member of the Hapi (Salt) clan, on May 13, 1915, at the age of nineteen. Ency and Dennis had two children together before his untimely death three years after their marriage. In 1922, when Ency was twenty-five, she married again, this time to Lounie Abbott, a member of the Nokko (Beaver) clan. The couple had five children and twenty years together before Lounie Abbott passed away in 1942.[34]

Between 1924 and 1938, Ency Abbott entered into seven mineral leases with Louisiana companies to perform oil and gas drilling on her property. She ensured that each of these leases contained provisions for cash payments to lease use of the premises, contingency payments depending on the outcome of the drilling tests, and a clause that gave her "gas free of cost from any such well for all stoves, and all inside lights."[35] Seventy years after she executed these leases, her daughters recalled their mother's frequent advice to "never sign anything" without great thought and deliberation.[36]

Ency Abbott was the last widely acknowledged medicine woman of the tribe. Her daughters recall this as a highly respected position within the tribe, especially in the days before most families were able to afford regular visits to doctors or hospitals. "People used to come get her at all hours of the day or night, and she would leave whatever she was doing to go and help them. Most of the time people had no money to pay her, so she just helped them anyway. She knew about a lot of the plants and things people could do for pain and sickness." Descriptions of the herbal remedies practiced often included the use of water or smoke and chanted prayers. Some recipes, moreover, could be used for protection as well as for curative purposes.[37]

One story relating to the protective powers of certain Coushatta medicinal rites was told during an interview, when we showed Ency's daughters copies of the account of San Antonio de Bexar in which he describes how twenty-five Coushattas "stood their ground" through three charges while the three hundred or so other Indian soldiers fled in disarray. Ency's daughters conferred with each other and agreed that the Coushatta soldiers must have had the kind of medicine that "makes you invisible," at which point they both shared memories of one of their uncles who could disappear in midstep as he walked right toward them.[38]

Some of Ency Abbott's medicinal knowledge may have come from her maternal grandfather, August Williams, whom Bureau of American Ethnography photographer M. R. Harrington described as a "doctor" in 1908. Her specific recipes and remedies have been closely guarded and seldom used by her descendants. As Ency's oldest surviving daughter stated, although they remember some of their mother's teachings, they "rarely need it now that the people can go to modern doctors."[39]

Visitors, including an anthropologist who made repeated trips to study the community, knew Ency Abbott as a gracious and willing host to visitors to the tribal community. Ency Abbott clearly passed her graciousness and hospitality on to her daughters. Ency Abbott's daughter Loris Abbott Langley became an equally gracious host to a linguistics student doing research for her master's thesis.[40] In being open to outsiders, Ency's daughter carried on the tradition of women as cultural mediators; just as an earlier generation had worked with Christian missionaries to preserve the language and culture, a new generation of Coushatta women worked with academics to accomplish the same purpose.

Ency Robinson Abbey Abbott survived twelve years after the death of her second husband, Lounie Abbott. She died on October 25, 1956. At the time of her death, Ency Abbott owned fifty-two acres of land in Allen Parish.[41]

ENCY ABBOTT'S DAUGHTERS CARRY ON THE TRADITION

As of this writing, only three of Ency Abbott's daughters, Louisa Robinson's granddaughters, remain alive, Elizabeth Marie Abbott Thompson (1926–), Loris Abbott Langley (1928–), and Edna Lorena Abbott Langley (1933–). By all accounts these three women are extremely intelligent, adept at handling relations with both the larger society and the internal tribal society, skilled at negotiating the necessary legal and economic systems, and were successful in raising their children to be the same way. Each of these women, like their mother, aunts, and grandmother before them, survived the death of her husband, remained strong for her family, and demonstrated unusual business acumen, with or without formal education. All three women contributed financially to the support of their families, much as Louisa Robinson had done in providing milk for her orphaned grandchildren.

Abbott's daughter Loris Langley drove the horse and wagon "school bus" for Coushatta schoolchildren, a job involving a lot of work for little pay. She recalls that her responsibilities included catching and harnessing the horses in all kinds of weather, beginning her long route in predawn hours, and feeding and tending to the animals. She cared for the wagon and team of horses without a fenced yard or pasture, often simply tying up the horses. The Bureau of Indian Affairs ran the school and allotted her a gallon of feed per day, not enough for the horses. She would start to get the team of horses ready at 5:00 a.m. each day, with the help of her brother, whose assistance was invaluable since she had neither electricity nor flashlights. She finished her long bus route at 8:00 a.m. each day. She assumed these responsibilities at the young age of eighteen because she was the only person willing to do the job for sixteen dollars a week.[42]

Additionally, Ency Abbott's daughters remember weaving longleaf pine-needle baskets to sell during times of financial strain. These women initially took advantage of traditional women's work to enter the local marketplace to support their families. Today, scholars and collectors alike highly prize Cou-

LORIS LANGLEY WITH GRANDDAUGHTER ELEYNA LANGLEY

Baskets made by the Langleys. Courtesy of the authors.

shatta longleaf pine-needle baskets for the tightness of the weave and the intricacy of the design. All three of Ency Abbott's surviving daughters are nationally recognized basket weavers, and one can find baskets by each of these women in museums and private collections throughout the United States.[43]

Weaving also provided the opportunity for daughters to learn from their mothers and granddaughters from their grandmothers. Women not only taught weaving technique and traditional patterns; they also transmitted their values, beliefs, and knowledge of life in the process. According to Loris Langley, "These baskets also helped us to learn the history of the tribe. We used to sit and talk when we made baskets together. . . . Sometimes while the women sewed, the men would make toys for the children, and we would tell stories. That's how my children learned the stories of our people, from my mother and my brothers while we were working."[44]

Along with the traditional stories of the Coushattas, Louisa Robinson also left a legacy of exceptional courage, determination, and ability to overcome challenges to her daughters and her daughters' daughters, on down to the present generation of Coushatta girls who are five generations removed. Although they are distant from Louisa Robinson in time, they still demonstrate her perseverance, intelligence, and endurance. It is impossible for any woman coming of age in modern American society to imagine all of the challenges and difficulties that Louisa faced in her daily life or to imagine the extent of the inheritance this remarkable Coushatta woman gave to her descendants. As one of her granddaughters remarked, "Now we have holidays for famous men like Abraham Lincoln and Martin Luther King. Our grandmother was never famous, but in her own way she was just as smart and did as much for her people."[45]

NOTES

We wish to express our gratitude to the Coushatta people. In particular, the willingness of Louisa Williams Robinson's descendents to share their knowledge and insights made this essay possible. We would also like to thank Theda Perdue and Daniel Usner for reviewing the chapter. Their suggestions helped to improve our interpretations and writing. *Alilamo.*

1. Ernest Stevens, Washington, D.C., to Emery A. Johnson, M.D., Rockville, Md., January 5, 1971, Indian Affairs: 1983–92, Governor's Commission on Indian Affairs, 19202-1-P, Louisiana State Archives, Baton Rouge (hereinafter cited as GCIA).

The 160 acres of land was issued to the heirs in fee simple in preparation for the termination of the tribe. Although the federal government provided no services between 1953 and 1972, Congress never officially terminated the Coushatta Tribe.

2. At a meeting of tribal elders on September 13, 2007, Linda Langley asked attendees whether they considered Louisa Williams Robinson unusually successful. This statement by Doris Battise was one of the responses.

3. Devon Mihesuah, "Commonalty of Difference: American Indian Women and History," *American Indian Quarterly* 20 (Winter 1996): 21. In accordance with the custom of the majority of contemporary tribal members, the terms "Native American," "Native," "Indigenous peoples," and "Indians" are used interchangeably and without derogatory implication, as are the terms "tribe" and "community."

4. Kathryn E. Holland Braund, "Guardians of Tradition and Handmaidens to Change: Women's Roles in Creek Economic and Social Life during the Eighteenth Century," *American Indian Quarterly* 14 (Summer 1990): 242. Richard A. Sattler argues against this central informal role, claiming that Creek women were excluded from even "informal participation" in political affairs ("Women's Status among the Muskogee and Cherokee," in *Women and Power in Native North America*, ed. Laura F. Klein and Lillian A. Ackerman [Norman: University of Oklahoma Press, 1995], 220). The Creek Confederacy was a coalescent society of diverse communities that included the Coushattas. Because the Coushattas took part in this confederacy, we are able to extrapolate from Creek culture in the eighteenth century to better understand the Coushattas when more specific information is unavailable. For an account of the formation and character of the Creek Confederacy, see David H. Corkran, *The Creek Frontier, 1540–1783* (Norman: University of Oklahoma Press, 1967), 3–5, Robbie Ethridge, *Creek Country: The Creek Indians and Their World* (Chapel Hill: University of North Carolina Press, 2003), 22–31, Claudio Saunt, *A New Order of Things: Property, Power, and the Transformation of the Creek Indians, 1733–1816* (Cambridge: Cambridge University Press, 1999), 17–19, and Steven C. Hahn, *The Invention of the Creek Nation, 1670–1763: Indians of the Southeast*, ed. Michael D. Green and Theda Perdue (Lincoln: University of Nebraska Press, 2004), 16–18.

5. Clara Sue Kidwell, "Choctaw Women and Cultural Persistence in Mississippi," in *Negotiators of Change: Historical Perspectives on Native American Women*, ed. Nancy Shoemaker (New York: Routledge, 1995), 116. See also Braund, "Guardians of Tradition and Handmaidens to Change," 246. For a description of de Soto's encounter with the Coushattas, see John R. Swanton, *Final Report of the United States De Soto Commission* (1939; rpt., Washington, D.C.: Smithsonian Institution Press, 1985), 50–52. See also Lawrence Clayton, Vernon James Knight Jr., and Edward C. Moore, eds., *The De Soto Chronicles: The Expedition of Hernando de Soto to North America in 1539–1543*, vol. 1 (Tuscaloosa: University of Alabama Press, 1993), 90–91, 282–83. For a discussion of McGillivray's identity, see Linda Langley, "The Tribal Identity of Alexander McGillivray: A Review of the Historical and Ethnographic Data," *Louisiana History* 46 (Spring 2005): 231–39. See also Michael D. Green, "Alexander McGillivray," in *American Indian Leaders: Studies in Diversity*, ed. R. David Edmunds (Lincoln: University of Nebraska Press, 1980), 43.

6. See Donald Hunter, "The Alibamons: Notes on the Occhanya, Pacana, and Coushatta in Louisiana during the Spanish Colonial and Early American Periods," unpublished ms., May 10, 2000, Tribal Archives, Heritage Department, Coushatta Tribe of Louisiana, Elton (hereinafter cited as Tribal Archives), especially Carondelet to Morales, June 20, 1797, AGI 2614, folio 130, 12. Citations from Hunter's work are presented here with his permission. Nearly a decade earlier, the influential Coushatta chief Alexander McGillivray mentioned that the Coushattas had a "great fear of the Americans, against whom they have the greatest animosity because of their disposition to usurp" (McGillivray to Folch, April 22, 1789, cited in John W. Caughey, *McGillivray of the Creeks* [Norman: University of Oklahoma Press, 1938], 227). The Treaty of San Lorenzo is commonly referred to in American history books as the Pinckney Treaty.

7. See David D. Smits, "The 'Squaw Drudge': A Prime Index of Savagism," *Ethnohistory* 29 (Autumn 1982): 281–306, and Michael P. Morris, *The Bringing of Wonder: Trade and the Indians of the Southeast, 1700–1783* (Westport, Conn.: Greenwood Press, 1999).

8. Kathryn E. Holland Braund, *Deerskins and Duffels: Creek Indian Trade with Anglo-America, 1685–1815* (Lincoln: University of Nebraska Press, 1993), 68; Braund, "Guardians of Tradition and Handmaidens to Change," 244–46.

9. Joshua Piker, *Okfuskee: A Creek Indian Town in Colonial America* (Cambridge, Mass.: Harvard University Press, 2004), 165–76; C. L. Grant, ed., *Letters, Journals, and Writings of Benjamin Hawkins* (Savannah, Ga.: Beehive Press, 1980), 2:46; Braund, "Guardians of Tradition and Handmaidens to Change," 239, 248–51. See also Theda Perdue, "Women, Men, and American Indian Policy: The Cherokee Response to 'Civilization,'" in *Negotiators of Change*, 90–114.

For an extended discussion of the role of "mixed blood" Indians, see Theda Perdue, *"Mixed Blood" Indians: Racial Construction in the Early South* (Athens: University of Georgia Press, 2003).

10. Jedidiah Morse, *A Report to the Secretary of War of the United States on Indian Affairs* (1822; rpt., St. Clair, Mich.: Scholarly Press, 1972), 373. Morse calculated the location and number of Coushatta in the summer of 1820 at 350 on the Red River, 510 miles above the mouth; 50 on the Nechez, 40 miles above the mouth; and 240 in two villages on the Trinity River, 40 or 50 miles above the mouth. See also Almonte's 1835 "Statistical Report on Texas," trans. Carlos Eduardo Castaneda, in *Southwestern Historical Quarterly* 28 (January 1925): 215, where the author estimates 500 "Cochates to the southeast of Nacogdoches," and William C. Davis, *The Pirates Lafitte: The Treacherous World of the Corsairs of the Gulf* (Orlando, Fla.: Harcourt, 2005), 358, 383.

11. *Biographical Sketches of the United States of North America and Texas Gathered by Friedrich W. Von Wrede* (Waco, Tex.: Texian Press, 1970), 7, 11.

12. J. Feagin to Cato Sells, June 19, 1917, Bureau of Indian Affairs files, Tribal Archives; Frances E. Abernathy, *Tales from the Big Thicket* (Austin: University of Texas Press, 1966), 73.

13. W. Eugene Hollon, *William Bollaert's Texas* (1956; rpt., Norman: University of Oklahoma Press, 1989), 115–16, 333.

14. See Gunlög Fur, "'Some Women are Wiser than Some Men': Gender and Native American History," in *Clearing a Path: Theorizing the Past in Native American Studies*, ed. Nancy Shoemaker (New York: Routledge, 2002), 75–103; Theda Perdue, *Cherokee Women: Gender and Culture Change, 1700–1835* (Lincoln: University of Nebraska Press, 1998), 3–11; Mihesuah, "Commonalty of Difference," 22. There is still a noticeable reluctance among tribal members to share information about traditional beliefs and practices related to medicine and such women's traditions as childbirth and menstruation. Although each of Ency Abbott's daughters is knowledgeable in these areas, they answer most questions with the general statement that "things were done differently then." We were cautioned not to provide detailed descriptions of certain practices and not to include specific names of individuals so as to avoid offending people by sharing their personal information with outsiders.

15. Geoffrey Kimball, "Members of the Koasati Ayiksa" (2003), 15th ed., Tribal Archives; Paul Leeds, *St. Peter's Congregational Church Records of Iowa, Calcasieu Parish, 1901–1958, Formerly Old Imperial Calcasieu Parish* (2004; rpt., [Kinder, La.]: Allen Parish Genealogical and Historical Society, 2005); St. Peter's cemetery grave markers, Elton, La.

16. Emma R. Haynes, *The History of Polk County*, unpublished TS 1937, 27, Tribal Archives.

17. Lydia Paz, "A Comparative Study of Southeastern Cultures" (master's thesis, Yale University, 1937), 9–10.

18. Jean Louis Berlandier, *The Indians of Texas in 1830*, ed. John C. Ewers (Washington, D.C.: Smithsonian Institution Press, 1969), 35.

19. Madero to Political Chief Ramon Musquiz, May 5, 1831, Spanish Collection, box 127, folder 35, 254ff., Texas General Land Office, Austin.

20. The Act for the Relief of the Coshattee Indians was eventually passed on August 30, 1856. Although the Alabama people were settled on their reservation by 1856, in June 1858, the Texas government was still trying to obtain "the voluntary consent of the chiefs or head men" for the removal of the Coushatta Indian tribe to Indian reservations on the Brazos River (orders to James Barclay, June 1958, in *The Indian Papers of Texas and the Southwest, 1825–1916*, vol. 5, ed. Dormon H. Winfrey and James M. Day [Austin: Texas State Historical Association], 246–47).

21. Surveyor's field notes, southwest district book 23, 28, Louisiana State Lands Office, Baton Rouge. Surveyor J. P. Parsons noted "A road E & W leading to Indian Village." Also there is a plat map of T7SR6W, showing a cluster of eight teepees in the sixteenth section, designated as "Indian Village," and a dotted line designated "Road from Lake Charles to Indian Village." In June 1875, Surveyor Parsons observed that "this township is mostly of high rolling land, covered with the very best of good yellow pine. . . . The Calcasieu River is but a small stream in this township . . . and can be forded at most any place in low water. There is an Indian Village, situated on a very pretty bluff in the 16th Section, numbering about 250 inhabitants" (66). Surveyor Parsons's team included an Indian man identified only as "Thompson," the same last name as Louisa's maternal grandfather.

22. Personal communication, Bel Abbey to Bertney Langley, October 1990; personal communication, Sam Thompson to Elizabeth Marie Thompson, September 1988.

23. Ernest R. Cushing, *Investigation of Alleged Loss by Koasati Indians of Louisiana of Lands Acquired by Them under Homestead Patents*, Division of Investigations, March 6, 1941, series 4C, box 48, folder 7, Joe Jennings Collection, Archives of Appalachia, East Tennessee State University, Johnson City.

24. Swanton's table of Coushatta households, ca. 1912, lists separate households for Alex Robinson (two persons) and Louisa Robinson (five persons). His listing of Coushattas by clan includes the word "divorced" penciled in after Louisa's name. See John R. Swanton, Koasati linguistic material and ethnographic notes and census data on the Koasati and Alibamu 1906–30, ms. 4153, Smithsonian Institution National Anthropological Archives.

Interviews with two of Louisa's surviving grandchildren elicited vague recollections of stories that their grandmother had been "divorced" in the Indian style (i.e., that she stopped living with her spouse) and that Alex Robinson had moved back to Texas without Louisa by the time of his death. However, the succession records for Alex Robinson state "that Mrs. Louisa Robinson be and she is hereby recognized as the surviving spouse and the owner of an undivided one-half of the community property," confirming the fact that Alex and Louisa Robinson were never officially divorced. See succession of Alexander Robinson, 15th Judicial District Court, record no. 300, Parish of Allen, and Geoffrey Kimball, "Members of the Koasati Ayiksa" (2003), 15th ed., Tribal Archives; Leeds, *St. Peter's Congregational Church Records*, 20.

25. Leeds, *St. Peter's Congregational Church Records*; Katherine S. Johnson and Paul Leeds, *Patteran: The Life and Works of Paul Leeds* (San Antonio, Tex.: Naylor, 1968); Linda Langley, personal communications with author, March–June 2006; Mrs. Wanda Johnson, widow of the Reverend Don Johnson, who served as pastor at the Indian church and who helped to run the school, interviews, n.d. Mrs. Johnson confirmed that the school was in continuous operation from September 1959 to May 1973 and served Coushatta students from prekindergarten to fourth grade; she also shared numerous memories of school events and showed photographs of social gatherings, individual students, and classes. The federal government rerecognized the community after a twenty-year cessation of services as the Coushatta Tribe of Louisiana in 1973; linguists identify the language as Koasati (SIL code is CKU). In accordance with this reality, we refer to the community and its members as Coushatta or Coushattas and to the language as Koasati. See the Christmas Story and Parables,

University Archives and Acadiana Manuscripts Collection, Special Collections Department, University of Louisiana at Lafayette. Recordings of two Koasati sermons given by Coushatta preacher Solomon Battise in 1973 are available at Global Recordings Network, http://globalrecordings .net/program/co2601. Clara Sue Kidwell, *Choctaws and Missionaries in Mississippi, 1818–1918* (Norman: University of Oklahoma Press, 1995) argues that Choctaws in Mississippi made Christianity "part of their changing culture" and gained from missionary efforts by "finding Christian churches as agents for their own survival" (201).

26. Record no. 3292, book A-5, 105, Allen Parish Courthouse Records.

27. 12:250–55, Allen Parish Courthouse Records.

28. "Indian Families, on Bayou Blue, near Elton La.," comp. Paul Leeds, January 15, 1941, original typewritten list with author's handwritten notations, in the collection of Wanda Johnson.

29. Ernest Stevens, Washington, D.C., to Emery A. Johnson, M.D., Rockville, Md., January 5, 1971, GCIA, application no. 13010, Louisiana State Lands Office, Baton Rouge. Although President William McKinley granted the patent in 1898, it was not filed in the Allen Parish courthouse until 1906. The letter in Sissy Alabama's file is handwritten and appears to match her signature, indicating that she did in fact compose the letter herself.

30. Leeds, *St. Peter's Congregational Church Records*, 61, 65.

31. Ibid., 22 and 36. Although Reverend Leeds placed the designation "TB" beside the ledger entry recording both Sissy's and Mittie's deaths, probably indicating tuberculosis as the cause of death, he noted the date of Mittie's death as the same date on which her daughter, Jane, was born, suggesting that complications from childbirth were a contributing factor to her death. Reverend Leeds also listed "TB" as the cause of Jackson Alabama's death on December 8, 1915.

32. Succession record no. 109, Allen Parish Courthouse Records. Louisa Robinson's sons, Mark and Jacob Robinson, her son-in-law Jimmy John, and her cousins Kinney Williams and Jeff Abbey attended the family meeting.

33. Inventory and appraiser's oath and first and second provisional accounts of Mark Robinson, dative tutor, in ibid. Reverend Leeds's records indicate that Sissy Alabama's youngest son, Nolan Alabama, died of tuberculosis on September 14, 1916, which means that within a two-year span Louisa had to bury her daughter, son-in-law, and two of her grandchildren.

34. *St. Peter's Congregational Church Records*, 37, 39. According to Reverend Leeds's notations, Dennis Abbey was killed by a horse on September 15, 1918, and Lounie Abbott was "found dead on road" on June 30, 1942.

35. 19:7, 74; 30:36; 34:614; 35:328; 43:182; 47:568, Allen Parish Courthouse Records. This quotation is taken from "Ency Abott to H. P. Mitchell et al. Mineral Lease," 19:7.

36. Loris Langley and Elizabeth Marie Thompson, interview by author, April 14, 2006.

37. Ibid.

38. Ibid.; San Antonio de Bexar's account is found in *The Missions of San Antonio* (San Antonio, Tex.: Alamo Press, 1982).

39. Photograph by M. R. Harrington, 1908. The plate's caption reads "Old man is a doctor" (National Museum of the American Indian, Smithsonian Institution, negative no. 2739). The Koasati Linguistic Archives have now completed an intensive study of Harrington's field journal and his linguistic notes and photographs. This study shows that he interacted closely with several tribal members; for example, he purchased fourteen items, including traditional medicine items, from Louisa Williams in 1908 and learned their description and use in Koasati (Loris Langley and Elizabeth Marie Thompson, interview by author, April 14, 2006).

40. Daniel Jacobson, Howard N. Martin, and Ralph Henry Marsh, *Alabama-Coushatta Indians:*

Ethnographical Report and Statement of Testimony (New York: Garland Publishing, 1974), 31; Willie Maye Kyzer, "A Descriptive Study of the Speech of the Koasati Indians of Louisiana" (master's thesis, Louisiana State University, 1952), 38.

41. Succession of Ency Robinson Abbey, record no. P-58–65, Allen Parish Courthouse Records.

42. Loris Langley, interview by author, August 22, 2006. Kinney Williams became the first Coushatta paid by the Bureau of Indian Affairs to transport Coushatta children to school around 1942 (Joe Jennings, superintendent of Indian schools, to Choctaw superintendent Archie McMullen, Philadelphia, Miss., August 18, 1943, series 3A, box 9, folder 2, Joe Jennings Collection, Archives of Appalachia, East Tennessee State University, Johnson City).

43. See Kidwell, "Choctaw Women and Cultural Persistence in Mississippi," 129. For a detailed account of how Coushatta baskets are made as well as of the economics of basket making, see Linda Langley, Susan LeJeune, and Claude Oubre, eds., *Les Artistes: Crafters Tell Their Tales*, vol. 2, LSUE Folklife Series (Springfield, Ill.: Phillips Brothers, 1996). For extended interviews with Ency Abbott's middle daughter Loris Langley, see Langley, LeJeune, and Oubre, eds., *Les Artistes*, 2:50–61, and for a biography of Ency Abbott's youngest daughter, Lorena Langley, see the Louisiana Folklife Center's Web site, http://www.nsula.edu/folklife/database/biography/langleyL.html.

44. Langley, LeJeune, and Oubre, eds., *Les Artistes*, 2:60.

45. Elizabeth Marie Thompson, interview with her and Loris Langley, April 14, 2006.

Clementine Hunter

(1887–1988)

Self-Taught Louisiana Artist

LEE KOGAN

❀ ❀ ❀

Following the devastation wrought by Hurricane Katrina, the Krewe of Rex leaders sat down to decide on a theme for the 2006 Rex Parade (the most prestigious colorful procession of floats through the city streets) for the annual New Orleans Mardi Gras celebration. Traditionally, the parade explores the worlds of mythology or distant cultures, but in light of the enormity of what had taken place at home, the organizers decided to honor their own. The theme would be "Beaux Arts and Letters," and the floats would feature the artistic and literary heritage of New Orleans, work inspired by its history, culture, and landscape. Up on the board went the usual suspects: Tennessee Williams, Walker Percy, John Kennedy Toole, William Faulkner, Anne Rice, Mahalia Jackson, John James Audubon. Joining this august company, however, was an artist with no formal education, an artist little known outside contemporary folk art circles, but a prodigious and powerful woman nonetheless, who recorded in paint much of the hundred years in which she lived and worked in Louisiana: Clementine Hunter. A float in her honor was a feature of the 2006 Fat Tuesday's parade.[1]

This was not the first time that Hunter received recognition within her state. In 1986, at the age of ninety-nine, Northwestern State University at Natchitoches awarded Hunter an honorary doctorate of fine arts. It was only the fourth time in the school's hundred-year history that an honorary doctorate was awarded and the first time that one was given to an African American. Hunter's degree had special significance to Dr. Mildred Hart Bailey, a professor and later a dean at the school. An ardent advocate of Clementine Hunter and her paintings, Bailey recalled that in 1955, due to segregation practices, Hunter was unable to attend an exhibition of her own art at the university during regular operating

CLEMENTINE HUNTER

Courtesy of Thomas N. Whitehead.

AFRICAN HOUSE MURAL, INTERIOR 1, BY CLEMENTINE HUNTER, 1955

Photo by James Rosenthal. Courtesy of the Historic American Building Survey, National Park Service.

AFRICAN HOUSE MURAL, INTERIOR 2, BY CLEMENTINE HUNTER, 1955

Photo by James Rosenthal. Courtesy of the Historic American Building Survey, National Park Service.

HARVEST TIME MURAL, AFRICAN HOUSE, BY CLEMENTINE HUNTER, 1955

Photo by James Rosenthal. Courtesy of the Historic American Building Survey, National Park Service.

AFRICAN HOUSE, EXTERIOR

Courtesy of Cammie G. Henry Research Center, Northwestern State University of Louisiana.

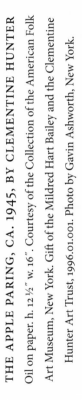

THE APPLE PARING, CA. 1945, BY CLEMENTINE HUNTER

Oil on paper. h. 12 ½ ″ w. 16 ″. Courtesy of the Collection of the American Folk Art Museum, New York. Gift of the Mildred Hart Bailey and the Clementine Hunter Art Trust, 1996.01.001. Photo by Gavin Ashworth, New York.

SATURDAY NIGHT, BY CLEMENTINE HUNTER, CA. 1965

Oil on board. h. 13½″ w. 17½″. Courtesy of the Collection of the American Folk Art Museum, New York. Museum of American Folk Art purchase in memory of Mr. and Mrs. R. A. Siegel, Atlanta, Ga., 1987.19.001.

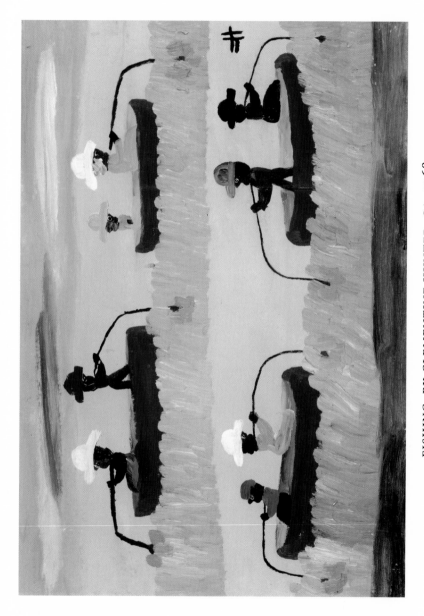

FISHING, BY CLEMENTINE HUNTER, CA. 1968

Oil on board. h. 24″ w. 16″. Courtesy of the Collection of the American Folk Art Museum, New York. Gift of Mary Bass Newlin, 1989.09.002. Photo by John Parnell, New York.

WASHING DAY, BY CLEMENTINE HUNTER, CA. 1971

Acrylic on board. h. 24″ w. 16″. Courtesy of the Collection of the American Folk

Art Museum, New York. Gift of Mary Bass Newlin, 1989.09.003.

hours. Bailey's colleague and friend, Ora Garland Williams, professor of English literature at Northwestern and an early Hunter patron, arranged for the artist to visit the exhibition of her work on Sunday, when the university museum was closed.[2]

Historians of Louisiana have much work before them to understand fully the extraordinary life of Clementine Hunter. Research efforts have barely, if at all, touched her life before she began to paint, the roots of her family tree, the effect that her mother, aunts, sisters, and friends likely had on her, or other aspects of her life not related to her painting and quilt making. Anne Hudson Jones's 1994 comment to a great extent still stands: "There is still room for a scholarly study of Hunter's life and work. . . . And issues of race, class, and gender need more careful analysis."[3] At this stage of research, we know Hunter primarily through her art, the writings of her patrons, and a few interviews. Her art continues to be a rich source for understanding this talented artist and the community that birthed, nurtured, and surrounded her.

This study focuses on Clementine Hunter's development as an artist, the men and women who encouraged her work and publicized it, and her artwork as a window on African American life at Melrose Plantation. The financial and emotional support of these dedicated supporters were essential to her motivation to continue painting and to her emergence to national prominence. Her art, although produced in the midst of a creative environment that flourished at Melrose for decades, remained in tone and content independent of the artist-guests who spent time there and advocates who supported her. It grew out of a seemingly inexhaustible wellspring of ideas, memories, and attitudes derived from her immersion in the community of African Americans she grew up with and labored among for half a century before she began painting.

It is not a given that self-taught artists are welcomed into the establishment world of arts and letters. It is almost unheard of for farm worker cooks from Cane River to gain stature within their state. Yet, Hunter's reputation is established, the result of a steady stream of publications and exhibitions, not to mention a lively market for her more than five thousand artworks. Collectors, dealers, friends, scholars, and museum professionals continue to support Hunter's art. Her art and life exemplified values that the parade organizers embraced. Hunter's work has inherent popular appeal; she had the strength, tenacity, and independence to become a folk hero.

Clementine Hunter was without peer as a diarist of plantation life, representing in visual form her more than half-century experience as a field hand, laundress, and cook at Melrose Plantation in the Cane River area near Natchitoches, Louisiana. "My paintings tell how we worked, played and prayed," she said.[4] Her subjects pick and gin cotton and harvest gourds, pecans, and figs. She painted women doing household chores: washing clothes, cooking, and caring for children. She painted people at leisure: dancing, playing cards, and socializing on Saturday night at the local honky-tonk. Religion was important to Hunter and her community; she painted not only nativity and crucifixion scenes but also people going to church, baptisms, revival meetings, weddings, wakes, and funerals. Hunter loved flowers—especially zinnias—and painted pictures of dazzling bouquets in large pots and in the garden around her small home. She also produced a number of abstract paintings, many commissioned by her friend James Register. For the most part, Hunter preferred to follow her personal muse and paint representational works in a spare, abstract style. In addition to her thousands of pictures, she left a quilt legacy in the form of several appliquéd pieced narrative textiles.

At age sixty-seven, when most of her peers were reducing their activity, the librarian and curator at Melrose commissioned Hunter to paint nine room-size murals for African House, one of the buildings in the Melrose plantation complex. The well-organized murals, painted during a sweltering summer, attest to Hunter's remarkable vitality. Hunter, who lived beyond her hundredth birthday, was motivated to make art until the last few months of her life. "God gave me the power," she said. "Sometimes I try to quit paintin'. I can't. I can't."[5]

Hunter's art is an important record of life at the turn of the twentieth century and the half century that followed, but it is her strong personal style, her unique vocabulary of form and handling of space, and a remarkable compositional and color sense that have assured her a place within the canon of self-taught artists.

Hunter's life spanned a century of enormous change. With the growth and industrialization of its cities, America emerged as the dominant world power. Although Hunter gave up kerosene lamps for electric lights and in later life enjoyed a television set, refrigerator with freezer, and automobile, most of the enormous change that occurred during Hunter's life passed by her and the other people in the Cane River area. Two world wars, the great depression, the civil rights movement, and the women's movement of the seventies barely if at all touched her life as a field hand, domestic servant, and artist. After growing too old to work as a domestic servant, Hunter lived modestly on social security and income from paintings she sold. She occasionally traveled, though not far. She preferred to stay home and re-create her memories in her artwork.[6]

Hunter is one of several self-taught artists in post-technological America who recorded and depicted memories of a fast-disappearing, unhurried time. Like Queena Stovall of Virginia (1887–1980), Mario Sanchez of Florida (1908–2005), and Anna Mary Robertson "Grandma" Moses of New York (1860–1961), Hunter began serious art making after the age of fifty, the point at which retirement or diminution of work, illness, the death of a spouse, or an accident typically creates time to pursue art making or other passions. Hunter has often been compared to Grandma Moses, who for thirty years documented rural life in upstate New York through the changing seasons. But there is a difference. Moses relied heavily on clippings from newspapers and other printed sources; her paintings only occasionally depict a specific time and place, and there are just two—or possibly three—self-portraits in her oeuvre. She traced elements, which she then assembled for her original, balanced, and colorful compositions. Hunter rarely used printed sources.[7]

Hunter produced only a few paintings of events other than from memory. A family photograph was the source for the oil on canvas *Brittain Family Portrait* (1975). An unusual subject, chickens dragging carts (*Chicken Haulin' Cotton* [1960], oil on upson board, and *Chicken Hauling Flowers* [1980], oil on canvas board), may have been inspired by popular sources that are still influential today. A recent Internet search by the author reveals multiple pictures of chickens pulling carts or wagons in paintings and on toys and ceramic lamps. Hunter may have seen and remembered an early amusing image on a wood engraving of a rooster pulling a cart, one of thousands of designs for flour sacks mass produced by S. George Milling Company of West Virginia (ca. 1895). A third example, a painting titled *The Good Darkie* (ca. 1950, oil on cardboard), was based on the statue called *The Good Darkey*, erected and dedicated in January 1927. The bronze sculpture stood on the corner of Washington and Front Streets in Natchitoches until 1968 when it was taken down and removed to the Louisiana State Rural Life Museum. Hunter was familiar with the prominently placed monument. The bulk of her work, however, drew from the wellspring of her life experiences.[8]

❀ ❀ ❀

Clementine Reuben was born in 1886 or early 1887 on Hidden Hill Plantation (also known as the Little Eva Plantation, Natchitoches Parish) to Mary Antoinette Adams and Janvier (John) Reuben. She was baptized in Cloutierville in 1887, when she was about two months old. At five or six, Clementine's family moved to Cloutierville. She attended school for only a short time, preferring work to school. When she was fourteen or fifteen, her father found work in the more fully developed community around Melrose Plantation. Hunter claimed she was Creole with Indian, black, and Irish ancestry. "All my people were creoles," she said.[9] "Creole" is a term used in so many different contexts that deciphering exactly what she meant by that is impossible. Creole people were culturally French, but they might be of white, African, or mixed-race descent. For Clementine, who spoke French before she spoke English, it was likely a reference to her culture. Interestingly, although she was a French-speaking Creole of color, socially she was not a part of the Melrose-area Isle Brevelle Creole community. Even though she is buried in the cemetery of St. Augustine, the local Catholic church, church records do not indicate that she was a member. Hunter may have over the years attended an occasional service there, but she also may have occasionally attended services at St. Matthew's, a Baptist church a few miles away.[10]

Hunter was the eldest of seven children and, "just like her mother," gave birth to seven children.[11] She had two children, Joseph (Frenchie) and Cora, with Charles Dupre, fifteen years her senior, who died in 1914. She was a single parent until 1924 when she married Emmanual Hunter, a woodchopper at Melrose, "a good Christian . . . he loved to work."[12] They had five children—Agnes, King, Mary, and two stillborn infants.[13]

Like her parents, Hunter's early work on the plantation was in its cotton fields, where she often picked 150 to 200 pounds a day. She often said she preferred picking cotton to other farm chores—hoeing corn, growing sugar cane, and harvesting pecans. In the late 1920s, Hunter moved out of the fields and into domestic service, working as a maid. She tended the vegetable garden, did laundry and ironing, and helped take care of Cammie Henry's children. She sewed lace curtains, made dolls and clothes for the children, created quilts, and wove baskets.[14]

❀ ❀ ❀

Hunter was one of three strong women who were pivotal in Melrose Plantation's history. The first two, Marie Thérèse Coincoin and Carmelite (Cammie) Henry, had a significant impact on Hunter herself. Coincoin, a slave born in 1742 and the subject of Elizabeth Shown Mills's essay in this volume, was matriarch to the powerful Creole family that founded the plantation. She had ten children with Claude Thomas Pierre Metoyer, a French bachelor who initially rented her and then purchased her in order to free her. After freeing Coincoin and some of their children, he gave them a small tract of land along what was then the Red River (later Cane River). Though Hunter believed the myth cultivated by Francois Mignon that Marie Thérèse Coincoin had owned Melrose, in truth it was Louis, Coincoin's oldest son, who in 1796 acquired the land that later became Melrose Plantation. Louis developed the land and built the small building today known as "Yucca House." In 1829, Coincoin's sons Augustin and Louis, both committed Catholics, built St. Augustine Roman Catholic Church, the spiritual center of the Cane River community of Creoles of color.[15]

The Metoyers prospered as a family of landowners, but in the 1840s, one young heir's free-wheeling ways cost them the plantation, which eventually became the property of John Hampton Henry Sr. Hampton named it Melrose in honor of Sir Walter Scott's burial site. In 1899, after the death of his father, the younger Henry and his wife Cammie moved to Melrose. He managed the plantation business and successfully harvested cotton and pecans. Miss Cammie, as she was called, renovated the rundown house and expanded the gardens and pecan orchards. At home, she did weaving and bookbinding and preserved plantation memorabilia in over three hundred scrapbooks. In a bold new venture, she invited artists and writers to the plantation to nurture their craft. Among them were the writers Alexander Woolcott, Rachel Field, and Lyle Saxon, the artists Alberta Kinsey and Caroline Dormon, and the photographer Carolyn Ramsey. In the late 1930s, Cammie hired Francois Mignon to be curator/librarian/organizer of culture at Melrose. It was Mignon who steadfastly nurtured Hunter's creative talent and offered her friendship.[16]

When Cammie Henry died in 1948, J. D. Henry, one of her sons, kept the plantation running and carried on her projects until he died in 1969. His death prompted the 1970 sale via auction of the plantation and its contents to the Southdown Land Company. The company understood Melrose's importance as a historic site as well as the important role women had played there, and in a charitable civic act, donated eight of the major buildings (including the main house, Yucca, and African House) and six acres of land to the Association of Natchitoches Women for the Preservation of Historic Natchitoches. In 1972, Melrose was added to the National Register of Historic Places; in 1974, it became a National Historic Landmark. Mignon, who had moved the fifteen miles from Melrose to New Haven House, Natchitoches, was not present at the public auction of the furnishings, but Hunter witnessed and recorded the 1969 event in a painting.[17]

❀ ❀ ❀

Unlike many gifted self-taught artists, Hunter had many advocates from the time she first picked up brushes and paint. Francois Mignon, who arrived at Melrose in 1939, was key among them. There are many versions of the story of Hunter's beginnings as a painter. Mignon recorded that she first started painting sometime around 1940:

Well do I remember when Clementine Hunter, already many times a grandmother, first tried her hand at painting. Alberta Kinsey of New Orleans had been here painting magnolias, using the antebellum outside kitchen as her studio. Late one afternoon, following Miss Alberta's return to New Orleans, it fell to Clementine Hunter to tidy up the place. About 7 o'clock that evening, clutching a handful of old discarded tubes of paint, she tapped at my door, said that she had found these twisted tubes while cleaning up and that she believed she could "mark" a picture on her own hook if she "sot her mind to it." . . . With a view to aiding her in her enterprise, I cast about and came up with an old window shade, a few brushes and a dab of turpentine.[18]

As the story continues, the next morning, Hunter appeared with a finished picture. In one of several interviews with author and gallery owner Shelby Gilley, Hunter said, "Early that morning, I took the picture I marked for Mr. Francois to his room. I didn't know it was so early cause I woke him up. I told him I finished his picture. He took it and unrolled the painting. I didn't know if he liked it or not until he said, 'Clementine, you keep painting like this and I can make you famous.' He then gave me a bunch of boards to mark. I nearly drove Hunter [the artist's husband] crazy. I had all these pictures in my head that I had to mark. I would go to work during the day, come home and fix Hunter his supper, then sit down and start to paint."[19] Over the course of her long career, Mignon unfailingly encouraged Clementine Hunter, bringing her supplies and checks for her works that he was able to sell.[20]

James Pipes Register, a writer who lived in Norman, Oklahoma, also took an interest in Hunter; although not wealthy, he paid Hunter a small monthly stipend, sent her supplies, and used his contacts to organize exhibitions for her work. Between 1944 and 1945, Register and Mignon corresponded extensively about Hunter and her progress as an artist. In 1945, Register secured some money for Hunter from members of the Julius Rosenwald Foundation. Hunter's paintings were featured in the New Orleans Arts and Crafts show in 1949, and at least two public showings in Brownwood and Waco, Texas, in the mid-1940s drew further attention.[21]

In 1953, Charlotte Willard wrote an article that appeared in *Look* magazine. In 1955, the Delgado Museum in New Orleans (now the New Orleans Museum of Art) held a one-person exhibition of Hunter's paintings. In 1961, the *Saturday Evening Post* featured her in an illustrated article. As early as 1945, Carolyn Ramsey wrote articles and provided illustrations for both *Look* and the *Saturday Evening Post*. In 1974, WDSU-TV in New Orleans produced a twenty-minute documentary on Hunter. Ora Williams became a patron and purchased paintings every time she visited the artist. Williams, who took the artist to see her own one-person exhibition at Northwestern State University, wrote the introduction and supported the printing of *Plantation Memo*, a selection of Francois Mignon's articles previously published in Plantation Memo and Cane River Memo, his newspaper columns.[22]

Hunter also developed a reputation as a creative cook; with Mignon, she published *Melrose Plantation Cookbook* (1956), which featured recipes she dictated to Mignon. Among them were Melrose favorites: "game soup, boiled bass, barbecued ham, piquant sauce, parsnip fritters, rice blancmange, apple biscuits, brown bread, fig cakes and puddings." Hunter learned to cook from her grandmother who served in a lavish antebellum household. The successful cookbook was reprinted several times and circulated well beyond Louisiana. A commendation letter from Alice B. Toklas brought Hunter and Mignon accolades from the French Académie Gastronomique and eligibility for a Cordon Bleu for one of the book's original recipes.[23]

Mignon's death in 1980 left a void in Hunter's life that was ultimately filled by a trio of collector-scholars: Mildred Hart "dede" Bailey; Ann Williams Brittain, daughter of Ora Williams and wife of Natchitoches attorney Jack Brittain; and Thomas N. Whitehead. They were devoted friends to Hunter over many years, visiting her, looking after some of her practical affairs, buying and promoting her work, and consistently offering her encouragement. All three were trustees of her estate. Bailey handled scholarly matters and assembled archival materials and a bibliography; Brittain was in charge of business affairs; Whitehead took care of marketing and promotion. Their individual roles overlapped. Even the deaths of two of these patrons were occasions for displaying Clementine Hunter's works. When Bailey died in 1995, she left works in her collection to museums that included the American Folk Art Museum in New York, the National Museum of Women in the Arts in Washington, D.C., and the National Afro-American Museum in Wilberforce, Ohio. After Brittain died in 2003, a number of paintings from the extensive Brittain collection of 345 paintings and three quilts were featured in a 2005 exhibition at the Ogden Museum of Art in New Orleans.[24]

❀ ❀ ❀

Hunter's paintings focused on work, recreation, and religion, illustrating how the people in the Cane River community lived. Although an occasional automobile and one airplane appear in her paintings, they generally depict earlier times. Hunter assumed the role of griot when she said, "The people who lived around here and made the history of this land are remembered by my paintings. I like that. I'm glad the young people of today can look at my paintings and see how easy and uncomplicated things were when we lived off the land. I wanted to tell them. I paint the history of my people. The things that happened to me and to the ones I know."[25]

Hunter, in one interview, acknowledged that she sometimes censored what she put in her paintings. In her signature work, *Picking Cotton*, adult women pick cotton, and no children are visible. Although on several occasions Hunter claimed she enjoyed picking cotton, she also said, "I didn't have no baby sitters like they do now. . . . Mine sat in the field, at the end of the row. Sometime I'd find some them fast asleep in the weeds. . . . I raise them all too . . . had a time. I no paint that."[26]

Cotton was basic to the Cane River community's economic life and thus was a natural subject for Hunter. Grown experimentally in Natchitoches as early as 1737, by 1804 or 1805 Emmanuel Prudhomme began to cultivate cotton commercially in the area, bringing prosperity to area landowners.[27] Later called King Cotton, the crop was basic to the southern economy throughout the nineteenth century and much of the twentieth century; its production supported a stratified social structure and, until 1865, the institution of slavery. After the Civil War, some blacks owned their own farms. Others became tenant farmers or sharecroppers, and still others became employees. The Hunter family worked for decades as field hands at Melrose.

Hunter always spoke positively about her cotton-picking experiences; she was proud of her ability as a field hand. Because cotton is planted and cultivated in rows, Hunter usually painted the cotton plants and pickers in horizontally layered arrangements in her paintings. There is implicit harmony between humans and nature in these paintings, the figures maintaining a relationship to the task at hand. Vibrant color transforms a scene involving arduous labor into a joyous celebration of work and a sense of community spirit.

The painting *Washing Day* (1971) recalls an era when women cleaned clothes outdoors in boiling water and hung them on an outdoor line to dry. Mignon wrote, "I re-capture the scene when, years ago, a lithe Clementine Hunter would be stoking the fire beneath the pot and, with a fragile but firm wrist, as dexterous with clothes-stick as later it was to be with a paint brush, would haul up from the black, simmering depths of the pot the snowiest white shirts imaginable."[28] In the painting, a woman stokes clothes simmering in an iron pot against a backdrop of clothes hanging out to dry. An iron pot is centrally placed in the picture. Iron pots were part of the landscape at Melrose. One in front of Ghana cabin served as a splashing pool for two pet geese; another was in the back of the cabin.[29]

Hunter's painting titled *Fishing* (1968) points to the importance of fishing in daily life in the Cane River. Fishing was not mere sport but was also an essential part of the local diet. In a light touch Mignon wrote, "It should be remembered . . . fish provides the 'resistance piece' for supper in many a home in the region, and often absence of good luck in angling may well spell out the difference between a toothsome repast and an empty stomach."[30] In this painting, Hunter depicts eight figures, two in each of four boats in two rows set on water and topped by a single band of blue-gray sky. Men and women are fishing; one woman has brought her child along. The figures in each boat face in opposite directions, achieving a rhythmic patterning that gives the painting an animated touch. The four horizontally placed brown boats and the vertical strokes of the water beneath lend a lively and striking counterpoint to this deceptively simple composition.

Hunter recorded moments of recreation in paintings of card players, dancers, and most frequently, Saturday night revelry. Lots of drinking took place inside and outside the local club, sometimes on the roof; there was fighting and an occasional violent flare-up—a shooting or stabbing. Hunter demonstrates her ability to compress time within a picture in *Saturday Night* (ca. 1965) where she painted one man shooting another, the victim on the floor. The painting may have been inspired by nearby Bubba's Lounge, a club/bar that still caters to the community just outside Melrose, or by the Friendly Place just across the river.[31]

Hunter was not an avid churchgoer, but she was profoundly spiritual. She was rooted in Protestant as well as Catholic traditions. When her husband Emmanuel died in August 1944, she was distressed that no words about him were planned for the proposed Catholic service; that very morning, she arranged for a Baptist burial at nearby St. Matthew's instead. She chose to be buried next to Mignon in the cemetery of St. Augustine's, a church that appears in the background of many of her baptism, funeral, and "going to church" paintings.[32]

The unusual painting *Blessed Martin Chapel* (1954) is an inspired work that features a tiny chapel built on a small projecting wing of Yucca House. The painting depicts the interior of the chapel, designed by Mignon as a place of refuge for local people of color, with a statue of the Chilean Martin de Porres, the first nonwhite person in the Western Hemisphere to be considered for canonization. Hunter, known for her compositions with flattened perspective, in this painting rendered a naturalistic perspective of the intimate chapel, with its central stained glass window, classical pillar, large cross, statue of St. Martin, and small painting of St. Veronica's veil that bears the likeness of Jesus's face.[33]

According to Mignon, the chapel has "a cross for the religious-minded, a Greek pillar for the intellectual and a picture for the simple souls. Perhaps St. Martin's Chapel will help bridge a gap that will at least offer something to a wider, even though more limited circle, if you will pardon the paradox." Mignon also hung a Hunter "baptism" painting on the chapel wall to provide relief from its austere feeling.[34]

Hunter painted baptism scenes over and over. Her wake and crucifixion scenes generally reflect the Catholic ritual. In Hunter's depictions, Jesus is usually black. Hunter said of one of these paintings, "That's Black Jesus, and the angel[s] . . . I don't know if black or white. 'Cause nearly everybody says 'Black Jesus,' so I thought I'd make him black like."[35] There are many possible sources for black Jesus—the Caribbean, South America, the charismatic black nationalist movement of Marcus Garvey, and a sanctified figure like Haile Selassie. Black Jesus may also have earlier African roots. Black Jesus is important to many southern black Protestants as well, and other self-taught artists have depicted him—including Bill Traylor (1854–1949), Mose Tolliver (1912–2006), William Hawkins (1895–1990), and Sister Gertrude Morgan (1900–1980).[36] Several of Hunter's crucified figures look female, with rounded contours. Hunter's possible personal identification with Jesus is hinted at in the *Cotton Crucifixion* (1970). Crucified thieves flank Jesus; they stand as black crosses on chapel-like structures filled with mounds of cotton. In *Black Jesus* (1965), in place of thieves, pots of zinnias, the artist's favorite flowers, flank the crucified figure.

The evolution of Hunter's style may be traced from her earliest work to her self-assured midperiod to her experiments with abstract paintings and then to her late style, when her brush strokes became loose and eventually less steady.

Hunter's color palette included black, red, white, green, yellow, gold, blue, and pastels of lavender blue and pink. She had an intuitive color as well as compositional sense. Balance between dark and light tones allowed Hunter to highlight the important elements and punctuate details against a pleasing background.

Hunter's earliest paintings were done with oil paint on paper and other surfaces. She often so thinned the oils with turpentine that the medium was frequently mistaken for watercolor. She sketched an outline in pencil, or in her words "marked" a picture, before applying paint. Her early brushwork is both smooth and vigorous. Although she seemed to prefer unmixed colors, she sometimes laid thinned paint color wet on wet, producing multiple shades in areas of a picture. Hunter didn't move from creating single-image paintings to more complex subject matter; she alternated between single flowers or figures and more complex compositions from the very beginning but seemed to favor more complex narratives to single-element formats. In early pictures, Hunter often used bright colors and often placed them against unpainted backgrounds that clearly demarcated earth, sky, atmosphere. She presented representational elements in abstract form, pared down to essentials.

Flat, unshaded forms presented close to the picture plane are hallmarks of Hunter's style. Generalized lighting—without shadow around principal compositional elements—also contributes to the flatness of the forms. In her mid and later years, Hunter demonstrated an occasional interest in perspective, as she did in the St. Martin Chapel painting, but in most of her pictures, she did not use perspective or foreshortening to create naturalism and volume. However, the artist's backgrounds—the banded and other areas of earth, sky, and water— reveal a surprising variety of color shades and textures that lend atmospheric dimension and variety to the picture surface.

In her early work on sheets of paper and other surfaces, Hunter often left backgrounds unpainted in order to conserve the precious paint. In middle and later years, she worked on canvas board, pressed wood, and upson board and painted the backgrounds. Hunter's flat, unshaded forms continue to be presented close to the picture plane. Narrative subjects and still life paintings appeared simultaneously from the beginning. In her compositional style, she often painted a central focal point figure or structure asymmetrically balanced on either side with figures, trees, or plants. In a wedding or revival scene, for instance, she framed a group of figures by using an overarching canopy or decorative device. She achieved rhythmic vitality by stylized patterning of figures in ordered rows and depth with layering of patterned groups, thus maintaining a flowing narrative. Hunter grounds her figures by placing small earthen mounds throughout the composition. Her universe is mapped by earth, midground, and sky. Angels float through Hunter's sky, their beehive hairdos animating them. Often, she shows various events in the narrative simultaneously, in, as mentioned before, some Saturday night, wash day, and baptism scenes. She also often shows interiors and exteriors of buildings at the same time, a familiar strategy among self-taught artists.

Like many autodidacts, Hunter took liberties with scale, enlarging figures or objects according to their importance in the picture. *The Good Darkie* towers over the surrounding trees; in *Calinda Corvier Was Over 100 Years Old* (ca. 1940), the vase of flowers takes on central importance. A pot of flowers often dominates a painting with architectural and figural house forms. In *Chicken Hauling Flowers*, an oversized chicken or rooster pulls a cart led by a tiny girl.

Liberties with perspective tie in with the artist's sense of humor. In an otherwise sedate rendition of *Melrose Complex* (ca. 1955), red underwear hangs from a clothesline, a figure hangs upside down in *Pecan Threshing* (ca. 1975), and at times, women stand taller than their partners at weddings and dances. Hunter seemed to delight in depicting ministers smaller than other major figures in a composition. In several paintings of Mary, baby Jesus, and the three wise men, instead of gold, myrrh, and frankincense the wise men bring a pineapple, a box of chocolates, and a birthday cake.

Hunter was sixty-seven when she undertook her most ambitious work: creating the nine African House murals at Melrose Plantation, a project conceived by Mignon. "After a cursory glance around the room, she thought the prospects promising."[37] In addition to the physical and mental energy she exhibited in completing the project, she also exhibited speed; she painted the nine large panels in less than two months of one hot summer: June 8 to July 21, 1955.[38]

The African House murals link Hunter with a tradition of nineteenth-century artisans who painted narratives on walls, lending radiance to house interiors. Murals painted on interior walls are among the most monumental of early American folk art. The best-known itinerant New England muralist, Rufus Porter (1792–1884), had a style distinguished by its large scale, bright colors, and bold design. Unlike Hunter's, Porter's murals were generic, often fanciful, frescoes. The African House murals feature various people in Hunter's life, although the likenesses are not realistic. An artist depicted at an easel under a tree in the mural *Melrose Plantation—Big House and African House* could be mistaken for Hunter herself, but according to Carolyn Ramsey, it is Alberta Kinsey, painting magnolias in the Melrose gardens. Ramsey reported that Hunter depicted herself in the mural serving drinks on a tray to Mignon and Lyle Saxon, another Melrose resident. Ramsey is shown taking photographs. A town character, Aunt Attie, who appears in the *Cane River Funeral* mural, vigorously drives a hearse to a funeral, and the plantation's last surviving former slave, Uncle Israel, hitches his horse and buggy before heading to the Primer ("Plymouth") Rock Church, where he was the preacher. In the *Wash Day* mural, Hunter paints a self-portrait outdoors at an easel, even though she usually painted inside her cabin with the support on her lap.[39]

The African House murals demonstrate Hunter's flexibility. Hunter adapted to the larger format with an ease that has eluded other self-taught as well as trained artists. Many of the murals' themes had been subjects of her smaller paintings; in making the transition to a larger format, Hunter wove vignettes of cotton picking, a pecan harvest, Saturday night at the honky-tonk, funeral, wash day, and baptism into a unified panoramic landscape of Cane River life that included an opening pictorial map of the area. She often made smooth transitions at the mural edges and wall intersections and did not hesitate to relocate structures for artistic and compositional reasons. For example, so the viewer can see it and accord it the significance it deserves, she placed the large sundial at the side of Yucca House instead of at the rear of the building among the buildings and gardens where it customarily sat.[40]

Hunter was adventurous. She worked in a variety of media—she made quilts, lace curtains, and dolls—before committing herself exclusively to painting. Her innate curiosity about painting was in itself evidence of a desire to try new things. She experimented with tubes of paint she found lying around Melrose as she went about her housekeeping chores. Her manipulation of color to create rhythmically patterned, balanced, and harmonious compositions demonstrates her interest in and fascination with possibilities of expression through paint.

By 1960, James Register noticed that some of Hunter's pictures seemed uninspired and repetitious. With sincere intent, he cut out colorful ads from magazines, rearranged the cut pieces, and taped the montages to a cardboard sheet giving them to the artist one at a time. Between 1962 and 1964, Register commissioned Hunter to paint "abstracts" from these. He meant this interference with her natural creative process to encourage her to move in other directions. Hunter painted about one hundred abstract pictures during that period but also commented that they were difficult to do. "Paintin' is a lot harder than pickin' cotton. Cotton's right there for you to pull off the stalk, but to paint you got to sweat yo' mind."[41] After the experiment, she returned to painting narrative pictures and still lifes, pictures that came to her through her mind's eye. However, on rare occasions, she painted an "abstract"—but only when she preferred to, not upon request.[42]

❀ ❀ ❀

Although Hunter's paintings are well known to many, the quilts she made before she began to paint seriously have received little attention. Scholars have attributed approximately two dozen quilts from the late 1930s to the artist. She stopped textile art, as did Grandma Moses, when arthritis made quilting and sewing too difficult. She made scrap-pieced and appliquéd quilts as well as quilts that combined both types. Hunter combined hand piecing with machine work after buying a sewing machine.[43]

In composition and color, Hunter's quilts resonate with her African American roots. Her pieced quilts, the chevron pattern, for example, with alternating harmonious colors, resonate with syncopated rhythmical patterning and spontaneous improvisation. Movement is created from the juxtaposition of the myriad colors and shapes in a zigzag pattern. The strip-piecing technique of quilt making "reflects a heritage of textile making that extends all over west Africa."[44] Similarly, the use of dark and light hexagonal pieces to create a mosaic pattern (widely known as Grandmother's Flower Garden pattern) also vibrates from the fluctuating color arrangement.[45]

Hunter's quilts were meant for utility and warmth, but Mignon and Register identified her pictorial appliquéd and pieced narrative quilts as wall hangings to be appreciated as works of art. Hunter sewed individually cut pieces to a larger background. She assembled narrative elements—representing buildings, plants, flowers, and people— into a colorful, well-designed format. Her pictorial quilts resemble West African textiles, like the Fon banners of Benin. They bear resemblance as well to the remarkable Bible quilts of Harriet Powers, another southern African American, born in Georgia in the nineteenth century.

It was color, motion, strong contrast, and narrative that Hunter sought in her quilts—not tiny, even stitches. Her aesthetic, like that of some other African American quilters, emphasized graphic design. The stitches are a means, not an end in themselves.

Hunter did not speak much of her quilting when interviewed. She discussed her cooking and working in the fields but not particularly her quilting.[46] However, in a rare self-portrait, in 1980, she depicted herself with her quilt on her lap.[47]

❀ ❀ ❀

Approaching her hundredth birthday, Hunter was often attended by her daughters and grandchildren. Even with her eyesight failing, Hunter continued to paint. As always, she painted on all manner of surfaces—cardboard, bottles, plastic containers, window shades, buckets, even an occasional ironing board. In later years, she sometimes painted a single subject but continued to favor multiple images. Toward the end, her hand became less steady. Her health weakened, and painting became physically very difficult.[48]

Hunter's commitment to work and to art combined with a strong sense of identity, independent spirit, close family and personal ties, spiritual faith, energy, and sense of humor sustained her throughout her long, active life. She utilized her talent and tapped into her inner expressive resources. Through art, she gained a measure of control over her life; she filtered her experience and expressed herself in a unique personal style. Folklorist Bill Ferris noted in his book *Local Color: A Sense of Place in Folk Art* that American artists are identified with place.[49] Within her large oeuvre, Hunter's sense of place shaped her personal vision. But her art transcends her life and that of her community. Through her art, Clementine Hunter offers universal, relevant messages for a local, regional, national, and global audience.

Her art reflects a love of life and the world within which she grew up and matured. She depicted strong African American women actively engaging in many aspects of traditional country life: working and playing outdoors, marrying, tending to children, nursing the sick, attending church, and laying the dead to rest. Her angels are female, Mary with baby Jesus is often depicted, and even Jesus occasionally appears to be female; all are African American. Her art also depicts a stable, well-balanced world grounded in nature. Her early life with her parents and siblings and her comfortable and enduring relationships with the fathers of her children complemented the stability evident in her art and likely contributed to her ability to re-create her memories by painting.

NOTES

I wish to thank Eva Baham, Elizabeth Shown Mills, and Judith Gentry for their careful readings of this essay and instructive suggestions.

1. Rex Organization, http://rexorganization.com/Parade.

2. Francois Mignon, journal, April 24 and May 9, 1945, folders 85–86, Francois Mignon Papers, document no. 3889, Southern Historical Collection, Wilson Library, University of North Carolina, Chapel Hill; Shelby R. Gilley, *Painting by Heart: The Life and Art of Clementine Hunter, Louisiana Folk Artist* (Baton Rouge: St. Emma Press, 2000), 34, 40, 42, 61.

3. Anne Hudson Jones, review of James L. Wilson's *Clementine Hunter: American Folk Artist*, in *Woman's Art Journal* 15 (Spring/Summer 1994): 54. Considerable archival material on Hunter and Melrose may be found in the Cammie G. Henry Research Center, Northwestern State University, Natchitoches (hereinafter cited as CHRC), and at the Southern Historical Collection, Wilson Library, University of North Carolina, Chapel Hill. Books and catalogs featuring Hunter's art are also useful. James L. Wilson's short biography, *Clementine Hunter: American Folk Artist* (Gretna, La.: Pelican, 1988), includes colorful plates of her art and excerpts from letters between Francois Mignon and James Register, along with remarks from the artist. Gilley, in *Painting by Heart*, draws on visits with the artist beginning in 1970 to present biographical information, a sprinkling of Hunter quotations, and color plates and has sections on unusual pictures and fakes. Thomas N. Whitehead and Art Shiver, who produced the thoughtful *Clementine Hunter: The African House Murals* (Natchitoches: Association for the Preservation of Historic Natchitoches in partnership with the National Park Service, 2005), have undertaken a major Hunter project that will culminate in a book that traces, through interviews and thousands of Mignon's papers, Hunter's professional career. Many significant exhibitions and books on twentieth-century self-taught artists include artwork by and entries on Hunter. See also Anne Hudson Jones, "The Centennial of Clementine Hunter," *Women's Art Journal* 8 (Spring/Summer 1987): 23–27.

4. Clementine Hunter, interview by John McCurnan for Shelby Gilley, 1982, witnessed and arranged by Thomas N. Whitehead and quoted in Gilley, *Painting by Heart*, 65.

5. Gilley, *Painting by Heart*, 60.

6. Ibid., 9.

7. Ibid., 66.

8. GramLee Collection of Early American Wood Engravings, West Virginia University, Morgantown; Francois Mignon to James Register, September 4, 1944, quoted in Wilson, *American Folk Artist*, 131; Wilson, *American Folk Artist*, 79. In 1926, Jackson Bryan, a Natchitoches businessman commissioned Hans Schular of Baltimore, Md., to make the sculpture of *The Good Darkey*, who was tipping his hat (Mary Linn Wernet, archivist, CHRC).

9. Wilson, *American Folk Artist*, 20. Thomas N. Whitehead, a trustee of Hunter's estate who knew the artist for twenty years, lived in Natchitoches, and visited her frequently, did not recall her attending church (Whitehead, interview by author, September 2006). Janet Colson, director of the Creole Heritage Center, reiterated that Hunter was not a member of St. Augustine's, although media reports stated that she was. Colson's husband, who knew Hunter for decades, confirmed that she was not a member. Colson, who lived in the area, said that Hunter was a member of St. Matthew's Baptist Church (Colson, interview by author, October 2006).

10. Wilson, *American Folk Artist*, 20, 74; James Register, "Clementine Hunter and the World around Us," *Natchitoches Times*, December 17, 1972, quoted in Gilley, *Painting by Heart*, 55, 57; Jones, "Centennial," 2324. Francois Mignon reports that "local legend says" the owner of Hidden Hill, Robert McAlpin, was the inspiration for the cruel character Simon Legree in Harriet Beecher Stowe's novel *Uncle Tom's Cabin* (*Plantation Memo: Plantation Life in Louisiana, 1750–1970, and Other Matter* [Baton Rouge: Claitor's, 1972], 113). In the 1910 federal census of the United States, population of Natchitoches County, microfilm reel 519, enumeration district 92, p. 32, the artist is listed as Clemence Reuben, age twenty, living in the home of Charles Dupre, age thirty-five, with their son Joseph (age three), their daughter Marita (age one), and others.

11. Wilson, *American Folk Artist*, 74; Jones, "Centennial," 23–24.

12. Wilson, *American Folk Artist*, 74; Jones, "Centennial," 24.

13. Wilson, *American Folk Artist*, 20, 24, 110; James Register, "Clementine Hunter and the World around Us," *Natchitoches Times*, December 17, 1972, quoted in Gilley, *Painting by Heart*, 55, 57. Emanuel Hunter, age twenty-seven, lived with his widowed mother and two boys, Emmon (age eleven) and Guss (age ten). See census citation in note 11, and Emmanual Hunter in the same census, reel 519, enumeration district 92, p. 33.

14. Clementine Hunter, conversation with Mildred Bailey, at Hunter's residence, March 5, 1978, tape recording, CHRC; Hunter interview, quoted in Wilson, *American Folk Artist*, 101; Wilson, *American Folk Artist*, 22, 24, 101, 117; Gilley, *Painting by Heart*, 57–58, 175.

15. See chapter 1 in this volume and Gilley, *Painting by Heart*, 19.

16. Lucy Gutman, ms. on Cammie Henry (PhD diss., University of Southern Mississippi, in progress), and Lucy Gutman, "Cammie Garrett Henry: The Evolution of a Plantation Mistress," unpublished ms.

17. Gutman, ms. on Cammie Henry, and Gutman, "Cammie Garrett Henry"; Gilley, *Painting by Heart*, 19–20, 39; Wilson, *American Folk Artist*, 25, 39.

18. Mignon, *Plantation Memo*, 99; Gilley, *Painting by Heart*, 44–45. See also Mignon letter, December 19, 1939, Francois Mignon Papers, Southern Historical Collection, Wilson Library, University of North Carolina, Chapel Hill.

19. Mignon, *Plantation Memo*, 99; Wilson, *American Folk Artist*, 27; Gilley, *Painting by Heart*, 45;

Hunter interview by John McCurnan for Shelby Gilley, 1982, witnessed and arranged by Thomas N. Whitehead and quoted in Gilley, *Painting by Heart*, 65. Hunter spoke the Francophone language Creole as her first language, which affected her English. It is likely that Gilley translated her dialect into standard English in this quote.

20. Mignon's role in furthering Hunter's success cannot be overstated. A person of unusual ability, he created a fictitious identity for himself, a romanticized version of Melrose, and an artistic persona for Hunter. This does not detract from her artistic talent and drive. See Gilley, *Painting by Heart*, 43–46, and *Clementine Hunter: The African House Murals*, 19–21.

21. Mignon to Register, November 9, 1945, quoted in Wilson, *American Folk Artist*, 146; Wilson, *American Folk Artist*, 29; Gilley, *Painting by Heart*, 49. Research is currently underway regarding details of Hunter's relationship with the Rosenwald Foundation. James Register received a grant from the foundation in 1944 and Thomas Whitehead and Arthur Shiver confirmed that Register shared money from his grant with Hunter.

22. Charlotte Willard, "Innocence Regained," *Look*, June 16, 1953, 102–5; Jones, "Centennial," 26; Mignon to Register, March 21, 1945, quoted in Wilson, *American Folk Artist*, 137; Mignon, *Plantation Memo*, i–iv; Wilson, *American Folk Artist*, 34.

23. Francois Mignon and Clementine Hunter, *Melrose Plantation Cookbook* (Natchitoches: Baker Printing, 1956), passim; Mignon, *Plantation Memo*, 136–39; Gilley, *Painting by Heart*, 46.

24. Wilson, *American Folk Artist*, 40–42.

25. Gilley, *Painting by Heart*, 46, 65.

26. Wilson, *American Folk Artist*, 101.

27. Mignon, *Plantation Memo*, 116. Natchitoches, the first permanent European settlement in the Louisiana Purchase, was established in 1714.

28. Mignon, *Plantation Memo*, 27.

29. Ibid., 26–27.

30. Ibid., 291.

31. Wilson, *American Folk Artist*, 90–91. Bubba's at 3410 Highway 119 is open on weekends and special holidays.

32. Mignon to Register, August 23, 1944, quoted in Wilson, *American Folk Artist*, 130.

33. Mignon, *Plantation Memo*, 304–5.

34. March 14, 1950, document no. 4127, Francois Mignon Papers, Southern Historical Collection, Wilson Library, University of North Carolina, Chapel Hill.

35. Wilson, *American Folk Artist*, 95.

36. Traylor and Tolliver, like Hunter, depicted a black Jesus crucified. Hawkins painted several versions of *The Last Supper* and Sister Gertrude Morgan often rendered Jesus in a secular setting. Hunter also often presented Jesus as a baby on Mary's lap.

37. Mignon, *Plantation Memo*, 106.

38. Art Shiver, "The Story of Clementine Hunter's African House Murals," in *Clementine Hunter: The African House Murals*, 22, 30–36; Mignon, *Plantation Memo*, 28, 31–32, 105–8; Gilley, *Painting by Heart*, 29.

39. *Clementine Hunter: The African House Murals*, 29, 31–34, 40–57; Carolyn Ramsey, "Melrose Murals Are Unveiled," *Baton Rouge Morning Advocate*, September 25, 1955; Mignon, *Plantation Memo*, 107–8.

40. Wilson, *American Folk Artist*, 34–36; See also *Clementine Hunter: The African House Murals*.

41. Gilley, *Painting by Heart*, 149.

42. Wilson, *American Folk Artist*, 37–38; Gilley, *Painting by Heart*, 50–51.

43. Gilley, *Painting by Heart*, 45. Quilt scholar Lynn Deal has recently studied a Melrose Planta-tion quilt (1952) and a pieced mosaic quilt (1970). Deal has written an in-depth study of Hunter quilts ("A Theory of Synergy: A Quilt Related Interpretation from a Modern Louisiana Plantation Based on the Creative Process and the Human Experience" [Norman: University of Oklahoma Graduate College, 2004]).

44. John Michael Vlach, *The Afro-American Tradition in Decorative Arts* (Cleveland, Ohio: Cleveland Museum of Art, 1978), 55.

45. Gladys-Marie Fry, "Not by Rules but by the Heart: The Quilts of Clementine Hunter," in *Clementine Hunter: An American Folk Artist* (Dallas, Tex.: Museum of African-American Life and Culture, 1993), 21.

46. Gilley, *Painting by Heart*, 73.

47. Deal, "A Theory of Synergy," 46.

48. Wilson, *American Folk Artist*, 40; Gilley, *Painting by Heart*, 17; Jones, "Centennial," 26–27.

49. William R. Ferris, *Local Color: A Sense of Place in Folk Art* (New York: McGraw Hill, 1982), xvii–xviii, xx–xxii.

Dorothy Dix
(1861–1951)

The World Brought Her Its Secrets

CHRISTINA VELLA

❁ ❁ ❁

The little matron who was known as "the best-loved woman in the world" had, for over fifty years, more readers than any writer of her day.[1] In the United Kingdom, members of Parliament used a debating stratagem named after her—the "Dorothy Dixer."[2] Shopkeepers in Italy and Australia, fooled by imposters, allowed false Dorothys to run up large bills. When Dorothy Dix went to the Philippines and Latin America as a simple tourist in the 1920s, she was mobbed by well-wishers and hailed as a great public figure. Even in the Far East, her popularity was phenomenal.

The millions of Americans who read her syndicated column, Dorothy Dix Talks, had no idea, usually, that she lived in New Orleans; they assumed she was writing from the newspaper office in their own hometown. Thus, among the two thousand letters a week she received at the height of her career, several would include a phone number with the anxious plea, "Please call me at home this afternoon or meet me at xyz drugstore, as I can't wait for an answer to appear in the paper."

Who remembers her now? Or does not confuse the newspaper adviser with Dorothea Dix, the reformer, whose name has proved more durable? Nothing, it seems, is so fragile as popularity. Dorothy Dix, the household name, whose motherly narrative voice was a vivid presence in every town and village, is now forgotten, like the thrift-store sugar bowls and flowered potholders that once sat beside her column on the breakfast tables of America. She got the country in the habit of turning for intimate consolation to a newspaper writer—that traditionally faceless recorder of impersonal information. Her self-assurance became a model for columnists who came after her; they tried to imitate her no-nonsense

DOROTHY DIX

Courtesy of the Historic New Orleans Collection,

Museum/Research Center, acc. no. 1990.128.1.

tone with a breezy style that never quite captured Dix's texture of kindly wit. Nevertheless, after Dix, the advice column, which had been a dispensable item in newspapers when she began writing in 1894, became an essential feature of all major dailies—some newspapers today regularly run two.

Dorothy Dix's wisdom consisted of ignoring almost all conventional wisdom—not a bad philosophy in any era. She thought, for example, that the family was an overrated institution. "There is no reason why you should have your temper continually rasped by antagonistic sisters and brothers when there are plenty of agreeable strangers in the world," she wrote. "Practically the only people who ever say . . . wounding things to us are in our own household."[3] A girl complained about the town gossips who were tormenting her. "Gossip is one of the most powerful influences in the world for good," came the answer. "It keeps the weak-kneed and wobbly on the straight and narrow path," whereas they would surely get into mischief if they didn't have to worry about what people might say.[4] No one tried harder than Dorothy Dix to dispel women's fantasies about marriage. A few words of love, she astutely observed, were more important to a woman than having a man work his fingers to the bone to show he loved her, whereas to men, love talk was merely a kind of courtship propaganda. "The man who told you he would make your life a dream of bliss . . . has forgotten he ever said it and expects you to, too."[5]

The world brought her its secrets, but she kept her own life a private matter. The little that has been written about Dix since her death is mostly twaddle, the expatiations of liberated brows who would mold Dix into protofeminism or shoo her into a white-columned myth of southern aristocracy. The exception is an overly fond biography by the journalist and author Harnett Kane, her protégé and lifelong friend. Kane was one of the first to earn a Dorothy Dix essay prize and the last to honor her with three hundred discreet, well-researched pages, written with more stylistic finesse than Dorothy Dix herself ever attained.[6]

❀ ❀ ❀

She was born Elizabeth Meriwether in 1861 in Woodstock, Tennessee, just a few feet from the Kentucky border (in fact, the state boundary ran through the Meriwether property). Dorothy Dix probably exaggerated her childhood poverty; however, when she said that she was brought up in an odd atmosphere of want and luxury, the remark had the ring of truth. The Meriwethers dined on antique china and were surrounded by fine things from the past, but they had no cash and the food itself was poor and scanty—a common enough situation in the Tennessee of Reconstruction. The family silver had been saved from marauding Civil War soldiers by a servant, Mr. Dicks, who had the presence of mind to bury it in a tomb rumored to be haunted.[7] Elizabeth Meriwether later borrowed her pen name from that retainer.

Far from being the southern lady of anybody's definition, Elizabeth was a tomboy who rode a retired thoroughbred before she could walk. Her first shoes were made by her adoring father from the hide of a squirrel he shot.[8] As a youngster, she trapped rabbits with her brother and boy cousins. Her mother was a semi-invalid who died as Elizabeth reached adolescence; her father then married one of his cousins, a hard-shell Baptist. Elizabeth was required to attend church but not school. However, for a time she was splendidly educated by an old man who came to stay on the farm. He was a distant Meriwether relative, as was everyone in the area, a well-mannered, whiskery, stooped fellow. He talked to himself and answered his own questions; but they were the questions of a trained, if desiccated, intellect. He took an interest in the young girl and within a few months had taught her to love great books in general and Dickens in particular.

The Meriwethers moved several times as their income diminished. Elizabeth's father tried first one business venture and then another. He nevertheless managed to send his country hoyden to the fashionable Hollins Institute of Virginia for one wretched semester of ridicule and humiliation. A good thing came out of that brush with formal education: Elizabeth won her first award for an essay.[9]

The woman who would become America's expert on romance had almost none of it in her own life. When her pretty younger sister got married, Elizabeth, turning twenty-one, still had no suitors. Just then, her stepmother's rakish brother came to visit for several weeks. Before long, a marriage of inconvenience had been more or less arranged. Ten years older than Elizabeth, George Gilmer was notably handsome, full of verve, ambition, and bravado. Later, after George's emotional instability was apparent to everyone, Dorothy Dix implied that she had succumbed to her stepmother's pressure in marrying him: "At the age of eighteen [one of her white lies] I tucked up my hair and got married, as was the tribal custom among my people."[10] Long before late marriages became prevalent in America, Dorothy Dix was recommending that couples wait until they were well into their twenties to wed.

In later years, on the rare occasions when she discussed her husband, she referred to "the hell of living with George."[11] But there are reasons to believe that despite the ordeal her marriage became, she loved him intensely. George Gilmer could not hold a job. The couple moved around constantly as he tried new positions and new business ventures, all of which met with failure. At times

Elizabeth and George were forced to live with her parents, who were themselves struggling financially. Elizabeth tried to earn a little by submitting essays and stories to magazines and newspapers. In 1889 she won a hundred-dollar prize from the Nashville *American* for a story about a thoroughbred and a boy winning a race.[12] Meanwhile, George's job changes became more frequent and his mood changes more pronounced. It was not George, however, but Elizabeth who had a nervous breakdown, in 1893, when she was thirty-two. She lay in bed, emaciated, unable to converse or get up, lips constantly moving in silence as her eyes searched the ceiling.

Will Meriwether was something of a ne'er-do-well himself, but his letters indicate that he was an even-tempered, charming, devoted father. He scraped up the money to take Elizabeth to the Gulf Coast for a rest. That was the first of many periods of separation from her husband, separations caused partly by practical difficulties and partly by marital stress. The trip was the turning point of Elizabeth's life. Close to her father and brother, Elizabeth slowly recovered. She played with the children she met on the beach. (It was to be one of the heartbreaks of her life that she never had children.) She submitted to card games with her father, gradually resumed writing, and visited with the lady in the next-door cottage—who happened to be Eliza Poitevent Nicholson, the dynamic owner and editor of the *Picayune*, the main newspaper of New Orleans. Mrs. Nicholson had been trying to attract women readers, that part of the population generally ignored by newspapers of the 1890s. She purchased, for three dollars, Elizabeth's "Story of Wartime," which described how a servant saved a family's silver.[13] And it was Mrs. Nicholson who brought Elizabeth to New Orleans for her first newspaper job—hunting up unreported births and deaths for the *Picayune*'s vital statistics page.

❀ ❀ ❀

In 1894, Elizabeth thus arrived at the *Picayune*'s rambling Camp Street building, climbed a flight of narrow, dingy stairs, and entered a newspaper editorial room for the first time. The place was a disorderly oven. Staffers were bustling about the cramped quarters, editors were swearing as they accidentally smeared the long proofs with their sweat, and everyone was talking out loud to himself as he worked. From the moment she saw the place, Elizabeth was in love.

She set out to learn everything about the newspaper business, poring over synonym books, memorizing editorials she liked, accepting every criticism with wide, docile eyes. She excelled in sentimental obituaries and bested her colleagues on the mortuary beat with the sheer number of deaths she discovered.

Her office mates joked that she killed people now and then rather than let her quota fall. She believed in her own motto: "Promise only what you can deliver. Then deliver more than you promise."[14]

She was promoted from obituaries to recipes. She learned to love cooking. From there she graduated to the Sunday feature section and covered the busy theater life of New Orleans. She learned to love theater, especially "two-handkerchief plays."[15] When she saw the legendary Maud Adams perform, she confided that "they had to remove me from the theater with a mop." It was her industry rather than her writing ability that prompted these promotions, for Elizabeth Gilmer's early articles tended to be mawkish and wordy. Nevertheless, rewards increased, until finally Mrs. Nicholson offered her the opportunity to write an advice column for women. Most articles intended for women, noted Mrs. Nicholson, were full of mushy platitudes about domesticity; they encouraged wives to be uncomplaining doormats. This advice column would neither exalt nor patronize women but would speak to them honestly, as practical and serious individuals. Alliterative pseudonyms were in vogue: Elizabeth chose Dorothy Dix. The column had various names until Dorothy Dix Talks finally stuck. Thus began fifty-five uninterrupted years of discussing the commonplace problems of getting along in life. Gradually, Mrs. Gilmer faded away and Miss Dix took over Elizabeth's personality. To readers, then friends, and finally even to her family and herself, she became "Dorothy."[16]

At first, the columns were digressive essays, not very polished, in which Dix might quote a long poem to illustrate a point. A column would typically begin, "The other Sunday I was walking in the park when I noticed a mother with her little boy." The sermon that followed was likely to mix tough-minded observation with trite maundering. But soon the writing developed a straight, sharp tone that became more noticeable with time. Relatives were brusquely advised to stay away from each other if they couldn't get along. Young people were reminded that they would one day be elderly: "What are you laying up for your old age?" she demanded to know, commenting sadly that people without savings were "forced to take the grudging charity of their own children" and discover "how steep are the stairs of another man's house."[17]

Very soon, Dix was writing constantly about marriage—how to arrive at it and then how to endure it. As blunt as her advice was, there were always traces of a sly smile playing between the words. "The foolproof way of getting a man is by flattery," she told women looking for husbands. "It is well to note that men oftener want to be praised for what they are not than for what they are. . . . A famous surgeon is prouder of his atrocious poetry than he is of the skill in his hands."[18] She offered men similar hard-nosed information. A widow made a bet-ter wife than a single girl, they were advised, because the widow "does not enter into marriage with impossible expectations and demands."[19]

In those years when women were streaming into offices as clerks and sec-retaries, middle-class people regularly debated whether working outside the home destroyed the feminine mystique and caused male chivalry to decline. "There are many thousands more women than men in the country," Dorothy Dix declared. "Are the superfluous multitudes of us supposed to sit on the curb-stones and suck our thumbs until some man comes along?" Men could practice their chivalry, she wrote, "by giving their women employees reasonable hours and fair wages."[20] She was angry that a woman in Britain could not aspire to a high diplomatic post: "Nothing but the stupidity of a nation that believes that breeches and brains are synonymous terms keeps her out of the job."[21]

When Dix's column took on the question-answer format, the overwhelming majority of her advice concerned love. Was it better to marry someone who adored you, though you felt only tender affection for him, or to marry someone whom you adored, even if his feelings were not intense? a reader asked. Marry the one you love, answered Dorothy Dix. "In almost every married couple, one kisses and the other submits to being kissed. Marriage lasts a long time. It seems longer with someone who bores you."[22] She counseled grieving widows to get jobs and keep so busy that they fell asleep at night from sheer exhaustion. Lov-ers who had been dumped should look at once for replacements: "There are just as good fish in the sea as have ever been caught." A woman with a past was instructed not to torment her fiancé by telling him about it, even though her conscience might be relieved. "Confession is always a weakness. The grave soul keeps its own secrets."[23]

A young man wrote that he had taken his girl to dinner, then to the theater, and afterward out to dance. Should he have taken the liberty of kissing her when he said goodnight? "No," Dorothy Dix answered. "I think you did enough for her."[24]

Sex was a subject fit only for unmarried girls, who were urged to stay away from it. Dorothy Dix never discussed physical relations after marriage. She used the term "lovemaking" in the old-time sense, to mean love talk, marriage pro-posals, heavy flirting, and all such activities that men undertook with embar-rassment so that they could find a wife and never have to resort to them again. Again and again, she tried to make women accept "the reality of matrimony," since there was hardly any hope of changing it.[25] "Woman's perpetual grievance against her husband is his indifference," she wrote. "He stopped all of his lovemaking at the altar with a suddenness that jarred her wisdom teeth loose, and in place of being a lady-love, she finds herself merely a household convenience. . . . This is never as she thought it would be. It just is as it is."

Dix's advice was commonsensical—as far as it went. She hardly ever tackled issues that could not be solved by compromise: alcoholism, homosexuality, addictions of any sort; spousal abuse, child abuse. Her columns were intended for average people with average woes. She wrote for those who, when facing conflict, were willing to change themselves, and could do so with honor, since changing anyone else was, she considered, a hopeless undertaking.

Dix's own love life was intermittent at best and fraught with more than average tension. After she was settled at the *Picayune*, her husband came to live with her in her rooming house near the newspaper's downtown offices. He worked hard to set up a little factory on Tchoupitoulas Street distilling turpentine. Some years later, Gilmer was recognized in government reports as a pioneer in the manufacture of turpentine products, his early work having laid the foundation for certain developments. His wild changes of mood had abated somewhat, but he remained, according to the few people close to him, a "difficult" person.[26] Dix's *Picayune* column steadily gained popularity; soon other newspapers were asking for permission to reprint it. In 1900, after she had been writing the column for five years, an irresistible invitation arrived to go to work as a reporter for the *New York Journal*, a national newspaper with a larger circulation than all the combined papers that had used Dix's work.

She accepted the offer with ambivalence, for George could not or would not join her in New York, and a trip home meant a two-day journey by train. She was required to travel constantly to cover the stories the *Journal* assigned her. The heavy workload at least allowed her to send substantial money to him and to her family. When, after a few years, George finally did leave his turpentine plant and move to New York, he took no part in the social life she had made for herself. (William Sydney Porter—O. Henry—was one of her close friends in those years.)[27] Visitors described her husband as amiable, certainly no raving maniac, but always silent, as if out of place. He was one of the few New Yorkers who never read anything she wrote.

One of Dix's first assignments for the *Journal* had been to follow Carrie Nation around Kansas for a week and report on her antisaloon campaign.[28] Dorothy Dix's articles called attention to the paradoxes in Carrie's makeup. Carrie was a maternal, unpretentious, sane-looking woman who led strikes against saloons (she called them "joints") only if she heard voices.

"What voices?" Dix asked.

"Voices from God," Carrie answered. "They tell me which joints to break up."

Dix compassionately described the simplicity of the woman who had prayed for a new husband when her first one, an alcoholic, deserted her and her baby. But Dix also captured the wacky atmosphere of a midnight temperance meeting in which each of Carrie's followers carried "a bright, new, business-looking hatchet." Carrie, on her knees, droned out prayers for over an hour, only to rise at around 3:00 a.m. and announce that God did not want any joints smashed that night. The frustrated legion went into a rage and brandished their hatchets at her.

After the series on Carrie Nation, the *Journal* offered Dix five thousand dollars a year. William Randolph Hearst, during one of his exciting descents on the office of the *Journal,* decreed that "the young lady" (Dix had begun lopping ten years off her age) was to be assigned to murders and trials—the true American detective stories. Dix thus began covering all the most notorious and grisly events of the time. She was in New Jersey for the case of a schoolteacher who beat, starved, poisoned, and bludgeoned her three-year-old stepdaughter. She covered the murder trial of a white slaver who lured his victims by offering stenography courses in the newspaper. (A fifteen-year-old trying to support her mother had answered one of his ads. Traces of her hair and scalp were found in his fireplace.) Sent to interview a bigamist, Dix met "a shabby little rat of a man who looked as if he had been left out in the rain all night."

"You married thirty-six women?" she asked incredulously. "How?"

"It's the easiest thing in the world, Miss Dix," the rat answered. "All you've got to do is talk to them about themselves."

Being immersed in criminal justice gave Dorothy Dix some worthwhile insights. Almost no man could provide reliable testimony about a woman's attire, she believed. He would say any dark dress was black. When the defense in one murder case suggested that a man was not killed by his girlfriend but by his own hand, Dix wrote: "Men have died and worms have eaten them . . . but not for love. . . . When a man commits suicide, it's about money."[29] As early as 1902, Dix advocated having women included on juries, since "it is practically impossible to convict a young and good-looking woman. . . . Her tears contain a chemical that dissolves the average man's backbone and common sense."[30]

One of Dorothy Dix's most famous cases involved no crime at all, although the woman at the center of it was jailed so as to keep away the swarming reporters. In 1914 in a small New York town, a prominent lawyer died suddenly. He had been a county judge and district attorney. From behind a partition in his office—a screen that did not even reach the ceiling—came a woman who had been living there voluntarily for four years, in a space no larger than a closet. She had set foot outside only twice during those four years. "Judge Couch," as he was known, was married and had grown children, but he spent most of his nights with his lover in the office. In the daytime, she wore rubber shoes so as not to make any noise until the moments in between his work when they could be alone. She read and sewed and knew nothing of the outside world except the information that reached her over the flimsy partition as the judge talked to his clients. She did, however, read the newspaper. The distraught, grieving woman agreed to be interviewed by Dorothy Dix because she and the judge had both loved her column. They had read it together every day and discussed it.

After seventeen years of crime reporting, Dix could boast, "I am on speaking terms with every criminal in America." But she was sick of the haunting murders, the traveling to out-of-the-way courthouses and jails, the relentless scenes of brutality. Throughout all the years, she had never stopped writing her syndicated advice column. She had begun to enjoy solving the problems of everyday life more than unknotting the mysteries of morbid crimes. When the *Journal* refused to allow her to abandon trial reporting, she decided to quit. She left New York, moved back to the place she considered home, New Orleans, and concentrated her energies on Dorothy Dix Talks, which was by then distributed by the Wheeler syndicate.[31]

❀ ❀ ❀

As far as the readers of the *Times-Picayune* were aware, she had never been away. In 1927, she acquired an assistant, Ella Arthur, who lived a few blocks from Dix's uptown home near Audubon Park. Mrs. Arthur screened the letters each day, replied to the routine ones with answers Dorothy Dix had given many times before, and selected a few dozen for Dix's own perusal and response. Dix gave careful thought to her answers, wept over missives that were especially sad, and sent many a special delivery letter to individuals whose situations seemed urgent.[32] She answered every one of the hundreds of letters with the help of only one assistant and a secretary who took dictation.

By the mid 1920s, her name and face were on billboards and the sides of buses. A New York optometrist put one of her columns on the cards he used for eye testing. A husband in South Carolina tried to get a court injunction to keep his wife from reading Dix's column to him every day. In 1925, when the Lynds made their famous sociological study, *Middletown* (which was actually in Indiana), they found Dorothy Dix everywhere, from the beauty parlor to the streetcar to the pulpit. Her column, the Lynds concluded, shaped "the habits and thought of Middletown in regard to marriage, and possibly represents Middletown's views more completely than any other one available source."[33] Louisiana had been moved to middle America. Dorothy Dix bought a house there and viewed the world through its windows.

In truth, New Orleans during the teens and twenties was lively and decadent as were few American cities. It was anything but a typical town. The neighborhoods surrounding the French Quarter were largely the precincts of prostitutes—Storyville being the one best remembered—animated at all hours by jazz and ragtime and ladies of the night and day. The French Quarter itself was a slum where derelicts stumbled out of flophouses each morning to share the sidewalks with dignified French families who were still hanging on to their language, their shuttered balconies, and their separateness from the bustling American suburbs that had built up around them and were taking over the city.

Dorothy Dix was part of a literary circle that included several newspaper people. The group was trying to reclaim the French Quarter from immigrants, criminals, and waterfront riffraff by encouraging writers and artists to settle there. Dix was friends with Lyle Saxon, Grace King, and Stanley Arthur, authors of classic books about Louisiana history and society. She was acquainted with the writers—Sherwood Anderson, William Faulkner, Julius Friend, Natalie Vivian Scott—who were creating a colony of literati in the old section.[34] However, there was no natural bond between the famous Dix and the still up-and-coming authors. They could not help envying the astonishing success of someone who had not even written one bad novel, much less a good one. On her side, Dix considered herself "an old newspaperman"—part of the ordinary life of ordinary people—not a writer, not part of an elite. Unlike the work of Saxon and Arthur and, later on, Harnett Kane and the romance novelist Frances Parkinson Keyes, her writing did not reflect the parochial interests of Louisiana or the South. She belonged to the whole of America.

Every Yuletide brought mail from plain people across the country inviting Dix to Christmas dinner. Each week brought marriage proposals, some with the plaintive request, "If you don't want me, please recommend me to another woman."[35] Her readers assumed she was a widow, but she was and remained oddly married. George's hostility toward her career was now well known to friends. Although her workload was greatly reduced when she stopped traveling on assignments, Dix's fame continued to rise and so did George's resentment. He suffered from excruciating arthritis, was bedridden at times, and would not be placated by either visitors or pleasure trips. His depression and pain left him, Dix said, "generally full of misery." He disliked having company and grievously complained, probably not without justice, that she ignored him.

Even for a more confident man than George Gilmer, it would not have been easy being "Mr. Dix," the consort of one of the world's most recognized women who all her life worked eighteen hours a day. For George, who thought he had failed at everything, the relationship must have been a curse. He would sometimes sit for hours in his parked car, brooding, or stay away from home for days at a time. When he was not depressed, he was subject to wrathful outbursts. Week by week, he became ever more agitated and violent. Confined to a wheelchair by arthritis, he had several bad falls during one period when he insisted on trying to walk. Eventually he did succeed in walking; he left their house and did not come back. Dorothy never saw him again. After some months, his family told her that he was living in Florida, but he did not want to have any contact with her. Then suddenly, still seething with anger against her, George headed back to New Orleans with apparently sinister intentions. His family intercepted him at the train station and committed him to a mental asylum. Some years later, in January 1929, he died in the sanitarium, still vilifying his wife. Friends recounted that, far from being relieved, she suffered long-lasting grief, guilt, and anguish.[36]

It is easy to speculate that Dorothy Dix clung to her marriage so as not to diminish her authority as a domestic counselor. However, her readers were hardly aware that she was married, and they certainly never knew when she was with her husband and when they lived apart. A voluntary separation was available to her at any time—the two were often separated anyway, because of her assignments. But, according to Harnett Kane, she consistently tried to get her husband to join her wherever she moved and to accompany her on her numerous trips abroad. She wanted more than just the formality of marriage; she wanted him. "In the final analysis," she had written, "we all depend for happiness on the people we love." And she commented more than once, "It is some peculiarity of the feminine constitution that makes a woman go on loving what has become unlovable."[37]

❀ ❀ ❀

Although her marriage had collapsed in bitterness, the widow Dorothy Dix continued dispensing connubial advice—the sound advice, generally, of a battlefield veteran—for another twenty-two years. Periodically, her pronouncements were gathered into books: *Hearts à la Mode* (1915); *My Trip Around the World* (1924); *Dorothy Dix: Her Book; Every-day Help for Everyday People* (1926); *How to Win and Hold a Husband* (1939). Like any normal person, she changed with the times. Whenever a country fights what is finally perceived as a pointless war, there is a backlash by young people against tradition, convention, and the authority figures who led their comrades into useless maiming and death. Dorothy Dix heard the din of iconoclasm that followed World War I. It was obvious to her that "men are changing their opinions about the desirability of modesty in women and establishing a single standard of conduct for both sexes. . . . Men may still theoretically admire what they call 'the old-fashioned girl,' but they leave her to spend her evenings with her parents."[38] Though Dix disapproved of promiscuity, she acknowledged, unsmilingly, that few postwar men could hold out for a girl who hadn't been "pawed over."

Her advice reflected the shifts in morality and values that each generation experiences; she was thus able to keep her place as a public oracle for five decades. Moreover, the media are always more conservative than the general public in matters of morality. Polls are taken; people lie in answering personal questions unless they are sure their own thoughts square with those of the community. Consequently, if the public is beginning to change its mind about intimate issues, newspapers and radio stand pat until the change is vividly apparent. Dix wrote as an individual, however. She could voice an opinion, privately held by thousands of thinking people, before it became the stock ideology of the press. She was lucky in that her column coincided with the decades in American history, the twenties and thirties, when readers in general reacted against hypocrisy. Since Dorothy Dix could be counted on to speak her mind (no one would dream of considering her hypocritical), everybody loved her, even when they disagreed with her.

❀　❀　❀

In the twenties, Dix addressed fairly minor problems of personal behavior. She reminded overly strict parents that times had changed: the average girl used rouge and lipstick as routinely as soap and water. She admonished a wife who complained about her husband's smoking. "Humph. It seems to me that any woman who is married to a man whose only vice is that he smokes is going a long distance out of her way to hunt up a grievance. She ought to be thankful that she hasn't got some real trouble . . . such as drinking, gambling, stinginess, or other women."[39] To Dix, stinginess in a husband was an unbearable fault. At a time when there was no day care for children except grandmothers, when mothers toiled at home and perhaps had to ask the breadwinner for spending money, a husband's stinginess was indeed a prickly and common issue. The mortal sin of wives, she indicated, was serving bad suppers. "When a man marries, he turns over his stomach to his wife," she wrote in 1926.[40] All hot food except canned soup was slow food then. For most working men, supper was the only hot meal of the day.

With the Depression still looming throughout the thirties, Dix gave heed to money issues. People had more serious problems than deciding whether they might neck and pet in cars. The specter of unemployment haunted the working class and kept people at jobs they loathed. Dix received poignant letters, such as the one from three elevator operators who feared the boredom of their jobs might make them insane.[41] Dix advised them to look for inadvertent signs of drama in the lives of the people who rode the elevator. By then, Dorothy Dix was an institution and her authority concerning any topic had been long established.

In the forties, she turned to the problems caused by absent husbands who had gone off to war. She roused men to join the army, noting that "in every war, it is the women who are the great conscription officers, who drive cowards into the army by their scorn." She herself despised "softies." She did, however, make the sage, if offhand, observation that if peace ever ruled the world, it would come because people finally realized "the futility of a struggle that ends in exhaustion, and wherein no man can tell victory from defeat."[42]

The perennial problem of all decades was unfaithful husbands. When men reached what she called "the age of indiscretion," they had "a sudden yearning for romance and flirtation—the last call to the dining car." She advised their wives to "sit tight," for the sake of the children, and wait for the phase to pass.[43] Once in a while, she advised divorcing, especially when the spouses truly hated each other, lest the children grow up "as shell-shocked as any soldier in war."[44] She rarely suggested that anyone seek professional counseling—the fallback bromide of modern advice givers. In those decades, most people found yearly dental cleaning an extravagance; psychotherapy was an unthinkable expenditure.

❀ ❀ ❀

The editor Arthur Brisbane had once told Dix, "Remember that a newspaper is read by very busy people, or very tired people or uneducated people. None of them is going to hunt a dictionary. . . . If you don't hit a reader between the eyes with your first sentence, there's no need of writing a second."[45] To her credit, Dix did not eschew big words; but neither did she follow Brisbane's advice to write succinctly. She never trusted a terse answer to do the job. She could tap out perfect one-liners that are delightful to quote, but she could not allow a period to put an end to the matter. However, the gentle redundancies that followed her quick jabs helped soften her flippancy. It was an earnest generation that read Dorothy Dix, a generation suspicious of cleverness but comfortable with benign repetition.[46]

Dorothy Dix's writing veered between extremes; she could be as maudlin as she could be sharp. Her readers loved that, too. "The Ordinary Woman" was one of her most popular homilies, a Valentine to mothers who trod "the Gethsemane of woman" in giving birth and afterward "did not falter in self-sacrifice."[47] But there were solid ideas even amid the puddles of sentimentality such essays comprised. Many mothers went years without a single night of unbroken sleep, Dix pointed out. They braved death without a second thought in caring for contagious little ones. The ordinary woman made huge sacrifices to educate her children, knowing all the while that in lifting them out of her sphere, she was creating a permanent chasm between herself and them, for they would one day be ashamed of her.

When Dix was tough minded, which was most of the time, she was the least romantic, most pragmatic of commentators. "The average girl is simply slopping over with romance," she noted in one essay, remarking in another that "without doubt, marriage is a cruel and bitter disappointment to nine-tenths of those who enter into the holy estate." In restaurants and theaters, "the alert, smiling people who are gaily chatting together are the unwed, or those who are talking to other people's husbands and wives."[48] The deadly rival most men could be sure to encounter in their marriage was not tall and dark but small and pink: "The first baby definitely and for all time puts the husband's nose out of joint."[49] Single women were told again and again to find jobs, work hard at them, and not whine about it, though they shouldn't fool themselves into thinking that working girls had an ideal life. "A husband," she generally concluded, was "a good thing to have around the house." At the same time, she commented that "the mistake most wives make is taking their husbands too seriously."[50] Like most people who came of age before the First World War, she had scant use for higher education; parents were foolish to deny themselves every comfort so that their sons could loaf through their courses and "acquire nothing but a college yell and a contempt for their hump-shouldered old dads."[51]

Women of today, whose historic memory may reach only as far back as the restrictive fifties, may not recall that in the twenties, thirties, and forties, Dix's prime years, women worked, especially if they were poor or of the lower middle class; they educated themselves (for indeed, educational opportunities were sadly limited for men, too); and they made no bones about disparaging men even as they promulgated free love—especially if they were women of the leisure class. Women with money, such as the *Picayune*'s Mrs. Nicholson, had their ideas taken seriously and exercised considerable power. Dorothy Dix's thoughts, therefore, were not particularly advanced for her time. But she was more forthright than most people in stating them and she directed them to poor and lower-middle-class women whose personal problems were only beginning to be candidly discussed in newspapers and radio.

Many of her opinions would not be welcomed today by women locked into a new set of banalities that are different from the clichés of their grandmothers. Sometimes Dix was flat wrong, from our perspective; but about many things, she was right. She advised women to stay married, unless their marital situations were utterly horrible. Children, she wrote, were almost always damaged irreparably by divorce, and mothers were not to be fooled into thinking otherwise.[52] She advised mothers to stay home with young children and she insisted that rearing children was the most noble of all professions. At the same time, no one could accuse her of not understanding women's yearning for intellectual stimulation and careers. As long as children need mothers and women need children, the problem of how to have a career and a family in a competitive society is likely to remain the crucible of young women. Dix found no solution, and neither, so far, has anyone else. At least she spoke up for children who have no voice in the matter.

❀   ❀   ❀

Nor would most women of today appreciate Dorothy Dix's attitude toward men. She understood and liked them and saw no reason to disabuse them of the notion that they were the smarter sex.

> If you will notice, it is only women who prate about equality between the sexes. Men take no stock in any such heresy. When a man tells a woman that . . . he looks up to her and worships her, it is one of the lover's perjuries at which Jove laughs. In reality, he doesn't mean a word of it. The very basic thing on which a man's love for a woman is built is his sense of superiority to her. He wants to feel stronger than she is, wiser than she is, to be more successful than she is. . . . That is why intelligent, big-brained men often marry morons and are happy and contented with them. . . . If women would only abandon their theories about what matrimony should be, and how husbands should act, and deal with them as they are, it would save a flood of tears.[53]

Dorothy Dix had marched in her day with the suffragists. She would stock the arsenal and do battle with men when a citadel was at stake, but not a theory.

"Very few men are sentimentalists," Dix wrote. "Most of them feel like fools when they are lovemaking, and so they get the ordeal over with as quickly as possible." A man considers that by marrying "he has given proof of his devotion and there is no use in saying anything more about it." The idea that his wife might cease to love him, she wrote, "actually never crosses the average man's mind."[54]

❀ ❀ ❀

Clear eyed and unmarried, she lived comfortably in New Orleans from the 1920s through the rest of her life. Her father was near her until he died in his nineties. Her brother eventually moved into an apartment below her, so close, she said irritably, that "we can practically hear one another change our minds."[55] From 1922 until 1943, she gave over one hundred talks to all kinds of organizations in New Orleans and served as an enthusiastic member of Le Petit Salon, a woman's club whose Thursday meetings she rarely missed. The older she grew, the more she enjoyed making fun of herself. Once a colleague came up behind her as she was staring at a store display of silk stockings. "Little lady," he said, "I'll buy you anything you want there." She whirled around. "Oh, it's only you. I thought for a moment I'd been insulted at last." She had no use for either cut flowers (she particularly disdained corsages) or music. "I'm like the man who knew only two tunes," she said. "One was *God Save the Queen* and the other wasn't." She had many friends, both men and women. She defined a friend as "somebody who knows all about you and likes you in spite of it."[56]

Dorothy Dix was unquestionably the most eminent newspaper person ever to write from Louisiana, and she was more celebrated than any other citizen of the state for over a half century. But fame in the popular culture is like a splash of rubbing alcohol on a carpet. It spreads; it is pervasive and pungent for a time; but it does not penetrate deeply. William Faulkner, Sherwood Anderson, Truman Capote, and others connected with New Orleans, writers who have never been read by the great majority of Americans, remain nevertheless intrinsic to the intellectual fabric of the nation; Dix, the household word, has evaporated with hardly a trace.

In 1944, she was knocked down by a bus and was never completely well again. She suffered a stroke at her desk early one morning in 1950. Paralyzed, she was hospitalized for many months while her column was kept going by articles she had stored up for a rainy day and by substitute writers who answered the letters that continued to pour in.

By then, she had lived to the age—we should all survive to it—when everything she said, no matter how tactless, was welcomed as evidence of a still droll,
lively sprit. A nurse came into Dix's hospital room, cooing, "Look what we have
here—pretty flowers."

"Oh," Dix answered, "I thought it was a bunch of Presbyterians."[57]

She had started out without the blessings of looks, money, or outstanding
intellect. She was gifted only with common sense and an uncommon drive to
succeed, and with these she won respect and renown in a man's profession.
Dorothy Dix died in December 1951, at the age of ninety, leaving an estate of 2.5
million dollars and a following of several million wistful readers.

NOTES

1. Pamphlet, "The Best-Loved Woman in the World," Philadelphia, 1929, Dorothy Dix Collection, Special Collections, F. G. Woodward Library, Austin Peay State University, Clarksville, Tenn.

2. A question posed to a minister by a backbencher or a member of his own party; often the
question has been suggested by the minister himself, who wants an opportunity to promote the
work he or his government is doing, or to criticize the opposition, or to draw notice to the backbencher asking the question. Since the 1950s the "Dorothy Dixer" has been a widely accepted tactic
used in the Australian House and Senate. The implication originally was that Dorothy Dix herself
made up many of the questions she answered in the newspaper (Harnett T. Kane with Ella Bentley
Arthur, *Dear Dorothy Dix: The Story of a Compassionate Woman* [Garden City, N.Y.: Doubleday,
1952], 232).

3. Dorothy Dix, *Dorothy Dix: Her Book; Every-day Help for Everyday People* (New York: Funk
and Wagnalls, 1926), 61, 148.

4. Ibid., 98.

5. Quoted by Kane, *Dear Dorothy Dix*, 61–62.

6. See papers presented at the Dorothy Dix Symposium, September 27, 1991, Todd County, Ky.;
Times-Picayune, June 9, 1929 (journalistic prize). Kane interviewed 233 people for his book.

7. Eloise Witherspoon, "Beloved Consolation: The Life of Dorothy Dix," Dorothy Dix Symposium, September 27, 1991, Todd County, Ky.

8. Kane, *Dear Dorothy Dix*, 19–21.

9. Collection of Elizabeth Meriwether Gilmer, "Lizzie Gilmer Wins English Composition Medal,"
1878–79, Hollins University publications, Hollins University Library, Roanoke, Va.

10. Anne Adams, "Elizabeth Meriwether Gilmer: Advice Columnist," *History's Women*, online
newsletter, n.d.

11. Kane, *Dear Dorothy Dix*, 227.

12. "How Dan Won the Christmas Stakes," Dorothy Dix Collection, Special Collections,
F. G. Woodward Library, Austin Peay State University, Clarksville, Tenn.

13. Correspondence, folders 1 and 2, 1863–1939, Dorothy Dix Collection, Special Collections,
F. G. Woodward Library, Austin Peay State University, Clarksville, Tenn.; "Dorothy Dix Recalls
Builder of Paper to Granddaughter," *Times-Picayune*, December 24, 1943. Newspapers typically in-

cluded a "women's page," sometimes along with a "children's page," as if the other pages were not intended for them.

14. Dix's remarks to Tulane journalism fraternity, *Times-Picayune*, May 22, 1931; Dix quoted in an address to Newcomb College students, May 5, 1931, www.quotationsbook.com under "Dorothy Dix."

15. *Times-Picayune*, June 27, 1933, Dix interview regarding the Little Theatre.

16. "Dorothy Dix's 40 Years in Newspaper Work Described on Its Anniversary," *Times-Picayune*, May 5, 1936, magazine feature; "Dorothy Dix recipes," folder 27, Dorothy Dix Collection, Special Collections, F. G. Woodward Library, Austin Peay State University, Clarksville, Tenn. It was a long time before the format and name of her column were set. For some months it was Sunday Salad: Made and Seasoned by Dorothy Dix; then Dorothy Dix's Letter Box; then Dorothy Dix's Common Sense Talks to Women. This title underwent several variations when it became apparent that men were also reading her.

17. *Times-Picayune*, March 6, 1935; Dix, *Her Book*, 344.

18. Dorothy Dix, *How to Win and Hold a Husband* (New York: Doubleday, Doran, 1939), 75.

19. *Times-Picayune*, March 12, 1925.

20. Dix, *Her Book*, 302.

21. Ibid., 318.

22. Ibid., 81.

23. See www.quotationsbook.com under "Dorothy Dix."

24. Quoted by Kane, *Dear Dorothy Dix*, 235.

25. Ibid., 210–11.

26. Ibid., 75.

27. "Authors I Have Known," *Times-Picayune*, April 21, 1927, quoting a talk by Dorothy Dix at the Newcomb Book Fair. Dix described O. Henry's death. At her parties, she regularly served a concoction she called "liquid fruitcake." "He drank eight cups in succession," she noted dryly, "and died almost immediately afterward."

28. "Investigative Writings of Dorothy Dix," folder 42, Dorothy Dix Collection, Special Collections, F. G. Woodward Library, Austin Peay State University, Clarksville, Tenn.

29. Ibid.

30. "Magazine Articles by and about Dorothy Dix," folder 30," Dorothy Dix Collection, Special Collections, F. G. Woodward Library, Austin Peay State University, Clarksville, Tenn.

31. Ten years after leaving the *Journal*, Dix agreed to cover one more case for the Wheeler syndicate: the Hall-Mills case in New Jersey in 1926. Dix did not object to traveling for pleasure and in fact left copious writings about her international trips; see "Travel Diaries," folder 30, Dorothy Dix Collection, Special Collections, F. G. Woodward Library, Austin Peay State University, Clarksville, Tenn.

32. The *Picayune*'s name was changed to *Times-Picayune* in 1917. Dix lived at 6363 Prytania Street (Kane, *Dear Dorothy Dix*, 261).

33. Kane, *Dear Dorothy Dix*, 253; Robert S. Lynd and Helen M. Lynd, *Middletown: A Study in American Culture* (New York: Harcourt, Brace, 1956), 87.

34. The last four founded or wrote for the *Double Dealer*, a literary journal of some distinction published in New Orleans in the twenties. Scott was one of those who wrote for the *Times-Picayune*.

35. Kane, *Dear Dorothy Dix*, 259.

36. The exact year of the final estrangement is hard to pinpoint because Dix and her husband had been separated off and on, although in steady communication, throughout the marriage. The final parting occurred in New York, near the time when Dix was about to move permanently to New Orleans, that is, about 1917 (Kane, *Dear Dorothy Dix*, 246).

37. Dix, *Her Book*, 242.

38. Ibid., 304.

39. *Times-Picayune*, March 12, 1925.

40. Dix, *Her Book*, 215.

41. *Times-Picayune*, March 6, 27, 1935.

42. *Times-Picayune*, September 20, 1939, Dix's editorial on women's place in war.

43. Dix, *How to Win and Hold a Husband*, 201.

44. Quoted by Kane, *Dear Dorothy Dix*, 281.

45. Quoted by Dix, in an address to journalism students, reported in *Times-Picayune*, May 22, 1931.

46. Kane, *Dear Dorothy Dix*, 275.

47. Newspaper articles, folder 26, Dorothy Dix Collection, Special Collections, F. G. Woodward Library, Austin Peay State University, Clarksville, Tenn.

48. Dix, *Her Book*, 32, 114, 246.

49. Ibid., 64.

50. Ibid., 177.

51. Ibid., 265.

52. "The Children Pay," ibid., beginning on 310.

53. Dix, *Her Book*, 299, 210.

54. Ibid., 12, 242.

55. Quoted by Kane, *Dear Dorothy Dix*, 249.

56. Calendar of the Dorothy Dix Collection, *Times-Picayune* Archives, New Orleans. Quoted by Kane, *Dear Dorothy Dix*, 45, 158.

57. Kane, *Dear Dorothy Dix*, 306.

True Methodist Women

(1895–1939)

Reflections on the Community at St. Mark's

ELLEN BLUE

❀ ❀ ❀

Though it sounds as if it might have been delivered from a pulpit, the phrase "Miss Mary Werlein's body turns to dust in Metairie cemetery, but her soul lives" was the lead for an article in the New Orleans afternoon newspaper on May 4, 1940. Reporting the death of "one of the most devoted charity workers this city has ever known," the *States* repeated its motif of continued presence, observing "her light still burns—in the spirit of the living."[1]

By the year 2000, however, Werlein had been forgotten by the Methodist community where she had been a driving force a century before, even though the two institutions she helped establish continued to serve the people of New Orleans. Mary Werlein is one of many powerful yet little-known Methodist women who shaped the city through a settlement house called St. Mark's Community Center. Along with meeting direct needs of the poor for health care, clothing, and education, they worked on causes like abolishing child labor, reducing infant mortality, and, of course, temperance, a subject vital to women working just a few blocks away from the notorious Storyville district where prostitution was legal until 1917. Though much of the work they began still continues, this essay focuses on their struggles and achievements between 1895 and the late 1930s, from the Progressive Era through FDR's New Deal. For Protestants, this was the era of the Social Gospel, a response to human needs occasioned by industrialization, urbanization, and immigration.

This chapter focuses in part on women whose careers as professional church workers brought them to the city for a time and in part on laywomen who lived in New Orleans all their lives. As a fabric needs strength in both warp and woof threads to be durable, Methodist women's endeavors required both deaconesses, who could devote full time and professional expertise to the work, and strong laywomen, who could raise funds and build lasting local networks, for success. The professionals were Methodist deaconesses (and one was a "city missionary," a designation used before the deaconess office existed). Laywomen who were important to St. Mark's included Mary Werlein, Elvira Beach Carré, and Hattie Parker, who were motivated by religious devotion and a "call" to be part of the Social Gospel. The laywomen supported the deaconesses, and not just financially. The professional deaconesses and the laywomen forged not only working alliances that enabled them to ease the harsh living conditions of immigrants and laborers but also deep and lasting friendships. These relationships created a community of women who understood and appreciated each other's abilities, desires, and commitments to social change.

Examining the Social Gospel through the lives of women like Werlein who embodied it clarifies some aspects now poorly understood, especially the dating of the end of the movement. This study of St. Mark's shows that the work of the Social Gospel was in full swing in the 1920s and that it was not until the New Deal, when government took over some of the work previously done in the private sector by volunteers, that the Social Gospel began a significant decline. Additionally, their training in the Social Gospel made the women of St. Mark's far more radical than other Louisiana women. The story of these Methodist women shows how powerful a religious motivation could be, for their devotion is what allowed them to push for real social change even when that put them in conflict with the values of their segregated and sexist society.

❀ ❀ ❀

The Methodist Church created the office of deaconess at the turn of the twentieth century, at the same time that the male hierarchy was beating back a push for women's ordination. Though they were "set apart" for professional Christian service, the deaconesses nevertheless remained laity. The Methodist Episcopal Church, South (MECS), consecrated its first deaconesses in April 1903. They received room and board for their full-time work, plus a small allowance to cover all other needs, including the required uniforms that made them easily identifiable as they made their way through dirty streets and into tenement houses—long black dresses and bonnets tied with a white bow under the chin.

Since these deaconesses took steps toward racial equality that, for Deep South white women, amounted to startling behavior, it is important to recognize that all Methodist women in this essay were members of the MECS, which broke off from the Methodist Episcopal Church (MEC) in 1844 over slavery and did not reunite with it until 1939. The MEC and its women's group also had a presence in New Orleans at this time, but their work was completely separate from that discussed in this chapter.

Located in the French Quarter on Rampart at Governor Nicholls Street, St. Mark's Community Center was an expansion of the earlier work at a Social Gospel mission located in the Irish Channel. St. Mark's had much in common with Hull House, the famous Chicago settlement founded by Jane Addams and Ellen Gates Starr. The term "settlement" might imply that these houses provided those who were poor with places to live, but in fact settlement houses were places that relatively affluent, well-educated people occupied in poverty-ridden areas. They "settled" among the people there so they could understand clearly the residents' needs before devising strategies to meet them. Deaconesses lived in community together, but a vital part of their mission was also to live in the neighborhood where they served and become a true part of that community.

Two settlement houses were founded in New Orleans in the 1890s; both were still operating when Katrina struck in 2005. St. Mark's remained a Methodist-identified operation, but Kingsley House, which began as an Episcopalian project, soon changed its status to "nonsectarian." Unlike Kingsley House, St Mark's has received little attention from historians. The church, too, overlooked and undervalued the role of religious settlements. Many clergy disagreed with the underlying theology, maintaining the church should address only spiritual needs. Additionally, historians have discounted the social services provided by religious settlements simply because it was women's work. During the Progressive Era, the Kingsley House board of directors was entirely male, while up until the 1960s, the St. Mark's board was entirely female; thus, not just the staff, but also the people who set policy for the agency were women.

These Methodist women who "stept out of their place" had to overcome serious challenges to their authority from male clergy, and their successes have rarely been documented. The records of St. Mark's were lost in the 1960s, and completing the research for the dissertation and upcoming book on which this chapter is based was like piecing a quilt from scraps and remnants. It took eight years and travel to eight states, using sources that included a shoebox full of mementos offered by a deaconess's daughter.[2]

Although some of the secular settlements tended to be identified with one individual, as Hull House was with Jane Addams, the Methodist women named in this essay accomplished what they did precisely because each one was willing to pour her talents and resources into a collaborative effort that would, in the long run, be seen as a group project rather than hers alone. The "Great Man" theory of history, which focuses on the work of individuals, can lead to the omission of significant contributions made by women who, by working together, accomplished important things. To include an essay about a group of such women in this volume is to recognize that Louisiana history was also made by women who acted primarily in the context of organized women's groups, not as individuals, and who shared the credit with others. To research and write about these women is more difficult, but it is as worthwhile and important as recording the histories of women who are somewhat better known.

The nineteenth-century "Cult of True Womanhood" required women of the late 1800s and early 1900s to be pious, domestic, and submissive and was deeply rooted in religious authority. Yet this role also offered opportunities for women to expand the boundaries of "woman's sphere" as they worked on behalf of the needy. Indeed, many "True Methodist Women" leaders, through their work in the settlement houses and particularly in their role as deaconesses, exhibited a kind of "soft feminism." Through response to what they saw as God's call to bring "life abundant" to French Quarter residents, the women of St. Mark's enlarged the acceptable sphere of Christian work for women.[3]

❁ ❁ ❁

In Louisiana, the MECS established the Woman's Parsonage and Home Mission Society (WP&HMS), the predecessor group of United Methodist Women (UMW), in 1891, and elected Mary Werlein corresponding secretary. The women soon designated a state organizer "because nothing but active, personal effort will multiply our societies, and develop that strength which we need." In 1894, the WP&HMS women appointed Werlein to this office, and she and the president traveled around Louisiana to form auxiliaries.[4]

The involvement of the WP&HMS with the ministry that would expand into St. Mark's began in 1895. A mission on Tchoupitoulas Street in the heart of New Orleans's "Irish Channel" was closing owing to lack of funding, so the MECS hierarchy gathered representatives from all WP&HMS groups in the city and implored them to take responsibility, warning it would cost three hundred dollars per year. The women voted unanimously to adopt the mission, named Werlein to a three-person committee charged with making "all necessary arrangements," and elected her district treasurer.[5]

Within two months, the *New Orleans Christian Advocate* editorialized that the mission was doing "a noble work." Revival services had resulted in numerous conversions. "Our sisters of the Woman's Parsonage and Home Mission Society have cause to rejoice as they behold the fruits of their labors. The work of the Lord has prospered in their hands."[6] However, the mission was not merely a place for street preaching and evangelism; it also carried on other urban ministries under the direction of a female "city missionary."

The Methodist women who supported urban ministries in New Orleans were well grounded in Social Gospel theory. On the WP&HMS reading list were works by Social Gospel theologians Josiah Strong and Washington Gladden. Also important to their work was Helen Campbell's *Prisoners of Poverty: Women Wage-Workers, Their Trades and Their Lives*, which may have inspired the Boarding Home for Working Women discussed later.[7]

For two years after the WP&HMS began operating the mission, Werlein, "by individual efforts, raise[d] the amount due for rent and gas, amounting to about $25 monthly." In 1897, she was instrumental in obtaining a building of its own, which would later be named in her honor. The daughter of the founder of Werlein Music, she never married but lived with relatives and spent much time engaged in good works. The *Advocate* explained that her "life, talents, and money are consecrated to the service of her Master." Her great-niece Betty Werlein Carter recalled that she visited regularly in the parish prison and led religious services there.[8]

Another great-niece, Leila Werlein Stone, remembered Mary as "one of those women who got better looking as she got older. She was a tiny woman, with blue, piercing eyes and gorgeous, snow-white hair which she kept immaculately groomed." Mary also volunteered at a residence for the elderly; on occasion, Stone accompanied her and found "the old ladies just adored her. She would . . . play the piano for them. She loved to play 'O Happy Day.'" Yet Werlein was not always a soul of kindness. Stone recalled a pastor referring to a prayer in the book of Jude that the saints might be preserved and observing that some saints were preserved in sugar and others in vinegar. "Aunt Mary," she said, "was a vinegar saint."[9]

Werlein found ways to give back some of her wealth to the less fortunate every day. She walked to her destinations, even distant ones, and gave the carfare to missions. Stone confirmed that she was "very frugal." Her epistle to those who had pledged contributions that was printed by the *Advocate* in May 1895 is revealing: "Friends, please do not fail to hand in your amount. Because it may be but little, do not believe it does not matter whether you are prompt or not. Remember there is '*multum in parvo*.'" She dismissed bluntly a common excuse—concern that because money went overseas, the giver could not monitor its use: "Many persons say they do not believe in foreign missions. This, then, is their opportunity. Cast in your mite monthly, and go to the mission and see with your own eyes and hear with your own ears what is being done. If you will not grasp this opportunity for home mission work, then know the truth that your words are spurious and forever after hold your peace about the foreign work, for we know too well that often this is only a quietus upon the conscience." Before signing "Yours in the work, Mary Werlein" to this undisguised challenge to put up or shut up, she said, "Cut this out and place it upon your looking-glass, and I will guarantee your district treasurer will not have to make a call upon you again."[10]

None of Werlein's papers except published letters has survived. One printed in July 1895 offers additional insight into her life's work. Asked to write about a women's conference in Ponchatoula, she responded: "It was a most delightful occasion, the spiritual feature being quite marked—in fact, it was equal to a camp meeting all the way through, and we bless God for the privilege of being there. Of course, we went to represent the work of the Woman's Parsonage and Home Mission Society. Never did anything lay nearer our heart than this cause, and we feel we shall never be quite satisfied until the whole of the state of Louisiana, at least, shall be canvassed, and an auxiliary planted in every church where it is at all practicable." Her five-day stay netted five new auxiliaries. Werlein was convinced that "there is not much that woman cannot accomplish when she goes at it with a heart full of love and energy, baptized by the Holy Ghost."[11]

Lillie Meekins, the city missionary in charge of urban ministries, lived at the Tchoupitoulas Street mission in what a WP&HMS member described as "one of the most depraved portions of our city."[12] The Irish Channel was reputed to be lawless. Laborers' homes surrounded the mills and small factories, and since Tchoupitoulas runs alongside the wharves on the Mississippi River, sailors and dockworkers frequented the area.

Meekins described the neighborhood as follows: "All of the families in the field are of the poorest[,] . . . those employed barely earning sufficient to supply the necessities, none of the comforts of life. The homes consist of one room. So many are unemployed." The outreach work of the mission eased the daily misery and struggle for survival of the immigrant poor enough so that "we might thereby lead some to salvation."[13]

The Irish Channel was also the setting for the Boarding Home for Working Women opened by the WP&HMS in 1897. The twelve-room building provided a safe and "suitable" place for single women who migrated to New Orleans looking for work. Often from poor or working class families in rural areas, unused to an urban environment, alone and on their own for the first time, these young migrants lacked connections and resources that could help them navigate the dangers—both physical and moral—of city life. To provide them with a clean, safe, and homelike environment, these "True Methodist Women" established a boarding house where young girls could "spend their hours of recreation in a manner both pleasant and beneficial to themselves."[14]

Like female reformers elsewhere in the nation, the Louisiana women disguised a radical agenda by couching it in conservative language. WP&HMS leaders operated within the norms of female behavior precisely because they found their efforts more effective that way. Using language about "home" was a common strategy; suffragists argued women's votes would make the country more homelike.[15] Still, flaunting domesticity while helping women work outside the home demonstrates that the women of New Orleans took a backseat to none in subtle subversion of patriarchal restrictions.

In 1903, the WP&HMS raised $200.85 for Lillie Meekins's annual salary. By 1906, they were contemplating "a much broader work" and sought pledges of twelve hundred dollars to hire a "trained worker." The term shows recognition of the need to professionalize women's positions within the church, as does their willingness to pay a training school graduate several times as much as Meekins.[16]

Sometime in 1906 or 1907, the Tchoupitoulas Street mission became the Mary Werlein Mission. The work continued nonstop under Meekins's direction because, as Meekins wrote, "There is ever much to be done, and ever will be, as long as this factory territory exists, with the crowded tenement conditions which ever follow such boundary." Both poor wages and "the daily discouragements which often come to these people in the monotonous drudgery of their lives" created a constant demand for spiritual and temporal help.[17]

Massive waves of immigrants entering the United States in this era provoked an often virulent reaction from nativeborn citizens, who were usually Protestant. Tension around the issue affected life in New Orleans, with its particularly complicated racial structure. It concerned MECS women that the Mary Werlein Mission was not reaching the many Italians moving to the city. Grim economic conditions forced 7 percent of Sicily's population to migrate between 1899 and 1910, and many came to Louisiana, recruited by a state campaign to attract immigrants who would compete with freed blacks for jobs. Around 1900, that part of the French Quarter bounded by Esplanade, Rampart, St. Peter, and the river was known as "Little Palermo."[18] Ministry with Italians became a priority for MECS women, and they selected a site within that district for a second ministry, which would be called St. Mark's.

They bought a three-story double with twenty-two rooms and a large interior courtyard at 619–21 Esplanade. It was so dilapidated it took three months to prepare it for occupancy. Two deaconesses and a house mother and her assistant moved into the structure with head resident Margaret Ragland on March 1, 1909, but they delayed work further so showers, health clinic equipment, and playground equipment could be installed. They occupied themselves by going door to door with cards describing the intended work. They hired a pastor,

N. E. Joyner, as superintendent and sent him to northern cities to study institutional churches and to London to study Toynbee Hall, an excellent example of settlement house work.[19]

By November, seventy-two people were learning English in a night school, the sewing school's ninety-six students were making dolls for orphans, and a cooking school was ready to open. As this list of classes indicates, the women who operated St. Mark's were particularly concerned about helping poor women and children. Women and children often worked, but their pitiful wages meant that they were likely to be dependent on and in greater need of assistance than working class men, who had more freedom of movement and earning power. Lacking money for transportation or medical services, women and children typically suffered from preventable or treatable maladies simply for want of care. Therefore, St. Mark's provided "a free clinic for women and children, a capable lady physician" volunteering three times a week. "We are trying to preach the gospel by both word and deed, believing that the latter is as effective as the former," Joyner wrote.[20] Head resident Berta Ellison put it even more bluntly in 1921 when she stated that the clinic served as "the opening wedge which helps to break down opposition and prejudice, and from its work and the follow-up visits of the nurse come by far the largest number of new comers to other departments and to church."[21]

Proselytizing the Christian gospel was clearly a driving force behind the work at the settlement house, and on Sunday evenings, St. Mark's welcomed people of all faiths to a worship service held in the courtyard. Although participation was not required to receive other services, forty-five to fifty worshippers, representing twenty-five countries, attended. This "Church of All Nations" reflected the ethnic makeup of the neighborhood, and the "All Nations" label thus belied the absence of persons of African descent. The Italian department received special emphasis, and the first membership roster had a preponderance of Italian surnames. Services were in both Italian and English, and workers distributed Bibles and tracts in Italian.[22]

When the City Mission Board met the next year, it indicated approval of the women's work by reelecting all its officers. In fact, Elvira Carré was reelected president for a nineteenth year despite asking to be relieved from the "onerous duties." Nurse deaconess Daisy Duncan said the St. Mark's clinic was growing under the direction of its volunteer physician, Ada Kiblinger. An additional deaconess was to take charge of the department of domestic science. Even despite a flood in 1912, which delayed meetings of the societies around the state and created a serious shortage of funds, work at St. Mark's continued unabated. Head resident Margaret Ragland reported five industrial schools, a night school, two boys clubs, two girls clubs, a club for men, and a mothers club, along with "348 visits made and 281 received . . . [and] 63 portions of the New Testament given."[23]

In 1911 or 1912, for unrecorded reasons, the settlement was put under the auspices of First Methodist Episcopal Church, South and the control of its pastor, J. W. Moore. This could have resulted from the denomination's absorption of the Woman's Mission Board into the male-run mission board in 1910, done over the objections of MECS women, who had little representation on the merged board.[24]

The crisis involved a tug-of-war over who had authority over the mission: men or women. Head residents held positions similar to CEOs of today's multitasked, nonprofit organizations. Moore was not able to fit into the woman-run structure, as his letter of July 9, 1912, to Bishop Warren Candler reveals. It begins, "I am in trouble with the women folks." He complained that St. Mark's had been run "as a Hull House" and that Ragland did not "want the church introduced into her institution." When he told her to start a Sabbath school, she threatened to resign. "She takes the position that the church is a decadent institution and that these Settlements are to take the place of the church." He said she "will not shake my hand but gives every evidence of a desire to shake me" and wrote, "I believe that with your pen you could puncture some of these silly pretensions and whilst I do not believe that you can work miracles, still some of these women might be won to sanity." Because "one year is all that any man can safely endure under the dominion of those the ungallant John Knox called 'The Monstrous Breed,'" he asked if Candler had a new church for him. "I dare-say, that by December I shall be a statesman out of a job." He closed, "Your hen-pecked brother, J. W. Moore."[25]

Given how often religious settlements have been dismissed by historians because they were "too religious," the irony is profound. Despite Moore's claims that she resisted Christianity, Ragland emphasized the spiritual aspects of her work in her reports, regularly including data about attendance at Bible classes and worship services. One of the first converts worked as a volunteer minister "at the hall on all occasions," and he and another pastor often led worship and conducted Bible studies and readings at St. Mark's.[26] To say Ragland forbade church functions is to contradict evidence in local, state, and national reports that reveals that she and other deaconesses saw their task as both true settlement work and evangelistic Christian mission.

Moore's letter shows not that Ragland was irreligious but rather that he disapproved of women leaders. Interestingly, 1912 was the year when the short-lived "Men and Religion Forward Movement" was in flower. This was an attempt to recruit more men into church and counteract the "overfeminization" of Protestantism. It is unclear whether Moore was part of the movement; still, it is certain the MECS women faced more than his personal negativity in 1911–12.[27]

Though the records are silent on the reasons, both Moore and Ragland lost their appointments that year. Martha Nutt replaced Margaret Ragland as head resident at St. Mark's, and First Methodist Episcopal Church, South received a new pastor—Mary Werlein's brother, the Reverend Dr. Shepard Halsey Werlein, who had served several of the largest southern congregations and used his prominence to advocate for reform. He returned from St. Louis to take the pastorate that so profoundly affected St. Mark's. We are left to speculate about how this came to pass, but it seems unlikely that Mary was a disinterested party. Presiding Elders were involved in assigning pastors, and since the women gave credit in 1913 to the Presiding Elder for keeping St. Mark's intact, they must have been politically astute enough to recruit him to their cause.[28]

The year after Moore left, St. Mark's moved to a larger structure at 908 Esplanade, but the staff was reduced to two. Despite adversities, the work was "better intrenched than it ever ha[d] been in the past." One reason for this optimism was the oversight of S. H. Werlein, whose opinions about women were diametrically opposed to Moore's. For example, he supported a resolution requesting full laity rights for women. A year later, St. Mark's had "scored perhaps its most successful year" and treated 2,533 clinic patients. The Mary Werlein Mission was profiting from additional space, and agitation began for more space for St. Mark's.[29]

The goals of the women included assisting "in the adjustment of the foreigner to American conditions."[30] This process, Americanization, is controversial today, because it can reflect, or mask, cultural imperialism. In 1906, the MECS bishops had called immigrants "a perilous menace" that might reduce America to paganism unless they were Americanized first. The MEC (northern) women also worked in New Orleans, and their reports contain extremely disparaging remarks about Italians. Yet these kinds of comments are not present in MECS women's reports. Even the worst of their remarks are comparatively soft.[31]

The strong animosity many whites felt toward blacks worked to the advantage of various ethnic groups who might otherwise have been even more discriminated against than they were. However, even though Italians had been specifically exempted from Jim Crow laws in 1898, they still endured much prejudice, in part because they were predominantly Roman Catholic.[32] Although for many Protestants, "non-Christian" was as applicable to Roman Catholic immigrants as to Buddhists or Muslims, the MECS deaconesses saw no need for practicing Roman Catholics to convert. They did not want immigrants to erase all traces of their heritage, and activities at St. Mark's encouraged immigrants to showcase their food, crafts, and culture. St. Mark's did, nevertheless, help all immigrants to learn English and to become citizens, and the settlement house was overflowing with those who desired this assistance.

Then an unexpected death occurred. On a Sunday afternoon in January 1916, Lillie Meekins, the city missionary who lived at the Mary Werlein Mission on Tchoupitoulas Street, suffered a tragic streetcar accident. The *New Orleans Times-Picayune* explained: "She was in the act of stepping to the ground when the car suddenly moved, catching her skirt on the platform. She raced beside the car, screaming to the motorman to stop. Her cries were heard a block away, but the car continued on its way. After running several feet the car outdistanced her, her skirt was torn loose, and she was thrown violently to the ground." She was carrying two gifts for an orphanage, one for a blind infant. In her conscious moments during the week she survived, she repeated, "O, my poor, blind baby, my poor, blind baby." Someone found the gifts and delivered them to ease her distress. The sixty-two-year-old "Angel of Tchoupitoulas street," a widow, had buried her only child, Nellie, "also a noted charity worker," six weeks before. Lillie Meekins's death was one of only a few local stories to make the front page that week. Her photo accompanied the first story. It depicts a solemn, slender woman with deep-set eyes and graying hair pulled back from her face. She wears a black blouse or dress with a white collar, which resembles a deaconess uniform sans the bonnet.[33]

Meekins as a city missionary could not have worn the bonnet. The deaconesses' "garb" was intended in part to offer them the same protection that habits gave Roman Catholic sisters. The garb became optional in 1925, and most abandoned it, but the deaconesses still were similar to Catholic sisters in a number of ways. Like the convent, their quarters offered refuge to women who sought a socially acceptable alternative to marriage and motherhood. Until 1959, Methodist deaconesses were required to be single; they did not promise never to marry, but they could no longer be deaconesses if they wed.[34]

The obituary described Meekins as a "charity worker," and her death is an interesting marker in the evolution from "mercy ministries" to "justice ministries." Language about "trained workers" was becoming more frequent in churchwomen's writings, and it referred to academic course work about root causes of social problems. The women of the MECS, when Meekins died, were developing such training and, though they grieved for Meekins, they pushed ahead with their work. They increased the staff at St. Mark's to four and expanded its programming. It soon became clear that St. Mark's needed a larger facility to accommodate its growth; the same room was used as an office in the morning, a meeting place for the clinic in the afternoon, and a boys' playroom at night. The women laid plans to expand.[35]

In April 1917, days after the U.S. entry into World War I, the denomination-wide Woman's Missionary Council met in New Orleans. An edition of the conference's daily newsletter profiled laywomen Elvira Beach Carré and Hattie Parker. Carré had once served as president of six organizations at the same time and was the "honorary life president" of five. She led the YWCA during its first two years in New Orleans and was a "lady delegate" to the World's Columbian Exposition in Chicago. The publication hailed her as "a tower of strength to Methodism in Louisiana" who was "universally esteemed and honored."[36]

Twenty-five years earlier, a local magazine had profiled Carré in its section on "what women are doing" and noted that she had successfully managed her husband's lumber mill after his death. Observing that she was a slender brunette of medium height with "large dark eyes . . . full of intelligence and kindliness," the author was apparently surprised to find that she was "essentially feminine in appearance and manner and one would never imagine that beneath that gentle face and quiet manner was the strength of will and intellect of a man." The author reassured readers that Carré had never "relinquished the management of her domestic affairs" and home life, no matter how busy she became. Her life provides a good example of women who enlarged their accepted "sphere" of activities while continuing to emphasize their devotion to traditional duties and roles. Carré was born in 1842, attended public schools, and graduated from a "female seminary" run by Madame Bigot. She died in 1924.[37]

After nineteen years as president of the Woman's Board of City Missions, Carré stepped down and Hattie Parker was elected to replace her. Parker was "well known as a forceful thinker and speaker along the lines of social betterment." It is interesting to see the adjective "forceful" applied positively to a female in a 1917 church publication. A New Orleans native, Parker had played a "prominent part" in efforts to establish a separate court for juvenile offenders and in advocacy for legislation abolishing child labor and had worked hard to reduce infant mortality. Election of an activist like Parker reconfirms MECS women's approval of reform/Social Gospel work.[38]

Historians have linked the waning of the Social Gospel and Progressive movements to the loss of optimism surrounding the end of World War I. Yet the demise of the movements has probably been dated too early, and certainly the Social Gospel activities of the MECS women in New Orleans only increased during the next two decades. In the 1920s, the center employed a head resident and three other deaconesses, including a nurse, and ran numerous programs, such as basketball, Boy Scouts, and Camp Fire Girls, and offered classes in woodworking, cooking, sewing, and home nursing. The deaconesses on staff visited hundreds of neighboring homes, and the health clinic treated thousands of patients.[39]

Further evidence that the MECS women were expanding their operations at this time is the fact that in 1923 St. Mark's moved to a new facility on Rampart Street, which is still in operation. It cost about $125,000 and was among the finest settlement houses in the South. Architects' drawings show each room's intended use. The domestic science school (a kitchen), practice dining room, and parlor were for teaching domestic arts to women. The city's first indoor swimming pool was a major feature, and one wing included a gymnasium and a stage. The clinic included a dental office, a sterilizing room, a consulting room, two examination rooms, and a large waiting area. Since Methodist deaconesses lived where they served, there was housing space for four, which included a roof garden and a sleeping porch.[40]

The exterior is reminiscent of a Spanish mission. One of the first women to live there, Annie Rogers, said its beauty was important. She remembered with delight an elderly woman who was thrilled to be among "nice things" for part of the day. The bringing of beauty was always part of the settlement agenda, reflecting the workers' intuitive understanding of the effect of physical surroundings on humans' interior lives. In 1976, Rogers spoke about the "abundant life" Jesus promised. In her understanding, settlement workers gained a more abundant life as they tried to provide it for others. "That abundant life is not just knowing Christ, but also having what you need, an opportunity to have your children get education, for you to grow physically and spiritually the most you can." She told stories of several people whose lives had been changed at her settlements. Indeed, while some historians deem the settlement movement a failure because it did not eliminate poverty, settlement women often measured success by positive impacts on individuals and told stories to demonstrate their achievements.[41]

Other life enrichment opportunities included banquets for Camp Fire Girls and their mothers. There were parties at sewing school; after instruction "the social feature enters in, as these mothers seldom get out of the home for any kind of recreation. They enter into games with the zest of children; so, for that reason, plenty of games will be on the program."[42]

When the impressive new structure was dedicated in 1924, a power blackout occurred during the ceremony. A worker sent to restore power found the lines had been deliberately cut by a nearby merchant. Head resident Berta Ellison refused to press charges against her neighbor and in fact worked to win him over. The deaconesses had a housekeeper who cooked and cleaned their quarters, thus relieving them of domestic duties, but Ellison did the shopping herself the next three months, frequenting that merchant. She "came back one day all smiles" saying, "'He's going to give me a discount on what we buy there and he

apologized for what he did.' And he turned out to be one of our best supporters."[43] It is not clear why he had objected, but St. Mark's had good relations with
its neighbors thereafter. However, the Mary Werlein Mission on Tchoupitoulas
Street suffered from the focus on the center and closed around 1925.[44]

In 1924, the Scarritt training school for MECS deaconesses moved from Kansas City into spacious new quarters in Nashville, Tennessee. The expansion enhanced deaconess education for decades. Examining their training proves that
the women at St. Mark's were far more radical than most Social Gospelers have
been thought to be.

Scarritt graduate Mary Lou Barnwell arrived at St. Mark's in 1927. Born in
Georgia in 1903, Barnwell dreamed of going to Asia as a missionary, but to serve
overseas, women had to weigh at least one hundred pounds, and she could not
gain that much. Instead, she went to New Orleans to run the boys' program
and serve as clinic receptionist. She moved in 1933 to Florida but returned in
1937 to be head resident in New Orleans. In 1939, Barnwell joined the staff of
the national mission board and in 1948 became head of the Commission on
Deaconess Work, a position she held for nearly twenty years. Her work took
her all over the world and gave her unparalleled opportunity to shape the work
of deaconesses. She "sought racial understanding, crossed economic barriers,
helped women interpret mores of different peoples and, in [the] face of opposition, exercised strong leadership."[45]

At age ninety-seven, Barnwell responded to a question about her understanding of the Social Gospel by saying, "It's just something you live." This deceptively
simple response mirrors the theological underpinnings of the Social Gospel.
During her formative period at Scarritt, Barnwell did her fieldwork at a Beth-
lehem House, the name given to Methodist settlements for black clientele. The
teacher who most influenced her was New Testament professor Albert Barnett,
who was "known throughout the South as a leader in liberal Christian action."
Frequently an advocate for organized labor who "fought for the rights of the
underprivileged, especially blacks" and a prominent white member of the National Association for the Advancement of Colored People (NAACP), he urged
students to become involved in civil rights activism. Deaconess Helen Mandlebaum, who grew up in New Orleans in the St. Mark's congregation, recalled
that she and other Scarritt students joined the NAACP in Nashville because of
Barnett's influence.[46]

Another student of his, Julia Southard Campbell, came to St. Mark's in 1935,
rose to head resident in 1939, and worked there until 1943. Born in Virginia in
1908, she recalled that Scarritt had an excellent relationship with historically
black Fisk University, exchanging professors and encouraging visits by students.

Throughout her career, she "was always on the side of good race relationships, thanks to the natural acceptance at Scarritt College, without 'preaching.'"[47]

Along with courses that taught skills, and Bible training that related the teachings of Jesus to social action, the Scarritt curriculum dealt with economics. Students read Walter Rauschenbusch's *Christianizing the Social Order*, the most radical of his writings, which called for reorganization of the capitalist system. They wrote one-thousand-word papers on a Christian social order that required them to describe in their own words the world as it would be if thoroughly Christianized. This training produced deaconesses who were anything but social conservatives as the turbulent 1930s approached.[48]

During the depths of the Great Depression, Doris Alford Branton moved into the pastor's apartment on the third floor when her husband became pastor. Branton recalled Nettie Stroup, the head resident, as "a dignified lady, very businesslike, and full of fun. She just loved to laugh." It was Stroup who wrote profiles of people impacted by the center in 1933, including one girl who had engaged in muskrat trapping, snake killing, drinking, and gambling before the women at St. Mark's encouraged her to abandon her wayward ways in favor of more cultivated and refined behavior. Taught to love reading, she returned to seventh grade at the age of nineteen and hoped to become a missionary. Branton said the nurse deaconess, Wortley Moorman, "was always ready to take people anywhere or do anything she could for them. She was gentle and kind, and the people loved her." Moorman was available to the sick day and night. Two medical students lived in rooms on the second floor and helped in the clinic.[49]

Branton recalled the diverse nature of the St. Mark's clientele. She often served as secretary of the women's clubs, because so many immigrants had not yet mastered written English. Campbell noted that many light-skinned blacks "passed" at St. Mark's with the staff's knowledge and cooperation. "We never turned anyone away, nor questioned anyone. We had many who 'passed.'"[50]

The clinic openly served blacks, so passing was not required. "St. Mark's was the only clinic in New Orleans with dental service available to Negroes[.] . . . Negroes were treated same as white and used rest rooms," Campbell said. She remembered that St. Mark's "had excellent race relations because of the Clinic. If a Negro came first, then the Negro saw the doctor first. Those things mattered not at all at St. Mark's." Serving people in the order they came meant more than blacks not having to wait. It also meant that different races used the dental chair and medical examining rooms successively, at a time when racist southern mores demanded that even waiting rooms in health facilities be segregated. Another article Nettie Stroup wrote for *The World Outlook* stated plainly: "The clinic provides our only direct contact with American Negroes. The Negro patients average about one-third of the total number of patients treated." She added, "Those who come to the clinic suffer not only with physical aches, but are often as much in need of love and sympathy as of medicine."[51]

Not surprisingly, in the 1930s, conservative critics frequently accused the MECS women who worked at St. Mark's in New Orleans and at MECS settlement houses in other large southern cities of being too far to the left. In 1933, the women's magazine published a response, "Women of the Left Wing," in which its strategy was to admit that the MECS women had done everything they were accused of, and more, while insisting that it was the Christian course to take.[52]

One primary criticism concerned the openness of the "left-wing" women toward working with people of color. Although some of their efforts can legitimately be criticized today from the other side—that is, for lacking the level of sensitivity and understanding of racial problems that have been achieved in the last three-quarters of a century—it is important to remember that in the 1930s, no one in the MECS was even suggesting desegregation of the separate settlements for blacks and for whites. Critics railed at the MECS women simply for "daring" to have white women raise funds to establish black settlements in black neighborhoods and further castigated them because some white women chose to work "among the Negroes" at those settlements. Some of the deaconesses who served at St. Mark's, including Martha Nutt and Margaret Young, worked at the Nashville settlement for blacks later in their careers and participated in a cooperative program that helped train Fisk University students. Since the MECS ethos dictated that white women serve at black settlements only if they volunteered, this is evidence that the women working in New Orleans were on the cutting edge of interracial cooperation in the 1920s and 1930s.

Compounding this outrageous behavior were meetings the white Methodist laywomen held with black women's groups to address racism after they "realized anew that if the chasm which yawns between shall ever be abridged that the white woman of the South must recognize her own strategic place in its accomplishment and set herself quickly to the task." Like other local white MECS women's societies across the South, the New Orleans chapters studied literature on the topic of race and made efforts to foster improved race relations. Although many wished progress were more rapid, one wrote, "In this recital of interracial work by the women of Southern Methodism, credit has not been given to the courage and enthusiasm of thousands of women who have *dared* in the name of their Master. Yet enough has been said to prove that the missionary organization has moved forward, and the leaders of Southern Methodist women may well be characterized as 'Left Wingers.'"[53] New Orleans's MECS leaders certainly fit the bill.

In that decade, the issue of race was less important than the basic struggle for survival. In 1937, the budget for St. Mark's Community Center totaled $4,940. Of this, $3,500 went for salaries, $300 for utilities, and $900 for janitorial service. Only $240 was earmarked for programming, and nothing at all for direct aid for the poor. Some deaconesses like Helen Mandlebaum, who grew up at St. Mark's, abandoned the church temporarily to work in New Deal agencies, where they provided direct financial assistance. "That's where the action really was," Mandlebaum recalled.[54]

In the 1930s, Methodist women also began to be more open about their ambitions for Christian service. "Where Shall Women Serve?" the title of an article in the November 1933 issue of *The World Outlook* asked. The article recounted that one hundred years before, in 1833, the national Methodist newspaper finally acknowledged the benefits of missionary wives accompanying their husbands overseas to do tasks men were prevented from performing by local custom. It speculated that in 2033 it would seem strange that in 1933 the church "put limitations upon the Spirit of God" by refusing to allow women to preach.[55]

Mary Werlein died in 1940 at the age of eighty-six. Under the headline "Charity Worker of New Orleans Dies at Age of 86," a *Times-Picayune* article said Werlein was "widely known for the charity work to which she devoted most of her life." The *States* ran two stories, including one titled "Devout Church Worker Expires." On page 4, a shorter but more vivid story was simply headed "Mary Werlein." It praised her charity work, saying: "In her burned the zeal of the Christian Martyrs, the courage of the Crusaders. She was a flame on the altar of brotherhood."[56]

Both newspapers used the term "charity worker," but the *States'* seemingly over-the-top rhetoric about "zeal of Christian martyrs" and "courage of Crusaders" may have been closer to how Werlein's activities were viewed in the early 1900s; it is not impossible that the writer remembered heated conflicts MECS women had with the Methodist establishment. "Charity worker" is inoffensive, but the more loaded terms "reformer" and "Social Gospel activist" could also have been applied to Werlein.

This study of St. Mark's refines many previously held assumptions about the Social Gospel. For one thing, the end of World War I did not mean the end of that important reform movement. Methodist women who manifested Social Gospel thought, theology, and principles were still on the upswing of the arc of their work in the 1920s, and the decade after the war was a high point in St. Mark's history. Examining the Social Gospel by studying its practitioners, rather than its theoreticians, will prove that New Orleans was by no means an exception. It was not the loss of reform zeal in the aftermath of World War I that caused the decline of the Social Gospel. Instead it was the New Deal and the acceptance by government of responsibility for the welfare of the poor that co-opted reformers' roles and institutionalized much of their work in the state.

The common conflation of the Social Gospel with Progressivism also needs rethinking. One major difference is the motivation of practitioners. The Progressive agenda was bound up with the idea that humanity is improving; the Methodist woman, on the other hand, who worked to facilitate the inbreaking of the Kingdom of God would not be discouraged by evidence that humanity could not dig itself out of its own morass. She might be saddened but would not be surprised.

The Methodist deaconesses' training program and their personal theologies and practices belie assertions that the real agenda of Social Gospelers was preserving a segregated social order. There is need for a much more nuanced consideration of "conservative" and "liberal" labels, particularly when applied to actions motivated by religious convictions. The later history of St. Mark's establishes links that earlier scholars had suggested but not clearly demonstrated between the Social Gospel and civil rights movements. The MECS deaconesses laid groundwork that allowed a major event in the civil rights struggle to be played out at St. Mark's. In 1960, the worshipping congregation at St. Mark's, with deaconesses as active lay leaders, supported the pastor as he and his daughter broke the white boycott of William Frantz Elementary that occurred when a black child, Ruby Bridges, began attending there.[57]

Moreover, the women of St. Mark's demonstrated that the true Methodist women of New Orleans were willing to operate from religious motivation even when that put them in conflict with the values of their segregated and sexist society. The civil rights movement, the Social Gospel movement, and the renewed push for women's ordination in the Methodist Church would all benefit from their courageous work for "life abundant."

NOTES

1. *New Orleans States-Item*, May 4, 1940, 4.

2. Ellen Blue, "The Gospel According to St. Mark's: Methodist Women Embodying a Liberating Theology from the Social Gospel Era to the Civil Rights Era at a Deaconess-Run Settlement House in the French Quarter of New Orleans" (PhD diss., Tulane University, 2002).

3. Barbara Welter, "The Cult of True Womanhood: 1820–1860," *American Quarterly* 18 (Summer 1966): 151–75; Jean Miller Schmidt, *Grace Sufficient: A History of Women in American Methodism, 1760–1939* (Nashville, Tenn.: Abingdon Press, 1999), 79–98. Schmidt, following Welter's classic definition of the "True Woman," refines it specifically for the women of Methodism, thus creating

the apt descriptor, "True Methodist Women." The laywomen who supported St. Mark's provide evidence for her usage of the term.

4. Mrs. H. A. Kennedy, "P. and H.M. Work in the Louisiana Conference," *New Orleans Christian Advocate*, October 3, 1895, 4 (her article contains an error; the society was established in 1891); "Louisiana Conference P. and H.M.S.," *New Orleans Christian Advocate*, February 7, 1895, 7. The *New Orleans Christian Advocate* was a weekly newspaper published by the MECS conferences in Louisiana and Mississippi.

5. *New Orleans Christian Advocate*, February 28, 1895, 2.

6. *New Orleans Christian Advocate*, April 25, 1895, 4.

7. Mrs. H. A. Kennedy, "P. and H.M. Work in the Louisiana Conference," *New Orleans Christian Advocate*, October 3, 1895, 4.

8. Florence Russ, "P. and H.M.S. Report," *New Orleans Christian Advocate*, April 8, 1897, 2; Betty Werlein Carter and Lorraine Moore, telephone interview by author, April 24, 1998.

9. Leila Werlein Stone, telephone interview by author, October 12, 2001.

10. Ibid.

11. Mary Werlein, letter to Lucinda B. Helm, June 26, 1895, in *New Orleans Christian Advocate*, July 11, 1985, 2.

12. Florence Russ, "P. and H.M.S. Report," *New Orleans Christian Advocate*, April 8, 1897, 2.

13. Mary Noreen Dunn, *Women and Home Missions* (Nashville, Tenn.: Cokesbury Press, 1936), 26–27. Meekins wrote her report sometime between 1893 and 1898.

14. Florence Russ, "P. and H.M.S. Report," *New Orleans Christian Advocate*, April 8, 1897, 2.

15. Sara Joyce Myers, "Southern Methodist Women Leaders and Church Missions, 1878–1910" (PhD diss., Emory University, 1990); Annette K. Baxter, preface, in Karen J. Blair, *The Clubwoman as Feminist: True Womanhood Redefined, 1868–1914* (New York: Holmes and Meier, 1980), xii; Rosemary Skinner Keller, "Conversions and Their Consequences: Women's Ministry and Leadership in the United Methodist Tradition," in *Religious Institutions and Women's Leadership: New Roles Inside the Mainstream*, ed. Catherine Wessinger (Columbia: University of South Carolina Press, 1996), 115. Keller notes that using language about "home protection" and making "the world more home-like" has "effectively released thousands of women in their callings from God."

16. *Journal of the Louisiana Annual Conference*, 1903; Mrs. J. Benton Hobb, "Woman's Home Mission Society," *Journal of the Louisiana Annual Conference*, 1906, 46; Sarah Sloan Kreutziger, "Going on to Perfection: The Contributions of the Wesleyan Theological Doctrine of Entire Sanctification to the Value Base of American Professional Social Work through the Lives and Activities of Nineteenth Century Evangelical Women Reformers" (PhD diss., Tulane University, 1991).

17. *Journal of the Louisiana Annual Conference*, 1907, 36; *Twenty-first Annual Report of the Woman's Home Mission Society*, MECS, 1907, 108.

18. Louise Reynes Edwards-Simpson, "Sicilian Immigration to New Orleans, 1870–1910: Ethnicity, Race and Social Position in the New South" (PhD diss., University of Minnesota, 1996), 43.

19. Annie Rogers, tape recording of presentation, March 1976, at Brooks-Howell Home (a home for retired deaconesses), Asheville, N.C., in possession of Helen Mandlebaum; *New Orleans Christian Advocate*, January 24, 1907, 5; *New Orleans Christian Advocate*, February 4, 1909, cover; N. E. Joyner, "St. Mark's Hall, Institutional Plant, in New Orleans," *Go Forward* 9 (November 1909): 3–4; records of the Women's Division of the General Board of Global Ministries, United Methodist Church Archives, General Commission on Archives and History, Madison, N.J. (hereinafter cited as WD/UMCA).

20. N. E. Joyner, "St. Mark's Hall, Institutional Plant," 3–4.

21. Berta Ellison, "Annual Report for St. Mark's Hall," minutes, eleventh annual meeting of the Woman's Missionary Society of the Louisiana Conference, February 1921, 64–65, 90, Magale Library, Centenary College, Shreveport, La.

22. Joyner, "St. Mark's Hall, Institutional Plant," 3–4; Margery Freeman, "The St. Mark's Family: A Story of Change," St. Mark's United Methodist Church, 1979; church membership rolls on file at St. Mark's United Methodist Church.

23. "Woman's City Mission Board," *New Orleans Christian Advocate*, March 3, 1910, 5; "New Orleans Notes," *New Orleans Christian Advocate*, April 28, 1910, 4; minutes, second annual meeting of the Woman's Missionary Society of the Louisiana Conference, 1912, 32, Magale Library, Centenary College, Shreveport, La.

24. Schmidt, *Grace Sufficient*, 228–29.

25. J. W. Moore to Bishop Warren Candler, July 9, 1912, box 19, folder 6, Warren A. Candler Papers, Special Collections, Robert W. Woodruff Library, Emory University, Atlanta. See also John Olen Fish, "Southern Methodism in the Progressive Era: A Social History" (PhD diss., University of Georgia, 1969), 43–44. Fish quoted Moore's letter, accepted its assertions uncritically, and concluded that at St. Mark's "the degree of influence of the church in the settlement was slight." He wrote, "The head resident probably viewed the establishment of a Sunday School at the settlement as an exertion of traditionalism that would strangle the program of the mission." Fish uses no data about programming at St. Mark's to back up this claim, and he demonstrates a failure to understand the deaconesses' mission. His study, which perpetuates the idea that Methodist settlement women were unspiritual and antichurch, is just one example of how the misrepresentation of their work has been compounded.

26. Allen F. Davis, *Spearheads for Reform: The Social Settlements and the Progressive Movement, 1890–1914* (New York: Oxford University Press, 1967), 15, 23; Judith Ann Trolander, *Settlement Houses and the Great Depression* (Detroit: Wayne State University, 1975); *Twenty-fourth Annual Report of the Woman's Home Mission Society*, MECS, 1910, 165; *Second Annual Report of the Woman's Missionary Council*, MECS, 1911–12, 358; *Third Annual Report of the Woman's Missionary Council*, MECS, 1912–13.

27. Gail Bederman, "'The Women Have Had Charge of the Church Work Long Enough': The Men and Religion Forward Movement of 1911–1912 and the Masculinization of Middle-Class Protestantism," *American Quarterly* 41 (September 1989): 432–65. J. W. Moore should not be confused with John M. Moore, who was later elected a bishop. Fish may have done so; he cites the actual John M. Moore frequently but also erroneously uses "John M. Moore" rather than "John W. Moore" to refer to the author of this letter in both text and footnotes.

28. *Third Annual Report of the Woman's Missionary Council*, MECS, 1912–13, 161; *Fourth Annual Report of Woman's Missionary Council*, MECS, 1913–14, 446; *Fifth Annual Report of the Woman's Missionary Council*, MECS, 1914–15, 362; minutes, third annual meeting, Woman's Missionary Society of the Louisiana Conference, 1913, 68, Magale Library, Centenary College, La.

29. *Fourth Annual Report of the Woman's Missionary Council*, MECS, 1913–14, 153; *Journal of the Louisiana Annual Conference*, 1913; Robert Henry Harper, *Louisiana Methodism* (Washington, D.C.: Kaufman Press, 1949), 109; *Fifth Annual Report of the Woman's Missionary Council*, MECS, 1914–15, 285; "Memorial to the Woman's Missionary Council," minutes, fourth annual meeting Woman's Missionary Society of the Louisiana Conference, 1914, 60, Magale Library, Centenary College, Shreveport, La.

30. Robert A. Woods and Albert J. Kennedy, eds., *Handbook of Settlements* (New York: Charities Publication Committee, 1911), 92.

31. "Episcopal Address," *Journal of the General Conference of 1906*, 24, cited in Fish, "Southern Methodism in the Progressive Era," 71; "Italian Kindergarten," *Woman's Home Missions*, April 1936, 11; Belle H. Bennett, "The Woman's Home Mission Society," 8, address delivered at the General Missionary Conference, New Orleans, April 27, 1901, pamphlet in WD/UMCA.

32. Edwards-Simpson, "Sicilian Immigration to New Orleans, 1870–1910"; George M. Reynolds, *Machine Politics in New Orleans, 1897–1926* (New York: Columbia University Press, 1936); Rowland Berthoff, "Southern Attitudes toward Immigration, 1865–1914," *Journal of Southern History* 17 (August 1951): 328–60; John Olen Fish, "Southern Methodism and the Accommodation of the Negro, 1902–1915," *Journal of Negro History* 55 (July 1970): 202–3; Arnold R. Hirsch and Joseph Logsdon, eds., *Creole New Orleans: Race and Americanization* (Baton Rouge: Louisiana State University Press, 1992).

33. "Mrs. Lily [*sic*] Meekins, Charity Worker, Dragged by Car: 'The Angel of Tchoupitoulas' Is Victim of Peculiar Accident," *New Orleans Times-Picayune*, January 3, 1916, 10; "Mrs. Lily [*sic*] Meekins, Charity Worker, Dies of Her Hurts," *New Orleans Times-Picayune*, January 10, 1916, 1.

34. Mary Agnes Dougherty, *My Calling to Fulfill: Deaconesses in the United Methodist Tradition* (New York: Women's Division, General Board of Global Ministries, United Methodist Church, 1997); Elizabeth Meredith Lee, *As Among the Methodists: Deaconesses Yesterday, Today, and Tomorrow* (New York: Woman's Division of Christian Service, Board of Missions, Methodist Church, 1963); Carolyn DeSwarte Gifford, ed., *The American Deaconess Movement in the Early Twentieth Century* (New York: Garland Publishing, 1987).

35. *New Orleans Christian Advocate*, March 29, 1917, 14; Helen Gibson, "St. Mark's Hall," *Seventh Annual Report of the Woman's Missionary Council*, MECS, 1917, 297.

36. *The Council Daily*, April 18, 1917, 3–4, WD/UMCA.

37. " What Women Are Doing: Gifted Louisiana Women," *New Orleans Louisiana Review*, April 29, 1891, 6; Isabel Gardner Larue, telephone interview by author, May 30, 2006; Alcée Fortier, *Louisiana: Comprising Sketches of Parishes, Towns, Events, Institutions, and Persons, Arranged in Cyclopedic Form* ([Madison, Wis.]: Century Historical Association, 1914), 3:502–3.

38. *The Council Daily*, April 18, 1917, 3–4, WD/UMCA.

39. Berta Ellison, "Annual Report for St. Mark's Hall," minutes, eleventh annual meeting of the Woman's Missionary Society of the Louisiana Conference, February 1921, 64–65, 90; Ruth Byerly, "Annual Report for St. Mark's Hall," minutes, twelfth annual meeting of the Woman's Missionary Society of the Louisiana Conference, February 1922, 72.

40. Winans Drake, "News from the Districts," *New Orleans Christian Advocate*, January 25, 1923, 4; Dougherty and Gardner, architects, Nashville, Tenn., architects' drawings for 1130 Rampart Street, 1923, St. Mark's United Methodist Church.

41. Annie Rogers, tape recording of presentation, March 1976, at Brooks-Howell Home, Asheville, N.C., in the possession of Helen Mandlebaum.

42. Berta Eliison [*sic*], *New Orleans Christian Advocate*, December 21, 1923, 13.

43. Delores Prickett, transcript of interview by Margery Freeman, 1979, St. Mark's United Methodist Church.

44. Margery Wright, Methodist Archives, Centenary College, Shreveport, La., e-mail to author, September 30, 2002. The *Journal of the Louisiana Conference*, 1926, is the first in which the Mary Werlein Mission is not listed.

45. Mary Lou Barnwell, interview by author, Asheville, N.C., August 25, 2000; *They Went Out Not Knowing . . . : An Encyclopedia of 100 Women in Mission* (New York: Women's Division of the General Board of Global Ministries, United Methodist Church, 1986), 33.

46. Mary Lou Barnwell, interview by author, Asheville, N.C., August 25, 2000; Alice Cobb, *"Yes, Lord, I'll Do It": Scarritt's Century of Service* (Nashville, Tenn.: Scarritt College, 1987), 49; Boone M. Bowen, *The Candler School of Theology: Sixty Years of Service* (Atlanta, Ga.: Emory University, 1974), 178–79; Helen Mandlebaum, e-mail to author, February 8, 2001.

47. Julia Southard Campbell, telephone interview by author, February 13, 2001; Julia Southard Campbell, letters to the author, n.d. (received February 5, 2001), n.d. (received February 16, 2001), March 22, 2001, and June 23, 2001.

48. Walter Rauschenbusch, *Christianizing the Social Order* (New York: Macmillan, 1921); Wallace MacMullen, L. F. W. Lesemann, and Miss A. M. King, *Directions and Helps: Course of Study for Deaconesses* (New York: Methodist Book Concern, 1922), 168–70.

49. Doris Alford Branton, interview by author, Shreveport, La., June 7, 2001; Nettie Stroup, "Life Changing at St. Mark's Community Center," *World Outlook* 23 (November 1933): 22.

50. Doris Alford Branton, interview by author, Shreveport, La., June 7, 2001.

51. Ibid.; Julia Southard Campbell, telephone interview by author, February 13, 2001; Julia Southard Campbell, letters to the author, n.d. (received February 5, 2001), n.d. (received February 16, 2001), March 22, 2001, and June 23, 2001; Nettie Stroup, "Glimpsing Our Work at St. Mark's Community Center, New Orleans," *World Outlook* 25 (August 1935): 20.

52. Sara Estelle Haskin, "Women of the Left Wing," *World Outlook* 23 (February 1933): 28–30.

53. Ibid.

54. "Estimates—1937: Education and Promotion/Home Field/Foreign Fields," pamphlet for use at meeting of the Women's Missionary Council, MECS, at First Methodist Episcopal Church, South, Dallas, March 1936, in WD/UMCA; Helen Mandlebaum, interview by author, Asheville, N.C., August 25, 2000.

55. "Where Shall Women Serve?" *World Outlook* 23 (November 1933): 23.

56. "Charity Worker of New Orleans Dies at Age of 86," *New Orleans Times-Picayune*, May 4, 1940, 3; "Devout Church Worker Expires," *New Orleans States*, May 4, 1940, 3; "Mary Werlein," *New Orleans States*, May 4, 1940, 4.

57. Darryl M. Trimiew, "The Social Gospel Movement and the Question of Race," in *The Social Gospel Today*, ed. Christopher Evans (Louisville, Ky.: Westminster John Knox, 2001), 27–37; Ronald C. White Jr., *Liberty and Justice for All: Racial Reform and the Social Gospel (1877–1925)* (San Francisco: Harper and Row, 1990); Ralph Luker, *The Social Gospel in Black and White: American Racial Reform, 1885–1912* (Chapel Hill: University of North Carolina Press, 1991); John Patrick McDowell, *The Social Gospel in the South: The Woman's Home Mission Movement in the Methodist Episcopal Church, South, 1886–1939* (Baton Rouge: Louisiana State University Press, 1981); Alice G. Knotts, *Fellowship of Love: Methodist Women Changing American Racial Attitudes, 1920–1968* (Nashville, Tenn.: Kingswood Books, 1996); Ellen Blue, "The Gospel According to St. Mark's"; Ellen Blue, "The Citizens Forum on Integration: 'Underground' Methodist Response to the *Brown* Decision in New Orleans," *Methodist History* 43 (April 2005), 213–26.

Cleoma Breaux Falcon

(1906–1941)

The Commercialization of Cajun Music

KEVIN S. FONTENOT AND RYAN ANDRÉ BRASSEAUX

❀ ❀ ❀

In 1928 Cleoma Breaux and her future husband, Joe Falcon, recorded the first Cajun music record: "Lafayette" backed with "The Waltz That Carried Me to My Grave." Over the next decade, Cleoma and Joe Falcon along with her siblings, the Breaux Frères, cut nearly one hundred Cajun records, making them the most prolific and influential family of Cajun musicians before the Second World War. Cleoma sensed the potential of the new industry and actively pushed the boundaries of Cajun music by incorporating influences from jazz, popular, and country music into her repertoire and also by recording in English. Popular with audiences, Cleoma Falcon likewise pushed social boundaries while enjoying a central position in the male-dominated world of Cajun music. As a divorced woman who actively participated in the masculine world of music and honky-tonks, Falcon posed challenges to old ideas about the roles played by Cajun and southern women, challenges that were more accepted by the men around her than by fellow Cajun women.

Cleoma Breaux Falcon straddled the urban and rural milieus that converged in Crowley, Louisiana. As an adolescent, she fell into the role of surrogate mother when her father abandoned his family. Cleoma worked at home, keeping house for her brothers, and then she helped contribute to the family income by playing music with her brothers in local dancehalls. Music became the glue that kept the family from falling apart. She married at age fifteen, but her effort to keep to women's traditional path failed. She challenged traditional mores when she divorced and took a second husband, accordionist Joseph Falcon, and during her public performances in violent and male-dominated Cajun honky-tonks. Cleoma Breaux Falcon represents the modern Cajun woman. She was a creative

CLEOMA BREAUX FALCON, LOULA FALCON, AND JOE FALCON

They pose for cultural geographer Lauren C. Post at their home in Rayne, La.,
ca. 1934. Courtesy of the Lauren Chester Post Papers, MSS 2854, Louisiana
and Lower Mississippi Valley Collections, Louisiana State
University Libraries, Baton Rouge, La.

individual who stayed in tune with contemporary American popular culture while carving a professional career in a male space. At the same time, however, she embraced the late Victorian ideal, making her home a center of domestic calm amid the bustling urban world of Crowley, Louisiana, and the raucous life enjoyed by the extended Breaux clan.

Crowley was something of an anomaly in French Louisiana. The town grew from an active railroad settlement founded by midwesterners in the 1880s into a regional commercial center boasting a considerable Anglo-American population and various strands of Protestantism, mixed with vernacular traditions introduced by working-class folk from the Afro-Creole and Cajun communities. These cosmopolitan currents profoundly affected the worldview of local residents and the protean strands of Cajun musical expression that emerged from blue-collar neighborhoods. Between 1928 and the late 1930s, the Acadia Parish seat of justice also became the epicenter of commercial Cajun music, as the city hosted a diverse array of musicians—there were the Hackberry Ramblers, Leo Soileau and the Four Aces, archetypal Cajun steel guitarist Julius "Papa Cairo" Lamperez, guitarists Floyd and Danny Shreve, Cajun music's first drummer, Tony Gonzales, the Breaux Family Band, and the Falcon family band—all of whom performed in different styles ranging from country-influenced Cajun swing to traditional Cajun.[1] Crowley's cosmopolitan character and cross-pollinated music scene was the artistic cradle that nurtured young Cleoma Breaux Falcon.

Modern American and traditional Cajun cultures overlapped in Crowley, where Cleoma Breaux came of age. She was born on May 27, 1906, to Auguste and Mathilde Schexnayder Breaux in the Acadia Parish seat of justice. Auguste and Mathilde married in 1897, and their family grew with the birth of Cleoma's brothers Amede, Ophy, and Clifford. Auguste played the accordion—the family's musical talent seems to have descended through the Breaux line as Mathilde never sang or played an instrument. The children all became multi-instrumentalists and initially played for the family's own entertainment. Amede was the primary accordion player, Ophy, the primary guitarist and sometime fiddler, and Clifford, the fiddler. Cleoma developed a solid rhythmic guitar style, closely related to the "hard" style preferred by later bluegrass guitarists. She also could play the fiddle and accordion, although she never recorded with these instruments.[2]

When Cleoma was eleven, her father abandoned the family, and Mathilde Breaux began to work as a domestic for various families in Crowley. Cleoma became a surrogate mother to her brothers, who even at an early age exhibited the rambunctious behavior that would make them legendary in the south Louisiana dancehall scene. Cleoma remained devoted to her brothers throughout her life, and they often turned to her for advice. She represented stability in their lives. The Breaux family hovered near poverty and depended on music for entertainment and, eventually, for a large part of the family income. They soon gained a local reputation as excellent musicians and started playing in the dancehalls of Crowley. Other musicians gravitated to them, and it may well be that is how Cleoma met her first husband, Oliver Hanks, who was also a guitarist.[3]

Little is known about Cleoma's relationship with Oliver Hanks. He probably belonged to the rather large Hanks family in Crowley that included several musicians. The couple married when Cleoma was fifteen, about 1921. She may have fallen for Hanks because he was a fellow guitar player and because his attention might have filled the gap in a young girl's life created by her father's abandonment. What, if anything, she learned from Hanks about playing the guitar is also unknown. The marriage was short, and Cleoma seems to have remained silent about her first husband for most of her life. In the family-centered Cajun world, divorce was rare and bad marriages usually ended with one partner just leaving. A divorced woman in this world bore a stigma. Cleoma, though, seems to have weathered the divorce well. Her success may have been based on her reputation as a "down-to-earth girl" who took her obligations to her family seriously. Also, in urban Crowley, divorce might have been more readily accepted than in some of the rural Acadian communities. Regardless, Cleoma Breaux did not suffer from a lack of suitors. She was not only a talented musician who performed with her popular brothers. Cleoma Breaux was also a stunningly attractive woman.[4]

Cleoma's beauty was recalled decades later by almost all who knew her. She was short in stature, with dark curly hair and dancing eyes. Surviving photos show a fashion-conscious woman who adopted the stylish urban clothes seen in motion pictures. Indeed, in the most famous photo of Cleoma and Joe Falcon, taken about 1928, she wears a white flapper-style dress, her hair coifed in a style strongly reminiscent of Clara Bow (who was at that time experiencing fame with her role in *It*), and sports high-heeled shoes.[5]

Cleoma consciously tried to keep up with modern styles. She made most of her clothes and undoubtedly frequented the department stores that opened in Crowley. The 1928 photograph indicates that she liked the liberated look of the flapper. Although her stocky size prohibited affecting a svelte Louise Brooks persona, her curly hair and rounded facial features allowed her to follow Clara Bow's lead. In both her physical appearance and her choice to play in dancehalls, Cleoma Breaux embraced the new era and the new roles for women that came with the 1920s. By playing in public, Cleoma challenged the old Cajun custom that relegated music made by females to the home place and the custom that dictated that Cajun women did not work outside the home.[6]

The Breaux family's musical reputation spread through the Crowley dancehall world. At some point in the mid-1920s the brothers began receiving regular visits from Joseph Falcon, an accordionist born near Rayne in 1900. Joe Falcon was gaining a reputation himself as a stellar musician, and he enjoyed the camaraderie of the Breaux brothers. He also fell in love with Cleoma, both the woman and the musician. He admired her steady, hard rhythm and her ability to follow chord changes. She was also a fine singer, although her voice at times tended to the nasal, a trait that at the time was common among many southern singers. Cleoma joined Joe's band and the sight of a beautiful young woman on the bandstand soon drew the attention of the dancehall crowd. Together, they literally "made beautiful music." And in 1928 they would also make history.[7]

During the 1920s, record companies sought new artists by conducting field recording sessions. Recording companies, such as Columbia, would send an artist and repertoire agent (referred to as an A & R man) to a city to audition new talent and make recordings. To ensure the profitability of such trips, the companies would schedule recording sessions with established artists at the same time. Sessions were generally held in hotel suites, with whole floors often reserved to serve as the recording area. A few weeks prior to the sessions, the companies placed advertisements in area newspapers calling for interested talent to appear at the session location for auditions. They often also notified regional record sellers and encouraged them to send local favorites to audition.[8]

In April 1928 Joe Falcon learned of a Columbia Records session to be held in New Orleans later that month. Most likely he learned of the session from his manager, George Burr. Joe, Cleoma, Burr, and a singer named Leon Meche traveled to New Orleans and auditioned for the A & R man. Meche experienced stage fright and was unable to sing, so Joe provided vocals and played accordion, backed by Cleoma's steady rhythm on the guitar. Initially, the record executive was less than impressed. Joe recalled the A & R "man said that in those days they wasn't making no records otherwise than with big orchestras, you understand. That's not enough music. He said, 'I can't use them.' Then Burr started talking with them. . . . And they decided that they would let us make one record. . . . When I got through with the record 'Allons a Lafayette,' they put it on the Victrola. . . . All them high bucks listened and listened and listened. And they came over to where we recorded and they said, 'Pardner, get ready, we're going for good now. We are going to make it. It sounds good.' And that's when we made it and it went over big."[9]

Joe and Cleoma cut two sides, enough for one record, on April 27, 1928. "Lafayette" backed with "The Waltz That Carried Me to My Grave" became the first commercial Cajun music recording. The record was a local hit, and record companies, desperate for new sales opportunities in the wake of competition from radio, began to record Cajun musicians. Columbia invited Joe and Cleoma to the company's New York City headquarters in August 1928 and the couple cut six more sides, including the now classic "Le Vieux Soulard et Sa Femme" (The Old Drunkard and His Wife). The song was a reworking of an older English folksong, "My Good Old Man," in which a wife laments her husband's reputation as a prodigious drinker. Joe and Cleoma exchanged vocals in the song, but she alone sang in "Marie Buller," which focused on a notoriously violent oil-field community near Mire, Louisiana (known as Marais Bouleur). Other titles recorded at the session included "A Cowboy Rider," "Fe Fe Ponchaux," and "La Marche de la Noche," the traditional Cajun wedding march played at the presentation of the newly married husband and wife.[10]

The success of the Falcon-Breaux recordings led the Columbia agents to invite Joe and Cleoma to record in Atlanta in April 1929. This time they took Cleoma's brothers Amede and Ophy along as accompanists, and the brothers also cut records on their own. In this session Cleoma's vocals shone brightly on "Prenez Courage" (Have Courage), "C'est Si Triste sans Lui" (It Is So Blue without You), and "Mon Coeur T'Appelle" (My Heart Aches for You). She also accompanied her brothers during their session, which included "Ma Blonde Est Partie" (My Blonde Left Me), the first version of the now classic "Jolie Blonde." Controversy over the authorship of the song remains. Cleoma is sometimes given credit for having written it, but the strongest case is for Amede as the primary author. He is also the singer on the record, despite the common belief that it is Cleoma. The session also allowed Cleoma to demonstrate her hard-driving rhythm on "Vas Y Carrement" (Step It Fast).

The year 1929 also marked the onset of the Great Depression, and Joe and Cleoma did not enter a recording studio for another five years. Indeed, the struggling record industry did not record *any* Cajun records between November 1930 and August 1934.[11]

With their recording successes came fame on the local dancehall circuit. Joe Falcon, Cleoma Breaux, and the Breaux Frères became local dancehall royalty. Joe proudly advertised himself as a "Columbia Recording Artist" on his handbills and posters. Joe was not the best accordionist in the region, but he was certainly talented, and he was an eager self-promoter. His status as the first Cajun artist to record underscored his reputation, and by the early 1930s, Joe and Cleoma were earning enough as musicians to make entertainment their primary occupation. They married in about 1931 cementing their personal and professional relationship. Shortly thereafter they adopted a daughter, Loula, and settled into married bliss.[12]

Cleoma's musical career dramatically demonstrates the transformation of women's roles in Cajun society from the nineteenth century into the modern era. Before she literally emerged onto the stage, Cajun women sang mostly only in the home. They passed on traditional songs to their children but rarely sang in any public setting. Public performance was reserved for men. As musicologist and folklorist Lisa E. Richardson has observed, "social pressure has played an important role in women's performance of music. Cajun men have always had the option of public performances without risking much social stigma. Women, on the other hand, have usually been emphatically discouraged, in both subtle and overt ways, from bringing their musical talents into a public arena. . . . Cajun women have, more often than not, chosen to express their musicality in the most socially acceptable manner available to them, among family and friends."[13]

Cajun women musicians were not alone in finding themselves limited to the "most socially acceptable manner." Other southern women were similarly restricted. In West Virginia, female fiddlers were limited to playing at the home place because fiddling was "man's business." A professional music career for a woman continued to be frowned on as late as the 1950s, when Loretta Lynn stated that country music was for men. During the late 1970s, Eliza Fontenot Carpenter told her grandson that "women can't sing country music, men do it better." Those women who did pursue a professional music career often found themselves stigmatized as "bad girls" for performing in honky-tonks. John Lair of the National Barn Dance carefully crafted a new image for Linda Parker to hide her past as a saloon singer. Acceptable roles for female singers were as part of a family band or as part of a large-scale radio barn dance like the Grand Ole Opry or the WLS-AM National Barn Dance. Both of these provided controlled environments, which placed women in traditional settings. With a family band, one could assume that the girls were monitored by their parents or brothers, and radio shows cultivated domesticity through down-home patter and homey references.[14]

Even in these contexts, women still found the profession difficult to navigate. Banjoist Rachel Veach joined Roy Acuff's band during the Depression, and Acuff transformed one of his regular band members into her "brother" to maintain respectability. Pete Kirby would be known as "Bashful Brother Oswald" for the rest of his career. When Lilly Mae Ledford joined the National Barn Dance, she found herself mercilessly victimized by teasing until Red Foley intervened and protected her as a "sister." In the male idioculture of country music, women had to prove themselves not only as musicians but also as good sports. Generally, if they were good musicians, they were soon welcomed into the fold and protected like Veach and Ledford.[15]

Cleoma's passage into professional performance was probably aided by the fact that she played with her brothers and later her husband. She also acted as a calming influence on her unruly brothers, so many probably saw her presence as a positive influence. Loula's remark that her mother was always seen as respectable supports this notion. "She always did for others," cooking and cleaning for sick neighbors, even finding Amede employment through the WPA.[16] Her brothers' reputation as fighters also helped create a protective zone around her, although she certainly proved capable of defending herself when necessary. As the swing era dawned and prohibition ended, the good-time scene of south Louisiana took on a hypermale stance, particularly on the western edge of the region.[17] Cleoma's background prepared her well for operating in such an environment.

Still, maintaining respectability remained Cleoma's priority. Randy Falcon remembers that women were jealous of his aunt for both her beauty and her fame. Male musicians likewise simultaneously envied and respected her musical prowess and the reputation she and Joe had earned from their recordings and performance successes. And some men, like Dennis McGee, coveted her as a beautiful woman. Her beauty and success as well as her early divorce forced Cleoma to walk a high wire of respectability, which she seems to have accomplished quite well. In the years since her death, virtually nothing negative has emerged about her, and even idle gossip has faded away.[18]

Despite her very modern occupation and engagement with urban culture, Cleoma Falcon settled easily into family life. She kept a neat home, made clothes for herself and Loula, canned fruit and vegetables, and generally doted on her daughter. Joe and Cleoma welcomed Mathilde Breaux into their home in her later years. As a Cajun woman interviewed for a book on gender roles in a Cajun town stated, "The old people should be at home if they can. . . . We can take care of our mothers ourselves and that's how it should be."[19] They soon invited Amede's son Preston to come live with them as well. The orderly domesticity of Cleoma's home and life contrasted sharply with disorder in the lives of her brothers. Amede presided over a large and perennially broken family. Ophy spent most of his life asking for little more than a decent meal, strong drink, and an opportunity to play music. Clifford's stable and neat home masked a troubled marriage with a controlling wife. Amede and Ophy suffered bouts with alcohol, while Clifford had to hide any drinking from his wife. Cleoma was her brothers' rock and confidant, always lending a sympathetic ear to their woes. She and Joe had brought Preston into their home to provide a playmate for Loula. But in taking him under their wing they also extricated him from a topsy-turvy home environment.[20] Stability had arrived for Cleoma, and her success gave her the freedom to create the home she wanted. And then Joe decided he wanted to move to a rural neighborhood not far from his boyhood home near Rayne.

"You couldn't take the country out of Daddy," daughter Loula later recalled.[21] Joe loved his vegetable garden and raising hogs. For three years the couple lived in rural Rayne, and Cleoma hated it. She missed her friends and weekly card games. More than anything else, the "city girl" missed the activity and urban interconnectivity of Crowley. The years in Rayne were rendered even more difficult after Loula contracted polio. Steel-guitar innovator Julius "Papa Cairo" Lamperez told Joe and Cleoma about the crippled children's hospital in Shreveport, and the couple drove their daughter there for treatments on a regular basis.

Loula's illness emotionally strained her mother. In accordance with hospital regulations, Cleoma and Joe could not comfort their daughter with hugs and caresses. The concerned parents thus sat in their daughter's room struggling to maintain their composure and their distance. Moreover, during extended hospitalizations, Cleoma could not stay with her daughter in Shreveport but had to return to Rayne. The stress of the separation wore heavily on the devoted mother. She needed the extended network of her family, and she longed to return to Crowley. Eventually they did, although Joe never gave up his dreams of the country, and ultimately he kept a pig hidden in a shed behind the home he was renting in town.[22]

The return to Crowley rejuvenated Cleoma. The family rented a small, three-room shotgun home, and Cleoma planted flowers in the yard. Soon the weekly card games started again. The Falcons bought a radio, listening religiously on the weekends to the Grand Ole Opry. Neighbors came to listen to the radio, and Loula remembers being the "big shots on the block" because of the radio. Mathilde Breaux remained leery of new technology and expressed frustration when she saw her daughter teaching Loula to operate the contraption. The trips to the Shreveport hospital continued, but in Crowley Cleoma had the broad network of family and friends to help her cope. One of those friends was accordionist and fiddler Lawrence Walker, who often sat up with Loula when she was ill. Loula remembered Walker as a "gentle, kind, humble man."[23]

Perhaps Cleoma's respectability remained intact because, although she pushed the boundaries of Cajun society by her public performances, she also committed herself to the family, that most basic of Cajun institutions. The family, including both the nuclear family and the sprawling extended family of blood kin and honorary relatives, lies at the heart of Cajun society. Cleoma's devotion to her brothers continued until her death, and she doted exceedingly on her daughter. Every morning, regardless of the time they had returned from a dance, Cleoma and Joe greeted Loula at the breakfast table before chauffeuring their daughter to school. She made Loula's clothes and brought her hot home-cooked meals every day at lunchtime, while other children ate cold lunches on campus. Singing was Cleoma's profession, and so she generally did not sing inside her home, except when Loula asked her to.[24]

Cleoma also maintained an orderly home. Perhaps this tendency came from her early responsibilities in her mother's home, but it may also have been a response to the rowdy nature of the dancehall environment. At home, Cleoma created a clean, stable escape from the world in the form of a comfortable, secure, domestic space. Her home was a Victorian ideal, and it stood in stark contrast to the disorder at Amede's house. Amede let his large brood run wild. Loula recalled enjoying her visits to Uncle Amede's decrepit rented house because she could jump on the beds. Ophy's home was always temporary and sparse, while Clifford's was ruled by a tightfisted wife who imposed order through her own will. Cleoma tried to maintain a peaceful and orderly haven for her family.[25]

Cleoma did break with tradition on one home matter. She taught her daughter English and not French. Indeed, Loula did not learn to speak French until she married. Loula speculates that her mother taught her English because she wanted her daughter to be "different." But more than likely there was a deeper reason. Cleoma, unlike other Cajun women of her time, had traveled widely around southwestern Louisiana and to New Orleans, San Antonio, Dallas, and New York. During the 1920s and 1930s, Cleoma saw the world and its possibilities—possibilities that were tied to speaking English. Women generally transmitted the primary family language to Cajun children. Although most Cajuns before the Second World War were probably bilingual, French was still the spoken language at home. That changed after the war when exposure to the opportunities of wider America became apparent to Cajuns. After the war French speaking plummeted. Although the reasons for this decline remain debatable, the conscious role played by mothers in making English the first language of their children must have been important. Many may have made the same choice that Cleoma did—she gave her child a chance to engage the economic opportunities afforded by the broader American culture.[26]

Lawrence Walker, who had been so helpful to Cleoma and Loula, was also a musical innovator who in the early 1930s was quietly forging a revolution in Cajun music that would force Joe and Cleoma to adapt to changing tastes. That revolution was still embryonic when Joe and Cleoma returned to the recording studio in 1934. The Depression had eased somewhat, and recording companies were once again interested in recording new material. The companies marketed these new records in a budget series designed to accommodate the pocketbooks of cash-strapped music lovers. Most major labels created subsidiary "dime store" lines like Bluebird (Victor) and Vocalion (Brunswick), but Decca became the king of the budget labels. Indeed, Decca aimed all of its issues at the budget-conscious buyer, selling its 78s for thirty-five cents, a bargain compared to the seventy-five-cent tag on earlier records. Decca's basic philosophy was that it could maintain its profitability by selling more records at a lower price. Decca's roster read like a who's who of American popular music; it included Bing Crosby and Louis Armstrong along with hillbilly stars like Stuart Hamblen and the future governor of Louisiana, Jimmie Davis.[27]

Bluebird got the Falcons back before the microphone on August 8, 1934. They recorded four sides at the San Antonio session. In December of that same year, the duo escorted their colleague and Afro-Creole accordionist Amede Ardoin by bus to New York City for a marathon Decca session. When the traveling musicians reached Hoboken, New Jersey, they boarded a ferry to cross the icy Hudson River. As the ferry crossed the river, the bus filled knee deep with freezing water. Cleoma recounted the adventure to Loula, who explained:

> Mom and dad, and a couple of members of the band, were on a Greyhound Bus and they were on a ferry going to Coney Island to make a record, the French records . . . and the ferry started to sink. And mom was sitting apart from daddy and it was pitch dark in the bus. Her thoughts were on me, that, you know, she might never see me again. She knew I was well cared for [back in Crowley], but she was still missing me. And they were rescued and brought to the recording studio and Mom made it into a song.[28]

The Falcons cut twelve sides, including the "Crowley Waltz," the song Cleoma had written for Loula. The session also saw Cleoma experimenting with blues material in the mode of Jimmie Rodgers ("Ouvrez Grand Ma Fenetre") and sentimental fare ("Mes Yeux Bleu"). These songs marked a growing tendency within Cajun music to incorporate hillbilly material (as country music was then called).[29]

By the time of the budget-label sessions, Joe and Cleoma had settled into their roles as professional musicians. Loula remembered her parents playing dances every night. The dancehall faithful continued to treat the duo "like royalty," and they were among the few musicians who could say that they earned their living strictly from music. Joe and Cleoma viewed their music as a "job they went to, and they didn't bring home" with them. The Falcons enjoyed the country music that had started to gain popularity in southern Louisiana, and Cleoma learned rapidly that people liked hillbilly songs that were translated into French. French was a language that Cleoma reserved for singing.[30]

The Falcons earned little money from their recordings. Most of their income derived from the dances they played throughout the region, such as those at Alex Hernandez's bar in Judice. The social norm distinguishing male and female space in public settings still was obvious inside Cajun dancehalls in the twenties. Unmarried women and men sat in segregated areas, only interacting on the dance floor under the watchful eyes of chaperones. "Yes, and the girls would come with their mothers and fathers, and they would go home with their mothers and fathers," explained Joe Falcon in an interview with cultural geographer Lauren Post. And, if an unmarried girl left the respectable confines of the hall unescorted, "It was good night Irene, and she couldn't come back."[31]

During the early 1930s, at the height of the Falcons' popularity, dancehalls were in the process of changing from highly regulated social spaces where mothers carefully watched their daughters and maintained propriety to male-dominated spaces where alcohol was freely sold and often liberally consumed. Musicians, even respected ones, were often seen as disreputable people. Women who publicly performed were considered suspect, and a woman as talented and beautiful as Cleoma Falcon certainly attracted hostile glances from jealous female dancers. She also received unwanted advances from male fans. At one dance, a drunken male patron wandered up to the bandstand and snarled some untoward remarks to Cleoma. Angry, she kicked the man in his face with her high-heeled, pointed-toed shoes, putting out his eye. Cleoma tried her very best to maintain a respectable image. She dressed nicely, always coifed her hair in the latest fashion, wore rouge, and seemed to enjoy her pointed high-heel shoes. But she could and would defend herself in an environment that was increasingly becoming rambunctious. Cleoma probably learned to defend herself while she tended to her brothers as a teenager. The Breaux Frères were well known for their propensity to fight at dances. If no one present wanted to fight, the brothers fought each other, especially if they had been drinking. Joe developed a strong taste for alcohol and often joined in the battles. Only Clifford seemed reluctant to fight and usually found himself caught in the middle as he tried to calm the protagonists.[32]

During the early 1930s, the American South's increasingly industrialized economy wrought dramatic shifts in Cajun music. Bilingual Cajun swing ensembles—string bands sans accordion modeled after western swing outfits in neighboring Texas and hot jazz bands from New Orleans—performed a variety of traditional tunes and American popular music that catered to the evolving demands of local audiences, who increasingly sought employment in the region's oil patch. By 1935, Crowley was at the center of the string band movement. The commercial hub became home to the Hackberry Ramblers, Leo Soileau and his Four Aces, and pioneering Cajun steel guitarist Papa Cairo.[33]

To remain viable performing artists, Joe and Cleoma transformed their sound to keep in step with the times. Cleoma sang hillbilly hits translated into French such as "Careless Love," "Nobody's Darlin' But Mine," and "Just Because," all standards of the western swing movement. They added Moise Morgan to their combo to incorporate the then-in-demand fiddle sound into their material. By their February 1937 recording sessions in Dallas, Cleoma was covering such popular songs as "Hand Me Down My Walking Cane," the Carter Family's "Bonnie Blue Eyes," and hot Cajun-French versions of the Fats Waller classics "Lulu's Back in Town" and "It's a Sin to Tell a Lie." Later that year in what would prove to be Cleoma's last commercial sessions, she recorded a French version of "Love Letters in the Sand," a popular song made famous by fellow Louisianian Gene Austin. During her final sessions, Decca granted the gifted musician the latitude to take the spotlight as lead vocalist on multiple sides, an opportunity that she had not enjoyed since the Falcons' second foray into Columbia's recording studios in 1928. These recordings placed commercial Cajun music's only feminine voice in the foreground of the cross-pollinated Cajun swing movement.[34] Cleoma seized the advantage afforded by her contemporaries like the Carter women (country music) and Lydia Mendoza (ethnic music), who helped pave the way for women in America's hegemonic male-dominated recording industry.

The last four years of Cleoma Falcon's life were difficult. In 1937 after returning from a recording session (probably in December), a moving vehicle caught her sweater and dragged the helpless pedestrian for nearly a quarter mile. Her body badly damaged, Cleoma took a long recuperation period. Her musical career slowed, and Joe began performing more often with an expanded band that included his brothers-in-law and featured as much country as Cajun material, his favorite songs being covers of Ernest Tubb honky-tonk numbers. He started to play the drums. He and Cleoma continued to do radio work, and she reportedly made several transcription recordings for airplay. But her health continued to suffer, and in 1941 she died at the age of thirty-five. Cleoma's passing profoundly affected Joe. The accordionist stopped drinking and smoking cigars, in part to save money so he could financially support fourteen-year-old Loula. Falcon paid homage to his late wife's memory by recommitting himself to their daughter, "because daddy wanted me to be able to have something."[35]

Cleoma Breaux Falcon's life straddled many worlds. She came of age in an urban southern town in a family that placed great confidence in traditional Cajun values, which were rooted in a rural frontier past. Her mother's training and her example in keeping the family fed, clothed, and together enabled Cleoma to join her brothers and later her husband in the effort to provide income for the family. Cleoma played and sang folk music and helped transform that vernacular expression into a commercial idiom that reflected interaction with a widening world. Her career took her out of the traditional Cajun homemaker role and onto the performance stage in venues that were predominantly male.

At the same time, she cultivated a stable domestic environment for her extended family. Cleoma Falcon is representative of the transformation of Cajun society in the twentieth century, a transformation that retained and adapted old values in a new context.

Despite her success as a musician, Cleoma Breaux Falcon was an anomaly in the Cajun music scene in the era before the folk revival of the 1960s. Few Cajun women took up public performance in those years, the only other major exceptions being Joe's second wife, Theresa, and his niece Solange. And their careers may have been advanced by Joe, who knew the value of a female singer from the success of his first wife. But the decision of most Cajun women in the forties and fifties to engage in the traditional jobs of full-time homemaking and motherhood rather than follow in her footsteps cannot be lain at Cleoma's door. She presented a strong model of a professional female musician who maintained her public respectability. Her success stands as a tribute to her ability not only to survive but to thrive in the male-centered world of Cajun music. Those spiked-heeled, pointed-toed, size-four shoes have proven very hard to fill.

NOTES

1. Mary Alice Fontenot, *Acadia Parish: A History* (Baton Rouge: Claitor's, 1976), 2:97–150.

2. Most information regarding Cleoma Falcon's personal and family life is drawn from an interview with her daughter, Loula Falcon Langlinais, conducted on June 20, 2006, by Ryan A. Brasseaux and Pat Johnson (hereinafter cited as Langlinais interview).

3. Ibid.

4. Ibid.

5. Duhon's remarks to Kevin S. Fontenot, Mermaid Lounge, New Orleans, 1997. The McGee quote is from Ann Allen Savoy, *Cajun Music: A Reflection of a People* (Eunice, La.: Bluebird Press, 1984), 91.

6. On the importance of department stores for the fashionable modern woman, see Joshua Zeitz, *Flapper: A Madcap Story of Sex, Style, Celebrity, and the Women Who Made America Modern* (New York: Crown Publishers, 2006), 202–8. Bow was at the height of her popularity from 1928 to 1930. She had first gained attention with the release of *It* in 1927. See David Stenn, *Clara Bow: Runnin' Wild* (New York: Doubleday, 1988). On the public performance of Cajun women see Lisa E. Richardson, "The Public and Private Domains of Cajun Women Musicians in Southwest Louisiana," in *Accordions, Fiddles, Two Step, and Swing: A Cajun Music Reader*, ed. Ryan A. Brasseaux and Kevin S. Fontenot (Lafayette: Center for Louisiana Studies, 2006), 77–82. One of the few examinations of gender roles in a Cajun town is in Marjorie R. Esman, *Henderson, Louisiana: Cultural Adaptation in a Cajun Community* (New York: Holt, Rinehart and Winston, 1985), esp. 39–54.

7. Biographical information on Joseph Falcon is drawn from Lauren C. Post, "Joseph C. Falcon, Accordion Player and Singer: A Biographical Sketch," *Louisiana History* 11 (Winter 1970): 63–79, Joseph Falcon, undated interview by Ralph Rinzler, Center for Louisiana Studies, Lafayette, and Langlinais interview.

8. For a general discussion of how these sessions worked, see Robert M. W. Dixon and John Godrich, *Recording the Blues* (London: Studio Vista, 1970), which discusses the numerous sessions held in the South during the 1920s and 1930s.

9. Post, "Joseph C. Falcon," 66.

10. All session and discographical information is taken from Tony Russell, *Country Music Records: A Discography, 1921–1942* (Oxford: Oxford University Press, 2004), 126–27, 334–36. See Barry Jean Ancelet, "Rednecks, Roughnecks, and the Bosco Stomp: The Arrival of the Oil Industry in the Marais Bouleur," *Attakapas Gazette* 22 (Spring 1987): 29–34, for a detailed discussion of the area.

11. For an example of the belief that Cleoma is both the author and singer, see vocalist Maria McKee's remarks in the liner notes to *Evangeline Made: A Tribute to Cajun Music*, Vanguard Records 79585-2.

12. Langlinas interview.

13. Richardson, "Public and Private Domains."

14. See Pamela Grundy, "'We Always Tried to Be Good People': Respectability, Crazy Water Crystals, and Hillbilly Music on the Air, 1933–1935," *Journal of American History* 81 (March 1995): 1591–1620. On West Virginia, see Erynn Marshall, *Music in the Air Somewhere: The Shifting Borders of West Virginia's Fiddle and Song Traditions* (Morgantown: West Virginia University Press, 2006), 104–19, quote on 197. For Lynn's comments, see Nicholas Dawidoff, *In the Country of Country: People and Places in American Music* (New York: Pantheon Books, 1997), 63. On Parker, see Kristine McCusker, "Bury Me Beneath the Willow: Linda Parker and Definitions of Tradition on the National Barn Dance, 1932–1935," in *A Boy Named Sue: Gender and Country Music*, ed. Kristine M. McCusker and Diane Pecknold (Jackson: University Press of Mississippi, 2004), 3–23. Carpenter's comments are remembered by her grandson, Kevin S. Fontenot. After she made this statement, Fontenot asked, "What about Kitty Wells?" "Well," Carpenter responded, "there ain't nobody like Kitty."

15. On Veach, see Elizabeth Schlappi, *Roy Acuff: The Smokey Mountain Boy* (Gretna, La.: Pelican, 1993), 73; on Ledford, see her comments in Cary Ginell's liner notes to *Red Foley: Old Shep*, Bear Family Records, BCD 16759 FL, 2006, 73. For the role of teasing in male idiocultures, see Gary Alan Fine, "In the Company of Men: Female Accommodation and the Folk Culture of Male Groups," in *Manly Traditions: The Folk Roots of American Masculinities*, ed. Simon J. Bronner (Bloomington: Indiana University Press, 2005), 61–76.

16. Langlinais interview.

17. Carl Lindahl describes this scene at its height in the years following the Second World War in "*Grand Texas*: Accordion Music and Lifestyle on the Cajun Frontiere," *French American Review* 62 (Winter 1991): 26–36.

18. Falcon interview (undated) by Ralph Rinzler, Center for Louisiana Studies, Lafayette, and Langlinais interview.

19. Esman, *Henderson, Louisiana*, 41.

20. This discussion of the Breaux family is based on the Langlinais interview and interviews with Lucien "Dale" Breaux and Randy Falcon, conducted by Pat Johnson in 2006. Dale Breaux is the son of Clifford Breaux and Randy Falcon is the nephew of Joe Falcon. All three interviewees attest to family problems and particularly the disorder that reigned in the Amede Breaux household. Loula remembered enjoying visiting Amede's home because she could "run wild" and contrasted it sharply with the atmosphere at Clifford's home.

21. Langlinais interview.

22. Ibid.

23. Ibid.

24. Ibid.

25. Ibid.; Breaux interview by Pat Johnson, 2006.

26. The decline of Cajun French needs further investigation, especially regarding the choices made by women in the shift to English. The decline of Cajun French is a central theme of Shane K. Bernard, *The Cajuns: Americanization of a People* (Jackson: University Press of Mississippi, 2003).

27. Langlinais interview.

28. Ibid.

29. Post, "Joseph C. Falcon," 74; Amede Ardoin also saw his life flash before his eyes. The black Creole composed and recorded "I'm Never Coming Home"—a lament capturing his own personal nightmare on the same sinking Greyhound bus—at the 1934 New York Decca session. See Amede Ardoin, *I'm Never Coming Home*, Arhoolie CD 7007, 1995.

30. Langlinais interview.

31. Lauren C. Post, "Joseph C. Falcon," in *Accordions, Fiddlers, Two Step, and Swing*, 330.

32. Randy Falcon interview by Pat Johnson, 2006.

33. For the changing southern economy during the first half of the twentieth century, see Jack Temple Kirby, *Rural Worlds Lost: The American South, 1920–1960* (Baton Rouge: Louisiana State University Press, 1987), and Neil Foley, *The White Scourge: Mexicans, Blacks, and Poor Whites in Texas Cotton Culture* (Berkeley: University of California Press, 1999). For Cajun involvement with the region's petroleum economy, see Carl A. Brasseaux, "Grand Texas: The Cajun Migration to Texas," in *The French in Texas*, ed. François Lagarde (Austin: University of Texas Press, 2003), 273–86, and Dean R. Louder and Michael Leblanc, "The Cajuns of East Texas," in *French America: Mobility, Identity, and Minority Experience Across the Continent*, ed. Dean R. Louder and Eric Waddell (Baton Rouge: Louisiana State University Press, 1993), 301–15. For shifts in Cajun music and the genre's connection to Texas, see Kevin S. Fontenot, "You Can't Go Wrong, If You Play It Right: Cajun Music and Zydeco," in *Ethnic and Border Music: A Regional Exploration*, ed. Norm Cohen (Westport, Conn.: Greenwood Press, 2007), 1–21, Ben Sandmel, liner notes, *Luderin Darbone's Hackberry Ramblers Early Recordings: 1935–1950*, Arhoolie 7050, 2003, Luderin Darbone, "A Brief History of the Hackberry Ramblers," in *Accordions, Fiddles, Two Step and Swing*, 399–406, Tony Russell, "Leo Soileau," in *Accordions, Fiddles, Two Step and Swing*, 383–88, and William A. Owens, *Tell Me a Story, Sing Me a Song: A Texas Chronicle* (Austin: University of Texas Press, 1983), 116–52.

34. All session information is taken from Russell, *Country Music Records*. The majority of Cleoma's Decca sides have not been reissued from the original 78s. A few songs like "Lulu's Back in Town," "It's a Sin to Tell a Lie," and "Hand Me Down My Walking Cane" are featured on the British JSP record label (*Cajun Early Recordings: Important Swamp Hits Remastered*, JSP 7726C, disk B, 2004).

35. Langlinais interview.

Caroline Dormon
(1888–1971)

Louisiana's Cultural Conservator

DAYNA BOWKER LEE

❀ ❀ ❀

The pivotal role of Caroline Dormon in Louisiana forestry and natural resource conservation has received extensive attention. Equally as important, but not as well remembered, is her dedication to "Indian work," as one of her associates described her efforts.[1] From the 1920s to her death in 1971, Dormon worked tirelessly to protect Louisiana's ancient archaeological sites, to create ethnographical records of modern Louisiana Native communities, and to provide those communities with economic assistance by promoting the sale of Native arts and crafts—most particularly, Chitimacha basketry. In pursuit of these goals, she built strong alliances with scholars and professionals in the Office of Indian Affairs (OIA), the Bureau of American Ethnology (BAE), and the Smithsonian Institution, making her knowledge and assistance crucial to the success of federally funded projects in her home state. Through her long association with John Reed Swanton, chief ethnographer for the BAE, Dormon exerted profound influence on anthropological research conducted in Louisiana as documented in a vast collection of correspondence, journals, publications, and artwork housed at the Cammie G. Henry Research Center. But why did Dormon become so involved with Louisiana Indians? And how in particular did her work impact Louisiana's tribes and ethnographic research in Louisiana? This essay explores the origins of her interest in Native Americans, her work with the Chitimacha, and the professional relationships that she fostered as a result of her "Indian work."

Born in 1888 at her family's summer retreat, Briarwood, in rural Natchitoches Parish, Dormon felt more at home outdoors than inside. Her parents, James and Caroline, encouraged their children—James, Virginia, Allen, Benjamin,

CAROLINE DORMON

Canoeing on an unidentified lake. Courtesy of Northwestern State University
of Louisiana, Watson Memorial Library, Cammie Henry Research Center
(Caroline Dorman Collection, DO.1).

George, and Caroline (two other children, Edwin and Paul, died very young)—
to explore the longleaf pine forests of Kisatchie Wold where they developed a
deep connection to the natural world. Even in her later years, Dormon seized
every opportunity to escape to Kisatchie Forest to camp, fish, and practice the
woods lore she had learned as a child.[2] She felt a strong affinity for the outdoors
and at an early age came to associate Indians with the natural world. She wrote,
"We were rather delicate children, of a nervous temperament; so . . . our parents
made it possible for us to spend every moment we were outside the schoolroom
in the woods. . . . And we didn't *play* Indians—we *were* Indians."[3]

While she relegated Indians to the realm of nature, at an early age her parents made certain that she gained a broader perspective. They subscribed to
and encouraged their children to read scholarly and government publications
exploring the history and diverse cultures of ancient Americans as well as the
myriad problems faced by the contemporary tribes. Coming of age at a time in
which many Americans believed that American Indian cultures inevitably faced
extinction, Dormon was influenced by the publications of the BAE most aptly
termed "salvage" ethnography.[4]

BAE researchers attempted to record and interpret archaeological sites before
humans and their machines could destroy them. Believing in the early 1900s
that American Indian cultures, if not the people themselves, were facing extinction, they documented native languages, songs, stories, belief systems, and
material culture. The annual BAE reports and bulletins found their way into the
Dormon library and fascinated the young Caroline. Like her love for the forests
of Louisiana, this childhood partially spent in the family library helps to explain
Dormon's affinity for Louisiana's first people.

Her lifelong interest in American Indians was thus heavily shaped by her belief that American Indians, tied in her mind to nature, were also, like old growth
forests, quickly disappearing. Her childhood recollection of not simply playing
Indian, but *being* Indian, positions her as one among many non-Indians in the
early twentieth century who sought refuge from the modern world in their
perceived primitive and natural state of Indianness.[5]

But Dormon was not just being Indian; she was actually interested in the lives
of modern Native individuals, and she in fact dedicated much of her life to Louisiana's tribal communities. Because her interest in Native Americans stemmed
from her perception of Indians as "a part of nature, she believed that natural
resource conservation and the cultural conservation of the original inhabitants
of Louisiana and other states were symbiotic and inseparable endeavors."[6] She
combined her efforts to promote forest and native plant conservation with her
campaign to protect ancient sites and to promote economic opportunities for

the Chitimacha, Tunica-Biloxi-Ofo, Koasati (or Coushatta), Choctaw, and the Houma of Louisiana, the Cherokee of North Carolina, and the Caddo in Oklahoma, who had been forced to leave their Louisiana and Texas homelands by the federal government. Dormon's efforts on behalf of these groups formed a significant part of her life's work to protect and preserve Louisiana's archaeological and cultural treasures.

Chronic ill health and her unconventional upbringing made it difficult for Dormon to hold a standard wage-paying job. After graduating from Judson College in Alabama in 1907, Dormon served briefly as a public schoolteacher before succumbing to the primal attraction of the pine forest of her birth. In 1918, the thirty-year-old Dormon "retired to private life," moving with her older sister Virginia, who had worked as a home extension agent and teacher, to Briarwood. Caroline planned to "put into usable form the store of information which I had been gathering all my life."[7] She turned Briarwood into a natural canvas, creating a preserve for native plants and taking a special interest in the Louisiana iris. The support of a sister, best friend, and confidant enabled her to fulfill her ambitions and sustained her through frequent illnesses. When Virginia married Dr. G. F. Miller in 1921, the younger sister accompanied the couple on their honeymoon. Although Dr. Miller persuaded his wife to relocate with him to Alabama, Virginia abandoned her husband to return home to Briarwood within a year of the ill-fated marriage. Virginia apparently believed that Caroline needed her more than Dr. Miller ever would.[8]

In 1920 Dormon established new connections that would sustain her interests in conservation and in Louisiana's native peoples. That year, the Louisiana Department of Conservation hired Dormon to coordinate educational outreach and public relations. She also joined the Society of American Foresters as the first female associate member. From this platform, Dormon engaged in years of aggressive lobbying of state leaders and the U.S. Forest Service, which resulted ten years later in the establishment of Kisatchie National Forest (the only national forest in Louisiana).[9] The same year that Dormon began to work in forestry, the Louisiana Federation of Women's Clubs (LFWC) appointed her state chairman of conservation, although she considered herself "in no sense a clubwoman."[10] These networks—bureaucratic and organizational—gave Dormon the necessary allies for the work on which she would soon embark: identifying and protecting American Indian sites and promoting the arts of the Native peoples of Louisiana.

These new associations encouraged Dormon in the early 1920s to seek out surviving tribal communities. Chauffeured by Virginia and occasionally accompanied by their matronly Aunt Dosia, she took to the back roads of Louisiana.

Her undated notebooks document extensive ethnographic field studies among the Tunica-Biloxi-Ofo in Avoyelles Parish; the Chitimacha in St. Mary Parish; the Koasati and Choctaw in Allen, Jefferson Davis, and Vernon parishes; the Houma in Lafourche and Terrebonne parishes; the Eastern Cherokee in North Carolina; and the Caddo in Oklahoma. Dormon worked with tribal elders to preserve oral traditions and language, record genealogies, photograph people and places, document craft traditions, and encourage the work of traditional artists, especially weavers for whom she brokered baskets through her many connections.[11]

The Dormons and their associates in the LFWC joined a movement challenging the assumptions and goals of an earlier generation that had promoted a federal policy designed to detribalize American Indians, liquidate reservations, and assimilate Native individuals into American culture through boarding-school education and other means, rendering them "productive," individualistic, and "proper" U.S. citizens. The OIA, aided by groups such as the Women's National Indian Association (WNIA), sought to assimilate Indians into mainstream American culture. The WNIA had advocated "civilized" industrial education (farming, dressmaking, textile arts, carpentry, housekeeping, etc.) and promoted the Indian Industries League. No longer insisting that Indians abandon their cultural traditions, members of a newer generation, including Neltje Doubleday, revalued traditional arts such as basketry as beautiful and marketable products that could provide support for Indian communities.[12]

Making an impassioned plea for using tribal arts to promote cultural pride and provide economic stability, Doubleday advised OIA administrators and clubwomen to develop basketry "industries" and market tribal arts. She persuaded Estelle Reel, superintendent of schools for the OIA, to add basketry classes to most Indian school curricula. Indian boarding school programs like the one at Hampton Institute, originally designed to assimilate Indian youth into American society by robbing them of language, religion, and tribal ties, began to include basketry in the industrial and domestic training regimens for Indian students. Basket weaving, now recognized as a domestically centered, highly marketable women's art, became a standard in the education of young Indian boarding school girls. American Indian basketry appeared in major department stores, school gift shops, and nonprofit stores like the Woman's Exchange in New York by the end of the nineteenth century. As a result of such efforts, philanthropic women of means helped to create new social, educational, and economic programs to address the needs of American Indians.[13]

By 1906, when Dormon was a young woman of eighteen, this movement had reached Louisiana. Doubleday established contact with the Chitimacha in

Charenton, whose basketry had been renowned since the early eighteenth century as a popular commodity in the regional market. She worked with Mary McIlhenny Bradford and Sarah McIlhenny, clubwomen and philanthropists from Avery Island, Louisiana, and neighbors of the Chitimacha. Together they developed a basketry industry in the Chitimacha village and expanded the market for Chitimacha basketry to northeastern collectors, museums, and retail stores, using the Bradford wealth and extensive contacts to exhibit and promote Chitimacha basketry nationwide. Although it is not known if Dormon knew about Doubleday, who died in 1918, she certainly knew of Bradford and her work with the Chitimacha basket weavers, which invigorated the tradition by making basketry more profitable and encouraged young women to take up the craft.[14] Knowing that other women had found ways to help Indians undoubtedly inspired Dormon to start making her own visits to the Chitimacha and other native villages.

Quickly discovering that she had no patience for the bureaucracy of state government, Dormon retired once again to Briarwood in 1923. By her own admission, her singular ambition was "to stay in the woods, fooling with plants and birds, . . . or once in a while slipping away on an Indian hunt."[15] Dormon was tireless in her crusade to educate the citizens of Louisiana about preserving the state's natural and cultural resources. Not wealthy like Doubleday or the McIlhenny sisters, Dormon drove herself unceasingly. Her educational campaigns took a toll on her already delicate health. "This publicity business is slowly killing me. . . . [but] all my friends . . . seem to think it necessary for me to be bandied about at teas, luncheons, and what not."[16] Determined to share her passions and knowledge and to earn a living on her own terms, Dormon continued to lecture and publish regularly. "I'm so crazy to write . . . and I can't help believing I can make a living at it. Tho not a *fat one*. But Oh to be free to *write some* of the things stored up waiting all these years."[17] Her presentations and close associations with women's clubs, the Girl and Boy Scouts, Camp Fire Girls, Daughters of the American Revolution, professional and educational associations, and garden clubs generated statewide interest in conservation that crossed age, gender, economic, and social boundaries. Dormon not only supported tribal artisans and marketed their crafts but also visited their villages to document endangered traditions and record dying languages. Through her network of friends and colleagues, she forged important connections between Louisiana Indians and those scholars and politicians who might improve the sad conditions under which they struggled and bring them some small measure of recognition and assistance.

These efforts also extended to attempts to change federal policies toward Indians. Dormon found a receptive audience in the LFWC, an affiliate of the General Federation of Women's Clubs (GFWC), a nationwide service organization that fostered ideals of volunteerism, charity, and philanthropy. The clubwomen sought to redress social and economic inequalities facing disadvantaged segments of the population, especially American Indians. In 1921, the GFWC created the Indian Welfare Committee, which worked to provide better health care and educational facilities for American Indians. Supported by the GFWC, John Collier, who later served as commissioner of Indian Affairs under President Franklin Roosevelt, established the American Indian Defense Association (AIDA) to provide legal services for American Indians. Under the auspices of AIDA, he sponsored a series of articles raising questions about the federal management of Indian affairs.[18] Dormon became involved in this movement at a very propitious time as federal assimilation policy was coming under sustained attack.

The criticisms of federal policy forced an official response. Secretary of the Interior Hubert Work commissioned the Brookings Institute of Government Research to carry out a study to examine American Indian social and economic conditions. A key recommendation of the final report, *The Problem of Indian Administration* (commonly called the Merriam report), was that the federal government support native crafts, especially basketry.[19] The report concluded that economic success in tribal families could only be achieved by supplementing a man's income with the contributions of women "able to follow at home traditional arts highly respected by discriminating white customers."[20] Dormon enthusiastically endorsed the Merriam report as a vindication of the work she had already begun.

Dormon received another appointment from the LFWC in 1937. This time she was called on to serve as advisory chairman for the Division of Indian Welfare. During her tenure, Dormon promoted a "New Deal" for American Indians, urged clubwomen to foster protection of ancient sites, and marshaled support for John Collier, then serving as commissioner of Indian Affairs. That same year he received the first of many letters from Dormon. She complained to Collier about "the propaganda put out by the enemies of the administration," which she described as "so little, mean, and at the same time so insidious [sic] that I can think of nothing to equal it—except the treatment of the Indians in the past." She asked Collier, "Where are the friends of the Indian? Why are they not filling the newspapers and magazines with the *truth*, to counterbalance the avalanche of slimy untruths being spread abroad by the enemies of the present Indian Policy?"[21] Collier's thanks for her "quiet and effective work in the interest of truth" marked the beginnings of a lively correspondence during his tenure as commissioner. She shared and encouraged Collier's support for Native arts, crafts, and traditions and kept him informed about local public opinion and the issues facing American Indians in Louisiana. They continued to correspond after his departure from the Indian office in 1945.[22]

In Louisiana, Dormon followed in the footsteps of Doubleday and Bradford in the 1920s and 1930s. She assumed the role of broker for tribal artisans, helping them market their crafts at both the state and national level. Through articles about tribal crafts traditions that she published in art and nature magazines and through her network of philanthropic women friends, Dormon worked to place Louisiana Indian material culture in museums and in the hands of collectors. She purchased or marketed handmade items like baskets and blowguns that evoked the tribal heritage and natural world of Louisiana Indians. John Swanton of the BAE aided her efforts, buying several items himself and arranging more substantial sales.[23] Dormon continued to promote tribal arts until well after World War II, by which time most of her closest tribal friends had either died or become too old to produce arts.

Dormon developed many enduring friendships with Native women during her lifetime, but she was particularly close to the Chitimacha basket makers who maintained what she considered to be the finest cane basketry tradition in the Southeast. Like Bradford before her, Dormon discovered that Chitimacha basketry was one of the most marketable of tribal crafts and made it an important part of her research, carefully documenting dyes, techniques, and processes in the Chitimacha language. Theirs was an ancient tradition practiced within almost the same cultural parameters as it had been for hundreds of years, as Chitimacha women continued to gather the materials, process plant dyes, and replicate designs rooted in the Mississippian Tradition, ca. 1000 to 1500 A.D. Dormon visited the Chitimacha village regularly and developed a close friendship with traditional chief Benjamin Paul, his wife, Christine, and his younger sister Pauline. A series of letters written to Dormon by Christine and Pauline between 1930 and 1942 document the deep concern and affection she felt for these women and they for her. The letters provide a rare glimpse into basketry from the weavers' perspective as few Louisiana Indians, and even fewer Indian women, were literate at that time.[24]

Dormon worked closely with Christine and Pauline to document Chitimacha basketry traditions. To preserve this knowledge, Dormon shared the results of her research with fellow artists and scholars and sought to answer their questions about Indian culture. She attempted, for example, to get samples of *pow-ash* (dock root) for Mrs. Smith, a guest at Melrose Plantation, the home of Dormon's friend, Cammie Garrett Henry, which also served as an artists' and writers' retreat. Mrs. Smith apparently had great knowledge about plant dyes. Dormon understood the difficulties the Pauls might encounter while trying to gather the plants, writing to Cammie Henry that the "poor things have no way to get anywhere, and they probably had to go some distance for the plants."[25] As Dormon had predicted, Christine wrote that Mrs. Smith would need to "wait until [we] go get them. . . . We all have bad cold here, so much bad weather."[26] Conditions were dire on the Chitimacha reservation, and for the Paul family particularly.

The Pauls' letters document the extreme poverty and poor conditions that pervaded the small tribal village at Charenton despite Dormon's efforts to help them economically. Several accomplished weavers died during the years of their correspondence, including Adele Darden, the granddaughter of the famed chief Soulier Rouge.[27] Although living month to month herself, Dormon stretched her own thin resources to help the weavers and their families, often sending gifts, small loans, and advances on baskets to be made.

As the wife of the chief, Christine Paul had for some time functioned as a kind of community broker, gathering the baskets from the network of weavers and transporting them to the McIlhenny sisters and later to Dormon. During the lean times of the Depression, however, Christine and Pauline used their own basketry to fill as many of Dormon's orders as they could. "I still macking [*sic*] Baskets try get my liveing [*sic*] but time its so hard here. I send big lots Baskets off and can get pay before end of this month and need some money to bring Pauline to the Doctor because she is so sick."[28] Later, Christine wrote: "Pauline . . . [is] little better . . . but she macking [*sic*] Baskets. . . . We might sell some for Christmas, I hope so."[29]

In most of the letters, baskets in production or in transit to Dormon are mentioned. "I am working on the Basket and try to not make one alike, I have twelve of them made."[30] The weavers appreciated any attention Dormon was able to bring to their craft. "The magazine [*Holland's*] is fine. I believed its [*sic*] called for more works in the baskets [business]."[31] Caroline Dormon continued to publicize, purchase, and sell basketry for the Chitimacha weavers until her close friends died: Christine Paul in the late 1930s, and Pauline in the early 1940s.

Not content with documenting tribal traditions, Dormon also sought to gain knowledge about Indian cultures from scholars. She originally initiated a correspondence with Swanton at the BAE for this purpose. Except for an occasional carbon copy of one of her letters, only his responses are archived in the Dormon collection. His letters do provide, however, a glimpse into Dormon's inquisitive mind and reveal the extent of her already impressive, albeit informal, anthropological education. She sent him pages of questions on topics ranging from ancient origins to linguistic peculiarities, constantly challenging him to remember and reexamine long-held assumptions.

Swanton, who had conducted ethnographic research with the Tunica, Koasati, and Chitimacha years earlier, obviously welcomed the opportunity to communicate with someone as interested as he was in Louisiana groups. His first letter to Dormon in 1929 made this clear. "Dear Madam," Swanton began. "We are glad to note your interest in the primitive people of your state . . . [and] will be happy to benefit from any new discoveries you make."[32] Their correspondence started shortly after the death of Swanton's wife, at a time when his enthusiasm for field studies was low and public funding for ethnographic research scarce. Dormon pressed the ethnographer, comfortably ensconced in his Washington offices working on his massive southeastern Indian handbook, to visit the isolated and impoverished Louisiana tribal communities. Swanton, for his part, seemed eager to return to Louisiana, but his travel time was limited to the summer months when his children were out of school.

The year after Dormon established contact with Swanton, he arranged to revisit the Louisiana tribes. Stopping first at Briarwood to collect his fellow enthusiast, he found Dormon suffering one of her inconvenient illnesses and unable to accompany him. Swanton kept her involved in his research, however, posting letters along the way in which he detailed travel adventures and accommodations, discussed his field observations, and recounted his unsuccessful quest into coastal Texas in search of surviving Attakapa speakers. Swanton found Dormon much improved on his return to Briarwood and passed his remaining time in Louisiana with Virginia, Aunt Dosia, and Caroline. He discovered renewed enthusiasm for his work while at Briarwood, a place he would visit again.[33]

Swanton was able to act on Dormon's recommendations for BAE-sponsored archaeological, ethnographic, and linguistic research in Louisiana and encouraged researchers to consider Dormon's expertise when undertaking their investigations. "If I am consulted regarding any work in your state or anywhere in your neighborhood I shall certainly suggest that you be invited to be present to take part."[34] Closer to home, he also sought to help Dormon find economic support by writing to Lyle Saxon to recommend Dormon for the Federal Writer's Project. "I am in hopes," he wrote Dormon, "you benefitted in consequence and, if so, some government money in Louisiana will not be wasted."[35] Swanton encouraged linguists Morris Swadesh and Mary Haas and archaeologists Winslow Walker, Frank Setzler, and John Ford to consult with Dormon before starting their work in Louisiana.[36] Although she considered this focus on her state long overdue, Dormon sometimes worried that their research might overshadow her own unschooled efforts to record the stories of tribal elders and her work to help preserve and perhaps publish these imperiled oral traditions.

When Swanton directed linguist Joseph Riste to work with the Louisiana tribes, he reassured Dormon: "You need not be concerned about anyone else collecting stories from the Tunica. Riste is interested only in velar r's and the classification of postpositions."[37] Telling her that "you are of assistance all the time in keeping an eye on Louisiana's antiquities and moulding public sentiment to [their] rescue and preservation,"[38] Swanton treated her as a colleague and commended her crucial role in helping to arrange and publicize Smithsonian-sponsored projects in her state.

After making repeated requests to Swanton to direct BAE archaeologists to the state to salvage archaeological sites threatened by highway construction, Dormon suddenly refused to work with recent arrival James Ford, thinking his research might conflict with the work of Setzler, whom she greatly admired. Not understanding her motives, Swanton wrote in exasperation: "I had gathered from your earlier epistles that, with the exception of a few favored spots, all Louisiana was being turned upside down with steam shovels, and now after Mr. Collins and I have moved heaven and earth to get an appropriation and a perfectly good archaeologist into Louisiana you are 'a little mixed' as to where to advise him to dig. . . . He is probably going to Louisiana with perfect confidence that you can lead him to no less than ten large and lucrative sites."[39] He took a more conciliatory tone the following week. "I had supposed it was sufficiently evident that we relied almost entirely upon you to put our field workers in contact with the mounds and other antiquities, create highways through the hillbilly intelligence and do all those necessary things."[40] She eventually agreed to assist Ford, but theirs was never a comfortable association.

Dormon served as the only female member of the de Soto Commission after Swanton insisted she be appointed. When the time to organize a committee of scholars and patrons came, Swanton called on Dormon to "become a full-fledged member of the Committee at once! Please!"[41] Flattered, Dormon agreed to serve, but due to health issues and the expense of travel, she declined Swanton's request that she act as secretary of the committee. The goal of the federally funded commission was to trace the route of Hernando de Soto's sixteenth-century expedition through the American Southeast. Dormon and Swanton had for some time exchanged theories and ideas about the route of the Spanish expedition and the tribes it encountered. She did serve on the fact-finding committee. Her duties included field trips to identify sites and explore possible expedition routes.[42]

The possibilities of Roosevelt's New Deal energized Swanton and Dormon who anticipated renewed funding for anthropological fieldwork. "Only a few months ago expert scientific work in archaeology and ethnology was threatened with total extinction on the ground of needless expense . . . and suddenly, in order to put an enormous amount of common labor to work, there is call for more scientific leadership than we can possibly supply."[43] Dormon did her part to fuel public interest in sponsored research in Louisiana, using her network of women's organizations to spread the word about contemporary Indians and ancient sites. "I am talking about Indians to my chapter of the DAR . . . and will take the opportunity to interest them in the De Soto Quadricentennial."[44] Swanton encouraged her connections: "You can be of the greatest help owing to your contacts with the DAR and other patriotic organizations."[45]

Over time, Swanton's letters to Dormon grew more familiar as their professional relationship evolved into a close friendship. Swanton chatted about his brothers, his home in Maine, the pitfalls of parenting, and the joys of grandparenting. He included tidbits of interest to be passed on to "Sister" and "Aunt Dosia," with whom he occasionally corresponded. Chronically ill and often depressed, Swanton's ennui sometimes crept into his letters. Worried at one point that her friend might be sinking completely into despair, Dormon took it on herself to write in confidence to Swanton's supervisor, M. W. Stirling. The director tried to allay her fears by pointing out that Swanton always overcame his depressions, which had grown less frequent since he had "checked himself into Mayo Clinic" some years earlier.[46] Swanton seemed to draw energy from the Dormon women and enjoyed traveling the highways in their company. They visited Louisiana tribal villages together and drove into Arkansas and Texas, "all the way to the Trinity River," retracing the route of the de Soto expedition.[47] For almost thirty years, until his death in 1958, Caroline Dormon and John Swanton remained colleagues, friends, and correspondents. Swanton's authority and extensive knowledge informed and validated Dormon's work, allowing her to break into fields of American anthropological and historical research theretofore dominated by male academics. At the same time, she advanced Swanton's interests and served as de facto agent for the BAE in Louisiana.

Most of the elders and artists who worked with Dormon preceded her in death by many years. The disappearance of so many friends, coupled with the death of her beloved sister Virginia who had chauffeured her around the state and her own precarious health, kept Dormon close to home in the last years of her life. This was a time of transition for both Caroline Dormon and Louisiana Indians.

Caroline Dormon spent the last two decades of her life at Briarwood engaging in the activities she loved: gardening, writing, painting, and promoting native plants. She continued to write and occasionally lectured about Louisiana's cultural resources, but for the most part she dedicated her energies toward natural resource conservation. She had been determined to die at Briarwood, but severe angina forced her to spend her final days in a nursing home in Shreveport, Louisiana. By the time of her death in 1971, however, she had ensured that Briarwood would be maintained as a nature preserve and that her voluminous collection of publications, letters, and manuscripts was archived in the Cammie G. Henry Research Center at Northwestern State University.

This brief examination of Caroline Dormon's work has identified the central role she played in protecting the physical reminders of Louisiana's first people and in bettering the lives and conditions of their descendants. Following in the tradition of social reformers and clubwomen like Doubleday and Bradford, Dormon fostered an appreciation of indigenous Americans, their histories, and their artistic traditions. She cultivated a network of committed clubwomen to help spread the word about the endangered sites that gave testimony to the social complexity and ancient heritage of Louisiana Indians while bringing attention and support to imperiled tribal communities. Through her friendship with Swanton and her correspondence with Collier, she advanced Collier's policy that heralded cultural pluralism over assimilation and brought the government's attention to Louisiana, ensuring that federal funds were dedicated to research in her home state.

Despite limited means and poor health, Dormon employed tenacity, determination, and intellect to increase awareness of America's first people, lobbying tirelessly for economic assistance and social parity for the tribes. Like Doubleday and Bradford before her, Dormon used tribal arts, especially basketry, to help Louisiana Indians maintain cultural identity and to give a boost to stagnant economies. Using marketing as a tool for cultural conservation, she helped sustain arts traditions, some of which might not have persisted otherwise. Although this essay highlights her work with the Chitimacha, Dormon brokered crafts and documented traditions for tribal communities throughout the state.

After World War II, tribal economies began to grow as men sought employment in the oil and gas and agricultural industries. Some tribal villages consolidated, like the Tunica-Biloxi-Ofogoula; others, like the Bayou La Combe Choctaw, merged into the local Creole community. The Chitimacha, however, remained on the same lands they had occupied for centuries.

Caroline Dormon did not live to see her labors in cultural resource conservation come to fruition, but the relationships she carefully built over the years formed a framework that supported Louisiana's cultural resources until more formal mechanisms for cultural preservation were put into place. By the end of the 1970s, the Koasati, Tunica-Biloxi, and Chitimacha had gained recognition as federally recognized tribes, followed by the Jena Band of Choctaw in the 1990s. National and state preservation laws protected the archaeological sites in Louisiana that Dormon had initially brought to the attention of the BAE and state authorities. Without her pioneering efforts, many precious cultural legacies might have disappeared.

Today, the Louisiana Division of Archaeology is charged with stewardship over site preservation. Casinos and other tribally owned businesses reinforce tribal economies. Arts like basketry are signifiers of identity and are no longer commodities necessary to the economic survival of the weavers and their families.

The tribes have successfully transited from dependency to sovereignty. Louisiana's Indian nations have their own cultural preservation offices and monitor and conserve their own traditions. Their efforts have been bolstered by Dormon's documentation of tribal traditions, her notes, and her photographs. Today, ancient ceremonial centers like those at Marksville and Poverty Point State Historic Sites bear witness to her efforts to protect ancient sites; but only a few tribal elders remember "Miss Carrie," and each year their numbers are thinned. It is hoped that this essay will bring attention to her legacy and encourage a closer examination of Caroline Dormon's "Indian work."

NOTES

Thanks to Dolores Janiewski and John Troutman, whose editorial assistance, comments, and suggestions were both constructive and insightful.

1. Marcia Myers Bonta, "Caroline Dormon, 1888–1971," in *American Women Afield: Writings by Pioneering Women Naturalists*, ed. Marcia Myers Bonta (College Station: Texas A & M University Press, 1995), 216–22; Fran Holman Johnson, *The Gift of the Wild Things* (Lafayette: Center for Louisiana Studies, 1990); Donald Rawson, "Caroline Dormon: A Renaissance Spirit of Twentieth-Century Louisiana," *Louisiana History* 24 (Summer 1983): 121–39; Mabel Butler to Caroline Dormon (hereinafter cited as CD), April 12, 1933, folder 434, Caroline Dormon Collection, Cammie Henry Research Center, Northwestern State University, Natchitoches (hereinafter cited as CD/CHRC). Although the Dormon collection at Northwestern State University is vast (1,614 folders, forty-two linear feet) and varied, it has its limitations. For example, some of the most interesting notes on tribal traditions are found on recycled materials like laundry receipts, pay stubs, or bits of scrap paper, and the notes are often undated and unattributed. Correspondence is mostly one sided, since Dormon made carbon copies of only some of her outgoing letters. This can prove frustrating to the researcher, as in the case of her correspondence with John Swanton. Attempts to find evidence of Dormon's letters to Swanton in the inventories of the National Archives, Smithsonian Ethnographic Archives, Swanton Family Collection at Harvard University, and the American Philosophical Society in Philadelphia were unsuccessful.

2. Bonta, "Caroline Dormon," 216–22.

3. Ibid. In all cases, emphasis is in the original document.

4. Erma T. O'Brien, "About Caroline Dormon," n.d., 1, folder 945, CD/CHRC. For publications of the BAE ethnographers, whose work was later termed "salvage ethnography," see for example Jacob W. Gruber, "Ethnographic Salvage and the Shaping of Anthropology," *American Anthropologist*

72, n.s. (December 1970): 1289–99, and George Marcus and Michael Fisher, eds., *Anthropology as Cultural Critique: An Experimental Moment in the Human Sciences* (Chicago: University of Chicago Press, 1986).

5. Philip J. Deloria, *Playing Indian* (New Haven: Yale University Press, 1998), 94; see also Marianna Torgovnick, *Gone Primitive: Savage Indians, Modern Lives* (Chicago: University of Chicago Press, 1990), Adam Kuper, *The Invention of Primitive Society: Transformations of an Illusion* (New York: Routledge, 1988), Leah Dilworth, *Imagining Indians in the Southwest: Persistent Visions of a Primitive Past* (Washington, D.C.: Smithsonian Institute Press, 1996), and Helen Carr, *Inventing the American Primitive: Politics, Gender, and the Representation of Native American Literary Tradition* (New York: New York University Press, 1996).

6. "Indians are a part of nature," CD to Miss Surggraf, July 27, 1937, folder 978, CD/CHRC.

7. Ibid.

8. Mary Linn Wernet, personal communication to author, July 15, 2006; Mrs. Jessie Johnson, personal communication to author, July 15, 2006.

9. O'Brien, "About Caroline Dormon," n.d., 2, folder 945, CD/CHRC; Bonta, "Caroline Dormon," 216–17.

10. CD to Miss Surggraf, July 27, 1937, CD/CHRC.

11. Unnumbered, undated notebooks, folder 1488, CD/CHRC.

12. Erik Trump, "'The Idea of Help': White Women Reformers and the Commercialization of Native American Women's Arts," in *Selling the Indian: Commercializing and Appropriating American Indian Cultures*, ed. Carter Jones Meyer and Diana Royer (Tucson: University of Arizona Press, 2001), 161, 170–72.

13. Ibid., 165–68; Karen J. Blair, *The Torchbearers: Women and Their Amateur Arts Associations in America, 1890–1930* (Indianapolis: Indiana University Center for Philanthropy, 1994); *Course of Study for the Indian Schools of the United States* (Washington, D.C.: U.S. Government Printing Office, 1901); Lori D. Ginzberg, *Women and the Work of Benevolence: Morality, Politics, and Class in the Nineteenth-Century United States* (New Haven: Yale University Press, 1990); Sarah H. Hill, *Weaving New Worlds: Southeastern Cherokee Women and Their Basketry* (Chapel Hill: University of North Carolina Press, 1997); Francis Paul Prucha, ed., *Americanizing the American Indians: Writings by the "Friends of the Indian," 1880–1900* (Cambridge, Mass.: Harvard University Press, 1973); Trump, "'The Idea of Help,'" in *Selling the Indian*, 159–89.

14. Mary Bradford to Christine Paul, December 4, 1906, McIlhenny Company Archives, Avery Island, La. Writing to weaver Christine Paul, Bradford notes, "Mrs. Doubleday says she wrote the chief. Tell him *I* will write to her and thank her for writing to him. . . . She's the one I sent the baskets to"; Dayna Bowker Lee, "The Ties That Bind: Cane Basketry Traditions among the Chitimacha and Jena Band of Choctaw," in *The Work of Tribal Hands: Southeastern Indian Split Cane Basketry*, ed. Dayna Bowker Lee and Hiram F. Gregory (Natchitoches: Northwestern State University Press, 2006), 43–71. Dormon hoped to make contact with Mrs. Bradford and benefit from her knowledge of the Chitimacha weavers and their traditions accrued over three decades of working with community artisans. "Must meet Mrs. Sidney Bradford, Avery Island," she noted to herself (notebook, n.d., folder 1488, CD/CHRC). The Great Depression put an end to this high level of community production as the demand for decorative Indian baskets ebbed. Chitimacha weavers no longer had a dependable national market, and many abandoned basketry altogether to seek wage-paying jobs, although Dormon continued to broker baskets for the Chitimacha weavers through the 1940s.

15. CD to Lyle Saxon (hereinafter cited as LS), March 2, 1934, folder 53, Melrose Collection, CHRC).

16. Ibid.

17. CD to Cammie G. Henry (hereinafter cited as CGH), August 18, 1929, folder 52, Melrose Collection, CHRC.

18. General Federation of Women's Clubs, "Women Working: 1800–1930," Harvard University Library Open Collections Program, http://ocp.hul.harvard.edu/ww/organizations-federation.htm; Mary Linn Wernet, "Lee Craig Ragan Levy: The Study of a Clubwoman's Participation in the Policy of Conservation after World War II" (master's thesis, Northwestern State University, Natchitoches, 1986); Hill, *Weaving New Worlds*; Joy Rehner, "American Indian Language Policy and School Success," *Journal of Educational Issues of Language Minority Students* 12 (Summer 1993): 35–59.

19. Lewis Merriam, *The Problem of Indian Administration: The Report of a Survey Made at the Request of Hubert Work, Secretary of the Interior, and Submitted to Him February 21, 1928* (Baltimore: Johns Hopkins Press, 1928).

20. Ibid., 532–33, quoted in Hill, "Weaving New Worlds," 287.

21. CD to John Collier (hereinafter cited as JC), n.d., 1937, folder 1436, CD/CHRC.

22. *Yearbook and Handbook for Club Women* (Washington, D.C., Division of Indian Welfare, 1938), 58; JC to CD, August 14, 1937, folder 1436, CD/CHRC; JC to CD, July 31, 1945, folder 1443, CD/CHRC.

23. John Swanton (hereinafter cited as JRS) to CD, July 31, 1945, folder 1372, CD/CHRC. For examples of Dormon's work on tribal crafts traditions, see Caroline Dormon, "The Last of the Cane Basket Makers," *Hollands: The Magazine of the South*, October 1931, 13, 66, and "Caddo Pottery," *Art and Archaeology* 35 (January/February 1934): 56–69.

24. Various correspondence, folders 1346–49, CD/CHRC; Pauline Paul to Christine Paul, October 25, 1909, Anonymous Collection, McIlhenny Archives, Avery Island, La. Although not all of Dormon's tribal contacts were female, she was particularly close to several women with whom she conducted research and for whom she brokered crafts. Among them, Emma Jackson, who served as the subject for the only known portrait that Dormon painted, and Billy Brandy, who provided her with word lists and stories, were both Choctaw women from Indian Village. Jackson's daughter, Rosa, married Joseph Pierite, a hereditary Tunica chief. Probably her closest friends, however, were Chitimacha weavers Christine and Pauline Paul. Christine Paul attended the parochial school established for a short time to serve Chitimacha children, and Pauline was educated at Carlisle Indian School in Pennsylvania.

25. CD to CGH, February 20, 1936, folder 54, Melrose Collection, CHRC; CD to CGH, March 23, 1936, folder 54, Melrose Collection, CHRC.

26. Christine Paul (hereinafter cited as CP) to CD, February 1936, folder 1346, CD/CHRC.

27. Dormon notebook , n.d., folder 1488, CD/CHRC.

28. CP to CD, March 3, 1935, folder 1347, CD/CHRC.

29. CP to CD, November 1935, folder 1347, CD/CHRC.

30. Pauline Paul (hereinafter cited as PP) to CD, November 24, 1930, folder 1345, CD/CHRC.

31. PP to CD, November 4, 1931, folder 1345, CD/CHRC.

32. JRS to CD, May 31, 1929, folder 1358, CD/CHRC.

33. JRS to CD, July 22, 29, and August 3, 5, 16, 1930, folder 1360, CD/CHRC.

34. JRS to CD, November 5, 1930, folder 1362, CD/CHRC.

35. JRS to CD, November 15, 1935, folder 1368, CD/CHRC.

36. Alicia Trissler, "Caroline Dormon and Louisiana Archaeology of the 1930s," (master's thesis, Northwestern State University, 1994).

37. JRS to CD, June 5, 1931, folder 1362, CD/CHRC. In linguistic terms, velars are consonants that are

articulated with the back part of the tongue against the soft palate, or velum. Postposition refers to the placing of a word or suffix after the word to which it is grammatically related.

38. JRS to CD, May 22, 1934, folder 1368, CD/CHRC.

39. JRS to CD, June 6, 1933, folder 1366, CD/CHRC.

40. JRS to CD, June 14, 1933, folder 1366, CD/CHRC.

41. JRS to CD, January 13, 1936, folder 1370, CD/CHRC.

42. CD to CGH, December 2, 1936, folder 54, Melrose Collection, CHRC; U.S. House of Representatives, *Final Report of the United States De Soto Expedition Commission*, by John R. Swanton, 76th Cong., 1st Sess., House Doc. 71 (Washington, D.C.: GPO, 1939; rpt., Washington, D.C.: Smithsonian Institution Press, 1985).

43. JRS to CD, September 8, 1933, folder 1367, CD/CHRC.

44. CD to JRS, January 26, 1936, folder 1370, CD/CHRC.

45. JRS to CD, February 19, 1936, folder 1370, CD/CHRC.

46. M. W. Stirling to CD, August 29, 1933, folder, 1367 CD/CHRC.

47. CD to CGH, December 2, 1936, folder 54, Melrose Collection, CHRC.

Mary Land

(1908–1991)

"When I Was Big Enough to Tote a Gun, I Did"

KAREN TRAHAN LEATHEM

❀ ❀ ❀

Mary Land's account of her introduction to Louisiana's hunting and fishing culture in the foreword to her book *Louisiana Cookery* indicates that at a young age this child born to a prominent old-line southern family was already on her way to leading a very unconventional life. A north Louisiana native, Mary Land is known chiefly as the author of this influential cookbook published by Louisiana State University Press in 1954. Her life and work offer a rare glimpse of a woman who defied the conventions of her class and era. She worked in a field—outdoor writing—dominated by men, competed in fishing rodeos, and married and divorced five times. Known for her lively personality, she left a strong impression on all who met her.[1]

Land was born in 1908 on Rough and Ready Plantation in the Red River Valley near Benton, not far from Shreveport. Her family tree included French Huguenots and Anglos. Her family's Louisiana roots predate the Louisiana Purchase. Many of Mary's ancestors fought in the American Revolution and one—David Smith—fought in that war as well as in the Battle of New Orleans. Among her more immediate forebears were three Louisiana Supreme Court justices—her great-grandfather Thomas Thompson Land and two great-uncles, John Rutherford Land and Alfred Dillingham Land. Her father, Thomas Taylor Land, mayor of Benton and a prominent district attorney of several nearby parishes, had hoped for a boy.[2] Faced with a girl, he decided to mold her into a fishing and hunting companion anyway. Her father's decision to raise her as he would a boy sowed the seeds for her unconventional life; never would Land feel constricted by notions about what proper girls or women could and could not do. As Land wrote in *Louisiana Cookery*, "At the mature age of four I felt no fainting fits from jabbing a fishhook into a worm—for I was reared by my father."³ Land dedicated her book to her sportsman father as well as to her cousin Gammon Nesbitt and his wife, Sunshine, bon vivants who also encouraged her to fish and hunt.

Her father's impact on her life extended beyond merely teaching her outdoor skills. Later in her life, she told a writer, "I had the good fortune of being reared by two men, my uncle and my father, and I think they taught me things like 'have no fear' and 'you have to put first things first'; a lot of that went into my thoughts about how people should live."⁴ Her father's influence looms large in part because her mother, Elizabeth Langford Land, suffered a stroke when Mary was young and remained an invalid until her death. Mary's strong relationship with her father, however, was not just the result of her father trying to compensate for her mother's inability to devote herself full-time to Mary. This kind of father-daughter bonding followed a trend that had begun in the late nineteenth century whereby middle-class or upper-middle-class fathers introduced daughters to an outside world—the races or other amusements, for example—that ignored Victorian proprieties.⁵ In Mary Land's case, the world of field and stream served as the rural counterpart to urban entertainments. Her hunting and fishing adventures with her father represented a break from her mother's upbringing and presented her an alternative vision of deportment and leisure life.

Even as Mary departed from genteel standards in cultivating shooting prowess, she and her cousin's wife, Sunshine (a big game hunter), were following in the footsteps of upper- and middle-class women who took up hunting as a fashionable sport in the late 1800s. In the 1870s and 1880s, women joined men in rifle clubs and became avid sharpshooters. By the 1890s, outdoor magazines featured women hunters, and by the 1910s, gun manufacturers began marketing their products to women.⁶

The members of Mary Land's family did not just impart to her a love of the outdoors; they also taught her to value literature, the arts, and education. Before the Civil War, her great-grandfather Thomas Thompson Land rode his horse from Holmes County, Mississippi, to Charlottesville to attend the University of Virginia, where he received his law degree. Mary's female relatives on her father's side especially encouraged her interest in literature and writing. One great-great-aunt, Sallie Jastremski, wife of newspaper publisher Leon Jastremski, wrote for the New Orleans weekly *Louisiana Review* in the late nineteenth century. Sallie's books—complete with marginal notes—were handed down to Mary. Her great-aunt Mattie Williams was widely recognized as the "mother" of the Louisiana Chautauqua in Ruston, a summertime educational program for teachers and citizens that flourished between 1890 and 1905. The Ruston

MARY LAND

Circa 1969. Courtesy of the John C. Guillet and the Vorhoff Library
and Newcomb Archives, Tulane University.

Chautauqua was part of a national movement that originated in Chautauqua, New York, in the 1870s and remained a widespread nontraditional educational forum in many communities through the 1930s. Williams was also a newspaper columnist, dedicated teacher, school administrator, clubwoman, and librarian who worked tirelessly to establish Shreveport's public library. Two of Mary's cousins, Florence Land May and her daughter Margery Land May, published fiction. Margery May's first publication was a short story in H. L. Mencken's *Smart Set*, and she went on to become a Hollywood screenwriter at Selznick in the late 1910s and early 1920s. One of her aunts, Mary Elizabeth Land, for whom Mary was named, attended Newcomb College and also wrote for newspapers but died of consumption at a young age.[7]

In keeping with her family's academic tendencies, Mary was a diligent student. At Foster Hall, an elite girls' school in Shreveport, she received a classical education, including four years of Latin. When she was fifteen, she began to attend the recently founded Gulf Park College for Women in Long Beach, Mississippi. The fledgling school attracted a lively group of young women from Shreveport, largely owing to the efforts of Gulf Park's president, Richard Cox, who met and talked with parents while visiting that city.[8] The well-regarded poet Vachel Lindsay taught there for a brief period, and Land developed her love of poetry in his classes.

Land's schooling was a significant influence in her life. Since the late nineteenth century, when girls began going to high school in greater numbers, the contours of female adolescence had changed. The culture of high schools—whether all girl or coeducational—encouraged girls to think differently about themselves, as "aspiring souls, desirous of making a mark on the world."[9] The competitiveness of school work and the focus on intellectual development meant that girls took themselves seriously as thinkers and began channeling their energies to vocational pursuits, which they now felt they could select "based on their own individual proclivities."[10] Mary Land, it is clear, embraced her schooling with a passion and turned to her favorite subject as she began to make a living.

Land began her professional writing career as a poet, selling her first poem to the *Christian Advocate* in 1937. She eventually published several volumes of poetry, including *Shadows of the Swamp* (1941), *Abode* (1972), and *Dreams* (1977). Over the course of her life, her poems appeared in various regional and national magazines and newspapers as well as in anthologies. Many of her poems focused on the natural world. Lines like "White plumed egrets / Guard sequined bayous" and "The cypress tree bent / In agony as the storm / Slashed at its heart" illustrate Land's fascination with the beauty of flora and fauna.[11]

In 1954 Land told a reporter, "My hobbies are fishing, hunting, cooking, and people. My work is writing."[12] The writer skillfully incorporated her hobbies into her job. She began working for the Louisiana State Department of Conservation around 1940 and shortly thereafter introduced a conservation education program in public schools throughout the state.[13] She also wrote articles on fish and game for the department's publication, *The Louisiana Conservation Review*. These pieces included recipes on fish and game, the genesis of her first cookbook.

Land began writing outdoors articles and columns for a number of other publications. She was briefly a staff writer for the *Mississippi Valley Sportsman* in the late 1940s. She contributed to *Southern Outdoors, Southwest Holiday,* and *Sportsman's News of Arkansas*; she wrote a syndicated column, Outdoors South, for Louisiana newspapers with Arthur Van Pelt, the outdoors editor of the *New Orleans Times-Picayune*; and she published a column by the same name in Mississippi newspapers. A number of regional travel magazines featured Mary's articles, including *South*, a New Orleans publication that focused on the American South and Latin America, *Mexico This Month*, and *Down South on the Beautiful Gulf Coast*.[14]

Land's writing mixed no-nonsense technical information about fishing and hunting with a nature lover's regard for the land and scenery. During one fishing trip just inland from the Mississippi Gulf Coast on Wolf River, she "placed the light cork on my line, the sinkers, hook and shrimp came next." But along the way she also encountered natural beauty, expressing what she saw with her poet's sensibility: "The day came reluctantly through a misty haze, and primitive stillness enveloped the forests."[15]

Mary Land's career shows how women developed their professional lives in the mid-twentieth century, even in a male-oriented field. In 1947 she was the only woman member of the Louisiana Outdoor Writers Association. That same year she was one of six women who attended the national convention of the Outdoor Writers Association of America. Yet she persisted and flourished, co-writing the column with Van Pelt, the dean of Louisiana outdoors writers. Her audience, though, was hardly all male. She encouraged women to hunt and fish, and the way in which she bridged the outdoors world and the kitchen represents the blurring between men's and women's domains in rural Louisiana.

In 1940, noting that only 5 percent of Louisiana fishing licenses went to women, she wrote in the *Louisiana Conservation Review*, "Women think, for some inane reason, that fishing is a man's sport. This misconception has been planted in the female mind for generations." She hypothesized that this "malignant attitude on man's part is [due to] the fact he recognizes woman's ability and cannot stand to have his piscatorial glory taken away." Thus men conspired to keep fishing gear out of women's hands. "Some men," she reported, "even go into acute and violent attacks at finding one of their wooden minnows moved a third of an inch in their tackle box." Land advised women to wait until the men in their families went away on business trips to raid the box and practice casting in the back yard. "Your casting a fly into a rose bush is not half so imbecilic looking as the carressing [*sic*] of flys and plugs by men during the months of their fishing confinement," she pronounced. When women mastered casting on dry land, it was time to hit the water. The result would be more than just a fish for dinner; the reader would, she asserted, come home with "a sense of independence." Nevertheless, she saw differences between male and female fishing experiences, an outlook that conformed to the predominant attitudes of the day: "A man will make his kill, guzzle a bottle of brew and blindly head homeward; a woman will be satisfied with one small perch and linger to revel in the infinitesimal loveliness of the bloom on Spanish moss or the haunting song of a rain crow at dusk." Yet at the end of the article, Land made her final pitch with a list of women who found satisfaction in winning competitions, including Mrs. H. F. Collister, winner of the Ladies Trophy at two recent tarpon rodeos, and Mrs. Sylvester La Brot, whose eighty-four-pound tarpon garnered her a trophy in the 1936 Grand Isle Rodeo.[16]

Land herself was accomplished at this newly popular form of sport fishing. In 1939, competing against seventy-five men, she won a tarpon rodeo in Lake Charles, Louisiana. She was active on the tarpon rodeo circuit for a time, catching the large fish in Grand Isle, Louisiana, Calcasieu Parish, Louisiana, the Aransas Pass in Texas, and the Florida Everglades. In 1947 she won the national Outdoor Writers Association tarpon rodeo in St. Petersburg, Florida.[17]

Land's unusual career and outdoor hobbies matched her unorthodox lifestyle. The quintessential flapper, a sixteen-year-old Land eloped with E. Timothy Kelly, a jazz clarinetist she met at the Washington-Youree Hotel's roof garden dance in Shreveport. Their daughter, Pat, was born the following year. The couple divorced three years later. Kelly continued to perform in various jazz bands, including that of Jack Teagarden and Bob Crosby.[18]

Land married George Thomas Lock III of Lake Charles, Louisiana, and Hot Springs, Arkansas, in 1931. He shared her interest in hunting and fishing, and the couple built a lodge on Lake Hamilton near Hot Springs. The couple had a son, George, in 1932, and the family settled in Lake Charles.[19]

George Lock came from a prominent Lake Charles family that had built its fortune in the lumber industry. His grandfather George Lock married the daughter of one of the area's lumber pioneers, Daniel Goos (pronounced "Goss"), and built a sawmill on Prien Lake in 1869. Goos had fifteen children, so his great-grandson George Lock III had extensive family ties in Lake Charles. Mary and George were thus well connected to the city's social scene. It was in Lake Charles that Land met oil heir and philanthropist Matilda Geddings Gray. The two women became fast friends. They shared intellectual interests and also enjoyed a number of outdoor activities together, from swimming and fishing to bird hunting. Food and cooking were part of their relationship as well. Gray's self-published 1940 cookbook, *Food for Gourmets*, cowritten with New Orleanian Ethel Wight Usher, lists Land in the acknowledgments. Though they were not as close after Land left town at the end of the 1930s, they kept in touch, and Land dedicated her second cookbook, *New Orleans Cuisine*, to Gray, "from whom I have learned a grace in living and a knowledge of *la vie creole*."[20] At least a couple of Land's *Louisiana Cookery* recipes bear a strong resemblance to Gray's versions—both cookbooks feature nearly identical crab soups named after the famous Tally Ho hunting club near New Orleans as well as matching duck hunters' camp gumbos. In the case of these two recipes, it is possible that the two shared the recipe in the 1930s or else that both of these recipes were in wide circulation at the time. Land paid further tribute to Gray in her 1969 cookbook, *New Orleans Cuisine*, crediting Gray for spiced tongue and featuring Matilda Gray's broiled quail.[21]

Although George Lock descended from lumber entrepreneurs and clearly had money, the family fortunes seemed to decline in the 1930s with the Great Depression. The young family lived in a modest cottage in Lake Charles (although with a nearby lake house for weekend retreats), and George ran a sporting goods store for a time. The couple and their children often fished, and it was during this period that Mary acquired her talent for sport fishing. Even as she enjoyed a south Louisiana lifestyle of hunting and fishing while raising her young children, she also devoted time to her literary pursuits. After becoming a charter member of the Junior League of Lake Charles, she resigned when she realized that club activities would take too much time away from her poetry writing, which she had returned to with renewed vigor.[22]

Land's Lake Charles years also brought Myrtis Storey into her life. Storey was the Lock family's domestic help. The African American woman helped care for the children, clean the house, and cook. She and her husband, Jim, lived in a small house in the rear of the Locks' house. Storey was a skilled cook, and Land collaborated with her in the kitchen, often suggesting different kinds of seasoning.[23]

Land's marriage to George Lock fell apart at the end of the 1930s. She took her children to Gulfport, Mississippi, first to the Markham Hotel, then a rented house. By 1940, she had moved to New Orleans and had taken a new education job with the Louisiana Department of Conservation, living first at the St. Charles Hotel, then in an apartment on Milan Street.[24]

Land came into her own as a journalist, contributing to the *Louisiana Conservation Review* at a time when the magazine was an odd mix of oil and gas news, horticulture, hunting, and fishing. A number of women wrote for the magazine during this period, including conservationist and native plant expert Caroline Dormon, who became a friend of Land's. The two women shared an interest in nature and conservation and an attachment to the northwest Louisiana landscape that persisted until Dormon's death in 1971.[25]

Land did not stay in New Orleans long but instead settled with her children in Pass Christian, where she bought a house in 1941. By this time, she was dating a cousin, attorney John Rutherford Land Jr. The two married that year and moved to Knoxville, Tennessee. Louisiana and the Gulf Coast pulled Mary back, however. She spent the spring of 1942 in Shreveport and then returned to Pass Christian. Around 1944, Mary and John moved to New Orleans, first living Uptown, then in the Upper Pontalba building on Jackson Square.[26]

Land's frequent moves and her multiple marriages demonstrate the difficulty of combining marriage and an independent working life during this era. She divorced John Land in 1948, then married businessman Walter Reed the following year. Sometime following the publication of *Louisiana Cookery*, Mary and Walter divorced, and she got married once more, to pianist John Guinn Hodges, whom she met in Hot Springs. They lived in Natchitoches in the 1960s, and after their divorce, Land stayed there.[27] Despite Land's marital troubles, her family relationships were warm and loving, from her two children to her elderly relatives. In a 1981 interview, she declared, "I have always been a very busy person, and I think that you've got to have two things: work and love. And no boredom."[28]

But it is possible to view Land's marital life from a different vantage point, one that sees Land primarily as a decisive actor rather than someone who could not juggle competing expectations during an era when combining marriage and career was not the norm. Mary was no shrinking violet, and she was willing to change life partners or her domestic circumstances when she saw fit.

From the mid-1940s to the late 1950s, Mary Land was a devoted citizen of the French Quarter (Vieux Carré) in New Orleans. During her lengthy stay in the Pontalba apartment building on Jackson Square, she had a number of unusual houseguests—including frequent visits from her son's pet lion. A small alligator—a Mother's Day gift from one of her friends—was in residence until his growth spurt made apartment life impractical, to say the least. Land earned a reputation as a vivacious host, sometimes inviting jazz revival musicians—a circle including Edmond "Doc" Souchon, Sharkey Bonano, and Oscar "Papa" Celestin devoted to "reviving" traditional New Orleans jazz—up for drinks after their concerts in Jackson Square. She enjoyed socializing with a wide range of people; as she remarked, she had her "daytime friends" and her "nighttime friends." Her daughter later said, "Mother didn't set out to be unconventional, she was simply born that way."[29] Her social circle at that time reflected the literary and intellectual range of French Quarter residents, including writers Lyle Saxon and Harnett Kane and famous Danish archaeologist Frans Blom of Tulane University's Middle American Research Institute, whom she met through the institute's benefactor, her friend Matilda Geddings Gray.

As she wrote about the outdoors, Land collected fish and game recipes, both because she recognized the need to deal with the catch and because she enjoyed cooking. She published recipes in many of her articles, and after more than a decade of compiling them, she went to Louisiana State University Press. The director, Don Ellegood, suggested that she expand the manuscript beyond outdoor cookery and incorporate all of Louisiana cuisine. Land characteristically approached the project with gusto, and the result was a classic Louisiana cookbook, one that recorded old-style dishes as well as embraced innovations. An indefatigable researcher, she documented Louisiana cuisine, north and south, as it existed in the mid-twentieth century. Her book stands the test of time, looking surprisingly modern with its emphasis on unusual herbs and wild greens.

Noted artist Morris Henry Hobbs illustrated *Louisiana Cookery*. His sketches of a cast-iron pot, the cuts of meat on a deer, and other culinary symbols added a touch of whimsy. Cookbook author and American food authority James Beard played a role in the book's publication, providing the reader's report. It was, he pronounced, "a massive work, truly an encyclopedia of invaluable information." Beard and Land became friends; after a visit, he wrote to her: "I loved your house; I loved the parties; I liked your husband immensely; I adored you."[30]

The volume evoked considerable interest, both in Louisiana and nationally. A *New York Times* review found it a "definitely worth while" investigation of "the cuisine of one of the regions of the United States richest in culinary lore." The reviewer singled out the chapter on game as "particularly interesting," especially given its information on more unusual game, such as bear and muskrat.[31] Writer Stephen Longstreet found Louisiana food the perfect antidote to the "sterile, sanitary ideas" of American cooking, characterized by "sand-filled stews, battery acid soups and color schemes on salads to match your drapes." Later, folklorists at Louisiana State University used the book in their courses.[32]

The cookbook was indeed encyclopedic and eclectic in its methods and techniques. A recipe for quick bisque that called for canned bouillon and tomato soup coexisted with such recipes as Idle Acres Plantation possum, which began with "scald, dress, and pick hairs off possum." Like many cooks of the era, Land embraced culinary shortcuts made possible by canned foods, but her recipes also reflect, as she put it, her "love and longing for the wilderness and a knowledge of how to use the groceries supplied by Mother Earth."[33]

Reflecting the south Louisiana enthusiasm for alcoholic drinks, the beverages chapter ran thirty-eight pages and included such concoctions as Hotel Roosevelt café brulot, Creole downfall (made from "corn likker" and ginger ale), and Cajun cherry bounce. But she hardly forgot the land of her birth; recipes for burgoo, Brunswick stew, and hopping John hailed from north Louisiana, brought there by migrants from other southern states.

She viewed Louisiana cuisine as the product of different cultures—Acadian, Creole, African, "Red Neck," Spanish, Italian, German, and American Indian. "Because of this potpourri of nationalities," she wrote, "there is no way that one may write an academic history of Louisiana cuisine. We might just call it *tout à fait.*"[34]

Some recipes came from friends and acquaintances, rural and urban, while "others were passed down to me along with my grandmother's iron skillet." She dismissed the precise measurements that had become standard in American cookbooks: "You will find my measurements indefinite, for that is 'our way.'" One reviewer warned readers that this book was not for novices: "A considerable knowledge of cooking is necessary to follow the recipes."[35]

One chapter, entitled "Gastronomic Gambles," reflected what Land termed the "spirit of gastronomic adventure" among Louisiana marsh dwellers. In it, she explained how to prepare food few would think of eating today, such as crows and owls, as well as delicacies now admired by Americans with sophisticated palates, such as eel and octopus.

Many recipe titles reflect the cuisine's grounding in place: Isle Dernière shrimp stew, Grand Isle pilau, Bayou Lafourche boogalee sauce, Breaux Bridge bisque, and Pontchartrain wiggle. The focus on game, fish, and such wild plants as bulrush, cattail, butterfly weed, and dandelion point to the strength of traditional Louisiana cuisine, which, like all great cooking, thrives off the surrounding land. She wrote in her introduction: "In creating any improvisations of native foods it is always best to mate fowl, fish, and game with the fruits of the fields and woods that are currently in harvest, for all these edibles complement each other."[36]

Land borrowed heavily from the hunters of south Louisiana. As the food writer John Thorne has recently noted:

> Cajuns have traditionally dealt with such uncertainties [the fluctuation in crawfish, differences in oyster harvests and fish catches] by hedging their bets. Jacks-of-all-trades, they trapped a little, oystered a little, and shrimped a little, and kept the larder full in the meantime with judicious use of the crawfish net and crab trap. They learned to make the most of anything the land had to offer, boasting that they would eat whatever failed to eat them first, and they have the recipes—braised bear steak, alligator sauce piquante—to prove it. . . . This self-sufficient aspect of the Cajun cook is reminiscent of pioneer cooking of the last century, but with one notable difference: the Cajuns are still cooking this way.[37]

Indeed, Mary Land's cookbook lists no fewer than seven bear recipes—bear doucement, bear ribs, bear steaks, German bear (with a ginger snap gravy), ragout of bear, roast of bear, and smoked bear. And her recipes for oyster pie, crawfish tails in rum, Cajun turtle stew, bass pecan, venisonburgers, and squirrel head potpie underscore the region's reliance on the bounty of the land as well as the book's origins in hunting and fishing columns.

Land was in many ways an anthropologist, documenting the foodways of a humble people. Her informants would not be likely to buy the cookbook—they were the very people who learned how to cook from their mothers, fathers, other relatives, and neighbors, not from books. *Louisiana Cookery* is sandwiched between Louisiana's first cookbooks—Lafcadio Hearn's *La Cuisine Creole* (1885), the Christian Woman's Exchange's *Creole Cookery Book* (1885), *The Picayune's Creole Cook Book* (1900), and Célestine Eustis's *Cooking in Old Creole Days* (1903)—and the new age of Louisiana cookbooks, heralded by Peter Feibleman's *American Cooking: Creole and Acadian* (1971) and Nathan Burton and Rudy Lombard's *Creole Feast* (1978). A handful of Louisiana cookbooks had been published in the 1920s and 1930s, but the recipes and cooking techniques of the period from about 1940 to 1970 reside largely in food memories and family lore, with the exception of a few community cookbooks, such as the *Acadian Bi-Centennial Cook Book* (1955), *River Road Recipes* (1959), and *Talk about Good!* (1969).[38]

Mary Land's *Louisiana Cookery* fit squarely in a new trend in cookbook publishing in the 1950s. The decade saw an explosion of cookbooks on all sorts of subjects, from casseroles to the cooking of Alice B. Toklas. Even more important, this time period marked the beginning of the gourmet explosion we usually associate with a later period, featuring international and ethnic cuisine. In addition to cookbooks highlighting specific regional cuisines, several general books on American regional dishes were published in the late 1940s and 1950s:

Sheila Hibben's *American Regional Cookery*; Mary Margaret McBride's *Harvest of American Cooking*; and Clementine Paddleford's *How America Eats*.[39]

But Mary Land was more than a gatherer of recipes, and she hardly set out to follow a publishing fad. Rather, the book grew organically out of her personal and professional life—as the title suggests, the book indeed represented Louisiana cookery, but that cookery was most definitely that of Mary Land, a Louisiana native firmly embedded in the state's foodways and hunting and fishing traditions.

Fifteen years later, Land focused on Crescent City food in *New Orleans Cuisine*. In this book Land presented recipes from well-known restaurants, such as shrimp canapé a la Irma from Arnaud's, tournedos Brennan from Brennan's, turtle soup from Commander's Palace, and red bean soup from Corinne Dunbar's. She also paid homage to a woman whose ingenuity and labor built the legendary Maylié and Esparbé's (which had become simply Maylie's by 1969) with Mme. Esparbé's bacalao. But the book was still vintage Mary Land, with rustic game and fish dishes, including rabbit sauce piquant, Pickoff's coon-ass duck, and outdoor fried fish. In addition, Land also relayed bits of folklore, including, for example, a section on New Orleans street foods, such as pain patate (sweet potato cake), calas tout chaud, and tac-tac.[40]

As with *Louisiana Cookery*, reviewers praised the book. Prominent New Orleans writer Harnett Kane, author of *Louisiana Hayride* and *Queen New Orleans*, called it "the finest Louisiana cook book ever written by anybody, any time."[41] According to the International Women's Fishing Association, it was "not just a cookbook, but the preservation of a way of life in New Orleans, of its traditions, customs, and cuisine."[42] Each chapter began with a literary quotation. Land gave detailed descriptions of food customs in south Louisiana and told stories about particular dishes and chefs. As always, Land was concerned with the stories behind the food and placing cuisine in context.

Even as she continued to explore Louisiana food, Land looked farther afield to the tastes of foreign lands. As Julia Child popularized French cuisine in the 1960s, Mary Land, who had featured recipes for tête de veau vinaigrette and pâté canard in her 1954 work, looked to even more exotic locales. A 1960 column in *Southern Outdoors* offered recipes for Tahitian coconut fish, sashimi, Cuban escabeche, Louisiana escabeche (made with Louisiana oranges and peppers), and serviche [*sic*] Acapulco style.[43] She later included some of these recipes in *New Orleans Cuisine*, along with a section on Mexican cookouts.

Immersed in the diverse culture of Louisiana, she perhaps yearned for an even greater degree of adventure. For years, she traveled to Mexico every win-

ter and at one point she stayed there year round. She once rented D. H. Lawrence's house in Guadalajara; on other occasions she stayed in Mexico City.
She felt a close kinship to Mexico, and the land and its people inspired her to
write an article-length manuscript called "Happy Land," a title that reflected
the "spontaneous gaiety" that she found in that country. To her, it was an exotic
place, where "the Mexican savors life while we, 'Norte Americanos,' rush madly
through each day."[44]

Land resettled on her beloved Mississippi Gulf Coast, in Ocean Springs, in
the mid-1980s.[45] She died there in 1991 at the age of eighty-three, leaving behind
cookbooks and articles that serve as a window on the foodways of Louisiana in
the twentieth century. An unusual woman, Mary Land nevertheless represents
a microcosm of Louisiana. She lived in the three major regions of Louisiana
(north, southwest, and southeast), enjoyed the solitude of the country and the
vibrancy of the city, and moved easily between the fishing boat and the kitchen.
Her friends were a diverse group, among them the prominent and affluent as
well as those she met during her back road rambles, where she met many who
lived off the land. A dedicated writer, she captured the essence of the food that
makes Louisiana cuisine so rich and varied, from its humble one-pot dishes to
its haute cuisine.

Mary Land's story is also one of modernity. Hers was the first generation
growing up in the shadow of the "New Woman," an ideal variously characterized by education, the notion that women could determine the course of their
own lives, support for woman's suffrage and other political issues, an interest
in sports and new forms of leisure, and new and more comfortable modes of
dress. Mary had to look no further than her own family for role models who
could be called New Women, from the educators, journalists, and novelists who
showed her that women could earn money from their intellectual pursuits to
her cousin's gun-toting wife, Sunshine. With such relatives and her father's tu-
telage in field and stream, her career choice seems only logical. Her personal
life also reflected new directions in women's lives. Her ability to refashion her
domestic circumstances and her embrace of writers and intellectuals both tes-
tify to her independent spirit. Just as she navigated the "sportsman's paradise"
of Louisiana, so, too, did she make her way through an era full of new implications for women.

NOTES

Some of the material in this essay originally appeared in an exhibition booklet: Karen Trahan
Leathem, *Two Women and Their Cookbooks: Mary Land and Lena Richard* (New Orleans: New-

comb College Center for Research on Women, 2001). The author is grateful to Susan Tucker and the Newcomb College Center for Research on Women for permission to reprint these portions. The author also thanks Emily Clark for her comments on a draft of this essay and Pat Land Stevens for information about and personal accounts of her mother, Mary Land.

1. Mary Land, *Louisiana Cookery* (Baton Rouge: Louisiana State University Press, 1954), vii.

2. *Jackson (Miss.) Clarion-Ledger* clipping, 1954, Mary Land Collection, Nadine Vorhoff Library, Newcomb College Center for Research on Women, Tulane University, New Orleans (hereinafter cited as MLC/TU). See also "Biographical Data," box 1, folder 1, MLC/TU, for basic biographical information. "Land, Alfred Dillingham," "Land, John Rutherford," and "Land, Thomas Thompson," *Dictionary of Louisiana Biography: Ten-Year Supplement, 1988–1998*, ed. Carl A. Brasseaux and James D. Wilson Jr. (Lafayette: Louisiana Historical Association in cooperation with the Center for Louisiana Studies, 1999); Pat Land Stevens, e-mail to author, March 16, 2007; "In the Spotlight this Week: Mary Land," *Register*, November 6, 1954, 46, Mary Land Collection, folder 9, Cammie G. Henry Research Center, Northwestern State University, Natchitoches (hereinafter cited as MLC/CHRC); Jerry Pierce, "People and Personalities," newsclipping, folder 5, MLC/CHRC.

3. Land, *Louisiana Cookery*, vii.

4. Mary Land, interview by Ronald Davis, ca. 1981, transcript, 1, box 2, folder 1, MLC/TU. The reference to the "uncle" is unclear, but it is probable that Land was actually referring to her cousin Gammon Nesbitt, who was considerably older than she was.

5. Pat Land Stevens, e-mail to author, July 14, 2006; Jane Hunter, *How Young Ladies Became Girls: The Victorian Origins of American Girlhood* (New Haven: Yale University Press, 2002), 121, 126. See also Peter Gay, *The Bourgeois Experience: Victoria to Freud*, vol. 1, *Education of the Senses* (New York: Norton, 1984), 102.

6. Laura Browder, *Her Best Shot: Women and Guns in America* (Chapel Hill: University of North Carolina Press, 2007), 3–11, 66–67, 70–74.

7. Kay Riser Smith, "Louisiana's Two Chautauquas," *North Louisiana Historical Association Journal* 5 (Summer 1974): 138; Patricia Lewis Strickland, "The Louisiana Chautauqua: Grounds for Education and Cultural Change, 1890 to 1905," *North Louisiana Historical Association Journal* 24 (Winter 1993): 14–15, 25; Rodney Cline, *Pioneer Leaders and Early Institutions in Louisiana Education* (Baton Rouge: Claitor's, 1969), 191–97; Edward Pinkowski, *Pills, Pen and Politics: The Story of General Leon Jastremski, 1843–1907* (Wilmington, Del.: Captain Stanislaus Mlotkowski Memorial Brigade Society, 1974); Pat Land Stevens, e-mail to author, July 14 and 30, 2006; Florence Land May, *The Broken Wheel* (Boston: C. M. Clark, 1910); Florence Land May, *Lyrics from Lotus Lands* (Boston: Poet Lore Company, 1911); Margery Land May, *Such as Sit in Judgment* (London: L. Parson, 1923).

8. Vita, folder 1, MLC/CHRC; Pat Land Stevens, e-mail to author, July 14, 2006.

9. Hunter, *How Young Ladies Became Girls*, 375–76.

10. Ibid., 376.

11. Mary Land Lock, *Shadows of the Swamp* (Dallas, Tex.: Kaleidoscope Press, 1940); Mary Land, *Abode* (Natchitoches: by the author, 1972); Mary Land, *Dreams* (Baton Rouge: Claitor's, 1977); Land, *Abode*, 31, 91.

12. "In the Spotlight this Week: Mary Land," *Register*, November 6, 1954, 12.

13. Pat Land Stevens, e-mail to author, March 16, 2007.

14. Unnumbered exhibit box, MLC/TU.

15. *Down South*, November–December 1964, 17, papers, box 2, folder 8, MLC/TU.

16. Mary Land Lock, "A Woman's Angle on Angling," *Louisiana Conservation Review* 9 (Autumn 1940): 17–18.

17. Lock, "A Woman's Angle," 18.

18. Pat Land Stevens, e-mail to author, July 31, 2006; "E. Timothy Kelly" vertical file, Hogan Jazz Archive, Tulane University, New Orleans.

19. "Mary Elizabeth Land," photocopy, labeled "Who's Who in World of Women," International Biographical Center, Cambridge, England, folder 1, MLC/CHRC; Pat Land Stevens, e-mail to author, July 31, 2006.

20. Matilda Geddings Gray and Ethel Wight Usher, *Food for Gourmets* (New Orleans: by the authors, 1940), 5.

21. W. T. Block, "Capt. Daniel Goos: An Early Lake Charles Sawmiller," William T. Block, http://hans.wtblock.com/wtblockjr/danielgoos.htm; Pat Land Stevens, e-mail to author, July 31, 2006; Donald J. Millet, "The Lumber Industry of 'Imperial Calcasieu': 1865–1900," *Louisiana History* 7 (Winter 1966): 59, 62; Usher and Gray, *Food for Gourmets*, xi, 191; Mary Land, *New Orleans Cuisine* (South Brunswick, N.J.: A. S. Barnes, 1969), 122, 185; Land, *Louisiana Cookery*, 40, 43–44.

22. Pat Land Stevens, e-mail to author, July 29, 2006.

23. Ibid.

24. Ibid., July 31, 2006.

25. Caroline Dormon scrapbook, Historic New Orleans Collection.

26. Pat Land Stevens, e-mail to author, July 31, 2006.

27. Ibid., July 31, 2006, March 23, 2007.

28. Ibid.; Mary Land, interview by Ronald Davis, ca. 1981, transcript, 1, box 2, folder 1, MLC/TU.

29. Pat Land Stevens, interview by Susan Tucker, n.d., transcript, MLC/TU.

30. James Beard to Mary Land, n.d., unnumbered exhibit box, MLC/TU.

31. June Owens, "News of Food," *New York Times*, January 4, 1955.

32. Stephen Longstreet, "Carbon on review to appear soon in the L.A. Daily News and on radio show: Let's Eat," MLC/TU; Pat Land Stevens, interview by Susan Tucker, n.d., transcript, MLC/TU.

33. Land, *Louisiana Cookery*, i, 43, 90. On the penchant for using convenience foods as shortcuts, see Laura Shapiro, *Something from the Oven: Reinventing Dinner in 1950s America* (New York: Viking, 2004), and Jessamyn Neuhaus, *Manly Meals and Mom's Home Cooking: Cookbooks and Gender in Modern America* (Baltimore: Johns Hopkins University Press, 2003), 174–76.

34. Land, *Louisiana Cookery*, xvii.

35. Owens, "News of Food," *New York Times*, January 4, 1955.

36. Land, *Louisiana Cookery*, xviii.

37. John Thorne, with Matt Lewis Thorne, *Serious Pig: An American Cook in Search of His Roots* (New York: North Point Press, 1996), 211.

38. Lafcadio Hearn, *La Cuisine Creole* (New York: W. H. Coleman, 1885); Christian Woman's Exchange, *Creole Cookery Book* (New Orleans: T. H. Thomason, 1885); *The Picayune's Creole Cook Book* (New Orleans: The Picayune, 1900); Célestine Eustis, *Cooking in Old Créole Days: La cuisine créole à l'usage des petits ménages* (New York: R. H. Russell, 1903); Peter S. Feibleman, *American Cooking: Creole and Acadian* (New York: Time-Life Books, 1971); Nathan Burton and Rudy Lombard, *Creole Feast: Fifteen Master Chefs of New Orleans Reveal Their Secrets* (New York: Random House, 1978); *The Acadian Bi-Centennial Cook Book* (Jennings, La.: Louisiana Acadian Handicraft Museum, 1955); Junior League of Baton Rouge, *River Road Recipes* (Baton Rouge: Junior League of Baton Rouge, 1959); Junior League of Lafayette, *Talk about Good!* (Lafayette, La.: Junior League of Lafayette, 1969). On Cajun cookbooks, see Marcelle Bienvenu, Carl A. Brasseaux, and Ryan André Brasseaux, *Stir the Pot: The History of Cajun Cuisine* (New York: Hippocrene Books, 2005), 52–53.

39. Alice B. Toklas, *The Alice B. Toklas Cook Book* (New York: Harper and Brothers, 1954); Neuhaus, *Manly Meals*, 167, 180; Sheila Hibben, *American Regional Cookery* (Boston: Little, Brown, 1946); Mary Margaret McBride, *Harvest of American Cooking with Recipes for 1,000 of America's Favorite Dishes* (New York: G. P. Putnam's Sons, 1957); Clementine Paddleford, *How America Eats* (New York: Scribner's, 1960).

40. Land, *New Orleans Cuisine*.

41. Harnett T. Kane to Mary Land, November 7, 1969, MLC/TU.

42. *Hooks and Lines*, August 1969, scrapbooks, box 2, MLC/TU.

43. *Southern Outdoors*, May 1960, 41, papers, box 2, folder 17, MLC/TU.

44. Mary Land, "Happy Land," papers, box 1, folder 7, MLC/TU.

45. Pat Land Stevens, e-mail to author, July 31, 2006.

Rowena Spencer

(1922–)

A Study of Changing Gender Roles in Twentieth-Century Louisiana Medicine

BAMBI L. RAY COCHRAN

❀ ❀ ❀

There was a time when becoming a medical doctor required little more than plunking down the money for a license and hanging out the proverbial shingle. Medicine in the early nineteenth century was more of a craft than a profession, and most doctors learned their trade through apprenticeships. Prior to the widespread acceptance of the "germ theory" of disease in the late nineteenth century, there was little a doctor could do to help cure illness anyway. In any case, most families seldom if ever called a doctor. Most "doctoring" was done in the home by women. When an outside expert was called in, it was frequently a midwife, come to care for a laboring mother or an ailing infant. Throughout much of human history, women were the primary health care providers for their families. Women served not just as doctors but as nurses and pharmacists, too, for they often grew their own herbs from which they made their own poultices, medicines, and tonics.[1]

The rise of standardized medical education and scientific developments during the nineteenth century largely pushed women out of their traditional roles in medicine. In 1847 Nathan Davis formed the American Medical Association to establish professional standards and encourage the states to adopt uniform licensing and educational requirements. Gradually, the states began to comply, and as they did so, male professionals replaced female healers. Men became the gatekeepers at each step of the process, and men determined who entered the profession. Although some all-female medical schools opened, like the Women's Medical College of Philadelphia, most medical schools in the nineteenth century refused to admit women. At the turn of the twentieth century, internships and residencies developed as additional hallmarks of training, and female graduates—regardless of which school they attended—found these positions out of reach for them.[2] In short, as the practice of medicine professionalized, women were excluded. They were the unprofessional healers, not the professional ones. Thus, they had to fight to get back into a field they had once dominated.

The career of Rowena Spencer illustrates the difficulties women experienced in the second half of the twentieth century when attempting to regain a place for themselves in the practice of medicine. Rowena Spencer's family provided a foundation of female doctor role models, high-quality education, and financial support for its daughters that was almost unique in the American South. She obtained superb medical education and training in American programs that accepted small numbers of women but treated their female students differently from their male students. She then entered a medical profession that continued to treat her differently in ways that debilitated her career. Post–World War II American certainty that the only acceptable roles for women were homemaker and mother combined with medical schools that accepted few women resulted in isolation and obstacles for Spencer and other women medical doctors. Spencer nevertheless made a successful career and had a positive impact on the improvement of medical practices in Louisiana and the profession in general. Like many women in demanding professions from 1940 through 1970, she could find no way to combine her profession with marriage and motherhood.

Spencer was part of a remarkable Louisiana family that produced two female doctors in two generations at a time when it was highly irregular for women in the South to pursue any kind of a career, much less a career in a field as thoroughly professionalized and masculinized as medicine had become by the early twentieth century. Rowena Spencer became Louisiana's first female surgeon and the first surgeon, male or female, in the state with a specialty in pediatric surgery. Spencer's career reflects shifts in the professions, in gender roles, and in society from World War II through the latter half of the twentieth century. Although often outside the dominant culture of American medicine, Spencer overcame the educational, professional, and sociocultural adversities of her generation and achieved both fame and success in her profession.

Rowena Spencer was born July 3, 1922, to Dr. Lewis Cass Spencer and Alice Beatrice Smead Spencer in Shreveport, Louisiana. Lewis Spencer, an orthopedic surgeon, moved his family to north Louisiana while trying to obtain a residency at the newly established Shriners Hospital in Shreveport. Rowena was the third of four daughters— "not the one you expect to be aggressive"—and in her adulthood became the eleventh doctor in her family.[3]

DR. ROWENA SPENCER

Courtesy of the Historic New Orleans Collection,

Museum/Research Center, acc. no. 2003.107, box 11, f. 123.

For generations, members of the Spencer family espoused progressive ideas regarding women, providing Rowena with nearly instinctive strength and determination to pursue a career in medicine. The women in the Spencer family became strong assets in times of need or distress, when male family members died or were away on business or fighting in wars. With little hesitation the women took financial or legal matters into their own hands to provide better lives for themselves and their children or for extended family members. At a time when women had few legal rights, the Spencer women bought and sold property, managed their own financial affairs, and ran their own plantations with little or no male assistance.[4]

Several female members of the Spencer family bequeathed money and property to surviving relatives, proving them capable of managing their own finances. Family-related documents also include a request for dissolution of community property in 1910 by Rowena Spencer Turberville. The Catahoula Parish district court awarded her "full authority . . . to conduct her own separate business and affairs,"[5] legally separating the financial assets of Rowena Turberville from those of her husband, Louis. At a time when men usually controlled the property of their wives, she applied for *femme sole* status to prevent her own money from being used to pay off her husband's debts. The tenacity of many of the family's female members no doubt affected later generations and their perceptions of women's roles in society and in the professional world.

When Rowena Turberville petitioned the court for a separation of community property while remaining married, she employed a seldom-used provision of the *Louisiana Civil Code* that dated back at least to 1808. Louisiana law protected a wife's dowry and income generated by business enterprises operated independently by her during the marriage from the claims of creditors against the community property of the marriage. The wife's right to a division of the community property without a legal separation or divorce was available only when the community property remaining was insufficient to pay all the debts.[6]

Higher education of females in the Spencer family also contributed to their roles as strong women. Spencer's great-uncle Judge William Brainerd Spencer advocated the continued education of women; two of his daughters, Adeline and Mary, received doctoral degrees and both taught at Newcomb College in New Orleans.[7] In addition, Sara Tew Mayo, Rowena's great-aunt, attended medical school at the Women's Medical College of Philadelphia. Mayo returned to New Orleans at the turn of the twentieth century with a medical degree and in 1905 helped to establish the New Orleans Dispensary for Women and Children. This health care facility, renamed the Sara Mayo Hospital in 1948, proved that female physicians could prosper in New Orleans and provided an excellent professional example for younger members of the Spencer family.[8]

Rowena's family moved back to New Orleans shortly after her birth and remained in the metropolitan area until 1928, when they returned to rural Catahoula Parish to assist her ailing paternal grandmother, Rowena Spencer Jones, with the affairs of the family plantation. The Spencer family lived near Utility, a small town now defunct, but in Rowena's childhood Utility, Louisiana, steadily held "a population of eight for three consecutive censuses."[9] Rowena's sisters were not excited about living in the country, but she was thrilled at the prospect. Rowena inherited her father's love of the outdoors and thoroughly enjoyed life on the plantation. She spent much of her youth outside, catching snakes and figuring out how to keep her bloomers dry so that she would not get in trouble for playing in the Little River.[10]

At an early age Rowena Spencer became enamored with young children. She often carried her younger sister Sara piggyback through the woods or carried the baby of a nearby neighbor up and down the riverbank on her hip.[11] She began babysitting as soon as she was old enough and saved enough money to pay for a good portion of her own undergraduate studies at Louisiana State University. When she was eighteen, Rowena also volunteered her time and money to aid in the care of an undernourished refugee infant. Her love of babies ultimately led her to a career in pediatric surgery, a medical specialty still in early development when she entered medical school.[12]

Rowena graduated from Block High School in Catahoula Parish in 1939, and the following autumn she enrolled in courses at Louisiana State University, the state's first fully coeducational college.[13] Coinciding developments in both medical education and women's education in the twentieth century are important factors in Rowena Spencer's career. The educational criteria for medical doctors changed greatly from the late nineteenth century through the post–World War II era, putting emphasis on extended training and membership in professional societies. Simultaneously, many all-female medical schools merged with male programs, effectively limiting the total number of women graduating as doctors of medicine well into the late twentieth century.[14]

The years between 1900 and 1965 proved difficult for women who chose to enter the medical profession. Despite the gains women made in nineteenth-century medicine, the number of female doctors decreased from 6 percent to 4 percent during this period and did not increase again until the late 1960s.[15] Even the increased number of female medical students during the World War II era did not create a significant change in the overall percentage of women in the field.[16]

Two main factors contributed to the decline in women's numbers in medical programs as Rowena began her postsecondary education in 1939. First, many all-female medical schools had been forced to close or had been consumed by larger coeducational programs, reducing the numbers of women admitted into medical schools. Second, at the turn of the twentieth century, the interests of various competing groups such as "professional associations, state licensing agencies, and colleges and universities" had come together to promote medical consolidation and reform.[17] This move served the self-interests of the men who dominated the profession. It suppressed many inferior institutions and reduced the overall number "of practitioners in a field believed already to be overcrowded."[18]

Despite nationwide setbacks in women's medical education, some opportunities were available to southern women interested in medicine. The Medical School at Louisiana State University accepted female students and was Rowena's first choice, but her father insisted that Rowena attend his alma mater, the Johns Hopkins University, because he considered it the only medical school worth attending.[19] She received a six-hundred-dollar scholarship to Johns Hopkins and entered the program in 1943.

The Johns Hopkins Medical School is significant in the medical history of the South, especially in the development of women's professional education in the region. The medical school opened in 1893 in Baltimore, Maryland, and was one of the first southern medical schools to accept women, a stipulation set forth by a few wealthy women who contributed money to establish the program. The medical school's female benefactors demanded very high preliminary requirements for both genders, causing many of its male administrators to protest for fear that the admission qualifications were too high to permit very many male applicants to be admitted. The admission policies of the Johns Hopkins program helped set a nationwide precedent for medical schools, but while the medical program's admission requirements were the same for men and women, its male and female students were not always treated equally in the classroom.[20]

The Johns Hopkins Medical School joined science, research, and clinical hospital practice in an unprecedented manner and was one of the first medical programs to establish a rigorous four-year training program. Hands-on experience such as internships and residencies quickly became an additional benchmark for medical training at the turn of the twentieth century, and Johns Hopkins incorporated this into its program as well. In fact, the term "residency" was first used at Hopkins "to describe advanced specialty training following an internship."[21] Although the program accepted female students and employed a few notable female physicians like Dr. Florence Sabin, a half century after the school's formation its internships and residencies were nearly always awarded to men.[22]

The Johns Hopkins medical education was innovative and reputable, but Rowena (unlike students in all-female educational environments) received little exposure to female role models. Other female graduates of Johns Hopkins also noted the "poverty of female role models."[23] Women's medical programs provided great incentives for students to see female physicians putting their training into practice and also allowed students opportunities to develop ideas about gender and social equality in a favorable setting. Rowena eventually became the first female surgical intern at Johns Hopkins, studying under the renowned surgeon Dr. Alfred Blalock and his assistant, Vivien Thomas. Although her career set a number of precedents for women in the medical profession at Johns Hopkins and in Louisiana, Rowena Spencer's accomplishments have been overlooked by most historians, who have chosen to ignore the significant contributions of female students, instructors, or physicians to medical schools or the profession in general.[24]

Rowena Spencer's years at Johns Hopkins marked for her the beginning of decades of experiences of gender discrimination in her training and work. These experiences demonstrate the lack of respect for female students at the institution and are also representative of the attitudes toward female students at many other coeducational schools.[25] Although Johns Hopkins had helped set the precedent for coeducation in southern medical schools, both obvious and covert forms of inequity still existed.[26] Pervasive stereotypes regarding female students were but one of the many ways in which Spencer and other female students were encumbered by gender discrimination. The dormitory for female medical students was nicknamed "the hen house" by male students, a term that implied female students were fussy and loud rather than academically inclined.

While enrolled in a medical art class she was "refused permission to go alone into the morgue [in a dark, dank, isolated part of the hospital basement] to draw gross specimens. . . . When adult males with hernias were presented in the clinic," the instructor forced her to stand behind a curtain and only listen to the instructions given on how to examine them.[27] Ironically, she performed over four thousand hernioplasties, or hernia removal surgeries, during her thirty-year career. During her fourth year of education at Johns Hopkins an instructor refused Rowena the opportunity to examine male urology patients, and she threatened to report the chief resident to the dean. When finally allowed to examine male patients, she faced a dual problem: Rowena did not know how to examine them at first and, on occasion, male patients refused to allow her to perform an examination because she was a female.[28] Male students never encountered instructors who forced them to stand behind a curtain during examinations of female patients.

The high standards for both male and female students at Johns Hopkins combined with the experience of its instructors and researchers quickly established it as a leading school in the development and instruction of specialized fields of medicine and experimental surgical techniques.[29] The coinciding creation of internships and residencies and their emphasis in the Johns Hopkins curriculum created an ideal atmosphere for the birth of new medical specialties, since many interns and residents trained in a specific field. This educational environment provided Rowena with opportunities available at few other medical institutions in the nation, although Rowena "did henpecking . . . and browbeating," as she described it, to receive a surgical internship.[30] Most physicians saw the development of new specialties as economically and scientifically beneficial, but there were some critics who argued that certain fields—such as pediatric surgery— were unnecessary medical innovations.

Spencer graduated from Johns Hopkins in 1947 and immediately applied for a surgical internship at the Johns Hopkins Hospital. Her personal interest in children led her to combine aspects of a traditionally female career option with a more masculine-oriented specialty. At that time, specialized fields such as orthopedics and surgery were still reserved for male doctors. Fields such as internal medicine, obstetrics-gynecology, pediatrics, and psychiatry attracted women because of the flexible schedules that allowed easier planning around familial responsibility.

Alfred Blalock initially discouraged her but ultimately yielded, and in July 1947 Rowena became the hospital's first female intern in general surgery. She learned much of her technique from Blalock's African American laboratory assistant, Vivien Thomas. Thomas developed surgical instruments still used in today's operations and, with Blalock, pioneered surgical techniques, but for many years he received little recognition for his skill owing to his race. Rowena had few women role models during her years at Johns Hopkins and claims that only Thomas gave her specific encouragement. Perhaps Thomas identified with the discrimination Rowena experienced at Johns Hopkins and took a keener interest in her success than in that of other more established, white, male physicians. Spencer credits few instructors with her success as a pediatric surgeon but "when complimented on her surgical technique, [Rowena] always pointed out that she learned her skills from Thomas."[31]

When she applied for a residency at Johns Hopkins, Blalock refused Rowena because she was a woman. Her specialty choice of pediatric surgery also might have played a part in her residency denial. Even though Johns Hopkins continued to be at the forefront of coeducation and emerging specialties, the debate among some professors regarding the unnecessary development of highly specialized areas of expertise affected the decision to deny Spencer continued training at Johns Hopkins.[32] Instead, Blalock contacted the Women's Medical College of Philadelphia—the alma mater of Rowena's great-aunt, Dr. Sara Mayo—but no surgical residencies were available at that time. He did, however, write an excellent recommendation in support of her application for a residency at the Children's Hospital of Philadelphia, which she was ultimately offered.[33] Spencer believed that Blalock wrote a strong recommendation primarily to be rid of the liability of a female student. While at the Children's Hospital, she specialized in pediatric surgery under the direction of C. Everett Koop, who later became U.S. surgeon general.[34]

In 1949, Rowena returned to Louisiana State University where she studied both pediatrics and general surgery, again the first woman to do so. She completed her medical training at the Karolinska Institute in Stockholm, Sweden, that country's first school to graduate a female physician.[35] Her time spent training in Europe was much less strenuous than her educational experiences in the United States. Spencer noted that in Sweden she encountered far less gender discrimination and actually worked with another female pediatric surgeon at the institute.[36] By the time Spencer completed her training, 17 percent of Sweden's medical graduates were females. During World War II, the number of women in American medical programs increased slightly, but in "the 1950s and 1960s women accounted for 5 to 8 percent of medical students and did not reach 9 percent until 1969–1970."[37]

In the late nineteenth century, other nations became less resistant to the idea of female physicians and provided an environment in which they were not subjected to the kind of educational and professional gender discrimination that many women experienced in the United States. Spencer claims her work schedule left her little time to develop relationships with men or women, but while in Sweden, Spencer developed a relationship with a male colleague named Raimo from Norway. It is unclear exactly how serious their relationship became, but in a letter to her parents in March 1954, she informed them that she was not going home with him or bringing him home with her.[38]

Upon her return to the United States, Spencer again faced gender and professional discrimination. The culture of postwar America, with its emphasis on traditional family roles and stay-at-home moms, did not lend support to female professionals and thus provided a less than favorable environment for the early development of Spencer's career. The post–World War II era pushed women back into domestic roles, and women who consciously chose to pursue a career often did so at the expense of having a husband and children.[39] Spencer became so focused on her career that other aspects of her life languished.

Female physicians came into conflict with "the gender-based structure of sexual-economic relations and the sexual division of labor . . . [and its] visions of womanhood, motherhood, and the life course" by fulfilling educational and professional goals rather than being wives and mothers.[40] In fact, identity work—defining a sense of identity through a meaningful profession, "was formerly restricted almost exclusively to men. A woman's identity was traditionally defined by marriage, as wife and mother. . . . It was not uncommon for a woman to drop out of medical school after marriage or drop out of practice for 8 to 10 years to take care of her family."[41] There are many instances of women who managed the demands of a career and family, but just as frequently women felt that they must deny themselves the privilege of family life to focus on their careers.[42]

Although some argued that women were well suited to medicine because of their nurturing character, others saw them as feminine anomalies for desiring professional positions. The professional world judged professional women unfavorably for exhibiting "masculine" traits such as "rationality, objectivity, technical authoritativeness, and aggressiveness in the face of emergencies."[43] Instead of seeing them as assertive, bold, or risk taking in their careers, as men would be seen, they viewed many professional women as argumentative or insulting to their superiors when daring to question them. Spencer characterized herself as "bossy" and "impatient," and her insistence on the reforms she believed important in pediatric surgery caused a number of incidents with male colleagues.[44]

In the post–World War II era, female physicians began to move away from being activists proposing and supporting reforms in medicine that characterized women's earlier participation in medicine. Spencer, therefore, was an activist at a time when professional activism by women was strongly discouraged. Throughout her career, she fought arduously for improvements in pediatric practices, often taking babies to and from operating or X-ray rooms herself to ensure that they received the best care possible.[45] Evidence of how much effort she put into her career is the fact that she worked eight years without a single day off.[46]

Another example of Spencer's drive to improve treatment of pediatric patients was her effort to get the profession to abandon the practice of drawing blood from the heels of babies, which caused scar tissue and lifelong pain. Spencer also attempted to establish a pediatric intensive care unit at Charity Hospital but was rebuffed by hospital officials who claimed that there were no adequately trained nurses to sustain the unit. Spencer offered to help train the nurses, but the unit never came to fruition. Instead the space it would have occupied was used to store Christmas toys for young patients in other wards.[47]

Spencer's career in pediatric surgery led her to become interested in conjoined twins. In 1954 she surgically separated the Duckworth twins—female conjoined twins from Mississippi—in order to save the life of the stronger twin. The operation was the first of its kind performed on newborns. Her interest in conjoined twins continued, and she wrote or cowrote articles on the topic for several medical journals, including *Clinical Anatomy, Neurosurgery Quarterly*, and the *Journal of Pediatric Surgery*. By the time of her retirement Spencer had clinical experience with fifteen sets of conjoined twins.[48]

Even after Spencer's retirement she continued research on conjoined twins, reviewing over a thousand cases. She publicly presented findings on the topic in 1991 and 1992. In 2003 she completed her book, *Conjoined Twins: Embryology, Pathogenesis, and Review of the Literature*, published by the Johns Hopkins University Press. She is now considered one of the world's leading authorities on the topic, and even in her retirement she continues to consult with physicians worldwide in their own cases and research related to conjoined twins.[49]

In the mid-twentieth century, the New Orleans medical community still resisted female physicians to some extent. Some local male physicians remained hostile to women in the field, but others readily referred their patients to Spencer. Her specialty in surgery brought the contempt of most general surgeons who felt that her training stole patients from their practices. She was even insulted by a male doctor in front of the parents of a critically ill patient when he told them that local "pediatricians must be scraping the bottom of the barrel to engage her services."[50]

Despite the criticism she received from some colleagues, many of Spencer's patients and their families readily voiced their appreciation for her efforts. Numerous letters in her family's collection of papers document their gratitude for her work as a pediatric surgeon. In 1992, almost thirty years after an operation performed on her daughter, Georgieanna Cooke noted that "all through her follow-up, you took such a loving interest in her development" and informed Spencer that "many grateful parents . . . think of you with happy thoughts everyday."[51] A former patient named Stan Saulny wrote to her in 1993 regarding a letter that Spencer wrote to the *Times-Picayune* entitled "Success in the Face of Bias." He stated, "I am inspired by your success . . . in becoming the first female surgeon in Louisiana. I am impressed with the empathy your letter conveys towards the black community, your insight into African-American issues, and your boldness . . . in discussing your views openly in Louisiana." He also informed her that his parents always spoke of her in high regard and that he felt fortunate that they selected her to treat him as a child.[52] Her success was also acknowledged in the 1984 World's Fair held in New Orleans, where the women's pavilion included Spencer in a select list of women of achievement in Louisiana.[53]

Thanks to Dr. Sara Mayo and her women colleagues in the early twentieth century, some professional barriers in New Orleans had been broken. Medical society membership and university teaching positions were more readily accessible to Rowena than they were to her great-aunt. She became a member of the Orleans Parish Medical Society in 1953, without being subjected to full proof of capability or worth like her female predecessors.[54] She also taught full-time at Louisiana State University from 1954 to 1968 and then part-time at Tulane University Medical School from 1968 to 1978.[55]

Many women who helped break barriers in American medicine in the late nineteenth century also had ties to organizations for women's rights. After the reforms of the early twentieth century that led to all-female and all-male medical schools being combined, many women lost sight of feminist reform in the profession.[56] The lack of female associates in her career presented Spencer with fewer opportunities for exposure to or discussion of women's equality in the workplace or other feminist issues. Many women like Spencer experienced "professional isolation, whereas the experience for men is highly social and socializing."[57] She reports that her schedule as a pediatric surgeon kept her too busy to become involved in political issues such as the equal rights amendment or the broader women's movement of the 1960s and 1970s. She also states that she had no female colleagues during her career, which meant she received less emotional and psychological support than female doctors, such as her aunt, received in the early twentieth century.

The life of a female surgeon in post–World War II America "was a lonely life. After work, while residents hung around together, Dr. Spencer was left out. . . . [In] Louisiana she wasn't even allowed in the doctor's lounge. While the other doctors gathered to talk and exchange information, she drank coffee with the nurses."[58] She had to struggle much harder to achieve success in her career, since exchanges of new information and ideas are frequently done informally, in lounges, changing rooms, and other spaces.

Spencer claims that she did not set out to be a pioneer in her field, but nevertheless her career included many of the "firsts" of her specialty. She became the first female surgeon in Louisiana and the first pediatric surgeon in the state, male or female. Spencer spent the early years of her career at the Louisiana State University Medical School, where she became the first female appointed to a full-time position on the surgical staff. From 1968–77 she practiced pediatric surgery at the Tulane University Hospital.[59] She opened a private practice in New Orleans, and another office in the New Orleans suburb of Metairie, operating both successfully until her retirement in 1984.

Spencer claims that her career was highly rewarding and that she would do it over again, but her years as a pediatric surgeon were not without hardships. Although the notion of women in the workforce had become more acceptable than when her great-aunt had been a physician, the predominant idea during Spencer's career was that the ideal role for women was homemaker. The Great Depression and World War II forced many women to seek paid positions that had previously been designated for men, but the postwar drive to return to a "normal" way of life pushed many women in the paid workforce back into domestic and economically dependent roles.[60] Spencer completed her medical training during this postwar period, and her career choice conflicted with this national trend. Her love of children led her down a career path in which she touched and saved the lives of many people, especially children. Her career became so time consuming that she found it impossible to combine a career that she loved with a long-term relationship. She never married or produced any children of her own.[61] Never a mother herself she explains: "My greatest satisfaction now comes from graduation and wedding invitations from my former babies, phone calls and visits (to see what I really look like now that they are adults) and a recent treasure—a baby named for me by the 25-year old mother whom I had operated on shortly after she was born."[62]

After retiring in 1984, Spencer took up numerous hobbies such as gardening, tatting—a form of lace making—and genealogy research. She became president of the Louisiana Fern Society and president of the Half-fast Knitters Guild of New Orleans. She claims that she does not miss practicing medicine, but she does miss the babies and occasionally returns to the hospital nursery to "ask for a baby, a bottle, and a rocking chair."[63] The personal experiences of Dr. Rowena Spencer shine light on four decades of development in the medical profession, including changes in the standardization of medical education and practices and changes in women's roles in the professions. Although sometimes feeling like an outsider in the dominant male culture of American medicine, her active involvement in the field helped to transform ideas regarding children's health in Louisiana and in the specific area of conjoined twins.[64] Perhaps because of the strong support and encouragement she received from her unique family, she overcame hurdles in education and the profession itself to help raise the quality of medicine available to Louisiana citizens.

NOTES

1. Magali Sarfatti Larson, *The Rise of Professionalism: A Sociological Analysis* (Berkeley: University of California Press, 1977), 160–63.

2. Delease Wear, *Women in Medical Education: An Anthology of Experience* (Albany: State University of New York Press, 1996), xiii; Ruth J. Abram, introduction, in *Send Us a Lady Physician: Women Doctors in America, 1835–1920*, ed. Ruth J. Abram (New York: Norton, 1985), 5. Both Abram and Wear discuss the complexity of gender issues in medicine. Although women were excluded from the field, there was still a demand by female patients for female doctors.

3. Sheila Stroup, "Babies Still Keep Her Up," June 17, 1993, box 10, folder 106, Spencer Family Papers, Historic New Orleans Collection (hereinafter cited as SFP/HNOC); Margaret Fuller, "Dr. Rowena Spencer: Rattling the Scalpels of Male Dominated Medicine," June 29, 1982, *New Orleans Times-Picayune/States-Item*, box 2, folder 17, SFP/HNOC.

4. Typed list of conveyances for Catahoula and La Salle parishes, box 6, folder 73, SFP/HNOC.

5. Dissolution of community property, box 8, folder 87, SFP/HNOC.

6. *Louisiana Civil Code*, art. 2425. Art. 131 of the *Civil Code*, also dating to 1808 or earlier, which authorized a wife to act as a "public merchant," enabled a married Louisiana woman to begin and operate a business separate from her husband's business. Two years after the court decision in favor of Rowena Turberville, the Louisiana legislature changed the *Civil Code* so that a wife would not have to obtain a legal separation of bed and board when living separately from her husband to keep her earnings as her separate property. This change in the law (although not directly on point with the Turberville case, since she continued to live with her husband) provided another avenue in the late nineteenth century for Louisiana married women to be able to support themselves (*Louisiana Statutes*, act 170 [1912]; Harriet S. Daggett, "The Modern Problem of the Nature of the Wife's Interest in Community Property: A Comparative Study," *California Law Review* 19 [September 1931]: 581, 487, 489).

7. "Adeline Spencer, Retired Newcomb Teacher Is Dead," box 4, folder 43, SFP/HNOC; Tinette Lichtenstein, "Among the Outstanding Alumni," *The Tulanian*, April 1940, 7, 12, box 6, folder 65, SFP/HNOC.

8. Stella Pitts, "Bans against Lady Doctors Couldn't Stop Sara Tew Mayo," *New Orleans Times Picayune*, March 7, 1976; resolution of the board, box 10, folder 104, SFP/HNOC.

9. Stroup, "Babies Still Keep Her Up," June 17, 1993, box 10, folder 106, SFP/HNOC.

10. Rowena Spencer, interview by author and Mark Cave, tape recording, New Orleans, April 29, 2004.

11. Fuller, "Rattling the Scalpels," June 29, 1982, *New Orleans Times-Picayune/States-Item*, box 2, folder 17, SFP/HNOC.

12. See Rowena Spencer, untitled, unpublished essay, box 28, folder 262, SFP/HNOC; Stroup, "Babies Still Keep Her Up," June 17, 1993, box 10, folder 106, SFP/HNOC.

13. Carmen Lindig, *The Path from the Parlor: Louisiana Women, 1879–1920* (Lafayette: Center for Louisiana Studies, University of Southwestern Louisiana, 1986), 77–78. Louisiana State University became fully coeducational in 1905.

14. Regina Markell Morantz-Sanchez, *Sympathy and Science: Women Physicians in American*

Medicine (New York: Oxford University Press, 1985), 87–89, 234–35, 254–55. Many women in the medical profession at this time incorrectly believed that merging all-female medical schools with male-dominated programs would provide greater opportunities for women in medicine.

15. Regina Markell Morantz-Sanchez, "So Honored, So Loved? The Women's Medical Movement in Decline," in *Send Us a Lady Physician*, 232.

16. Marjorie A. Bowman and Deborah I. Allen, *Stress and Women Physicians* (New York: Springer-Verlag, 1985), 5. Bowman and Allen note that both female students and instructors experienced intellectual sexism in the university setting during this period. More women were allowed into medical programs during World War II but only because there were vacancies that could not be filled by men serving in the armed forces. Many programs chose to remain small or downsize as a result of the depression and the war, and so there was not a substantial increase of females in the field.

17. Morantz-Sanchez, "So Honored, So Loved?" 233; Paul Starr, *The Social Transformation of American Medicine: The Rise of a Sovereign Profession and the Making of a Vast Industry* (New York: Basic Books, 1982), 112–27.

18. Morantz-Sanchez, "So Honored, So Loved?" 233, 243; Rosemary Stevens, *American Medicine and the Public Interest* (New Haven: Yale University Press, 1971), 55–73; David Rosner and Gerald Markowitz, "Doctors in Crisis: Medical Education and Medical Reform during the Progressive Era, 1895–1915," *American Quarterly* 25 (March 1973): 83–107; Larson, *The Rise of Professionalism*, 161.

19. Rowena Spencer, "Rowena Spencer," unpublished essay, 2002, folder 2, SFP/HNOC. The Tulane University Medical School also accepted female students at this point, but Rowena's father would not consider any schools other than Johns Hopkins.

20. Bertram M. Bernheim, *The Story of the Johns Hopkins: Four Great Doctors and the Medical School They Created* (New York: Whittlesey House, 1948), 31; Morantz-Sanchez, *Sympathy and Science*, 254. Maryland's cultural identification with the South did not warrant its secession from the Union over the issue of slavery.

21. Paul Starr, *The Social Transformation of American Medicine*, 116.

22. Fuller, "Rattling the Scalpels," June 29, 1982, *New Orleans Times-Picayune/States-Item*, box 2, folder 17, SFP/HNOC.

23. Morantz-Sanchez, *Sympathy and Science*, 254–55.

24. See Alan M. Chesney, *The Johns Hopkins Hospital and the Johns Hopkins University School of Medicine: A Chronicle*, vol. 2, 1905–14 (Baltimore: Johns Hopkins Press, 1963), 2:13. Although Johns Hopkins was established as a coeducational medical program, Chesney devalues the contributions of its female students by his lack of acknowledgment of their enrollment or accomplishments in the medical school.

25. Morantz-Sanchez, *Sympathy and Science*, 88.

26. See Rowena Spencer, "Rowena Spencer," unpublished essay, 2002, folder 2, SFP/HNOC.

27. Ibid.

28. Ibid.; Bernheim, *The Story of the Johns Hopkins*, 33. Bernheim claims that "there has been no occasion for the girls to step aside or to refrain from examining men patients." Dr. Spencer's experience may not be indicative of all female medical students at Johns Hopkins, but it is nonetheless the case that she was not allowed initially to examine male patients.

29. Chesney, *The Johns Hopkins Hospital and the Johns Hopkins University School of Medicine*, 2:12, 14.

30. Fuller, "Rattling the Scalpels," June 29, 1982, *New Orleans Times-Picayune/States-Item*, box 2, folder 17, SFP/HNOC.

31. Rowena Spencer, interview by author and Mark Cave, tape recording, New Orleans, April 29, 2004; *Footprints through Time: Rowena Spencer (1922–)* , http://pbs.org/wgbh/amex/partners/legacy/l_colleagues_spencer.html, July 30, 2003.

32. Bernheim, *The Story of the Johns Hopkins*, 110.

33. Anonymous, "Rowena Spencer," unpublished essay, 2002, folder 2, SFP/HNOC.

34. Ibid. See also *Footprints through Time: Rowena Spencer (1922–)*. This web page also discusses a PBS documentary film entitled *Partners of the Heart*, about two of Dr. Spencer's instructors at Johns Hopkins, Dr. Alfred Blalock and Vivien Thomas, his laboratory technician.

35. Thomas Neville Bonner, *To the Ends of the Earth: Women's Search for Education in Medicine* (Cambridge: Harvard University Press, 1992), 54. The study of medicine was opened to females in Sweden in 1870.

36. Rowena Spencer, interview by author and Mark Cave, tape recording, New Orleans, April 29, 2004.

37. Bonner, *To the Ends of the Earth*, viii, 54, 168. Among other sources, Bonner uses data from Beverly C. Morgan, "Admission of Women into Medical Schools in the United States: Current Status," *Woman Physician* 26 (1971): 305.

38. Dr. Rowena Spencer to Dr. and Mrs. Lewis C. Spencer, March 23, 1954, box 10, folder 116, SFP/HNOC.

39. See Anne Firor Scott, *The Southern Lady: From Pedestal to Politics, 1830–1930* (Charlottesville: University Press of Virginia, 1970), 37; Suzanne Poirier, "Women's Reproductive Health," in *Women, Health, and Medicine in America*, ed. Rima D. Apple (New York: Garland Publishing, 1990), 225; Gail Collins, *America's Women: 400 Years of Dolls, Drudges, Helpmates, and Heroines* (New York: William Morrow, 2003), 398. Collins claims that "after having survived the Depression and kept the economy running in World War II, women seemed to have been catapulted back in time to the nineteenth century, to the cult of the True Woman and the corset that went with it."

40. Adele E. Clarke, "Women's Health: Life-Cycle Issues," in *Women, Health, and Medicine in America*, 15.

41. Alexandra Symonds, "Emotional Conflicts of the Career Woman," in *This Side of Doctoring: Reflections from Women in Medicine*, ed. Eliza Lo Chin (Thousand Oaks, Calif.: Sage Publications, 2002), 239.

42. See Ellen Singer More, *Restoring the Balance: Women Physicians and the Profession of Medicine, 1850–1995* (Cambridge: Harvard University Press, 1999), 1–2, 13–41. More includes a biographical sketch of Sarah Dolley, who was one of many nineteenth-century physicians with a husband and child. More also states that men were seldom the subjects of research regarding them as victims of "sexual harassment, the 'mommy track,' . . . sex stereotyping, glass ceilings [or] unequal pay." Research of this sort most frequently focuses on women because of their traditional roles in the family and society. Women are frequently the subjects of studies regarding pay scales and child care because they remain the primary family caregivers. Although women are studied in terms of the composite role of woman/physician, men in the medical field are infrequently studied on the basis of balancing the variety of roles they fill. Lo Chin's *This Side of Doctoring* also includes numerous firsthand accounts of women who balanced a career, marriage, and family in the twentieth century.

43. Judith Lorber, *Women Physicians: Careers, Status, and Power* (New York: Tavistock Publications, 1984), 1.

44. See Kathryn A. Carolin, "Kath's Graduation," in *This Side of Doctoring*, 242.

45. Fuller, "Rattling the Scalpels," June 29, 1982, *New Orleans Times-Picayune/States-Item*, box 2, folder 17, SFP/HNOC.

46. Rowena Spencer, interview by author and Mark Cave, tape recording, New Orleans, April 29, 2004.

47. Fuller, "Rattling the Scalpels," June 29, 1982, *New Orleans Times-Picayune/States-Item*, box 2, folder 17, SFP/HNOC.

48. *Joined: The World of Siamese Twins*, http://www.channel4.com/health/microsites/H/health/magazine/conjoined/index.html. Copies of these articles can be found in 2002, folder 2, SFP/HNOC.

49. *Footprints through Time.*

50. Ibid.

51. Typed letter from Georgieanna Comeaux Cooke to Dr. Rowena Spencer, March 30, 1992, box 1, folder 12, SFP/HNOC.

52. Handwritten letter from Stan Saulny to Dr. Rowena Spencer, December 21, 1993, box 1, folder 12, SFP/HNOC. Saulny chose to follow in Spencer's footsteps and attend medical school. He also told her that he would take her inspirational letter with him wherever his career took him.

53. "Salute to the Women's Pavilion," July 28, 1984, printed program, box 10, folder 108, SFP/HNOC.

54. John Wilds, *Crises, Clashes, and Cures: A Century of Medicine in New Orleans* (New Orleans: Orleans Parish Medical Society, 1978), 217.

55. Fuller, "Rattling the Scalpels," June 29, 1982, *New Orleans Times-Picayune/States-Item*, box 2, folder 17, SFP/HNOC.

56. Delease Wear, *Privilege in the Medical Academy: A Feminist Examines Gender, Race, and Power* (New York: Teachers College Press, 1997), 33. Wear states that modern American medicine "has remained seemingly immune from a broad-based feminist critique from within, given the fervent intellectual feminist debate in college and university settings and in the larger U.S. culture[;] . . . indeed the huge and powerful institution of U.S. medicine . . . is controlled by a huge majority of white men. Yet as I look at these same extraordinary women, I am aware that not many would call themselves feminist."

57. Lo Chin, introduction, in *This Side of Doctoring*, xxii. See also Roberta E. Sonnino, "Life in the Boys' Club," in *This Side of Doctoring*, 226–28. Sonnino also experienced "professional jealousy [of her] and gender discrimination," and like Spencer her success came "at great physical and mental costs." In Sonnino's experience, involvement in women's professional organizations was frowned on.

58. Stroup, "Babies Still Keep Her Up," June 17, 1993, box 10, folder 106, SFP/HNOC.

59. *Footprints through Time.*

60. Sue Headlee and Margery Elfin, *The Cost of Being Female* (Westport, Conn.: Praeger Publishers, 1996), 185–86.

61. Anonymous, "Rowena Spencer," unpublished essay, 2002, folder 2, SFP/HNOC.

62. Ibid.

63. Ibid.

64. Abram, introduction, in *Send Us a Lady Physician*, 5.

Oretha Castle Haley

(1939–1987)

"Ain't Gonna Let Nobody Turn Me Around"

SHANNON FRYSTAK

❁ ❁ ❁

On a Wednesday evening, in the spring of 1961, members of the New Orleans chapter of the Congress of Racial Equality (CORE) staged a demonstration in front of a department store on Dryades Street in downtown New Orleans's central shopping district. The student-led organization had been picketing downtown stores nightly for over a year requesting black access to jobs and an end to segregation. Picketing ended when the store closed and, following an organizational strategy session, the students dispersed for the evening. Three of the picketers that evening, sisters Doris and Oretha Castle and fellow CORE member Julia Aaron, returned to the Castle family home in the Lower Ninth Ward, an area of the city possessing a rich history of civil rights leadership. Virgie Castle, the girls' mother, left a note requesting that the girls hang some curtains in the kitchen. Doris went into the bedroom she had shared with her sister growing up and that they continued to share off and on as adults. Doris and Julia sat on the floor near the bed and Oretha lay down. Knowing that her sister was less than domestically inclined, Doris recalls initially thinking that Oretha was once again trying to shirk household chores. As Doris later stated, "My sister was a glorious person for the world, but . . . there was nothing about my sister that was domestic."[1]

Doris finished a cigarette and tried to rouse her sister, but Oretha seemed to be in pain, holding her stomach and moaning. Finally, Oretha stood up, her large frame causing her to tower somewhat over her smaller sister. As Oretha headed toward the bathroom, Doris noticed a puddle of water on the floor where Oretha stood. They argued over whether or not they should call a doctor, and although Oretha finally relented, it was too late; the baby's head was

ORETHA CASTLE HALEY

1974. Courtesy of Okyeame Haley.

already out. Oretha asked Doris to "hold her tight," and that evening, after picketing and a CORE meeting, she gave birth to her second child, a son she named Martin Luther. For nine months, while she attended school and worked daily in the movement, no one, not the members of her immediate family nor the members of her CORE family, had known that she was pregnant. Doris would later discover that Oretha had asked the dean of Southern University at New Orleans SUNO, where she attended school, for a week's leave knowing somehow that she would give birth that week. "She had it all worked out, all planned out," remarked Doris. "Her position about it was, 'I'm pregnant, I'm gonna have the baby, I'm going to school, I am doing all of these other things, now what do I do to keep it all together, keep it going?'" She returned to school the following Monday and resumed her spot on the picket line. As Julia Aaron stated, Oretha "was definitely a very, very outstanding woman."[2] Oretha let little, not even pregnancy and childbirth, slow her down. With the help of her extended family and others in her close-knit Ninth Ward neighborhood, she would continue to be an activist on the front lines of the civil rights movement in New Orleans while simultaneously mothering her two little boys.

Oretha Castle was born in Oakland, Tennessee, on July 22, 1939. When she was seven years old, the Castle family, including her younger siblings—sister Doris and brother Johnny—moved to New Orleans. The family lived in the Lower Ninth Ward, a neighborhood that, unlike other areas of the Deep South, was considerably integrated. According to Doris Castle, "The neighbors were fairly well mixed up together. The block I grew up in . . . there was white people two doors down, on the other side of the street . . . [and] on the next block. People just got along fairly well."[3]

Like the majority of black southerners in the 1940s, Oretha's family worked extremely hard to make ends meet. Her maternal grandparents had been sharecroppers and her paternal grandparents independent farmers. In New Orleans, Oretha's father found work as a longshoreman while Oretha's mother, Virgie, worked as a barmaid for Leah and Dooky Chase, celebrated black restaurateurs and supporters of the local civil rights movement. The Castles worked long hours, and unlike many other black families in New Orleans, eventually saved enough money to purchase their Lower Ninth Ward home. There was "a lot of self-awareness, a lot of independence instilled in all three of us." Doris Castle believed that because their parents worked so many hours, the "three of us [were] fiercely independent":

> [Our parents] taught [us to] always depend on yourself and not somebody else. If you want to do something, determine what it is you want to do and what you need

to do it. What things you need to bring you towards whatever goal it is you [are] trying to achieve. In large part, the way we saw them move through certain points in life, let us build the confidence that we needed . . . that we could accomplish the goals we set.[4]

Oretha hailed from a long line of independent, strong women. Although her father's parents had managed to escape the oppression of white employers, her mother's family had been forced to depend on white people for security, economic and otherwise. It was this dependency that formed her maternal grandmother's philosophy of race relations and personal dignity. "Don't ever bow to anybody when you feel that you are right," Oretha's sister recalls her grandmother telling her. "I'd rather pick with the chickens than be beholden to somebody." Oretha's paternal grandmother, Callie Castle, also supported the civil rights movement, and in the mid-1960s she filed a lawsuit to desegregate Charity Hospital in New Orleans.[5]

It was Oretha's mother, however, who instilled in Oretha her assertiveness and strength, albeit seemingly with quiet dignity. According to Julia Aaron, "Their mother was definitely strong. You could see where they [got] it from."[6] When her children participated on the local, and later, national, civil rights stage, Virgie offered what assistance she could. The Castle home acted as the unofficial headquarters for CORE, and during CORE's 1961 Freedom Ride Campaign, it served as "Freedom Ride Central." "Their house was open for meetings, anything we needed to do, we did it there. That was our real headquarters," stated Aaron. According to Doris, "Nobody ever asked them [her parents] if it was all right for 375 people to parade through their house, would you feed them and stuff like that. Somehow it was understood that they weren't going to jail, or march on the picket lines, but . . . [they] were going to play some part in making this all come about." According to Doratha Smith, a fellow member of CORE, "We spent a lot of nights at that house. That's one lady [Virgie] who should get a lot of credit. Even though she was in the background, she did a lot."[7]

Oretha graduated from Joseph S. Clark High School in 1958 and a year later enrolled at SUNO. Founded in 1959, SUNO is a liberal arts institution that was created for the education of African American students by an act of the state legislature during the school desegregation crises that erupted in Louisiana in the wake of the *Brown* decision. The school began somewhat modestly with one building and 158 students on a seventeen-acre plot located in the middle of the newly developed middle-class black community, Pontchartrain Park.[8] When the student-dominated phase of the civil rights movement erupted in the spring of 1960, Louisiana's historically black colleges and universities, including

SUNO, quickly joined the fray. In fact, students attending SUNO dominated the student-led movement in New Orleans, and the New Orleans chapter of CORE in particular.[9]

New Orleans had a history of civil rights activity dating back to the turn of the century. Although membership in, and action by, the larger and more established National Association for the Advancement of Colored People (NAACP) dominated the state movement, grassroots activists at the local level had been confronting segregation and discrimination in New Orleans in myriad other ways. The Louisiana civil rights movement was born and bred in New Orleans's Seventh and Ninth wards where the Castles and a number of other well-known activists lived. Jim Crow reigned supreme in the more cosmopolitan city of New Orleans, just as it had in other areas of the Deep South, and black Louisianians actively and vocally confronted the racism and discrimination they encountered. In the 1930s, African American residents of the Ninth Ward founded the Ninth Ward Civic League (NWCL), an early voter registration organization created with the sole intention of educating and registering black voters. Through the 1940s and 1950s, New Orleans's black and white residents worked together to challenge the racial status quo in their city in a variety of civil rights organizations, including the National Urban League, the Young Women's Christian Association, and the National Council of Jewish Women. Because of their efforts and the efforts of other organizations in the New Orleans community, by the time the Supreme Court handed down its decision in *Brown v. Board of Education* more than twenty-five thousand African American New Orleanians had successfully registered to vote.[10]

Louisiana has received scant attention from historians of the civil rights movement until recently, even though some of the major figures of the movement, including Oretha Castle, hail from this state. The lack of attention from scholars is puzzling, given that civil rights activism in Louisiana not only preceded but often provided inspiration for later and more famous, media-saturated, events in the movement. For example, the Baton Rouge bus boycott of 1953 provided the model for the Montgomery bus boycott of 1955, which launched the civil rights career of Dr. Martin Luther King Jr.; New Orleans's CORE members tested transportation facilities in Louisiana and Mississippi prior to the onset of the legendary Freedom Rides of 1961; and Louisiana's voter registration/education projects began in the 1950s, long before the renowned voting rights drive of Freedom Summer '64 in Mississippi. Finally, Louisiana's CORE, and the New Orleans chapter in particular, was considered one of the most important chapters in the South, if not the most important chapter.[11]

In the late 1950s, a number of younger members of the New Orleans black community affiliated themselves with the New Orleans NAACP through its Youth Council. Working with the Consumers League of Greater New Orleans (CLGNO), a black organization founded in 1959 in the wake of the Louisiana State Legislature's assault on the NAACP's integrated membership, local activists conducted "Don't Buy Where You Can't Work Campaigns." Supported by older members of the NAACP and the city's black ministerial leadership, the CLGNO declared war on the predominantly white-owned businesses on Dryades and Canal Streets, picketing and boycotting for access to jobs, the stores, the lunch counters, and restaurants. Members of the CLGNO also conducted "kneel-ins" at all-white churches in the city.[12]

Oretha Castle, who had recently given birth to her first child, Michael, and three other local college students, Jerome Smith, Rudy Lombard, and Hugh Murray, a white Tulane University student, joined the CLGNO pickets during the Easter holiday in April 1960. They achieved only limited success. Although the number of African Americans hired by the Dryades street merchants increased, albeit nominally, the lunch counters and restaurants had yet to desegregate. When the traditional forms of protest failed to produce results, Oretha and other young black students, working with the CLGNO and the NAACP Youth Council, decided to escalate the direct action protests by sitting in. The controversial sit-in movement, which had begun in the winter of 1959–60, was spreading rapidly across the South. Oretha explained later the reason for her decision to ramp up the protests: "The same systematic problem of segregated lunch counters and other segregated facilities existed in New Orleans as in other places in the South. I guess because this was an activity that was in the forefront[;] . . . the lunch counters . . . was something that we certainly felt needed to be dealt with in New Orleans."[13]

Yet, to their dismay, when the student members of the NAACP and the CLGNO met with the older leaders of the New Orleans movement to discuss organizing sit-ins locally, they quickly discovered that the older generation found such a move too radical for their tastes and discouraged them from undertaking this new form of activism. "They didn't want to have anything to do with it," Oretha explained. "We had a desire to do something in terms of the lunch counters . . . and we couldn't take the kind of action we wanted to within the NAACP framework. Of course, they felt that this was real kind of militant and radical action to be talking about sitting in and all that kind of stuff. So, independently we decided to organize ourselves."[14]

Rebuffed by the NAACP and resolute in their decision to intensify pressure on city officials, in the summer of 1960 Oretha Castle, along with Rudy Lombard and Jerome Smith, organized a small cadre of student activists into a new (for

New Orleans), more radical organization. The students decided to affiliate with CORE, a national organization, after a visit from member Marvin Robinson. Rudy Lombard, a dynamic black Xavier University student led the new chapter, which from the outset included both black and white women and men, many of whom would go on to become leaders in the state and national movements. The majority of the founding members of CORE, however, were a group of strong and militant-minded African American women like Oretha, her sister Doris, sisters Jean, Alice, and Shirley Thompson, Julia Aaron, Doratha Smith, Katrina Jackson, Joyce Taylor, Ruthie Wells, and Sandra Nixon. In the end, many of these women, Oretha included, emerged as significant actors in the larger struggle for black equality.

With the formation of the New Orleans CORE chapter, the sit-in movement arrived in the city. In early fall, black and white members began sitting in at the Woolworth's on Canal Street. The city's moderate mayor, DeLesseps "Chep" Morrison, already mired in the city's school desegregation battle, reacted by enforcing two acts passed by the state legislature earlier that year, which banned all further picketing and sit-ins in the state. Undeterred by the mayor's threats, CORE continued to demonstrate, and on Saturday, September 17, 1960, police arrested Oretha Castle, Rudy Lombard, Cecil Gardner, and Sidney Goldfinch, charging them with "criminal mischief" for sitting in at the McCrory's lunch counter on Canal Street. Police additionally charged Goldfinch, a white student, with "criminal anarchy" for demonstrating alongside the African American students. Per CORE's methods, the four students chose "jail, no bail" to dramatize to the New Orleans community how "unjust segregation was."[15]

What began as an arrest for a seemingly minor infraction turned into a much more significant history-making event with Oretha Castle at the center. On September 24, 1960, A. I. Kleinfeldt, assistant district attorney for New Orleans, denounced CORE as one of the United States' most subversive organizations. As a result, New Orleans city officials charged Castle, Lombard, Carter, and Goldfinch with advocating opposition to the state of Louisiana and conspiracy to commit criminal anarchy. A local judge refused to throw the case out of court, ruling that "it is not an abuse of police power to enact laws for the preservation of public peace" and that persons who "refuse to leave an establishment are subject to arrest and prosecution under the law."[16]

The case, *Lombard v. Louisiana*, worked its way up through the state courts, eventually to pass along to the U.S. Supreme Court. After the Louisiana Supreme Court upheld the convictions of the four arrested students, CORE attorneys John P. Nelson Jr., Lolis Elie, Robert Collins, and Nils Douglas filed an appeal to the Supreme Court. In 1963, the Supreme Court handed down its decision. Justice Earl Warren wrote the opinion, which overturned the Louisiana conviction, arguing that the arrest was a violation of the Fourteenth Amendment and an attempt, essentially, to "quash the sit-ins."[17]

The case made the New Orleans chapter of CORE one of the national organization's most prominent chapters and Oretha one of the state's most notorious female residents. A young mother, soon to have a second child, Oretha appears to have successfully combined her domestic life with her activist life. Her family was more than willing to assist with the duties of child rearing, but the children also at times accompanied Oretha to meetings and demonstrations. The role of mother and citizen were ideologically compatible for a number of female activists who chose to work for racial justice while simultaneously performing the more socially acceptable role of mother. Black activist mothers in particular seemed to blend the role of wife, mother, and activist citizen seamlessly. It appears that African American women were immune to the sort of scrutiny afforded white activist mothers who were largely expected to abide by more critical socially proscribed mores, which rendered any kind of activity negative if it detracted from the primary role of "mother."[18]

The New Orleans CORE chapter experienced a further boost when the national CORE planned its most famous campaign—the Freedom Rides—scheduled to terminate in New Orleans on May 17, 1961. Modeled after the two-week long southern Journey of Reconciliation held in 1947, which also tested compliance with a Supreme Court ruling regarding interstate transportation, the rides were meant to test interstate travel facilities from Washington, D.C., through the Deep South. New Orleans CORE members, and the Castle house in particular, prepared for the arrival of the riders who left Washington, D.C., on May 4, 1961. When the rides ended abruptly on Mother's Day, May 17, after riders were brutally attacked in Anniston, Alabama, the battered riders flew to New Orleans; many stayed at the Castle home to recuperate. However, the New Orleans CORE chapter was unwilling to give up so easily. Members met to discuss the termination of the rides and decided to resume them. The following week, seven members joined the Nashville Student Union and the Student Nonviolent Coordinating Committee (SNCC) in Montgomery, Alabama, to continue the rides south to Mississippi.[19]

Throughout the summer of 1961, New Orleans served as home base for the Freedom Riders, but the oppressive conditions had not improved in the Crescent City. Demonstrations and protests continued while *Lombard v. Louisiana* played out in the state courts, and riders poured into the city from Mississippi. Oretha continued her work as mother/activist in the New Orleans movement, often serving as the leader of a number of demonstrations that were occurring with greater and greater frequency. New Orleans CORE members housed and fed the Freedom Riders through the summer of 1961. In early August, CORE staged a protest outside of New Orleans police headquarters to protest the beatings of two white male Freedom Riders who had recently arrived in the city; of the fifteen students arrested at the demonstration, nine were women, including Oretha, still awaiting sentencing in the case of *Lombard v. Louisiana.*[20]

By the end of 1961, Rudy Lombard decided to leave New Orleans to pursue graduate school, and Oretha Castle assumed the role of New Orleans CORE president, a rare position for a woman to hold in a largely male-led movement. In the wake of the Freedom Rides, the New Orleans chapter of CORE was, arguably, the most respected and dynamic chapter within the national organization. Moreover, Oretha found herself in charge of an organization that, according to historian Kent Germany, contained "some of the most aggressive and legendary activists in the entire civil rights movement," including Oretha herself.[21] As a number of fellow CORE members recall, it was Oretha's strong and determined leadership that "held things together" through the rough times that came to define the New Orleans CORE in 1962.

One of Oretha's first decisions as the new president of CORE came in December 1961, when she organized and led "Operation Freezeout," a new technique employed by the national organization wherein demonstrators would occupy all of the seats at a lunch counter, order a drink, and sip it until the store closed, in effect, economically crippling an establishment. White racist reactions varied in New Orleans, but, not unlike other areas of the Deep South, the activists were subject to verbal and physical abuse. For example, they had coffee poured on their heads and cigarettes put out on their backs. In one particularly violent demonstration, Oretha and her fellow CORE members were splashed with a burning liquid, later discovered to be carbolic acid; they were also sprayed with insecticide and threatened by the store manager with a gun. Moreover, the waitresses had dumped ammonia, iodine, and chocolate on their heads. The noxious fumes forced the store owner to close early. On returning to CORE headquarters, Oretha contacted the police, the national CORE office, the FBI, and Attorney General Robert Kennedy, all to no avail. Undeterred, Oretha announced to the media that the students would not only continue to picket and sit in but would begin a hunger strike as well.[22]

According to Matt "Flukie" Suarez, a member of CORE during this campaign, Oretha

> was the guiding force. She was the backbone. She was it[;] . . . she was a woman of
> extraordinary capabilities. She had a quality about her that most people, I think,

developed a natural trust in her and they wanted to be a part of whatever it is she was doing and they wanted to try and help because she had that aura about her. And it was deserved because she was always doing something serious. And she didn't half-step or bullshit; she was about serious business.[23]

Without a doubt, Oretha's personality and style challenged traditional notions of gender. It appears that she ignored the gendered divisions of labor that were typical in the civil rights movement structure and successfully overcame any barriers presented her. Certainly, as acting president of the most prestigious CORE chapter in the country, Oretha was part of the top tier of the movement, regardless of her sex.

By 1962, the New Orleans CORE had experienced a rapid increase in its student membership, both black and white. As president, Oretha presided over an organization that was nationally known. In early 1962, the New Orleans chapter of CORE became nationally recognized not for its dynamic nature and vigilant student members but rather for its bucking of national policy, and Oretha was at the center. At the same time, the chapter was increasingly subject to internal strife. As a portent of issues to come in the larger movement, the New Orleans chapter had to contend with dissension over the interracial nature of their organization.

Since its inception in 1942, CORE had championed its interracial nature. According to CORE's original statement of purpose, "Gandhian non-violence and interracial action are the twin ideological beliefs underpinning CORE's organizational structure." For CORE members, racial issues in the United States were a "human problem" rather than a "Negro problem"; subsequently, a commitment to interracial membership was a fundamental aspect of its organizational composition. As founder James Farmer wrote, "We cannot destroy segregation with a weapon of segregation."[24] In reality, however, the New Orleans chapter was one of only a handful of CORE chapters that were interracial in composition, and the members of the New Orleans group soon found themselves wrestling over divergent notions about leadership, membership, and strategy. They had created a "Beloved Community," but ultimately that community failed.

From the outset, the New Orleans chapter of CORE was made up of students both from the historically black colleges (Dillard, Xavier, and SUNO) and from New Orleans's predominantly white institutions (Tulane, Loyola, and Louisiana State University of New Orleans, now the University of New Orleans). There were even times when a majority of members were white. But the leadership consistently remained black. As Oretha Castle remembered, "CORE was an interracial body at that point. We thought, here are these white kids . . . to feel that they [whites] are doing us wrong." When white and black student activists sat in at a whites-only lunch counter and neither were served, it was clear to Oretha Castle that "the whites were part of the action." However, she also remembered this as her "first lesson in . . . the whole role of white folks in the black peoples struggle." Although Rudy Lombard had served as president of the New Orleans chapter since it began in 1960, there were a handful of white students "showing us what to do. . . . From the very beginning."[25]

In New Orleans, the black members recognized the problem of white dominance and interracial cooperation early in the organization's existence. After the Freedom Rides and less than a year of organizational stability, African American members of CORE started to question the justifications for white involvement not only in their organization but in the movement as a whole. According to Oretha, conflicts initially arose when two white students, Sidney "Lonnie" Goldfinch, a Tulane student, and "Skip," a photographer in charge of publicity and public relations for the group, began to assert their authority. "At first," stated Oretha, "that was just the way [it was] for the most part. Honestly, my reaction to it was, 'Oh, there Skip and Lonnie goes.' I guess, though . . . I began to develop some kind of feelings about Lonnie always wanting to tell people what to do, but I didn't really suppose it ever got too much beyond that until . . . several months later." Indicative of problems that would arise in the wider movement across the South in 1965, Oretha Castle stated that

> you had all the whites coming in with their tremendous amount of education and sophistication and then you had the blacks who we really felt, "Boy, we is some dumb compared to those white kids." They would come in meetings and they'd be talking about the philosophy of this political philosopher as opposed to that and we never even heard of what they were talking about. And too, it was that kind of intimidation on our part by what we thought was their smartness . . . but underneath . . . we'd be mumbling certain things, "Boy, they sure want to run everything and tell us what we have to do."[26]

Many whites in the movement had the education and skills that blacks had been historically denied. This situation often created a scenario in which blacks in the movement viewed whites as taking over organizational leadership and decision making. In fact, historical social conditioning contributed to the divisions that were probably bound to arise and that ultimately did. As a strong black woman, however, Oretha was convinced of the need to develop leadership within the black community.[27]

The resentment felt by a number of black CORE members surrounding the paternalistic white students was only part of the problem. Again as a portent of controversies to come, the issue of interracial sexual relationships plagued the New Orleans CORE. Historically, the South's system of segregation had been designed primarily to prevent interracial sex. The taboo against sex between black men and white women was central to whites' control of blacks, even as white supremacy authorized unlimited white male access to black women. After white Mississippi locals accused fourteen-year-old Emmett Till from Chicago of whistling at a white woman in 1955, for instance, two white men rousted him from his uncle's home at midnight and lynched him. Thus, when hundreds of white female college students arrived in the South to work in close contact with young black men, there was bound to be tension beyond that created by the usual cultural differences. For some, however, having an interracial relationship was a way to challenge "these taboos as vestiges of a racist society." According to sociologist Doug McAdam, for these white activists, "interracial sex became the ultimate expression . . . [and] conclusive proof of their right to membership in the 'Beloved Community.'"[28] For Oretha, however, it was a distraction from the real issues at hand.

Ultimately it was the conflict over interracial relationships that ignited a firestorm within the local organization. The New Orleans chapter often hosted interracial social gatherings, but, according to Oretha, soon "it seemed as though the CORE chapter . . . was the place if you were white and you wanted to get some black meat, that was where you were to come, especially if you were male and wanted to get next to a black female." And although Oretha admitted that interracial sexual liaisons had been going on "ever since we [as black people] had been here," this was not what the movement meant to her. "I didn't appreciate none of that shit from the very beginning. . . . I agreed to the fact that what we were fighting, and what the struggle was all about for people, [was] to be able to do whatever they wanted to do. That [interracial sex] was not what CORE was all about[,] . . . certainly [not what] my interests and my struggle was about." Finally, at a CORE-sponsored interracial gathering one evening, a male member openly admitted to Oretha that the promise of an interracial liaison was what "sold him on CORE. He never heard of CORE before, but he saw all them black men with them white women and he said 'if that's what CORE is, that's what I want.'"[29]

It was this incident that convinced Oretha Castle to purge white students, as well as a few black members, from the organization. In February 1962, Castle strategically called a meeting of the all-black membership committee, during which they decided "that as far as we were concerned, [interracial sexual liaisons] wasn't what the struggle was all about. So what it amounted to, we put every last one of the white people out. Every last one of them." According to Julia

Aaron, "You can't tell a person who they [are] going to fall in love with or have a relationship with but it was becoming a real problem in that it was affecting our effectiveness as a group." Oretha admitted that white paternalistic attitudes had contributed to the decision. "There were all of the other things that had been building ever since perhaps the first meeting we had where from the very beginning the white students were very clear that they knew what was best for us to do. . . . But I think that part of that had to do with many of us [feeling] that we just did not know or were not capable of participating to the level that whites were at."[30] Another New Orleans CORE member, Doratha Smith, recalled that most of the whites were from well-to-do families, and that, after whites were expelled from CORE, "I questioned whether they were really interested in what we were about or if it was something new to them."[31]

Immediately, Oretha was mired not only in a local but also a national controversy of her own making. Area CORE members wrote to the national organization to express their resentment over what one member deemed "arbitrary rule[,] . . . puppets manipulated by an unknown person for unknown purposes." Although this member noted that tensions in the interracial group had "steadily built, due in part to the change in leadership and organizational structure," Oretha had expelled white members without the consent of the larger CORE membership. Julia Aaron later recalled that the goal was "to maintain the integrity of the organization and kind of realized that it wasn't about relationships. It was about achieving freedom for our people. I am sure that they did the best that they could, that it was the best decision they could make at the time, but I am not sure it was right."[32]

In response to the expulsions, the national office sent Richard Haley to New Orleans, an act that would affect Oretha's life in myriad ways. (Richard Haley remained in New Orleans and eventually he and Oretha married.) CORE, unlike SNCC, did not reject hierarchy in principle, and so the obvious assertion of authority by a small number of members, as well as the seemingly unilateral decision to expel the white members, permitted action from above. Oretha's actions proved problematic for an organization that prided itself on its interracialism, and Haley conveyed the national organization's stance that the interracial makeup of the organization was central to its philosophy, although he understood where Oretha was coming from. "As a group[,] . . . black people have been caught in a kind of psychological situation, which we tend to expect leadership to come from white people," Haley recalled. "This traditional, habitual relationship between black and white had to be broken."[33] Oretha, it seemed, understood this better than most. After further consideration, however, and many debates among the larger membership, the suspensions were declared "invalid," and, over time, white students slowly rejoined the New Orleans chapter. Although some feel that the group never fully recovered, the organization continued to address issues of racial inequality in the city. "I think it zapped a lot of its strength," stated Raphael Cassimere, CORE member and president of the NAACP Youth Council at the time. To be sure, the New Orleans group had gone from a small group of committed young activists bound by the experience of the Freedom Rides to a larger, but less effective and less cohesive, group.[34]

Despite the problems of 1962, the New Orleans CORE continued to groom student activists and Oretha remained president. Throughout 1963 and 1964, members of CORE, the CLGNO, and the NAACP Youth Council persisted in their nightly demonstrations. The students eventually expanded these demonstrations to include the city's more established hotels, the city theaters, and the all-white Pontchartrain Beach. In 1963, Oretha and her sister Doris filed a lawsuit to desegregate the Schwegmanns supermarket chain, which eventually closed rather than integrate its lunch counters. In yet another highly publicized media event, in November 1963, Oretha led the members of CORE in a Freedom March to city hall, followed by a sit-in to protest the segregated cafeteria located in a "tax-supported building." As the media looked on, police dragged a highly respected local minister, the Reverend Avery Alexander, down the steps of city hall. Police also arrested thirty-six CORE members, including Oretha, who was, along with her sister and another CORE member, carried out of the building in their chairs after refusing to leave. As Oretha told the media, "We mean business. The segregated barriers in public places must come down." Early the following year, a state court ruled it illegal to discriminate in a tax-supported building.[35]

By 1964, the more militant, direct-action phase of the movement in New Orleans began to wind down, and a number of CORE members left to work in rural areas of both Louisiana and Mississippi. Unlike in Mississippi, however, women in Louisiana played visible and integral roles as field directors, directors of Freedom Schools, and leaders of voter registration projects in a number of parishes, including those infamous for being extremely dangerous and for being hotbeds of Ku Klux Klan activity. In the late spring of 1964, Oretha left her position as president of the New Orleans CORE and joined the staff in Ouachita Parish as acting field secretary. In addition, Oretha worked with the national organization as a scout for the Fourth and Fifth Congressional districts assessing the needs of the black residents in those areas of the state. When she moved on to Ouachita Parish working in the voter registration clinics, Oretha found herself under constant surveillance and harassment by the local police. Despite the dangers, Oretha continued her fieldwork, canvassing and directing a number of local offices. The national CORE office was so impressed with her leadership abilities that in November 1964 they hired her as field director for all of northern Louisiana, a position held by only one other woman in CORE.[36] In this capacity, Oretha's main duty was to scout for the 1965 summer voter registration project that CORE had planned.

Throughout 1965, Oretha worked in a number of towns in northern Louisiana. She supported "Don't Buy Where You Can't Work" campaigns in Monroe, Louisiana, reported on incidents of violence and harassment across the state, petitioned the Department of Health, Education, and Welfare on behalf of Jonesboro residents regarding the segregation of their local health center, and even investigated the hiring and advancement practices in Ouachita Parish of the Olin-Mathieson Company, the largest employer of blacks in that area of the state. When the Deacons for Defense and Justice organized in the Sixth Congressional District where Oretha was based, she supported CORE's altered stance regarding its long-held philosophy of nonviolence and worked alongside the deacons in Bogalusa. In the spring of 1965, after more than a month of picketing, testing public accommodations, and mass rallies, she, along with CORE leaders James Farmer and Ronnie Moore, led a march of five hundred local blacks to Bogalusa's city hall despite the overwhelming presence of the Klan and the palpable tension that existed there.[37]

In 1965, Oretha returned to New Orleans to work on antipoverty programs in the city. Like a number of activists from this generation, Oretha employed the skills that she had learned in the grassroots civil rights movement to address the antipoverty initiatives that President Lyndon Johnson had outlined in his 1964 Great Society speech. One of the first projects Oretha tackled was developing public recreational facilities for black children in New Orleans, of which few existed at the time. Despite the numerous gains made possible by the movement in New Orleans, the public parks system remained segregated. Rather than integrate, New Orleans public swimming facilities had closed. In the spring of 1966, Oretha, along with friend and fellow activist Dorothy Mae Taylor, took on the New Orleans Recreation Department. Working through the Target Areas Recreation Committee (TARC), a local organization created in the wake of the War on Poverty initiated by Lyndon Johnson, the two women met with city officials and organized a number of mass demonstrations demanding the integration of all city departments and the reopening of the swimming pools. While their demands went largely unmet, Oretha was once again leading a grassroots effort on behalf of New Orleans black citizens.[38]

Oretha Castle Haley's activism went beyond civil rights. Seen by one historian of the 1960s as "probably the most influential female activist in New Orleans," she was also a pioneer and a leader in the War on Poverty efforts in the city. She often worked alongside Richard Haley, whom she married in 1967, to fight for affordable, quality health care, fair and community-based education, and greater public safety. Oretha had two more sons, Okyeame in 1969 and Sundiata in 1971. With a strong family support system, Oretha appears to have successfully managed and integrated the various parts of her life: wife, mother, and activist.[39]

Married with four children, Oretha Haley continued to effect political change in New Orleans. As a leader in the Black Organization for Leadership Development (BOLD), one of the many "acronym" organizations created in New Orleans during the War on Poverty years, Oretha led a coalition of local activists who ultimately succeeded in their campaign to stop construction of a new Mississippi River bridge that would have displaced thirty-five hundred people, 90 percent of whom were black. In March 1970, approximately one thousand people marched to protest construction of the bridge; another three thousand signed a petition. Oretha attended that demonstration with her children in tow. In the end, the city council voted against bridge construction.[40]

In 1971, Dorothy Mae Taylor chose Oretha to lead her campaign for the state legislature. At the same time, Oretha fought city officials on the redrawing of voting districts in New Orleans. With Oretha's help and political clout, Taylor won the election, becoming the first African American woman state legislator. In the 1980s Oretha served as deputy administrator at Charity Hospital, an institution that predominantly serves the New Orleans poor, black community. During her tenure she instituted reforms that created better health care for New Orleans black citizens. In addition, she also helped found the New Orleans Sickle Cell Anemia Foundation.[41]

Oretha Castle Haley died on October 10, 1987, after a long battle with ovarian cancer. Yet the legacy of her work lives on in a city that, even in the wake of Hurricane Katrina, would not be where it is today without her tireless devotion to equality and human rights. "What I wanted then," Oretha stated in 1978, "was the basic dignity that every human being ought to have. That basic human dignity to function as a free person."[42]

In 2001, city officials honored her memory and renamed Dryades Street, the site of many a civil rights demonstration, Oretha Castle Haley Boulevard. In Center City, local residents also voted to rename an elementary school in her honor. Her leadership in the fight for equal rights for black New Orleanians cannot be overstated. In a movement predominantly led by men, and in a state largely overlooked in civil rights literature, Oretha Castle Haley stands out for her brazenness and determination. According to friend and fellow activist Matt

Suarez, Oretha was "really, really different. In Nashville you had Diane Nash Bevel. In New Orleans, you had Oretha Haley. I consider them both to be unsung heroes."[43] Oretha's sister Doris perhaps describes her best:

> Somebody just meeting her . . . could rightly conclude that she was probably one of the most arrogant, domineering, abrasive people you ever wanted to meet. . . . [T]o say she was callous was an understatement and almost always tactless. But, that was style as opposed to being really Oretha. For those of us who knew her, knew that that style was cultivated, nourished over a period of years . . . that allowed her to accomplish most of the things that she did in her lifetime. She was by no means a person without substance. But that image that a lot of people have of her says that she was very, very strongly rooted in her identity. She was very clear about who she was and where she was going, and she was equally clear about how she was going to get there. She knew what buttons to push[;] . . . people . . . looked up on her as a leader. People . . . came to view her as a leader or a spokesman, and she was really all of those things.[44]

Oretha was not, however, unique or extraordinary in her role as a female leader in a social movement structure. Black women have historically endured unique forms of discrimination in both the private and public spheres, and they have also challenged the oftentimes competing and complementary forces of racism and sexism.[45] There were many women like Oretha whose leadership abilities were indispensable to the civil rights movement in their communities. Indeed, gender was part and parcel of why women joined the struggle. For Oretha, being a mother did not preclude activism; rather, it spurred it. Like many other black female activists, she sought to create a better America for her children. Thus, the roles of "mother" and "citizen" were ideologically compatible, as were motherhood and racial justice.[46]

Historian Laurel Thatcher Ulrich has said that "well-behaved women seldom make history."[47] By many standards, Oretha Castle Haley was not a well-behaved woman. She routinely defied socially devised notions of femininity and "ladylike" behavior and refused to dampen down her powerful and sometimes abrasive personality. Her leadership qualities were recognized by all who knew her, and they were the primary reason she became the president of a major civil rights organization at a time when no other women were in such positions. Civil rights work in the Deep South in the 1960s was dangerous work, and partly for that reason was considered a man's job. Yet Oretha elbowed her way to the top slot while simultaneously balancing her role as a woman—daughter, sister, wife, and mother. Though their stories have scarcely begun to be told, there were undoubtedly many other black women leaders like her across the South.[48]

Oretha further challenged gender assumptions when she chose to work as a field director in rural Louisiana, a job that, while not anomalous, was still rare for women to hold. Moreover, when the civil rights movement proper waned toward the end of the 1960s, Oretha continued to push the envelope and buttons, challenging local and state politicians to fulfill the promises made during the movement. All the while, Oretha performed the roles of wife and mother. Like a number of other women who were married with children and worked in the movement, such as Diane Nash Bevel, she embodied the sociohistoric definition of leader, ultimately and undoubtedly influencing later generations of both male and female activists by example and through perseverance and action.

NOTES

I wish to thank Adam Fairclough, Cynthia Griggs Fleming, Okyeame Haley, and this volume's editors, Janet Allured and Judith F. Gentry, for their invaluable comments, clarifications, and suggestions. I am also extremely grateful to those individuals who allowed me to interview them over the years regarding their participation in the Louisiana civil rights movement and even more so regarding their friendships and associations with Oretha Castle Haley.

1. Doris Jean Castle-Scott, interview by Kim Lacy Rogers, January 19, 1989, Kim Lacy Rogers–Brenda Stevens Collection (hereinafter cited as RSC), Amistad Research Center, Tulane University, New Orleans (hereinafter cited as ARC, and Julia Aaron Humbles, interview by author, March 11, 2003.

2. Castle-Scott, interview by Kim Lacy Rogers, January 19, 1989, RSC, ARC, and Humbles, interview by author, March 11, 2003.

3. Castle-Scott, interview by Kim Lacy Rogers, January 19, 1989, RSC, ARC.

4. Castle-Scott, interview by Kim Lacy Rogers, January 19, 1989, RSC, ARC.

5. Ed Hollander to Marvin Rich, August 5, 1964, Congress of Racial Equality Papers (hereinafter cited as CORE Papers), reel 40, ARC.

6. Humbles, interview by author, March 11, 2003.

7. Castle-Scott, interview by Kim Lacy Rogers, January 19, 1989, RSC, ARC; Humbles, interview by author, March 11, 2003; Kim Lacy Rogers, interview by Doratha Smith Simmons, July 27, 1988, RSC, ARC.

8. See www.suno.edu/AboutSUNO/history.htm.

9. Michael L. Kurtz and Morgan D. Peoples, *Earl K. Long: The Saga of Uncle Earl and Louisiana Politics* (Baton Rouge: Louisiana State University Press, 1992), 201, 199.

10. Information on the makeup of the initial CORE chapter in New Orleans comes from a variety of interviews, including author interviews with Katrina Jackson, December 8, 2001, Sybil Morial, December 4, 2001, Julia Aaron Humbles, March 11, 2003, Raphael Cassimere, March 5, 2003. In 1958, Governor Earl Long supported the construction of New Orleans branches of Louisiana State University and of Southern University. Although both schools, built within a mile of each other, were legally integrated, the intention was to have black students attend SUNO and whites attend Louisiana State University. However, when two hundred black students registered that fall at Louisiana State University, it appeared that Long had unintentionally established the "first public, state-supported

university in the Deep South that admitted all students without regard to race." Integration in the public elementary and secondary schools was different; although privately supportive of desegregation, the governor publicly signed a number of segregation bills into law (Kurtz and Peoples, *Earl K. Long*, 201, 199); "Registration of Negroes in the City of New Orleans," NAACP report, July 9, 1954, NAACP Papers, New Orleans (hereinafter cited as NAACP/NO). For information on the early activism of women in Louisiana see Shannon Frystak, "African-American Women Civil Rights Activists in Louisiana," in *Southern Black Women in the Civil Rights Era (1954–1974): A State by State Study*, ed. Bruce A. Glasrud and Merline Pitre (College Station: Texas A & M University Press, forthcoming), Shannon Frystak, "A Dissenting Tradition: Women and the Black Struggle for Equality, 1924–1968," in *Louisiana, Race, and Civil Rights*, ed. Michael S. Martin (Louisiana State University Press, forthcoming), and Shannon Frystak, "The Integration of the League of Women Voters of New Orleans, 1953–1963," in *Searching for Their Places: Women in the South Across Four Centuries*, ed. Tom Appleton and Angela Boswell (Columbia: University of Missouri Press, 2003), 261–84.

11. Perhaps the most important and comprehensive work on the Louisiana civil rights movement is Adam Fairclough, *Race and Democracy: The Civil Rights Struggle in Louisiana, 1924–1972* (Athens: The University of Georgia Press, 1995). See also Kim Lacy Rogers, *Righteous Lives: Narratives of the New Orleans Civil Rights Movement* (New York: New York University Press, 1993), Greta De Jong, *A Different Day: African American Struggles for Justice in Rural Louisiana, 1900–1970* (Chapel Hill: The University of North Carolina Press, 2002), Lee Sartain, *Invisible Activists: Women of the Louisiana* NAACP *and the Struggle for Civil Rights, 1915–1945* (Baton Rouge: Louisiana State University Press, 2007), and Shannon Frystak, "'Woke Up This Morning With My Mind on Freedom': Women and the Struggle for Black Equality in Louisiana, 1924–1967" (PhD diss., University of New Hampshire, 2005).

12. Madelon Cochrane, interview by author, December 11, 2001; Cassimere, interview by author, March 5, 2003.

13. Oretha Castle Haley, interview by James Mosby, May 26, 1970, Ralph Bunche Civil Rights Documentation Project, Moorland-Spingarn Center, Howard University, Washington, D.C. (hereinafter cited as RBCRDP).

14. Castle Haley, interview by James Mosby, May 26, 1970, RBCRDP.

15. "New Orleans Stores Picketed," press clipping, September 11, 1960, CORE Papers, reel 20, ARC; "Mayor Morrison Clamps Lid on 'Sit-ins,'" *Louisiana Weekly*, September 17, 1960, ARC; Gordon Carey to local contacts, November 4, 1960, CORE Papers, reel 20, ARC.

16. "Four More CORE Members Arrested in 'Sit-in,'" *Louisiana Weekly*, September 24, 1960, ARC; report of James T. McCain, New Orleans, Louisiana, September 8–25, 1960, CORE Papers, reel 20, ARC; "4 Sit-Ins Lose Round in Court, Trial Set December 7," *Louisiana Weekly*, December 3, 1960, ARC; "CORE to Carry Sit-In Fight to Supreme Court," *Louisiana Weekly*, January 21, 1961, ARC; "High Court Weighs Louisiana Sit-In Case," *Louisiana Weekly*, November 24, 1960, ARC.

17. "Louisiana Supreme Court Upholds Convictions of Four Sit-Ins," "High Court Weighs La. 'Sit-in' Case," "Supreme Court Action Clears Four Students," *Louisiana Weekly*, July 8, 1961, November 24, 1962, and May 25, 1963, ARC.

18. In a conversation I had with Oretha Haley's son Okyeame on November 13, 2007, he stated that there were family pictures that showed his siblings at random demonstrations with his mother. Unfortunately, most of both his mother's and father's papers, including family pictures, were destroyed in Hurricane Katrina.

19. August Meier and Elliott Rudwick, CORE: *A Study in the Civil Rights Movement, 1942–1968* (Urbana: University of Illinois Press, 1973), 33–35, 135–40.

20. "Freedom Riders Charge N.O. Cops with Brutal Beatings" and "Arrest 15 for 'Sit-Ins' at Police Headquarters," *Louisiana Weekly*, August 19 and September 2, 1961, ARC.

21. Kent Germany, *New Orleans after the Promises: Poverty, Citizenship, and the Search for the Great Society* (Athens: University of Georgia Press, 2005), 34.

22. Alice Thompson, interview by Kim Lacy Rogers, July 25, 1988, RSC, ARC; Katrina Jackson NaDang, interview by author, December 8, 2001; Cassimere, interview by author, March 5, 2003; Matt Suarez, interview by author, December 3, 2001; "Doused with Acid After New Technique," *Louisiana Weekly*, 30 December 1961, ARC.

23. Suarez, interview by author, December 3, 2001.

24. Meier and Rudwick, CORE: *A Study in the Civil Rights Movement, 1942–1968*, 126 and 11.

25. Castle Haley, interview by James Mosby, May 26, 1970, RBCRDP.

26. Ibid.

27. Arnold S. Kaufman, *The Radical Liberal, the New Politics: Theory and Practice* (New York: Atherton Books, 1968), 83; author conversation with Okyeame Haley, November 13, 2007.

28. Doug McAdam, *Freedom Summer* (New York: Oxford University Press, 1988), 93–94.

29. Castle Haley, interview by James Mosby, May 26, 1970, RBCRDP; Castle Haley, interview by Kim Lacy Rogers, November 27, 1978, RSC, ARC.

30. Castle Haley, interview by Kim Lacy Rogers, May 26, 1970, RSC, ARC; Humbles, interview by author, March 11, 2003.

31. Doratha Smith, interview by Kim Lacy Rogers, July 27, 1988, RSC, ARC.

32. Carlene Smith to Jim McCain, 22 February 1962, CORE Papers, ARC; Humbles, interview by author, March 11, 2003.

33. Richard Haley, interview by Kim Lacy Rogers, May 9, 1979, RSC, ARC.

34. Cassimere, interview by author, March 5, 2003.

35. "36 Arrested in Direct Action Movement," "Desegregation of City Hall South," and "City Hall Cafeteria Desegregated," *Louisiana Weekly*, November 9, 1963, and February 22, 1964, ARC; Oretha Castle quoted in *Louisiana Weekly*, November 30, 1963, ARC.

36. Louisiana's Citizenship Education Program, July 20, 1964, field report, CORE Papers, December 13, 1964–January 24, 1965, submitted by Oretha Castle, ARC; "Castle's Projected Schedule for February–March 1965," n.d., CORE Papers, ARC; field report, January 19, 1965, CORE Papers, ARC; 6th Congressional District Papers, State Historical Society of Wisconsin, Madison, Wisconsin.

37. "Efforts to Settle Problems at Conference Table Fails" and "Tensions Eased," *Louisiana Weekly*, April 17 and May 1, 1965, ARC.

38. Germany, *New Orleans*, 84–86.

39. Germany, *New Orleans*, 254.

40. Germany, *New Orleans*, 254–56; author conversation with Okyeame Haley, November 13, 2007.

41. See "Notable African Americans from Louisiana," http://nutrias.org/info/aarcinfo/notabl2 .htm#haley.

42. Castle Haley, interview by Kim Lacy Rogers, November 27, 1978, RSC, ARC.

43. Suarez, interview by author, December 3, 2001.

44. Castle-Scott interview by Kim Lacy Rogers, January 19, 1989, RSC, ARC.

45. Jacqueline Jones, *Labor of Love, Labor of Sorrow: Black Women, Work, and the Family, from Slavery to the Present* (New York: Vintage Books, 1985).

46. Rhoda Lois Blumberg, "White Mothers in the American Civil Rights Movement," in *Research in the Interweave of Social Roles: Women and Men*, ed. Helen Lopata (New York: JAI Press, 1980),

33–50. Blumberg calls the women who were mothers and activists "sex-role transcenders," basically for bucking the mother/woman stereotype.

47. Laurel Thatcher Ulrich, "Vertuous Women Found: New England Ministerial Literature, 1668–1735," *American Quarterly* 28 (Spring 1976): 20–40.

48. Most of the early work that concentrated on female civil rights activists came out of the social sciences. See Belinda Robnett, *How Long? How Long? African-American Women in the Struggle for Civil Rights* (New York: Oxford University Press, 1997), Doug McAdam, *Freedom Summer*, Rhoda Lois Blumberg, "White Mothers in the American Civil Rights Movement," Rhoda Lois Blumberg, "Careers of Women Civil Rights Activists," *Journal of Sociology and Social Welfare* 7 (September 1980): 708–29, Rhoda Lois Blumberg, "Women in the Civil Rights Movement," *Dialectical Anthropology* 15 (June 1990): 133–39, Rhoda Lois Blumberg, "Rediscovering Women Leaders of the Civil Rights Movement," in *Dream and Reality: The Modern Black Struggle for Freedom*, ed. Jeanne Swift (New York: Greenwood Press, 1991), 19–28, and Bernice McNair Barnett, "Invisible Southern Black Women Leaders in the Civil Rights Movement: The Triple Constraints of Gender, Race, and Class," *Gender and Society* 7 (June 1993): 162–82.

Louisiana Women and Hurricane Katrina

(2005–)

Some Reflections on Women's Responses to the Catastrophe

PAMELA TYLER

❀ ❀ ❀

The pages you are reading were intended to feature a nice piece on Corinne Claiborne Boggs, an essay that I, a political historian and longtime Lindy Boggs fan, enthusiastically volunteered to write back in 2005 for inclusion in this collection. Events of that year, however, included the submerging of valuable manuscript collections at Tulane University's Howard-Tilton Library in Katrina floodwaters after the unthinkable happened in New Orleans. Learning that our Lindy's papers were off being freeze-dried somewhere in Texas, in an effort to save them for use by future scholars, forced me to postpone the sketch of Congresswoman Boggs's life and career. It also gave me the chance to craft an essay of appreciation for the efforts of women who coped resourcefully with the effects of two devastating hurricanes in 2005. Without those women's unpaid efforts, the recovery of the Gulf South, though still painfully incomplete, would be an even more daunting task than it is. Mopping up is, and always has been, women's work.

❀ ❀ ❀

First, the background. The tropical storm season of 2005 was unusually active. We were already up to "K" on the roster of named storms, when, in late August 2005, yet another mass formed off the Cape Verde Islands, made its way across the Atlantic, gathering strength as it came, and gained the velocity to become Katrina, the eleventh named storm of the season. A modest category 1 hurricane, Katrina crossed the tip of the Florida peninsula early Friday, August 26, and immediately began to grow exponentially. Feeding off superheated tropical waters and enlarging to terrifying proportions, she accelerated across the Gulf of Mexico toward the U.S. Gulf Coast. Louisiana residents awoke to the news on Saturday, August 27, that Katrina was already a category 4 storm, with the miles of open water still ahead of her certain to render her even more lethal. Landfall would occur early on Monday, August 29.

My partner and I bolted to Dallas within an hour of my reading the dire warnings that blared from the *New Orleans Times-Picayune*'s Saturday headlines. Many in Katrina's path evacuated; others, either by choice or by force of circumstances, did not. But, at virtually the last minute, the storm turned slightly to the east; miraculously, she spared New Orleans her worst winds. Like many New Orleans women, I recall watching CNN coverage on that Monday. Learning that Katrina had "hiccupped," I felt gleeful, but in a bittersweet way. Having spent time on the Mississippi coast, I knew that New Orleans's deliverance would be the ruin of sweet little Waveland, funky Bay St. Louis, and gracious, old Pass Christian, as well as the casinos, the beaches, and the important Gulf cities of Pascagoula, Biloxi, and Gulfport. But at least our New Orleans had been spared.

However, as the entire world soon learned, New Orleans had not escaped: in fact, New Orleans was doomed. Unknown to a trusting population, fatal design flaws existed in the expensive levee system, built over the decades by the U.S. Army Corps of Engineers for our city's protection. In the aftermath, disbelieving investigators revealed the shocking fact that the corps had anchored some floodwalls in nothing more substantial than sand and peat. Try this for a joke that makes no one laugh: our floodwalls fell down even though the hurricane went to Mississippi. When the pressure of storm surges blew out those costly structures, the vast brown contents of Lake Pontchartrain and the brackish Katrina-driven storm surge filled the topographical "bowl" of the Crescent City. It wasn't Mother Nature that flooded the Crescent City; it was flawed, fallible human nature, which the ever-so-reluctant Army Corps of Engineers at last acknowledged in a report delivered in June 2006.[1] In journalist Jed Horne's vivid phrase, "The levees had not been overtopped; they had collapsed—flopping over like the tailgate on a pickup truck."[2] Without the Corps' blunders, Katrina would have left nothing really extraordinary behind: downed leaves, limbs, and power lines; roof damage here and there; and serious street flooding in the lowest areas. But because of those failures, Lake Pontchartrain, a body of water fifty miles long and twenty-five miles across, began pouring into New Orleans, a city below sea level. Thirty billion gallons of water put 80 percent of the city, an area seven times the size of Manhattan, underwater.[3]

Even as tens of thousands of people begged for rescue, the entire animal population of the Louisiana SPCA shelter was safe. Laura Maloney, SPCA executive director, had swung into action over the weekend. As the storm approached, knowing that her agency had a policy of evacuating the shelter for storms category 3 or higher, she actually implemented that plan, arranging for trucks to transport every one of the 263 dogs and cats to safe quarters in Houston. "Each animal got its own digital picture shot. We made sure each pet's paperwork was in order. And we ID'd each collar; we had a tracking system, in case any animal got separated from their paperwork." The shelter on Japonica Street, in the Ninth Ward, experienced floodwaters up to the rafters; no animal housed there would have survived had Maloney not acted.[4]

Our frightened, disbelieving city drowned on live TV. In the days after the floodwalls failed, CNN and others beamed out searing images of bewildered people, stranded, stricken, suffering. And, yes, I am still furious to this day that it took our federal government, the Superman waiting in the wings, so unconscionably long to get out of its Clark Kent drag and into action. Like many women, I wept at what I saw, tears springing from pain, hurt, compassion, and anger.

Many wept in the days after Katrina departed. Our senior senator, Mary Landrieu, wept. When she described what she viewed from a helicopter above the Seventeenth Street Canal breach, she tried unsuccessfully to stifle her tears. "Is that the most pitiful sight you've ever seen in your life? Just one little crane!" she quavered, as she registered the enormity of the catastrophe, seeing a wall of water pouring unchecked as one overmatched piece of machinery worked in futility to plug the gap. "Just one!" Mayor Ray Nagin had a famous meltdown on live radio, venting his tortured feelings in a torrent of expletives before fetching up in shaky sobs. During a televised interview, Aaron Broussard, an elected official from an adjacent suburb, gave way to copious, disheveled weeping as he recounted a colleague's mother's death during the flood.[5]

Governor Kathleen Blanco, who frequently appeared with moist—although not actually weeping—eyes received harsh criticism in the days immediately after the storm. Undeniably, the Bush administration orchestrated much of it in a hardball effort to shift blame from its own abysmally inadequate response to the catastrophe. Members of the press who asked pointed questions about the governor's tug-of-war with the president over who would control the Louisiana

National Guard during the crisis admitted that "high White House sources" had provided them with their leads.[6]

Blanco can be faulted for uncertainty in the hours immediately after Katrina hit, as can all other elected officials in the region, and she can be faulted for sins of omission before the storm struck, as can others. However, it is interesting to note how shrilly the Blanco critics zeroed in on her appearance and demeanor. These are the traditional targets for men who want to criticize women in authority. A voluble source of such puerile criticism is the author, Doug Brinkley. In his hastily written account of the catastrophe's first week, Brinkley described Blanco as "ashen-faced . . . [despite] circles of rouge," "plump," "schoolmarmish," and "charmless." He faulted "her uninformed emotionalism," accused her of radiating "a sense of dread," and judged her "god-awful on television."[7]

In fact, Governor Blanco displayed a quiet and steely courage throughout the ordeal. Unlike Ray Nagin, Aaron Broussard, and New Orleans police chief Eddie Compass, she managed to keep her dignity in the most trying of circumstances. It remains acceptable for men to pound tables to vent emotions, but a woman in public cannot allow such a display. Men in high positions also get a pass when it comes to tears, according to a recent study by university psychologists.[8] We still stereotype men as the courageous sex, but Mayor Nagin, cool, tall, and fit, could not bring himself to go in person to rally the desperate people enduring agonies in the Superdome. Governor Blanco, by contrast, quietly and without press along to document her bravery, went directly there to walk among survivors in the heat and filth, to hear their anger and their fear, to show herself. Hard duty, yes, but duty she did not shirk.

If Blanco did not exude the hearty confidence of her Mississippi counterpart, Governor Haley Barbour, perhaps that had something to do with the fact that as a Democrat in a region of red states, she knew that the White House was fast politicizing every aspect of the disaster, to her distinct disadvantage. How far the White House operatives would end up sticking their knives into her amazed many. Being done dirty behind the scenes while absorbing hourly bulletins of things gone from bad to worse surely would make one less than perky or stentorian on television. Governor Blanco kept her balance throughout trying circumstances.

The first stop that George W. Bush chose to make on his visit to the Gulf Coast was in Mississippi to meet with that state's highest leaders, all white Republican men. There, among friends, the president surveyed the damage and allowed as how he looked forward to the restoration of good friend Senator Trent Lott's four hundred thousand dollar second home on the beach; they would sit together on the porch, he said warmly. On the other hand, his dealings with Blanco, a Democratic woman, were frosty at best. For the president's return trip to the region, his staff delivered a calculated snub by simply not informing Governor Blanco about his visit at all. Learning only at the last minute that he was about to arrive, she canceled a flight to Houston, where she had intended to meet with evacuees, and stayed behind to meet the president instead. Despite such provocations, Blanco did not cast aspersions on George W. Bush.[9]

Meanwhile, although slow to arrive, National Guard units from other states were ensconced in New Orleans within a week, running checkpoints on roads into the city and denying entry to all but those possessing "official" credentials. I later discovered that enforcement of the order was anything but systematic; bold and clever folk talked their way around the guardsmen. A college professor watched in disbelief as her husband, flashing nothing more than a business card and a manner full of bravado, was able to bark, "Thank you, soldier!" and drive right past the barriers.

In October 2005, authorities at last lifted the barricades; New Orleans refugees could return to their homes, if they had the fortitude for it. My partner and I made the drive from Tulsa, in a borrowed SUV piled high with garbage bags, ventilator masks, work gloves, bottled water, tools, first aid supplies, and lots and lots of wine. For six weeks, we had worried in absentia over the fate of our house. From aerial photographs posted on the web, we knew that our neighborhood had flooded; we saw the water in the streets, but how high did those waters go? Unable to contact our far-flung neighbors to ask if they had any news of the neighborhood and gaining no useful information from television (which, maddeningly, seemed to limit its coverage to broadcasting the same images of the French Quarter and the Lower Ninth Ward again and again), we had no idea what we would find when we turned onto our beloved street.

We arrived on a gorgeous blue day, with mercifully low humidity, and found that we were among the luckiest. The water had reached no farther than the third step of the house; yea, verily, we were spared. Of course, our rank, food-filled refrigerator, which had sat unelectrified in the sweltering heat for six weeks, demanded our attention. Plugging our nostrils with gobs of pungent mentholatum and masking our faces, we manhandled the wretched appliance onto a dolly and out to the curb, where it joined the sixteen others that I could see from the front steps. We cleared the ravaged courtyard and grounds of dead limbs, dislodged shingles, and other debris. At dusk we departed, since we had no hot water or working stove. Gas service would not be restored to us for another two months. As we drove away in the silent twilight to seek refuge in a friend's house across town, no lights burned on our dark, dark block; we realized that we were alone in the neighborhood.

All over New Orleans, variations of this drama played out in the fall of 2005. Thousands of returnees discovered absolutely ruined homes, indelibly marked with the foulest stains, the exterior water line showing the depth of the floodwaters, the interior holding muck and detritus within walls that once had enclosed the comforts of home. All over town, stunned people dragged sodden sheetrock and carpet out to the curbs. But wallboard and rugs are replaceable; out there at curbside, I also saw ruined wedding photos and letters from camp, baby shoes and Barbie dolls, keepsakes and treasures particular to each house and its family.

Nesting is the most normal instinct in the world. But as the city quickly learned, getting back home would be complex. When would electricity and gas be restored? When would the battered city water system, with leaks on every block, again provide potable water? When would buses and streetcars run, and on which routes? Which neighborhoods would get police protection? Which schools would open, and when? When could a shopper again buy groceries in her own neighborhood instead of having to make the ten-mile drive to a functioning suburban store? When would mail delivery resume? Which hospitals would reopen? When would garbage again be collected on a regular basis? How would the enormous needs be funded?

City government provided precious few answers. Embroiled in a hot campaign for reelection, the incumbent mayor Ray Nagin trod ever so carefully around controversial questions. Not daring to risk offending any potential voter by being the bearer of bad news, Nagin shamelessly led voters to believe that the entire city would soon be rebuilt and that full city services would be available to all. His challenger, Mitch Landrieu, brother of Senator Mary Landrieu, was no bolder in confronting harsh truths. Realists noted that the downsized city could not afford to provide services to far-flung sectors with few returnees; they urged leveling with the public and admitting that "shrinking the footprint" was inevitable. Experts agreed. Urban planners offered various proposals for abandoning some neighborhoods. This, of course, prompted understandable shrieks of pain from those whose neighborhoods were slated to become "green space," at which Nagin avowed that everyone who wanted to return to his home could indeed return. Our Humpty Dumpty on the Bayou would be put together again. But no one said how, or when, or by whom. Or at what cost. Or on whose nickel.

While the sphinxlike city government stoutly refused to say which communities would be guaranteed city services if they tried to rebuild, it also refused to rule out any zones in which rebuilding should not be undertaken. In the final analysis, it was this dearth of leadership that galvanized many women. One after another, they came to the same realization independently: "We cannot wait for the elected officials; we must act."

LaToya Cantrell, 34, an African American transplant to New Orleans who moved from California in 2000, headed the Broadmoor Improvement Association. A national historic district with genuine ethnic and racial diversity, Broadmoor featured a mix of shotgun houses and craftsmen, Mediterranean, and California bungalow styles and was home to over seven thousand people. Because it had flooded heavily, some in high places floated the notion that Broadmoor, an attractive community more than 120 years old, should become a "green space"; they talked darkly of the "gamble" and "risks" involved in re-populating. To demonstrate the viability of their neighborhood, Cantrell saw that Broadmoorians needed to gut, restore, and return to their homes as rapidly as possible and persuade numbers of their neighbors to do likewise. "There has been no direction given from City Hall, so neighborhoods have to fend for themselves. We're on our own," Cantrell said.[10] She and neighbors developed an aggressive strategy to save Broadmoor, soliciting residents' input, painstakingly gathering information about scattered citizens' plans for the future, and keeping a grueling schedule of weekly meetings to foster maximum involvement. They made valuable connections with personnel at the Kennedy School of Government, which dispatched teams of students and staff to assist in planning. The Harvard contingent left New Orleans impressed with the Broadmoorians' ambition and actions. Reflecting his dissatisfaction with city officials, David Elwood, the Kennedy School's dean, mused aloud that "there aren't enough Cantrells in leadership positions."[11] Her determination and enthusiasm galvanized a true grassroots movement, yielded the first comprehensive neighborhood recovery plan in the city, and inspired many to imitate her stated determination to "work my butt off."[12]

The Holy Cross neighborhood, a Ninth Ward district nestled against the Mississippi River levee below the Industrial Canal, had a feel of history about it; even floodwaters eight feet deep could not obliterate that. Before Katrina, a predominately African American population occupied its wooden homes, built in the late nineteenth and early twentieth centuries; 42 percent were homeowners. Like other neighborhoods, its fate hung on the collective determination of its residents. Few had flood insurance, all had suffered grievous losses, and yet the city waited for them to "earn" support by repopulating Holy Cross, thereby providing evidence that a majority intended to return. Pam Dashiell, feisty president of the Holy Cross Neighborhood Association, had a way of direct speech and direct approach. She made herself knowledgeable about the threat posed to her community by the "storm funnel" effect of the Mississippi River-Gulf Outlet, a project the Corps of Engineers defended but a waterway Dashiell and most of her neighbors wanted closed. In learning to face off with military builders, she had absorbed nuances of engineering and environmental issues, so much so that she could claim a high degree of mastery. She put this information to good effect defending her community's best interests in public forums.

In 2006, an entity called Global Green USA sponsored a sustainable-design competition in which architects vied to create affordable, energy-efficient housing to be built for returning Ninth Ward residents. Celebrity Brad Pitt funded the prizes, helped to raise building funds for the six trial houses, and brought an aura of glamour and excitement to the project. Pam Dashiell made sure that Global Green solicited feedback from the Holy Cross community at each step and was herself deeply involved. When a local reporter bluntly asked how Global Green could surmount generations of resistance to change to make the project more than just an architectural oddity in the Lower Nine, Dashiell leaned across the table and offered her common-sense view. "The way you do it, as opposed to what has happened so far, is: You just do it. You have to start somewhere. If we don't start, we'll never, ever finish."[13]

Spared catastrophic flooding because of their elevations, historic neighborhoods like the French Quarter, the Garden District, and Uptown were livable as soon as the utilities restored electricity, gas, and potable water; for most addresses in these areas, that restoration came in October or November 2005. Women of the comfortable classes returned to pick up interrupted lives on oak-shaded streets like Palmer, Newcomb, Eleonore, and Octavia, but disorder confronted them every time they ventured out of their bubbles of comfort. A trip to the post office or grocery store became an ordeal. Potholes, garbage, no functioning traffic signals, curtailed hours at stores, block after block of abandoned homes, carcasses of thousands of flooded and useless automobiles. The seeming absence of a strategy for dealing with the disarray appalled many. In interviews, women mentioned being struck by a feeling of disbelief and dread when they told themselves, "There is no plan." Determined to help, women with confidence, means, and social skills stepped into the leadership void. Fueled by lethargy in government, an old and familiar pattern repeated itself: women's activism flourished.

Socially, Ruthie Frierson's position in New Orleans was unassailable; her husband was a former Rex, king of Carnival, making the couple a special sort of New Orleans royalty. She had also earned a reputation as the top-selling agent for residential real estate in New Orleans. Yet the stalled recovery in her city worried her to such an extent that she stepped away from work and embarked on a time-consuming, unpaid effort at reform. Tearful stories from distraught homeowners galvanized Frierson; she took call after call from men and women who asked, "Should we sell, or rebuild? Can the levees be made safe? What will our taxes be? How much aid will government give?" Heartsick, she had no answers for her clients. She concluded that the chaotic state of New Orleans tax assessments and the tangled lines of responsibility for maintenance of the region's levees seriously hindered recovery. Moreover, she feared that the city government's reputation for clownish incompetence and blatant malfeasance acted as an impediment to the flow of desperately needed federal largesse.

In New Orleans, no fewer than seven elected assessors kept the property tax rolls, raising or lowering assessments in their districts whimsically and autocratically, in full agreement with the long-honored local custom of "greasing." Miles of manicured levees fell under the jurisdiction of no fewer than eight entities, whose members' performance in office gave rise to the suspicion that matters other than proper levee maintenance occupied them. Indeed, the patronage-obsessed Orleans Levee District spent its time, and funds, on an airport, two marinas, a police force, and a grand, costly, and permanently broken Mardi Gras fountain.

Just before Thanksgiving 2005, a legislative committee in Baton Rouge killed a reform proposal to consolidate the levee boards; the measure never even made it to the floor for debate. Disgusted at such a cavalier attitude when the need for change was so great, Frierson convened a group of some 120 citizens at her home. Outraged at the legislature's rejection of levee consolidation, they launched a petition drive to force the governor to call a special session of the legislature; they demanded reconsideration of levee board reform and consolidation. Calling themselves Citizens for 1 Greater New Orleans, the reformers (almost all of them women) elected to wear signature red jackets for public appearances in which they advocated consolidation of disparate boards and sprawling, wasteful bureaucracies. They lobbied with intensity, collected fifty-three thousand signatures within three weeks, and, of perhaps greater importance, raised hundreds of thousands of dollars to promote the levee amendment.

Their efforts proved fruitful. Governor Kathleen Blanco, thinking ahead to reelection, allied herself with the group and their cause, wore red, and called the session. Under terrific pressure from the red-jacketed women, who attended every committee hearing and session in the capital for two-and-a-half weeks, the legislature did the unthinkable in February 2006: it approved milestone legislation to dissolve the long-standing local levee kingdoms and create a regional flood protection authority, staffed by professional hydrologists and engineers, subject to voter approval of a constitutional amendment. On October 1, 2006, a banner headline in the New Orleans press told the outcome: "Voters Merge Levee Boards."[14]

In November 2006, voters went to the polls to consider another amendment, this one also pressed by Citizens for 1 Greater New Orleans, to consolidate the seven city tax assessors' positions into one. Frierson's group had paved the way for this reform by holding public meetings to promote the idea, by cultivating the editorial boards of all the state dailies, by running a savvy ad campaign, and by staying relentlessly "on message," which was "Why pay seven to do the job of one?" The stunning results revealed a statewide vote of 78 percent in favor, and 68 percent of Orleanians in support, of the assessor consolidation reform. A local political writer commented in response, "If someone had been bold enough to predict 18 months ago [passage of the two amendments], he or she would have been hauled off to a quiet place for a long rest. Go figure."[15] With their mission of overcoming inertia and politics as usual partially completed, one hopeful red-jacketed member commented, "If we want to rebuild this city, we can't go back to the way it was."

The catalyst for Becky Zaheri's activism was garbage. The horrendous blight of the sodden, rotting, violated cityscape assaulted her senses on every visit back to New Orleans. Thirty-eight-year-old Zaheri had rented an apartment in Baton Rouge so that her two children could enroll in school in the fall of 2005 while her husband remained in New Orleans to work as an emergency physician. Once the power was on at their Uptown house, Becky and the children commuted to New Orleans for weekends with him. Municipal sanitation services, notoriously inadequate in the best of times, had proved completely unequal to the task of clearing away mountains of garbage and the moldy contents of gutted houses, which festered at curbside for weeks on end. Zaheri's decision to e-mail a few friends suggesting a clean-up day brought fifteen women to pick up litter over Thanksgiving. From that modest beginning, the project snowballed. By Christmas, the group was staging two clean-ups a week and seeing upward of two hundred people turn out.

Christening themselves the Katrina Krewe, Zaheri's group soon harnessed the help of the nation. Displaying solid organizational skills, the group set up committees, mastered the art of publicity, established a sophisticated Web site (www.cleanno.org), and worked up a sweat twice a week, clearing block after block of city streets. By early 2006, a phenomenal growth was apparent; volunteers were coming from around the country and turnouts for any given clean-up easily numbered a thousand people. Zaheri, a fit, photogenic woman possessed of direct, clear speech, made guest appearances on the Ellen DeGeneres show and spoke with broadcasters for many national media outlets, boosting the Katrina Krewe's national profile. Beginning by spending over two thousand dollars herself on equipment, Zaheri then tapped area businesses for supplies of bottled water, garbage bags, work gloves, and rakes; from an auto dealer, she received a loan of vans in which to transport and store the Krewe's supplies. In February 2006, the Katrina Krewe filed for status as a 501c3 organization, making donations tax exempt. During Mardi Gras and spring break weeks, college students arrived to pitch in, foreign tourists added their muscle power, and locals continued to rally to the cause. Zaheri directed the project with the assistance of ten board members, all women and most of them young mothers like herself. Volunteers sometimes included young and old, black and white, men and women, but the overwhelming motive power of the Katrina Krewe was female.[16]

Anne Milling, a slim sixty-five-year-old with social connections and an impressive resume of community involvement, convened six guests, all women, at her home in January 2006 and pitched an idea: how would it be if a group of civic-minded women went to Washington and personally invited members of Congress to come to New Orleans to see the damage firsthand? The women responded enthusiastically. The scope of the disaster made large federal appropriations imperative for a successful recovery, but, four months after the flood, lawmakers in Washington were still bickering over the necessary amount of aid, and comments from many indicated a strong reluctance to finance the rebuilding of New Orleans. Clearly, local officials were too dysfunctional to lobby effectively. Convinced that a mere descriptive report could never convey the extent of the need, Milling's friends agreed that seeing New Orleans for themselves might move congressmen and congresswomen to vote for desperately needed recovery funds. If lawmakers should accept the women's invitation to visit, they would offer their captive audience pithy presentations from informed community leaders. Rather than giving guests just an eyeful of misery and making a general appeal for aid, the women intended to offer a carefully mapped city tour and an educational seminar on the need for wetlands restoration, levee construction, and financial aid for homeowners.

Milling wanted articulate, confident women to make the trip. The core group included women who had years of experience in civic affairs and nonprofit organizations, who all knew each other well. Using their contacts to enlist others, they quickly enrolled 130 volunteers for the Washington trip. At that early stage, the small steering committee was all white, but the larger group that traveled included Hispanic women, African American women, and women from the local Vietnamese community. Christening themselves Women of the Storm, they cautiously formulated a dress code intended to avoid fueling any negative stereotypes. Avoiding voicing assumptions about who might wear what, they simply mandated that "nothing could be showing. Everybody has their own style and some of that might include plunging necklines or a lot of jewelry, so we said no jewelry, no plunging necklines. We wanted to be perceived as very serious."[17] As it turned out, the entire group *was* serious. On the flight up, "nobody was chitchatting. Everybody was talking issues." The women had talking points (information about the vast extent of water damage, the unique importance of New Orleans to the nation and the world, coastal wetland restoration, levee protection, and more); they arrived primed and ready. In pairs, they fanned out to keep their appointments in congressional offices.

Milling herself had raised the cost of the chartered airliner, commenting in a telling aside, "If I can't raise $80,000 in a couple of hours, I'm no kind of a fundraiser." Many participants commented that the trip ran "like clockwork." Complex logistics—transfers to ground transportation, routes through city traffic, sequences of meetings with congressional members or staffers, a press conference on the Capitol steps that CNN broadcast live, delivery of box lunches—ran smoothly. In an interesting reversal of gender roles, men had arranged the logistics, leaving the Women of the Storm to concentrate on business. They proceeded with meeting, establishing rapport, and selling an idea to members of Congress, "relaxed," in the words of one participant, "because . . . all the inner workings [were] nailed down." A compact, efficient visit wrapped up at day's end; by rush hour in Washington, the women were on their flight home.[18]

In her approach, Milling embraced many stereotypes about the South and its women. "It's a natural thing for Southerners to do, ask people to come and visit. Why not ask [members of Congress] to come down?" Describing their persistence, she commented, "One of the things women do well is nag. We nagged and nagged the congressmen. . . . And we do it with southern grace."[19] "We play off the southern charm," her colleague Nancy Marsiglia conceded. After a pause, she added, "And then we hit them with the wealth of our knowledge." Olivia Manning, mother of NFL quarterbacks Peyton and Eli Manning, found that interest in her sons' athletic careers gave her entrée almost everywhere on Capitol Hill. Other women used every connection they could conjure up to get face time with lawmakers. One in the group had roomed in college with Laura Bush's chief of staff, which allowed a small delegation to meet with the First Lady's staff. Everywhere that they gained an audience, the Women of the Storm carried an invitation: please come to Louisiana as our guest; see the extent of the devastation so that you will understand why our region asks for more aid from the federal government.

Within six weeks, what began as a trickle of congressional visitors became a

steady stream of official guests. Milling and her steering committee were masters of hospitality, reliable workhorses who could be counted on to drop everything to host a last-minute dinner for a visitor, to accompany someone's chief
of staff on a two-hour tour of devastation, and to say the right thing. Lining up
guides for the tours, arranging press conferences, and getting the most effective
speakers to educate the visitors about the needs of the city demanded meticu-
lous attention to detail. Because Louisiana's U.S. senators, one a Democrat and
the other a Republican, had an edgy relationship ("Big babies . . ." "No, like ado-
lescents!"), the women marshaled tact for every exchange with senatorial staffs,
a careful balancing that kept good relations with both lawmakers. When Milling
fielded a phone call from a documentary filmmaker who wanted to follow four
or five of the women as they went through a typical busy day, the group hooted
in derision and rejected the idea without further discussion. When a local group
proposed a gala luncheon to honor the women, they again rejected the idea;
collectively and individually, they already had plenty of accolades. They stroked
egos of visiting officials; they allowed credit to go to those who seemed to want
it; they smiled and pushed toward their goal, which was to get every member
of Congress to visit the flooded city and then to commit to funding recovery
efforts for New Orleans.

The web site for Women of the Storm featured a scoreboard listing senators
and representatives who traveled to inspect conditions in New Orleans, 57 senators and 132 representatives as of November 2007; most of these members came
in response to the women's "come and visit" campaign. Senator John McCain
stated emphatically after his March 2006 visit, "It's necessary for every member
of Congress to come down here. You can't appreciate the enormity of it until you
come down here. We have an enormous long-term environmental challenge
here. I am for doing what is necessary."[20] His remarks summed up the response
of most congressional visitors.

As this essay goes to press, in fall 2007, the women of New Orleans are still
active in rebuilding their city. LaToya Cantrell's Broadmoor neighborhood is
definitely reviving, largely through injections of private capital for needed projects. Funds from the Carnegie Foundation in New York, rather than from government, fueled the 2007 reopening of the area's flood-ruined branch library,
which serves as a community social and cultural center. Restoring the library
was a centerpiece of the plan developed by Cantrell's neighborhood association
and Harvard's Kennedy School. To execute their ideas, they secured funding
from President Clinton's Global Initiative and a range of partners, in addition to
Carnegie.[21] A National Public Radio report compared Cantrell to a "queen" and
noted that neighbors credit her personal efforts with bringing their salvation;

when she walks by, they "weep in gratitude for the work she's done to save this area from the bulldozer."[22]

Across town, another neighborhood activist also chalked up a victory in 2007. Pam Dashiell returned to her severely depopulated Ninth Ward neighborhood from a long exile in St. Louis to continue her battle against the U.S. Army Corps of Engineers and MR-GO, the waterway it created in 1968 to shorten the distance from the Gulf of Mexico to New Orleans. Dashiell was one of eight plaintiffs in a lawsuit against the corps to force its closure; while she waited for a ruling, she frequently participated in forums to educate the community about the environmental dangers it posed. In July 2007, she savored the news that the Corps of Engineers was at last recommending that Congress take steps to close the forty-year-old channel, labeled by many as a "hurricane highway."[23]

Meanwhile, the overwhelming success of the Katrina Krewe had exhausted Becky Zaheri and the board of the Katrina Krewe. Twice-weekly clean-ups required a ton of advance work. Zaheri scouted locations, driving slowly around the city to locate appropriately large swaths of badly littered blocks that could fully occupy the labors of upward of a thousand eager volunteers for three hours each time out. Her team coordinated delivery of supplies, tried to arrange with the city for trucks to come to the right locations to collect the bagged litter after each outing, and dealt with the sheriff's department for traffic control around their work areas. Frustratingly, cleaned blocks had a way of becoming littered all over again. New Orleans, mockingly called "the city that forgot to care," had never had a good record on sanitation or habits of cleanliness, but in the wake of the flood, illegal dumping was rampant.

As frustration built over relittering, Zaheri's own family obligations demanded more from her. Feeling guilt over what she saw as neglect of her husband and children, aged six and eight, she nevertheless drove herself to respond personally to the avalanche of e-mails of inquiry and encouragement she received daily, at times numbering three hundred. "[The children] were very upset with me; there were a lot of tears. My husband was very upset; there were many days when honestly I could not speak a word to him, because if I didn't get through those 350 e-mails today, then there's gonna be 600 tomorrow. . . . And the phone calls . . ." At last, she had to back away from her creation. "I had to cut back. I just couldn't do it any more."[24]

Zaheri and the board of the Katrina Krewe reduced clean-ups to one per month during the summer of 2006 and eliminated them entirely in the fall. They began a new mission in the 2006–7 school year, aiming to teach good habits to young children. Organizing the Kat Krewe ("Kids Against Trash"), they distributed "Keep It Clean" T-shirts, devised clever activities for building litter consciousness in the minds of children, and hired members of Tulane University's Theater Department to write an antilitter skit for performances before elementary school audiences.[25] Envisioning a younger generation of Orleanians acting on their antilitter slogan, "See it, snag it, bag it," the Katrina Krewe demonstrate the most traditional of maternal attributes: faith in the future, belief in the teachability of children, and the widely held assumption that it is women's job to instill good habits in them. In addition to their work with children, the Katrina Krewe has purchased billboards, placards for buses and streetcars, and three hundred "No Dumping/Littering" aluminum city signs. Their vigorous example has inspired many neighborhoods, businesses, churches, and schools to begin clean-up efforts of their own.

The Women of the Storm returned to Congress in September 2006, determined to corral the holdouts into making a visit to their still-devastated city. With their trademark "blue-tarp" umbrellas and rectangular lapel pins, they were a recognizable presence on the Hill. Like Katrina Krewe members, Women of the Storm confessed to surprise at how much of their time the group consumed, but unlike the Katrina Krewe, those in the inner circle of Women of the Storm no longer had young children at home. Explained one member, "Everybody just makes room in their schedule. . . . We've been successful so people are looking for us to do more. . . . We just have to do it." Although one member noted, "We are not looking for full-time jobs or careers," another said, "I think we all think that we've got to move this to another level, that there's another issue to take on after this. What it will be, I don't know."[26] In March 2007, the Women of the Storm, in partnership with four New Orleans universities, submitted an application to the Commission on Presidential Debates to host a candidates' debate in fall 2008, having previously arranged for commitments from corporations and foundations for financial support. When the commission sniffed that New Orleans was "not ready" to host such a complex event and rejected the bid, Anne Milling noted that New Orleans had successfully hosted conventions of twenty thousand ophthalmologists and twenty-five thousand realtors, plus the Sugar Bowl, since Katrina. She labeled the commission's attempt at justification "incorrect, unsupported, damning." Undaunted, Women of the Storm continue to hold events to attract attention to the needs of their storm-damaged region.[27]

Citizens for 1 Greater New Orleans, the red jackets who roared, endorsed the words of their leader Ruthie Frierson, who said, "We are taking responsibility for our recovery. There is power in the citizen voice."[28] Invigorated by the ringing success of the consolidation reforms, the group subsequently made criminal justice reform its top priority. The dysfunctional state of the local judicial system revealed itself in an appalling statistic: in 2006, a year with 160 murders in a severely depopulated city, exactly one conviction resulted. In 2007, the city's murder rate per capita was 20 percent higher than that in any other U.S. city. The chair of the Senate Judiciary Committee called Crescent City crime the "most serious threat to recovery since the storm."[29] Partnering with several respected local organizations to announce an anticrime package aimed at convicting and incarcerating career criminals in New Orleans, Frierson's group pressed for innovations such as a Court Watchers program, which would train citizens to monitor judicial procedures for fairness and propriety, and an effort to motivate citizens to volunteer for jury duty. They worked to obtain funds for creating a special unit of assistant district attorneys for prosecuting repeat offenders. Describing their approach as "assertive, not aggressive," group members stated for the record that this was "just the beginning. We are in for the long haul."[30]

❀ ❀ ❀

The women featured in this essay fit into a familiar and long-standing pattern, with roots stretching back to the nineteenth century. Over the decades, in countless towns and cities, middle-aged, economically comfortable women, confident, articulate, and generally not employed outside the home, used their influence and connections in order to achieve goals for civic betterment through women's voluntary associations. By the twenty-first century, New Orleans women of this type were leading major nonprofit initiatives, sitting on corporate boards, and moving easily among the city's political and economic powers. Their resumes showed experience and solid achievements in a variety of fields, including journalism, law, public relations, accounting, catering, education, and real estate. Successful in their own right, some, married to leaders in banking, oil, utilities, commerce, and the professions, also enjoyed prominence because of affiliated status. In their post-Katrina activism, the most active of these women easily devoted forty hours a week to an unpaid "invisible career." Like their nationally known forebears Jane Addams, Mary Church Terrell, and Eleanor Roosevelt, they chose to work through women's voluntary associations. Like earlier New Orleans activists Jean and Kate Gordon, Martha G. Robinson, and Emily Blanchard, the strategy of choice for most was female separatism, a preference for working with other women to wield influence and achieve goals of civic betterment.[31] Although liberated from the oppressive clothing of previous generations and thus vastly different in appearance, although wielding cell phones, sending faxes, and reading e-mail, they nonetheless resembled reformers of previous generations in their demonstrations of intelligence, dedication, and capacity for hard work, and particularly in their eagerness to challenge the status quo in a quest for something better.

The new element visible in this post-Katrina manifestation of women's activism is diversity. Unlike an earlier generation of New Orleans women, the women reformers after Katrina consciously attempted to avoid errors born of racism and elitism. Earlier reformers and activists had often practiced exclusion and behaved with condescension toward women who did not share their race and class identity. The historical record documents a series of troubled and suspicious alliances between white and black women suffragists, for example. And, within the more recent feminist movement of the sixties and seventies, the difficulties that middle-class white women experienced in agreeing with black and working-class women on a shared agenda indicate their differences in experience and perception.[32] The white women of the inner circle of Women of the Storm moved from the outset to have African American women represented in their group. Similarly, Citizens for 1 Greater New Orleans began with women of like background and expanded to become "metro-wide, diverse, and irresistible." The Katrina Krewe harnessed the volunteer work of literally thousands who represented all regions, races, and experiences. By the twenty-first century, diversity had become the "new normal."

The appraising comment of one activist, a successful executive fully accustomed to long hours and hard-driving ways among her business associates, sums up the commitment women brought to their volunteer reform activities. Of her colleagues in Citizens for 1 Greater New Orleans, she said forcefully, "This is by far the most disciplined, relentless group of individuals I've ever worked with."[33] Her positive evaluation is applicable to many women. It is beyond question that women's unpaid labor, given so willingly, has helped to speed the recovery of New Orleans. This grievously wounded city, while still far from mended, is already more vibrant and hopeful because of their efforts.

NOTES

1. "Katrina Report Blames Levees," CBS News, June 1, 2006, http://www.cbsnews.com/stories/2006/06/01/national/main1675244.shtml.

2. Jed Horne, *Breach of Faith: Hurricane Katrina and the Near Death of a Great American City* (New York: Random House, 2006), 147.

3. Ibid., 84–85.

4. Douglas Brinkley, *The Great Deluge: Hurricane Katrina, New Orleans, and the Mississippi Gulf Coast* (New York: William Morrow, 2006), 1–3.

5. Horne, *Breach of Faith*, 91–92.

6. Ibid., 96–97.

7. Brinkley, *Great Deluge*, 88–89, 267, 279, 289.

8. "Probing Questions: Are Adults Judged Negatively for Crying?" *Research Penn State: The Online Magazine of Scholarship and Creativity*, http://www.rps.psu.edu/probing/crying.html.

9. John McQuaid and Mark Schleifstein, *Path of Destruction: The Devastation of New Orleans and the Coming Age of Superstorms* (New York: Little, Brown, 2006), 316–17.

10. Coleman Warner and Keith Darce, "Locals Not Waiting to Be Told What To Do," *New Orleans Times-Picayune*, March 12, 2006.

11. Libby Hughes, "Could Katrina Come to Cape Cod?" *Cape Cod Today*, September 15, 2006.

12. Molly Lanzarotta, "Students Help the Grass Roots Grow," *Harvard University Gazette*, April 3, 2007, http://www.news.harvard.edu/gazette/2007/04.05/99-neworleans.html.

13. Chris Rose, "The House That Brad Built," *New Orleans Times-Picayune*, September 1, 2006.

14. Frank Donze, "Voters Merge Levee Boards," *New Orleans Times-Picayune*, October 1, 2006; http://www.citizensfor1greaterneworleans.com/site/PageServer.

15. Clancy DuBos, "Da winnas and da loozas," *Gambit Weekly*, November 4, 2006, http://www.bestofneworleans.com/dispatch/2003-11-25/politics.html.

16. Becky Zaheri, interview by author, June 10, 2006, New Orleans.

17. Nancy Marsiglia, interview by author, March 16, 2006, New Orleans.

18. Diana Pinckley, Pamela Bryan, Nancy Marsiglia, and Becky Currence (Women of the Storm members), interviews by author, March 15, 16, 21, and 14, 2006, New Orleans.

19. April Capochino, "Stormers Not Ready to Stop Congress Push," *New Orleans City Business*, June 12, 2006, http://www.neworleanscitybusiness.com/viewStory.cfm?recID=15811.

20. McCain quote posted on http://www.womenofthestorm.net.

21. "$2 Million Carnegie Corporation Grant Catalyzes Community Redevelopment Effort in Heart of New Orleans," June 19, 2007, http://www.clintonglobalinitiative.org/NETCOMMUNITY/Page.aspx?pid=1583&srcid=1384.

22. Larry Abramson, "For One New Orleans School, an Uncertain Future," National Public Radio, May 17, 2007.

23. Susan Finch, "Class Action Suit Seeks MR-GO's End," *New Orleans Times-Picayune*, July 13, 2006; Paul Rioux, "Corps' Final Report to Congress: Close MR-GO," *New Orleans Times-Picayune*, July 3, 2007.

24. Becky Zaheri, interview by author, June 10, 2006, New Orleans.

25. The Katrina Krewe Web site, www.cleanno.org, posted comments from mothers who reported their children's enthusiasm and changed behavior after viewing the litter skit. "My kids came home *so* excited about cleaning up the city. . . . [They] are now picking up trash everywhere we go." "A bag of garbage broke yesterday and the garbage men just left it behind. When he got home from school, he put on his 'Keep It Clean' T-shirt and picked up all the garbage in the street."

26. Nancy Marsiglia, Becky Currence, Pamela Bryan, and Tania Tetlow, interviews by author, March 16, 14, and 21, 2006, New Orleans; Tania Tetlow, panelist, Women of the Storm panel discussion, Newcomb College Center on Research for Women, New Orleans, March 7, 2006.

27. Harry Shearer, "The Debate about the Debate Continues," *Huffington Post*, November 27, 2007, http://www.huffingtonpost.com/harry-shearer/the-debate-about-the-deba_b_74349.html.

28. Ruthie Frierson, interview by author, June 29, 2007, New Orleans.

29. Bob Dart, "Post-Katrina New Orleans Turns into Crime Haven," *Washington Times*, June 21, 2007, http://www.washingtontimes.com/news/2007/jun/21/post-katrina32new-orleans32turns-into32crime-haven.

30. Ruthie Frierson, interview by author, June 29, 2007, New Orleans; remarks of Stephanie Haynes and Karen Noles Bewley, November 29, 2006, Newcomb College Center for Research on Women, audio tape.

31. For information on New Orleans activists, see Pamela Tyler, *Silk Stockings and Ballot Boxes: New Orleans Women and Politics, 1920–1963* (Athens: University of Georgia Press, 1996).

32. See Bonnie Thornton Dill, "Race, Class, and Gender: Prospects for an All-Inclusive Sisterhood," *Feminist Studies* 9 (Spring 1983): 131–50, and Rosalyn Terborg-Penn, "Discrimination against Afro-American Women in the Woman's Movement," in *The Afro-American Woman: Struggles and Images*, ed. Sharon Harley and Rosalyn Terborg-Penn (Port Washington, N.Y.: Kennikat Press, 1978), 17–27.

33. Remarks of Karen Noles Bewley, Newcomb College Center for Research on Women, New Orleans, November 29, 2006, audio tape.

Contributors

JANET ALLURED earned her doctorate at the University of Arkansas. She is associate professor of history at McNeese State University in Lake Charles, Louisiana, where she coordinates the women's studies program. She is the author of several articles and conference papers on southern women and is currently working on a history of second-wave feminism in Louisiana.

ELLEN BLUE holds an MDiv from the Perkins School of Theology, Southern Methodist University, and a PhD from Tulane University. She is the Mouzon Biggs Jr. Associate Professor of the History of Christianity and United Methodist Studies at Phillips Theological Seminary in Tulsa and the coauthor of *Attentive to God: Thinking Theologically in Ministry*. An ordained elder in the Louisiana Annual Conference of the United Methodist Church, she is currently completing a book about St. Mark's in the Social Gospel and civil rights eras.

PATRICIA BRADY, who received her doctorate from Tulane University, was director of publications at the Historic New Orleans Collection before retiring to write *Martha Washington: An American Life*. She has published extensively on southern women and American first ladies as well as edited several documentary publications, including two volumes of the papers of Martha Washington's granddaughter, *Nelly Custis Lewis's Housekeeping Book* and *George Washington's Beautiful Nelly*. She is president of the board of the Tennessee Williams/New Orleans Literary Festival and a member of the board of the Louisiana State Museum.

RYAN ANDRÉ BRASSEAUX is a doctoral candidate in American studies at Yale, where he directs the Yale Public Humanities Initiative. Brasseaux is coauthor of *Stir the Pot: The History of Cajun Cuisine*, coeditor (with Kevin S. Fontenot) of *Accordions, Fiddles, Two Step and Swing: A Cajun Music Reader*, and author of *Cajun Breakdown: The Emergence of an American-Made Music*.

BAMBI L. RAY COCHRAN is a doctoral candidate at Tulane University. Her essay in this volume is based on her master's thesis, "The Spencer Family and a Century of Change in Louisiana Medicine."

MARY FARMER-KAISER received a doctorate in history from Bowling Green State University. She is associate professor of history as well as the James D. Wilson/BORSF Professor of southern studies at the University of Louisiana at Lafayette. She has published several articles on southern African American women in the age of Reconstruction. Her book *Freedwomen and the Freedmen's Bureau: Race, Gender, and Public Policy in the Age of Emancipation* is forthcoming from Fordham University Press.

KEVIN S. FONTENOT has a master's degree from Tulane University and is an instructor at Tulane University's School of Continuing Studies, where he teaches Louisiana and U.S. history. He has published articles on country music history in *Country Music Annual* and *Country Music Goes to War* and is coeditor (with Ryan André Brasseaux) of *Accordions, Fiddles, Two Steps, and Swing: A Cajun Music Reader.*

SHANNON FRYSTAK earned a doctorate from the University of New Hampshire and is assistant professor of African American history at East Stroudsburg University. She is the author of several articles on female civil rights activists in Louisiana. Her book *Woke Up This Morning with My Mind Set on Freedom: Women and the Struggle for Black Equality in Louisiana, 1924–1967* is forthcoming from Louisiana State University Press.

JUDITH F. GENTRY earned a doctorate from Rice University and is professor of history at the University of Louisiana at Lafayette and a cofounder of the Southern Association for Women Historians (SAWH). She has published scholarly articles on the Civil War, antebellum Louisiana, and women's history, one of which won the Ewing Publication Prize for the best article in the *Journal of Southern History*. She has served as president of the Louisiana Historical Association and of the SAWH.

LEE KOGAN has masters' degrees from Columbia University and New York University. She is curator of special exhibitions and public programming at the American Folk Art Museum. She was previously director of the Folk Art Institute at the American Folk Art Museum and served as consultant for the American Folk Art Museum's *Encyclopedia of Twentieth-Century American Folk Art and Artists*. She was for a decade adjunct assistant professor of art and art professions at New York University. She is the author of several books on American folk art and folk art entries for the *Encyclopedia of Southern Culture*.

LINDA LANGLEY holds a doctorate from Brown University. She is an anthropologist documenting the Koasati language in cooperation with the Coushatta Tribe of Louisiana and McNeese State University, where she is a research professor of anthropology. She has authored two documentary films, three book chapters, and several articles on the history and culture of the Coushatta Tribe of Louisiana and is coeditor of a four-volume folklore series highlighting aspects of tribal life. She has also published numerous articles and book reviews in scholarly journals.

KAREN TRAHAN LEATHEM, who earned a PhD at the University of North Carolina at Chapel Hill, is a historian at the Louisiana State Museum. She has coauthored essays in *New Orleans Cuisine: Fourteen Signature Dishes and Their Histories* and *The American South in the Twentieth Century.*

DAYNA BOWKER LEE received her doctorate from the University of Oklahoma and is an assistant professor of anthropology and folklore at Northwestern State University in Natchitoches, Louisiana. Recent publications include *The Work of Tribal Hands: Southeastern Indian Split Cane Basketry*, edited with H. F. Gregory, which includes her essays "The Ties That Bind: Cane Basketry Traditions among the Chitimacha and Jena Band of Choctaw" and "Five Caddo Baskets from Indian Territory."

CAROLYN MORROW LONG studied studio art and art history at Auburn University, the University of Missouri, and the University of Mississippi. She was employed for eighteen years as a conservator of paper artifacts and photographs at the Smithsonian Institution's National Museum of American History and retired in 2001. Long is the author of *Spiritual Merchants: Religion, Magic, and Commerce* and *A New Orleans Voudou Priestess: The Legend and Reality of Marie Laveau.*

ELIZABETH SHOWN MILLS is the former editor of the *National Genealogical Society Quarterly* (1986–2002). An independent researcher, writer, and lecturer, she has published essays on southern and family history in scholarly journals in the fields of history, sociology, and genealogy as well as in literary journals and in university press books. Her last two books were the prizewinning *Evidence Explained: Citing History Sources from Artifacts to Cyberspace* and *Isle of Canes*, a historical novel centering on Marie Thérèse Coincoin.

CLAUDE OUBRE earned a doctorate from the University of Southwestern Louisiana. He is professor of history and political science at Louisiana State University at Eunice. He is the author of *Forty Acres and a Mule: The Freedmen's Bureau and Black Land Ownership* and *A History of the Diocese of Lafayette.* He is the coauthor of *Creoles of Color in the Bayou Country* as well as of numerous articles in scholarly journals and coeditor of a four-volume folklore series.

JAY PRECHT holds a PhD from Arizona State University and is assistant research associate at McNeese State University in Lake Charles, Louisiana, where he works through a Documenting Endangered Languages grant for the Coushatta Tribe of Louisiana. He has presented papers at the annual meetings of the Organization of American Historians, the American Anthropological Association, and the American Society for Ethnohistory. He is currently revising his dissertation, a twentieth-century history of the Coushattas, for publication.

EMILY TOTH earned a doctorate from Johns Hopkins. She is professor of English and women's studies at Louisiana State University-Baton Rouge and the author or editor of eleven books, including two Kate Chopin biographies, two collections of Chopin's unpublished writings, and the first edition of Chopin's last story collection. Toth teaches the only regularly offered course on Louisiana women writers in the United States and is also the author of *Ms. Mentor's Impeccable Advice for Women in Academia, Ms. Mentor's New and Ever More Impeccable Advice for Women and Men in Academia,* and the only biography of author Grace Metalious: *Inside Peyton Place: The Life of Grace Metalious.* Her monthly Ms. Mentor advice column appears on the *Chronicle of Higher Education*'s career network site.

PAMELA TYLER holds a PhD from Tulane University and is associate professor of history at the University of Southern Mississippi. She is the author of the award-winning *Silk Stockings and Ballot Boxes: New Orleans Women and Politics, 1920–1963.* She has published articles on Eleanor Roosevelt's difficult relationship with the American South and is currently editing the diary of Cynthia Sanborn Ware, which covers the coming-of-age years of a young southern woman in the 1920s and 1930s.

CHRISTINA VELLA earned a doctorate from Tulane University, where she teaches occasionally. A consultant for the U.S. State Department, she lives in New Orleans and lectures extensively around the country. She is the author of several books, including *Intimate Enemies: The Two Worlds of the Baroness de Pontalba.*

MARY ANN WILSON, who received her doctorate from Louisiana State University, is professor of English and women's studies at the University of Louisiana at Lafayette where she has taught since 1985. Her research interests are nineteenth- and twentieth-century American women writers and southern literature. She is the author of *Jean Stafford: A Study of the Short Fiction* (1996) and numerous articles on writers such as Kaye Gibbons, Rebecca Wells, Joyce Carol Oates, and Alice Walker as well as Grace King. She was the recipient of the University of Louisiana at Lafayette Foundation Distinguished Professor Award in 2001 and most recently was named the Friends of the Humanities/BORSF Endowed Professor in the Humanities.

Index

Aaron, Julia, 303, 306, 309, 315

Abbott, Ency Robinson Abbey, 155, 165, 167; Coushatta medicine woman, 166

Acadiana region, of Louisiana, 123, 129

Acadians. *See* Cajuns (Acadians)

Acadia Parish, 239, 250

African American women, 1, 10–11, 54, 63, 65, 276; African cultural survivals among, 13–14, 20, 21, 23, 190; in civil rights movement, 309–10; during Civil War, 82; as Creoles, 176–77; difficulties in writing their history, 4; at Melrose plantation, 177, 191; in New Orleans following Hurricane Katrina, 330, 334, 340; religious belief systems of, 60, 186; slave ownership among, 20, 57. *See also* Cantrell, LaToya; Coincoin, Marie Thérèse; Haley, Oretha Castle; Hunter, Clementine; Laveau, Marie; Taylor, Dorothy Mae; Voudou

African House murals (Hunter), 178, 188

Afro-Creoles, 13, 20, 55, 239, 247

Alabama, Annie, 165

Alabama, Sissy Robinson, 164–65

Allen Parish, 162, 167, 257

Almonester, Andrés, and Mme. de Almonester (parents of Baroness Pontalba), 31, 33, 34

American Federation of Teachers, 4

Amite Female Seminary, 97

Arkansas, 123, 264, 275

At Fault (Chopin), 122, 124, 125–26

Awakening, The (Chopin), 129, 130–32, 133, 134

Bailey, Mildred Hart, 175, 183

Balcony Stories (King), 141, 146

Baptists, 121, 180, 185, 198

Barbour, Haley, 327

Barnett, Albert, 228

Barnwell, Mary Lou, 228

basket making: Chitimacha, 253, 257–61, 265–66, 267n14; Coushatta, 155, 157, 159, 160; cultural significance of, 169; economic importance of, 164, 167. *See also* Dormon, Caroline

Baton Rouge, La., 5, 9n9, 307, 333

Bayou Folk (Chopin), 126–27, 128

Blanco, Kathleen, 326–28, 332

"Blessed Martin Chapel" (Hunter), 185

Boarding Home for Working Women, 219, 220

Bradford, Mary McIlhenny, 258, 261

Briarwood, 253, 256, 258, 262, 264–65

Brittain, Ann Williams, 183

Brokenburn Plantation, 75–88. *See also* Stone, Kate (Sarah Katherine)

Brown v. Board of Education, 307

Bureau of American Ethnology (BAE), 253, 255, 260–64, 266

Cable, George Washington, 140

Cajuns (Acadians), 3, 5, 122–23, 129, 279. *See also* Falcon, Cleoma Breaux